Romance-Germanic Bilingual Phonology

Studies in Phonetics and Phonology
Edited by Martin J. Ball, Linköping University, and Pascal van Lieshout, University of Toronto

The aim of this series is to provide both accessible and relevant texts to students of linguistics, phonetics and speech sciences, and to publish more advanced texts and edited collections. The textbooks aim to cover a wide variety of topics relevant for such an audience, and to introduce these topics in a practical way to enable students to undertake a range of analysis procedures. The more advanced books will present state-of-the-art research in the topic concerned.

While we intend to cover a wide range of topics in phonetics and phonology, there will be an emphasis on phonetic studies of under-reported languages, or the bringing of new data to explore phonetic characteristics on the one hand, and on phonological studies that employ more psycholinguistic, cognitive and functional approaches on the other (and, of course, on the interaction between phonetics and phonology). The recent increase in interest in laboratory phonology we see as particularly to be welcomed. Each volume will be authored by leading authorities in the field, who have a grasp of both the theoretical issues and the practical requirements of the area and, further, are at the forefront of current research and practice.

Published:
Challenging Sonority: Cross-Linguistic Evidence
Edited by Martin J. Ball and Nicole Müller

Forthcoming:
Prosodic Variation (with)in Languages: Intonation, Phrasing and Segments
Edited by Marisa Cruz, Pedro Oliveira and Sónia Frota

Romance-Germanic Bilingual Phonology

Edited by
Mehmet Yavaş, Margaret Kehoe and Walcir Cardoso

SHEFFIELD UK BRISTOL CT

Published by Equinox Publishing Ltd.
UK: Office 415, The Workstation, 15 Paternoster Row, Sheffield, South Yorkshire S1 2BX
USA: ISD, 70 Enterprise Drive, Bristol, CT 06010

www.equinoxpub.com

First published 2017

British Library Cataloguing-in-Publication Data
A catalogue record for this book is available from the British Library.
ISBN 978 1 78179 282 7 (hardback)

Library of Congress Cataloging-in-Publication Data
Names: Yavaş, Mehmet, editor. | Kehoe, Margaret, editor. | Cardoso, Walcir, editor.
Title: Romance-Germanic bilingual phonology / edited by Mehmet Yavaş, Margaret Kehoe and Walcir Cardoso.
Description: Sheffield, UK ; Bristol, CT : Equinox Publishing Ltd, [2017] | Includes bibliographical references and index.
Identifiers: LCCN 2016020801 (print) | LCCN 2016030659 (ebook) | ISBN 9781781792827 (hb) | ISBN 9781781795064 (e-PDF) | ISBN 9781781795071 (e-epub)
Subjects: LCSH: Bilingualism–Psychological aspects. | Grammar, Comparative and general–Phonology, Comparative. | Romance languages–Phonology. | Germanic languages–Phonology.
Classification: LCC P115.4 .R65 2017 (print) | LCC P115.4 (ebook) | DDC 430/.0415–dc23
LC record available at https://lccn.loc.gov/2016020801

Typeset by S.J.I. Services, New Delhi
Printed and bound by Lightning Source Inc. (La Vergne, TN), Lightning Source UK Ltd. (Milton Keynes), Lightning Source AU Pty. (Scoresby, Victoria).

Contents

Acknowledgements

We would like to express our gratitude to the authors who have contributed to this book. Their enthusiastic response with original contributions made it possible for us to set the goals of this volume. We are extremely grateful for their contribution.

Our deep thanks also go to the following scholars who gave their help in the review of the chapters:

Niclas Abrahamsson, University of Stockholm, Sweden
Katsura Aoyama, University of North Texas, USA
Esther Brown, University of Colorado, USA
Susana Cortes, University of the Balearic Islands, Spain
Rory DePaolis, James Madison University, USA
Janet Grijzenhout, University of Konstanz, Germany
Nina Grønnum, University of Copenhagen, Denmark
Denise Kluge, Federal University of Santa Catarina, Brazil
Conxita Lleó, University of Hamburg, Germany
Heather Newell, University of Quebec at Montreal, Canada
Andréa Rauber, University of Tubingen, Germany
Thais Cristófaro Silva, Federal University of Minas Gerais, Brazil
Ellen Simon, University of Ghent, Belgium
Annie Tremblay, University of Kansas, USA

We are very appreciative of their generosity.

Mehmet Yavaş, Margaret Kehoe and Walcir Cardoso
Miami – Geneva – Montreal
March 2016

1
Introduction

Mehmet Yavaş, Margaret Kehoe and Walcir Cardoso

For many people living in a monolingual environment, bilingualism may seem exotic. It may be regarded as a phenomenon restricted to a few countries such as Canada, Switzerland and India. The facts, however, speak differently: bilingualism is present practically everywhere to a greater or lesser degree. For decades, scholars have struggled with the definition of bilingualism. While Bloomfield (1933) defines a bilingual as someone who has native-like control of two languages, Weinreich (1968) and Mackey (1970) relax the criteria and consider a bilingual as an individual who alternately uses two languages. In this book, we do not dwell on the different definitions of bilingualism; rather, we adopt a view that includes both extremes of the debate along the lines of Beatens-Beardsmore's (1982) approach: 'bilingualism as a concept has open-ended semantics.'

This volume is about phonetic and phonological aspects of bilingualism, an underrepresented area in contact linguistics. Our focus is on the investigation of phonetic and phonological issues that are in contrast between Romance and Germanic languages. More specifically, we aim to cover well-established phonotactic, segmental and suprasegmental conflicting situations between four Germanic (English, German, Danish and Swedish) and four Romance (Spanish, Portuguese, French and Italian) languages in order to evaluate several assertions that have been advanced in the literature.

Cross-linguistic interactions have been one of the most discussed themes of bilingual phonology. Different theoretical models have been proposed to account for the interaction between an individual's two sound systems, whether acquired simultaneously or sequentially. Among these, Flege's Speech Learning Model (hereafter SLM) (1995, 2007) is probably the most well-known. According to this model, a bilingual's two languages (L1 and L2) share a 'common phonological space', and thus they interact with one another throughout the lifespan. As such, the model is concerned with 'ultimate attainment', and consequently it focuses on long-term bilinguals. SLM treats phonological acquisition with a view of phonetic approximation and interference based on perceptual judgements. It is built on the ideas of categorical perception and equivalence classification in the determination of a how a learner will react to and ultimately acquire sounds in an L2. In this model, L1 and L2 phonetic segments can be related along a continuum, within which sounds are classified as 'new', 'similar' or 'identical' on the basis of the differences between L2 novel sounds and existing L1 sounds, and the model predicts how the learner will react. The different categorizations are made in terms of acoustic similarity or perceived cross-language similarity. If L2 sounds are categorized as 'similar', their assimilation to the existing L1 phonetic categories will be through a process of equivalence classification, and will be produced as the L1 sound (never as an authentic L2 sound). New categories will be formed for less similar and 'new' L2 sounds.

Although the model holds the view that adults can retain the capability for accurate perception of L2 contrasts (i.e. no critical period after which the learner will be unable to acquire an L2 sound system), it also states that L2 development will be constrained by age of learning. It is predicted that learners are more likely to have native-like perception with early age of learning. The later the age of learning, the less likely a learner is to perceive the differences between L1 and L2 sounds, because the learner's L1 categories will be more developed and are likely to impede the formation of new categories for L2 sounds. SLM also states that L2 development is further constrained by the amount and type of input and output in each language.

There seem to be four possible outcomes regarding the interaction of bilingual's two languages, each of which has found support from specific studies.

1. L1 may display a unidirectional influence on L2: when languages are not acquired simultaneously, the L2 will be acquired through the filter of the L1 (interference). This situation receives support from several studies (Flege 1987, 1991; Flege and Eefting 1987; Flege and Liu 2001).
2. L2 may operate independently of L1: it is predicted that L2-dominant bilinguals, those who are truly immersed in their L2 and who experience limited to no use of their first language, will have productions that are free of L1 interferences and may experience L2 influence on their L1 (Flege and MacKay 2004; Guion, Flege and Loftin 2000).
3. L1 and L2 may reciprocally affect one another: since SLM states that a bilingual's language-specific phonetic categories are stored within a common phonological space, these categories may influence each other through a variety of merging and dissimilation processes (Flege 1991).

4. There may be no clear relationship between L1 and L2 in bilingual speech production: this envisions the operation of L1 and L2 independently of one another in the production of highly competent or 'balanced' bilinguals, i.e. the belief is that such bilinguals can switch languages completely free of interlanguage phonetic interference (Grosjean and Miller 1994; Magliore and Green 1999).

Differences in the functional properties of sounds (i.e. phonemic mismatches) are also likely areas of interaction between a bilingual's two languages. For example, the English contrast between /t/ and /ʧ/ (e.g. tip [tɪp] versus chip [ʧɪp]) is underdifferentiated by learners whose L1 is Portuguese, because the two sounds are allophones of the same phoneme in their L1. Research has shown that learning the phonemic split is more of a challenge than learning that two sounds which are separate phonemes in the learner's L1 are allophones of the same phoneme in the target language (Eckman, Elreyes and Iverson 2003; Major and Kim 1999).

Finally, besides the different types of mismatches discussed above, structural elements of varying nature with respect to their markedness are expected to feature prominently in potential areas of interaction in bilingual phonology. For example, acquiring the voicing contrast in obstruents in syllable-initial position will be easier than the more marked final position.

All the above demonstrate that bilingual phonology is structurally governed by three components: L1, L2 and universal principles, characterized in terms of markedness constraints. Although these factors influence speech production, the role of each may vary at different stages of development, a pattern captured by the Ontogeny Phylogeny Model for second language acquisition (Major 2001). According to this model, in the earlier stages of L2 acquisition, L1 interference is the dominant factor, and the role of universals is minimal. Gradually, the influence of L2 and universals increases, and the role of L1 decreases. In later stages, the only element on the rise is the influence of L2, with concurrent decline of L1 features and universals.

The main research model applied to speech production in young bilinguals has not been the SLM of Flege (1995), but Paradis and Genesee's (1996) model, which, in reality, is not a model but a framework for describing patterns of cross-linguistic interaction. Paradis and Genesee define cross-linguistic interaction (or interdependence) as 'the systemic influence of the grammar of one language on the grammar of the other language during acquisition, causing differences in a bilingual's patterns and rates of development in comparison with a monolinguals' (1996: 3). They consider three potential manifestations of cross-linguistic interaction, which are summarized below:

1. Transfer: the incorporation of a grammatical property into one language from the other.
2. Acceleration: the situation in which a certain property emerges in the grammar earlier than would be the norm in monolingual acquisition.
3. Delay: the situation in which a certain property emerges in the grammar later than would be the norm in monolingual acquisition.

Many studies on the phonological acquisition of young bilingual children have interpreted their findings using Paradis and Genesee's (1996) framework of cross-linguistic interaction (Kehoe 2002; Fabiano-Smith and Goldstein 2010; Keshavarz and Ingram 2002; Paradis 2000).

We now turn to the contributions of this volume where some of the issues discussed thus far are evaluated and/or adopted to explain aspects of the phonology of bilinguals in a particular context. The original empirical studies in this volume all come from populations exhibiting contact situations between a Romance and a Germanic language and put a variety of principles discussed above to test. The first three chapters address cross-linguistic interaction in the development of aspects of prosody in young bilinguals. While Kehoe and Lleó's and Dodane and Bijeljac-Babic's chapters concentrate on simultaneous bilinguals, the study by Splendido focuses on both simultaneous and early sequential bilinguals.

The first two chapters investigate early prosodic development in bilingual children, specifically from an acoustic-phonetic perspective. Kehoe and Lleó examine whether bilingual input influences the development of vowel reduction processes in German and Spanish and, consequently, the rhythmic patterns of the two languages. German is a stress-timed language, in which unstressed syllables may contain reduced vowels, whereas Spanish is a syllable-timed language, in which unstressed syllables contain non-reduced vowels. Kehoe and Lleó measure both quantitative and qualitative aspects of vowel reduction (vowel duration and formant frequencies values) and find that there is evidence of mutual influence between languages: the stress-to-unstress duration ratios are not as extreme in the bilinguals as in the monolinguals, suggesting that the unstressed syllables become shorter in Spanish due to the influence of German, and the unstressed syllables become longer in German due to the influence of Spanish. The German reduced vowels are also more open-like in vowel quality in the bilinguals than in the monolinguals, possibly due to the influence of Spanish. Dodane and Bijeljac-Babic's study of the acoustic correlates of stress in French-English bilinguals also observes interaction between the bilinguals' two languages. In two-syllable words, French is characterized by word-final stress, cued by duration, whereas English is characterized by word-initial stress cued by pitch, amplitude and duration. The authors find that the bilingual children exaggerate the differences between the two languages producing more extreme stress-to-unstress duration ratios than the monolingual children. Their results also show that the bilingual children realize a pitch accent on the initial-syllable of their French productions, thus, showing influence from English onto French. Interestingly, the interaction effects observed for vowel duration by Kehoe and Lleó on the one hand, and Dodane and Bijeljac-Babic on the other hand, were quite different: while the former shows that the two systems approximate each other, the latter shows that the two systems diverge from each other. Similar types of effects have been reported in second language acquisition (Flege 1995).

The chapter by Splendido deals with the acoustic measure of voice onset time (VOT; see also the chapter by Kupisch and Lleó). This measure has received a great deal of attention in bilingual research, but there have been no studies to date that have tested young French-Swedish bilinguals and, in particular, that have contrasted simultaneous bilinguals with young sequential bilinguals (Swedish children acquiring French in a school immersion setting). In this study, bilingual children display VOT patterns consistent with cross-linguistic influence. In particular, both the simultaneous and early consecutive children produce exceptionally long VOTs in Swedish, which Splendido interprets either as a delay or as a dissimilation (i.e. deflecting) effect. This effect is analogous to the exaggerated differences observed by Dodane and Bijeljac-Babic in stress acquisition by French-English bilinguals. Regarding the comparison of simultaneous and early sequential bilinguals, Splendido observes an initial stage (after 10 months of initial exposure to the L2) in which the sequential bilinguals produce VOTs in French similar to those in Swedish. In this respect, they resemble adult learners acquiring a second language. However, after this 19-month period of acquisition, the process aligns itself more closely with the simultaneous bilinguals, in that only minimal differences are observed between these speakers and the monolinguals.

The following four chapters focus on cross-language interaction in adult bilinguals. Investigation of VOT in bilinguals is also the subject of Chapter 5 by Kupisch and Lleó. However, the focus here is on the two languages of adult bilingual speakers of Italian and German with exposure to both languages from birth, i.e. simultaneous bilinguals. The study compares German-Italian bilinguals who grew up in Italy (with German as their minority language) to those who grew up in Germany (with Italian as their minority language). The objective is to verify whether the language spoken in the childhood environment matters for the development and maintenance of the phonetic systems of the bilinguals. Results show the effects of interaction between the two languages, as the observed VOT values differ from those of monolingual speakers, even if the speakers have been exposed to both languages from birth. Although there is variation among the participants' patterns, cross-language influence is more commonly unidirectional, from stronger to weaker (i.e. heritage) language. The fact that influence is sometimes bidirectional indicates that more than one factor is at play. In cases when the stronger language is affected, relative markedness of features in the target language is given as the explanation.

Chapter 6 by Yavaş looks at the production of American English laterals by early Spanish-English adult sequential bilinguals. The central question investigated is whether early bilinguals are able to develop new phonetic categories for a phonologically same (coronals in both languages) but phonetically different L2 sound (clear lateral in L1, but dark lateral in L2), or if starting a few years late will create impediments in the formation of native-like productions in their L2. The results of an acoustic investigation reveal significant differences between the productions of the monolingual control group and those of the bilinguals. No correlation is found between the age of English acquisition and the in-/accuracy of the participants' production; nor is there an effect of the frequency of the target words. There is, however, a relationship between the syllable position (onset vs coda), and the front/back quality of the preceding/following vowel with respect to participants' approximation to native-like productions. Targets in coda position with a preceding back vowel (darkest English lateral which is most different from that of Spanish) show the most 'within monolingual range' productions. Overall, the results are in support of the Speech Learning Model (Flege 1995, 2007) which states that dissimilar sounds are easier to acquire because there are salient differences between the two languages, and the Similarity Differential Rate Hypothesis (Major and Kim 1999) which suggests that dissimilar phenomena are acquired at faster rates than similar phenomena.

Evaluating the predictions of SLM, together with another prominent model (PAM-L2), is the objective of Chapter 7 by Garibaldi and Bohn. They evaluate these two models through examining the perception and production of the Danish front rounded vowel /y/ by highly experienced L1 speakers of Spanish and English who have reached a level of ultimate attainment in Danish. Acoustic comparisons of natively produced Spanish and English /i, u/ and Danish /i, y, u/ are conducted, and L2 speakers' perceptual assimilation of Danish /i, y, u/ to Spanish /i, u/ and to English

/i, u/ are examined. The results are in line with the predictions derived from PAM-L2 and SLM, in that Spanish L1 speakers, for whom Danish /y/ is a 'new' (SLM) or 'uncategorized' (PAM) vowel, discriminate Danish /i, y/ and /y, u/ near ceiling, and produce a Danish-like /y/. On the other hand, English L1 speakers for whom Danish /y/ is a 'similar' (SLM) vowel which assimilates to the same native category as Danish /u/ ('Category goodness', PAM), fail to produce a Danish-like /y/.

Following on from Garibaldi and Bohn, Chapter 8 by Kartushina also examines Danish vowels; in this case, the Danish vowel /ɔ/ as produced by native French speakers. Kartushina is also interested in adult learners' ability to acquire L2 sounds which are acoustically similar to native ones (the French /o/ versus the Danish /ɔ/). She explores another aspect of L2 acquisition, however; that is, the effects of L2 experience on the production of native sounds. Thus, her focus is on mutual influences between native and non-native vowels. She examines this question by conducting a study in which native French speakers are trained to produce Danish /ɔ/ over three training sessions. Kartushina then investigates the effects of training on the Danish /ɔ/ and the French /o/ vowels. She finds that an individual's production of French /o/ in terms of its position in the acoustic space and its compactness (inverse of variability) influences the production of Danish /ɔ/ both before and after training. Those French speakers who produce more variable /o/ vowels before training benefit more from training than those speakers with compact vowels. With regard to French /o/, the overall results indicate that this vowel is not modified after training. However, when training-related changes are examined across individual speakers, the author observes that native and non-native categories undergo similar degrees of change and in similar directions. Speakers who produce the Danish /ɔ/ with higher openness after training produce the French /o/ with higher openness as well. These results, like those of Yavaş and of Garibaldi and Bohn support the SLM, and suggest that native and non-native categories interact with each other in a common (acoustic) space even from the earliest stages of learning.

Chapters 9 through 11 examine the representation and/or instantiation of phonological knowledge in the speech of L2 users. In Chapter 9, Carlisle examines the effects the Sonority Cycle (Clements 1990) on the acquisition of /s/+consonant onset sequences in the English spoken by a group of Brazilian Portuguese speakers. Moving to the right edge of the syllable and targeting a similar group of L1 speakers, Chapter 10, by John and Cardoso, investigates the representation of syllable-final consonants in Portuguese-English speech. Finally, the chapter by Garcia and Guzzo examines the acquisition and subsequent representation of stress and word-level constituency in an English-Canadian French contact situation.

The chapter by Carlisle addresses the acquisition of bilateral and trilateral /s/+consonant onset sequences (sC) in the English spoken by a group of Brazilian Portuguese speakers. The study has two purposes: to determine whether native speakers of Portuguese use prothesis significantly more frequently after consonants than after vowels, and whether the frequency of prothesis before sC(C) onsets actually depends on the degree of sonority of the preceding environment (the more preferred the sonority profile of the preceding environment, the greater the frequency of correct production of the target onsets, as observed in previous studies involving Spanish speakers – e.g. Carlisle 1991, 2010). Based on resyllabification phenomena (triggered by phonological environment) and Clements' (1990) Sonority Cycle, the results of the study confirm the author's hypothesis that sC clusters are more accurately produced in less marked environments such as after vowels, and when the target cluster is preceded by a highly sonorous segment (the greater the sonority of the preceding demisyllable, the higher the frequency of accurate sC production). As such, the results are in accordance with those found for Spanish learners of English and Swedish, highlighting the universality of the constructs adopted in the study.

In their chapter, John and Cardoso investigate the acquisition of the stops /p k/ in medial coda and word-final position by Brazilian Portuguese (BP) learners of English in the contact context of Montreal. The primary purpose is to shed light on the syllabic status of word-final consonants, which have been variably analysed as codas (the orthodox view – Blevins 1995; Selkirk 1982) or as onsets of empty nuclei (the Government Phonology view – Harris and Gussmann 1998; Kaye 1990). Although /p k/ occur in BP, their distribution is restricted to word-initial and -medial onsets (e.g. [kapa] 'cover'). Consequently, BP learners of English have difficulty with both medial and final /p k/ (e.g. *ca*[p]*tain, magi*[k]), the tendency being to epenthesize the vowel [i] (e.g. *ca*[pi]*tain, magi*[ki]). Through a series of tasks, the authors gather data to test whether BP learners exhibit differential or simultaneous acquisition of medial and final /p k/. Under the orthodox view, medial and final /p k/ should be acquired simultaneously, since they share a prosodic representation (i.e. both are codas). Medial and final /p k/ are, however, shown to be acquired differentially, a finding consistent instead with the analysis of final consonants as onsets of empty nuclei.

Chapter 11, by Garcia and Guzzo, investigates the acquisition of stress and word-level constituency in English (L2) in contact with Canadian French (L1), a language which is often assumed to have no lexical stress and no foot structure. Under this analysis, learners need to learn contrastive stress, the rhythmic patterns of their target L2, and the respective phonetic cues involved. Based on production data, this study finds no phonetic evidence for word-level prominence in Canadian French, indicating that the learners' baseline regarding prominence has no robust phonetic cues that could facilitate the acquisition of L2 stress. The study also shows that advanced L2 learners of English make use of duration and intensity to mark both primary and secondary stresses, a pattern which mirrors that of native English-speaking controls. In addition, the alternating rhythmic patterns observed in the L2 data indicate that learners accurately assign word-level prominence to English words, implying that learners have acquired the target foot structure.

The following two chapters are concerned with linguistic and extra-linguistic factors that influence L2 learning. In Chapter 12, Baker-Smemoe examines the effects that extra-linguistic factors such as age of L2 acquisition or arrival in the target country, as well as cognitive, social and experiential factors, may exert on learning. Chapter 13, by Silveira and Gonçalves, on the other hand, focuses on the effects of phonological environments, orthography, and L2 proficiency. These studies target L2 English in contact with Spanish and Portuguese, respectively.

The chapter by Baker-Smemoe is based on Flege's SLM (1995, 2007), which postulates that learners can acquire accurate second language speech perception and production throughout their lifetime, but factors like degree of first language and L2 interaction change with age of acquisition and affect learners' ultimate success. As such, the study sets out to identify whether L2 speech accuracy is related to age of acquisition (AOA) and whether this relationship differs for early versus late L2 learners. It also aims to determine the relative importance of cognitive, social and experiential factors in L2 speech accuracy and whether this differs between the two groups. The study measures English global foreign accent, and English vowel perception data from Spanish L1 speakers who migrated to the USA at different ages (0–69). Results reveal that different factors affect learners with different AOAs; early learners are more affected by AOA and cognitive factors (e.g. ability to imitate, working memory capacity and phonological memory), while older learners are more affected by social variables such as their identification with the L2 culture.

Silveira and Gonçalves address a different set of factors that may exert influence on L2 learning. The authors investigate the production of English word-final nasals by a group of 24 Brazilians living in the United States. The study focuses on the production of syllable-final /m/ and /n/ and the roles played by phonological environment following the target nasal, orthography and L2 proficiency. Because nasal codas undergo a vocalization process in Brazilian Portuguese (e.g. *sem* 'without' is produced as [sẽj]), Brazilians tend to vocalize these L2 nasals, rendering words such as 'fun' as [fã]). Vocalization, however, is predicted to be affected by orthography such that the presence of the grapheme -e (e.g. the 'silent' -e in words such as 'come') is more likely to reduce the frequency of the phenomenon. In these cases, vowel insertion (i-epenthesis) is the preferred strategy, which results in creation of an extra syllable (e.g. 'line' /lajn/ → [laj.ni]). The authors test 20 CVC words (10 of them spelled with the silent -e grapheme) embedded in carrier sentences, distributed among three following phonological environments: a pause, a vowel and a consonant. While their results reveal that the phonological environment does not play a significant role in the phenomena under investigation, they do corroborate their initial hypothesis that both vocalization and vowel epenthesis depend upon L2 proficiency (e.g. with higher incidence of i-epenthesis and vocalization among the least proficient participants), and that orthography plays an important role in the syllabification of these forms, as the words spelled with silent -e lead to few vocalized forms but higher rates of vowel epenthesis.

The final chapter of the volume by Bullock and Olson is a thought-provoking study that challenges current linguistic approaches to cross-linguistic interaction in bilingual speech. Linguistic approaches to bilingual phonetic and/or phonological variation assess the factors that contribute to deviation from a monolingual target ('foreign accent') and usually offer explanations of cross-language interaction based on learner variables such as language dominance and age of acquisition. In contrast, Bullock and Olson take a look at phonetic variation in bilingual speech through sociophonetics. The sociophonetic approach holds that gradient phonetic variation, which is often not treated as linguistically meaningful, serves to identify properties of the speaker, such as sex, stance, group affiliation etc. The authors argue that an analysis of bilingual speech should also incorporate these socially conditioned sources of variation. This chapter focuses on several points of phonetic divergence between the sound systems of Spanish and English – voice onset time, intonation and labial fricative production – as empirical illustrations of the impact of social/stylistic variables, including language mode and education and literacy, on phonetic performance among Spanish-English bilinguals in the USA.

To sum up, this book brings together contributions from up-and-coming and well-established researchers in the area of bilingual phonology. It includes studies on child and adult bilinguals as well as L2 learners, and incorporates diverse themes as cross-linguistic interaction, the representation of phonological knowledge in L2 learners, linguistic and extra-linguistic factors which influence L2 learning and bilingual speech.

The common thread running through all these studies is the contact situation, involving the phonologies of Romance and Germanic. Given the diversity of the themes, the findings of the various studies cannot be summarized in a single sentence; however, one clear-cut generalization we can authenticate is that bilingual speech is not the same as monolingual speech, and the studies in this volume have helped us to understand the linguistic, extra-linguistic and sociolinguistic factors that contribute to monolingual and bilingual differences, as well as the linguistic models that account for these differences. We hope these studies will stimulate further discussion on this important topic in linguistic research, the phonology of bilinguals.

References

Beatens-Beardsmore, H. (1982). *Bilingualism: Basic Principles.* Clevedon, Avon: Tieto Ltd.

Blevins, J. (1995). The syllable in phonological theory. In J. Goldsmith (ed.), *The Handbook of Phonological Theory*, 206–44. Cambridge, MA: Blackwell.

Bloomfield, L. (1933). *Language.* New York: John Wiley.

Carlisle, R. (1991). The influence of environment in vowel epenthesis in Spanish/English interphonology. *Applied Linguistics* 12: 76–95.

Carlisle, R. (2010). Word-final sonority as an environmental constraint to prosthesis. In A. Rauber, M. Watkins, R. Silveira and R. Koerich (eds.), *The Acquisition of Second Language Speech: Studies in Honor of Professor Barbara O. Baptista*, 243–66. Santa Catarina: Universidade Federal de Santa Catarina.

Clements, G. (1990). The role of the sonority cycle in core syllabification. In J. Kingston and M. Beckman (eds.), *Papers in Laboratory Phonology I: Between the Grammar and Physics of Speech*, 283–333. Cambridge: Cambridge University Press.

Eckman, F., Elreyes, A. and Iverson, G. (2003). Some principles of second language phonology. *Second Language Research* 19(3): 169–208.

Fabiano-Smith, L. and Goldstein, B. (2010). Phonological acquisition in bilingual Spanish-English speaking children. *Journal of Speech, Language, and Hearing Research* 53: 1–19.

Flege, J.E. (1987). The production of 'new' and 'similar' phones in a foreign accent: Evidence for the effect of equivalence classification. *Journal of Phonetics* 15: 47–65.

Flege, J.E. (1991). Age of learning affects the authenticity of voice onset time (VOT) in stop consonants produced in a second language. *Journal of the Acoustical Society of America*, 89: 395–411.

Flege, J.E. (1995). Second language speech learning: Theory, findings, and problems. In W. Strange (ed.) *Speech Perception and Linguistic Experience: Issues in Cross-Linguistic Research*, 233–77, Timonium, MD: York Press.

Flege, J.E. (2007). Language contact in bilingualism: Phonetic system interactions. In J. Cole and J.I. Hualde (eds.), *Laboratory Phonology* 9: 358–81. Berlin: Mouton de Gruyter.

Flege, J.E. and Eefting, W. (1987). Production and perception of English stops by native Spanish speakers. *Journal of Phonetics* 15: 67–83.

Flege, J.E. and Liu, S. (2001). The effect of experience on adults' acquisition of a second language. *Studies in Second Language Acquisition* 23: 527–52.

Flege, J.E. and MacKay, I (2004). Perceiving vowels in a second language. *Studies in Second Language Acquisition* 26: 1–34.

Grosjean, F. and Miller, J. (1994). Going in and out of languages: An example of bilingual flexibility. *Psychological Science* 5(4): 201–6.

Guion, S., Flege, J.E. and Loftin, J. (2000). The effect of L1 use on pronunciation of Quechua-Spanish bilinguals. *Journal of Phonetics* 28: 27–42.

Harris, J. and Gussmann, E. (1998). Final codas: Why the west was wrong. In E. Cyran (ed.), *Structure and Interpretation in Phonology: Studies in Phonology*, 139–62. Lublin: Folia.

Kaye, J. (1990). Coda licensing. *Phonology* 7: 301–30.

Kehoe, M. (2002). Developing vowel systems as a window to bilingual phonology. *International Journal of Bilingualism* 6: 315–34.

Keshavarz, M. and Ingram, D. (2002). The early phonological development of a Farsi-English bilingual child. *The International Journal of Bilingualism* 6: 255–69.

Mackey, W. (1970). Interference, integration and the synchronic fallacy. In J. Alatis (ed.), *Bilingualism and Language Contact*, 195–227. Washington DC: Georgetown University Press.

Magliore, J. and Green, K. (1999). A cross-language comparison of speaking rate effects on the production of voice onset time in English and Spanish. *Phonetica* 56: 158–85.

Major, R.C. (2001). *Foreign Accent: The Ontogeny and Phylogeny of Second Language Phonology*. Mahwah, NJ: Lawrence Erlbaum.

Major, R.C. and Kim, E. (1999). The similarity differential rate hypothesis. *Language Learning* 46: 465–96.

Paradis, J. (2000). Beyond 'one system or two?' Degrees of separation between the languages of French-English bilingual children. In S. Dopke (ed.), *Cross-linguistic Structures in Simultaneous Bilingualism*, 175–200. Amsterdam/ Philadelphia: John Benjamins.

Paradis, J. and Genesee, F. (1996). Syntactic acquisition in bilingual children: Autonomous or interdependent? *Studies in Second Language Acquisition* 18: 1–2.

Selkirk, E. (1982). The syllable. In H. van der Hulst and N. Smith (eds.), *The Structure of Phonological Representations (Part 2)*, 337–83. Dordrecht: Foris.

Weinreich, U. (1968). *Languages in Contact*. The Hague: Mouton.

Mehmet Yavaş is a professor of linguistics at Florida International University.

Margaret Kehoe lectures at the University of Geneva and works as a speech-language pathologist with bilingual children.

Walcir Cardoso is a professor of Applied Linguistics/Teaching English as a Second Language in the Department of Education at Concordia University, Montreal.

2
Vowel Reduction in German-Spanish Bilinguals

Margaret Kehoe and Conxita Lleó

2.1 Introduction

Descriptions of phonological rhythm recognize the role of unstressed as well as stressed syllables in conveying the temporal and spectral qualities that contribute to our sense of the rhythm of speech. One principal way in which the difference between stressed and unstressed syllables is maximized is through the shortening and centralization of unstressed vowels. In stress-timed languages, such as English and German, a high proportion of unstressed syllables contain reduced vowels; in a syllable-timed language, such as Spanish, unstressed syllables contain non-reduced vowels.

This study examines the development of unstressed vowels in monolingual and bilingual children (aged 2;6 to 3;0) acquiring German (with vowel reduction) and Spanish (without). The aim of the study is to determine whether bilingual input influences the development of unstressed vowels in these two languages. That is, does bilingual input lead to greater vowel reduction in Spanish and lesser vowel reduction in German due to interaction between the two language systems? To determine this, we will compare the realization of unstressed vowels by monolingual and bilingual children.

2.1.1 Phonological Rhythm and Vowel Reduction

Beginning with Pike (1945), who established a clear difference between machine-gun (alias syllable-timed) and morse-type (alias stressed-timed) languages, there have been numerous attempts to quantify rhythmic differences between these two language types. First attempts to identify the level of isocrony (syllables vs stress units) were unsuccessful, which led to new approaches of conceptualizing and measuring rhythm. One of these was the phonological approach, which did not regard rhythm types as phonetic primitives but as derivatives of certain phonological properties, the three most important being syllable structure (more complex in stress timing), vowel reduction (typical of stress timing) and word stress (more extreme differences between stress and unstress in stress timing) (Dasher and Bolinger 1982; Dauer 1983). In recent times, there has been renewed interest in establishing a phonetic basis to rhythm, which takes into consideration the above-mentioned phonological properties. Methods used nowadays are based on the measurement of vocalic versus consonantal intervals, both of which are more variable in stress- than in syllable-timed languages (Grabe and Low 2002). Proportions of vocalic intervals within sentences (%V) are relevant, too, as syllable-timed languages have a larger proportion of vowels than stress-timed languages (Ramus, Nespor and Mehler 1999). Regardless of which rhythmic approach one ascribes to (phonological or acoustic measurement approach), vowel reduction plays an important role in contributing to differences in rhythm types.

2.1.2 Phonological Rhythm in Monolingual and Bilingual Children

Numerous studies have applied acoustic measurement approaches of rhythm to the speech of monolingual children acquiring languages traditionally considered syllable- or stress-timed (Bunta and Ingram 2007; Kehoe, Lleó and Rakow 2011; Mok 2013; Payne, Post, Astruc, Prieto and Vanrell 2012). These studies show that cross-linguistic differences in rhythmic patterns are evident in the speech of three- to four-year-old monolingual children and may even be present in two-year-old children (Payne et al. 2012).

In contrast, studies of rhythm in bilingual children show a slower timeline of acquisition. Kehoe et al. (2011) observed that bilingual German-Spanish three-year-olds displayed similar rhythmic patterns in both languages, producing greater vocalic variability in their Spanish and less vocalic variability in their German than was documented in the monolinguals, thus suggesting a 'merger' of rhythmic patterns. Bunta and Ingram (2007) found instead that their four-year-old Spanish-English bilinguals were able to distinguish the rhythmic patterns of their two languages, although their vocalic variability in English was still characterized by lower values than those of their monolingual counterparts. Schmidt and Post (2015b) corroborated the findings of Kehoe et al. (2011) and Bunta and Ingram (2007) in their study of bilingual Spanish-English children, aged two to six years. Rhythmic differences were not present in the two-year-olds, were emerging in the four-year-olds and were clearly present in the six-year-olds. Using a different constellation of languages, Mok (2013) also found that bilingual Cantonese-English children aged 2;6 – Cantonese being a syllable-timed language – did not make clear rhythmic distinctions between their languages. Thus, the current findings suggest that rhythmic differences in bilingual children develop only after the age of 2;6, somewhat later than in monolingual children.

One concern with applying acoustic measures of rhythm to the speech of young children is that it is not clear what components of rhythm actually pose difficulty for them. As a consequence, investigators have focused on the individual properties that interact in the production of rhythm (syllable structure and vowel quality in Mok 2011; prosodic heads and edges in Schmidt and Post 2015a). The current study is an attempt to do just this – namely, to study one aspect of phonological rhythm, vowel reduction, in bilingual German-Spanish children.

2.1.3 Unstressed Syllables in German and Spanish

Spanish unstressed syllables represent a subset of German unstressed syllables: Spanish contains full vowels whereas German contains full and reduced vowels. Indeed, Bartels, Darcy and Höhle (2009) report that the majority of trochaic forms in German (i.e. over 80%) have final schwa, which includes schwa only, R-coloured schwa and syllabic consonants. Spanish and German unstressed syllables in word-final position are contrasted in Table 2.1.

Table 2.1. Final unstressed vowels in Spanish and German.

Type of Unstressed Vowel	Spanish	German
a. Full Vowel	coch[e], vac[a], perr[o]	Aut[o], Kiw[i], Kaff[e]
b. Schwa		Ent[ə], Kat[ɐ], Apf[l̩]

Vowel Reduction in Spanish

Navarro Tomás (1916, 1917) carried out a detailed analysis of the quantity of stressed and unstressed vowels in Spanish. He took into consideration differences related to syllable structure, vowel quality as well as word length. He showed that vowels are longer in open than in closed syllables; however, syllable structure will not be taken into consideration in the current study, given that child production in Spanish hardly contains closed syllables at the early stages. Word length is an important factor, which will be considered in this study.

Navarro Tomás (1916, 1917) found that the ratio of stress to unstress in trochees could range from 1.0 up to 3.0. He reported that although unstressed vowels are generally short, phrase-final unstressed vowels can be long, resulting in smaller stress-to-unstress ratios in this position, namely, 0.66 to 1.0. In amphibrachs (or trisyllabic words with penultimate stress), the ratio of stress to unstress (initial pre-tonic syllable) is 1.79. In the case of quadrisyllables comprised of two trochees (e.g. *zapatero*), the ratio of the initial secondarily stressed and following unstressed vowel is about 1.0.

Several phoneticians have noted that unstressed vowels in Spanish, beside being shorter than stressed ones, display some qualitative modification. Navarro Tomás (1918: 44–6) differentiates lax vowels from tense or normal ones, and notes that whereas /i/ and /u/ become more open when they are lax, /e/ and /o/ tend to become more closed. Other phoneticians have observed a tendency to centralization in unstressed vowels, as for instance, Delattre (1969) and Quilis and Esgueva (1983), and more recently Menke and Face (2010) and Simonet and Cobb (2015). They all underscore that the quality difference between stressed and unstressed vowels is minimal in Spanish, and is not comparable to the extreme differences found in German or English. Table 2.2 exemplifies this minimal difference showing mean formant (F1 and F2) values of stressed versus unstressed /e/, /a/ and /o/, according to Delattre (1969); the table also contains the mean F1 and F2 values of these stressed vowels according to Quilis and Esgueva (1983) and Martínez Celdrán (1995). The reason we focus on /e/, /a/ and /o/ is that they are more frequent than /i/ and /u/, and, in the current study, we wish to analyse sequences of two repeated vowels (stressed–unstressed) within a word, which in the case of /i/ or /u/ would have been impossible to find in the child productions.

Table 2.2. Mean Hz values of F1 and F2 for Spanish stressed /e, a, o/ according to Quilis and Esgueva (1983) and Martínez Celdrán (1995), and for stressed versus unstressed vowels according to Delattre (1969).

	Delattre				Quilis and Esgueva		Martínez Celdrán	
	F1 str	F1 unstr	F2 str	F2 unstr	F1 str	F2 str	F1str	F2str
/e/	475	475	1950	1800	492	2252	457	1926
/a/	750	650	1400	1350	664	1168	699	1471
/o/	475	475	950	1000	511	981	495	1070

Figure 2.1 shows the classical diagram of the five vowel phonemes of Spanish, indicating the various directions imposed by centralization to the unstressed vowel in the general trochaic structure SW.[1] Formant values correspond to the stressed vowels produced by adult Spanish speakers, according to Quilis and Esgueva (1983).

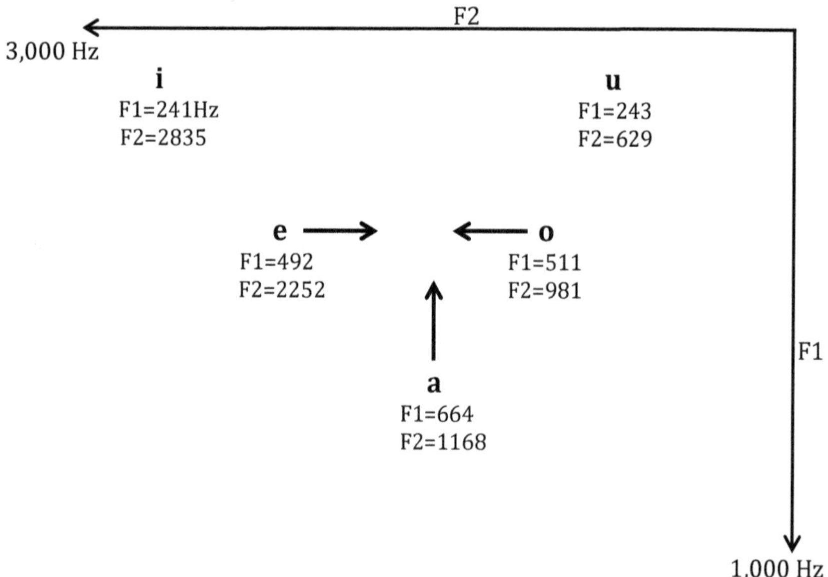

Figure 2.1. Vowels of Spanish indicating direction of centralization for vowels /a/, /e/, /o/ in unstressed syllables.

Vowel Reduction in German

In German, it is necessary to distinguish between two types of unstressed syllables: (a) those that contain underlying schwa and (b) those that contain underlying full vowels. In the German child data, the most frequent types of unstressed syllables are schwa syllables and, consequently, they will be the ones under focus in this study.

The defining phonetic characteristics of schwas include their short duration and centralized vowel quality. Schwas are very short in connected

1 As usual in Metrical Phonology, 'S' stands for strong or heavy, and 'W' for weak or light, which here refer to stressed and unstressed syllables, respectively. In Spanish, two-footed words (e.g. *mariposa* 'butterfly') bear main stress on the third syllable, whereas in German, two-footed words (e.g. *Badewanne* 'bathtub'; *reingeflogen* 'flown into'), in particular, compounds or derived words, bear main stress on the first syllable.

speech. Koopmans-van Beinum (1994) reports a mean duration of 47 ms for Dutch schwa in spontaneous speech, similar to the value reported by Bürki, Fougeron, Gendrot and Frauenfelder (2011) for French schwa (i.e. 51 ms) in radio broadcasted news. Schwas may be long, however. Flemming and Johnson (2007) document phrase-final schwas in English of 153 ms. Concerning vowel quality, schwas are mid-central vowels. Phonetic studies in English suggest the importance of distinguishing between two kinds of schwa: final and medial schwa (Flemming 2009; Flemming and Johnson 2007). Word-final schwa has mid-central vowel quality with a relatively stable F2 (around 1772 Hz) and a less stable F1, which varies according to speaker and speech rate. In contrast, medial schwa is characterized by extreme variability of F2 and a relatively stable F1 (around 428 Hz). The variable F2 arises due to coarticulatory effects from neighbouring consonants, which may be particularly evident in schwa (in contrast to full vowels) because of its reduced length and also because it does not contrast with other vowel qualities especially in English (Flemming and Johnson 2007).

Vowel Reduction in First Language Learners

There is little research on vowel reduction in young children's speech. At the moment, we do not know at what age children display vowel reduction patterns similar to those observed in adults and when children produce vowels that are perceived as schwa. Studies based on phonetic transcription indicate that English-speaking children (aged 2;2–3;9) reduce syllables in function and multisyllabic content words about 50% of the time (Allen and Hawkins 1978). Higher rates of reduction have been reported for German-speaking children. Kehoe (2002) found that two-year-old German-speaking children reduced vowels with a mean accuracy rate of 64%. Studies on the phonetic characteristics of reduced syllables in children are rare. Levelt (2008) reported a mean value of 233 ms for utterance-final schwa in the speech of one Dutch-speaking child, a value considerably shorter than an utterance-final full vowel (i.e. 328 ms).

Vowel Reduction in Second Language Learners and Bilinguals

Studies in second language acquisition, which have focused on transfer of vowel reduction between L1 and L2, may be pertinent to bilingual first language acquisition. Numerous studies show that non-native speakers of English do not reduce unstressed vowels to an appropriate extent (Bond and Fokes 1985; Flege and Bohn 1989; Kondo 2000). For example, Kondo (2000) found that Japanese speakers of English were more likely to produce longer schwas in English than native speakers and to produce vowels with formant values more similar to the Japanese vowel /a/ than to the English schwa. Flege and Bohn (1989) also showed that Spanish learners of English produced lower stress-to-unstress ratios for word pairs of the type satan-satanic (e.g. [ˈse̱tɪn][sə̱ˈtænɪk]) than monolingual native English speakers.

There have been fewer studies on L2 German but they show that, in the case of vowel reduction, non-native speakers of German may display more extreme vowel reduction. This was observed by Kaltenbacher (1997) for English learners of German. The English native speakers were more likely to reduce vowels in pre- and post-tonic position in German target words when the expected pattern was the production of a full vowel. As Delattre (1969) revealed, reduction of full vowels is more extreme in English than in German. In the case of underlying schwa, Gut (2003) found that Chinese, Polish and Italian speakers of German produced significantly lower stress-to-unstress ratios (approximately 1.5) than native German speakers (1.87), indicating that they were not reducing vowels sufficiently to produce acceptable schwas.

The phonetic quality of Spanish vowels in second language learners has been the focus of several recent studies (Menke and Face 2010; Ronquest 2013; Simonet and Cobb 2015). Findings are inconclusive, with some studies showing few differences between native speakers and second language learners (Menke and Face 2010; Simonet and Cobb 2015) and others showing salient differences (Ronquest 2013). These contradictory findings are also present in studies with native Spanish speakers, with some studies documenting clear differences in vowel quality according to stress (Simonet and Cobb 2015; Ronquest 2013) and others documenting fewer differences (Menke and Face 2010).

One of the rare studies that has examined vowel reduction in bilingual children did not document extensive centralization of Spanish vowels in Spanish-English bilinguals, aged 6 to 12 years (Menke 2010). All children displayed some degree of centralization of unstressed variants; however, statistically significant differences between stressed and unstressed vowels were few and inconsistent across age-groups. The author concludes that exposure to English did not overly affect Spanish vowel production in this population.

Vowel Reduction and Phrase Position

When measuring duration of unstressed vowels, several factors need to be controlled, such as prosodic boundary and word length. Studies have established a positive relationship between the depth of the prosodic boundary and degree of segment lengthening, with utterance-final position engendering the greatest degree of lengthening, and other prosodic positions such as phonological phrase and prosodic word engendering less lengthening (Cambier-Langeveld, Nespor and van Heuven 1997). Word length also influences segment length: vowels are longer in shorter than in longer words (Lehiste 1972).

Prosodic position may also be important when vowel formants are considered. As discussed previously, formant values of schwa syllables may vary considerably depending upon whether they are word-final or -medial (Flemming 2009). In particular, F2 of medial schwa may be extremely variable due to coarticulatory effects from neighbouring consonants. Thus, the current study controls both prosodic boundary and word length when measuring acoustic parameters related to vowel reduction.

2.1.4 The Current Study

This study compares the phonetic characteristics of vowel reduction in German and Spanish monolingual and bilingual children, aged 2;6 to 3;0. Given that monolingual German children are starting to display vowel reduction at age 2;0 (Kehoe 2002), we assume that bilinguals should also be displaying vowel reduction at this age or slightly later; hence the age range selected, 2;6 to 3;0. We measure quantitative and qualitative aspects of vowel reduction across different phrasal conditions. In Spanish, we consider all five Spanish vowels, but in the vowel formant measures, we concentrate only on /e/, /o/ and /a/ because they are well represented in child speech. In German, we concentrate on the realization of underlying schwa syllables because they are the most frequent type of unstressed syllables in German.

The general research questions are:

1. Are unstressed (schwa) vowels longer in bilingual than in monolingual German due to the influence of Spanish? Conversely, are unstressed vowels shorter in bilingual than in monolingual Spanish due to the influence of German?
2. Do unstressed (schwa) vowels have more extreme (less centralized) formant frequency values in bilingual than in monolingual German due to the influence of Spanish? Conversely, do unstressed vowels have more centralized formant frequency values in bilingual than in monolingual Spanish due to the influence of German?

The prosodic conditions studied are: (a) SW words in phrase-final position (i.e. SW final), (b) SW words in phrase-medial position (i.e. SW), (c) WSW words and (d) SWSW words. In German, conditions (c) and (d) are grouped together because there are not sufficient numbers of these forms in child speech to analyse them separately. For the duration analyses, we measure the ratio of the duration of stressed to unstressed vowels. In WSW words, we calculate the ratio of the stressed to the initial unstressed vowel. In quadrisyllables (SWSW), the ratio of the initial stressed to the medial unstressed vowel is calculated.

2.2 Method

The database consists of longitudinal recordings of three monolingual German, three monolingual Spanish, and three bilingual German-Spanish children tested from the onset of first words (see Lleó 2012, for a more detailed description of the corpus). The monolingual German and bilingual children were recorded in Hamburg, Germany, and the monolingual Spanish children were recorded in Madrid, Spain. The children were audio-recorded in their homes, while interacting with a parent and an experimenter. The bilinguals were children of Spanish-speaking mothers and German-speaking fathers. Each parent followed the *une personne, une langue* rule by addressing the child in his/her respective language.

2.2.1 Procedure

For the purposes of the current study, two- to four-syllable words were extracted from the database at age range 2;6 to 3;0 years. An attempt was made to analyse 20 items in each prosodic condition per child – i.e. 20 SW final, 20 SW, 20 WSW, 20 SWSW: in total 80 words in Spanish per child; 20 SW final, 20 SW, 20 (S)WSW: in total 60 words in German per child. However, this number was not always obtained due to sampling gaps in the database. In particular, it was hypothesized that R-coloured schwa and syllabic consonants might contain different phonetic characteristics to pure schwa. Hence, schwa syllables were restricted to syllables containing schwa. This reduced considerably the number of schwa syllables available for analysis.

Concerning prosodic condition, trochees were divided into two groups, phrase-final and phrase-medial. WSW and SWSW words could be either phrase-final or phrase-medial. In Spanish, vowel formants were measured in a subset of the words included in the duration analysis. The subset included words containing one of the vowels /a/, /e/ or /o/ in stressed and unstressed position. Examples of possible words include: /a/ cama, (ven)-tana; /e/ ese, (pati)nete; /o/ solo, (tam)poco.

The selected two- to four-syllable words were segmented into stressed and unstressed syllables using Praat (Boersma and Weenink 2007). The segmentation of syllable boundaries was determined by examination of the time wave-form and spectrogram. Clear periodicity in the waveform, and onsets and offsets of the second formant, were used to define the boundaries of the vowels. The extraction of duration and formant values for stressed and unstressed vowels was carried out with the help of a Praat script.[2] Vowel formants were measured at the midpoint of the vowel. In Spanish, vowel formants of stressed and unstressed vowels were measured, but in German, only vowel formants of schwa were measured.

A subset of productions (n=100 syllables) was reanalysed by a second tester. The subset included productions of stressed and unstressed German and Spanish vowels from two different children. Inter-rater reliability was high, based on a Pearson correlation coefficient [$r(100)=0.950$, $p<0.001$].

2.3 Results

2.3.1 Quantity of Unstressed Vowels in Monolinguals and Bilinguals

Spanish

Results of the acoustic analyses of duration for Spanish are shown in Table 2.3. It displays the mean ratios of stressed to unstressed vowels, the standard deviation of the ratios, and the number of items on which the ratio is based. Table 2.3 shows that Spanish monolinguals produced ratios of less than 1.0 for phrase-final trochees (mean=0.87); ratios of about 1.0 for phrase-medial trochees and for the initial SW form in quadrisyllabics, and ratios of more than 1.0 (mean=1.19) for WSW words.[3] In other words, the

2 We are very grateful to Dr Torreira, from the Max Planck Institute for Psycholinguistics, Nijmegen who provided us with the Praat script, and to Dr Schmidt and Dr Woerner, from the Research Center on Multilingualism (University of Hamburg), who adapted it to our needs.

3 In Spanish the ratios of stressed to final unstressed syllables in WSW and SWSW words were also measured. They were approximately 1.0 (mean ratio for monolinguals is 1.05 and 0.97, and for bilinguals 1.08 and 1.05, for WSW and SWSW words respectively).

unstressed vowel was longer than the stressed vowel in phrase-final position, about the same length as the stressed vowel in phrase-medial position, and shorter than the stressed vowel when in word-initial position.

Results in bilingual Spanish show increased ratios in all conditions: a ratio of 0.98 (instead of 0.87) for phrase-final trochees, of 1.04 (instead of 1.0) for phrase-medial trochees, of 1.10 (instead of 1.01) for the initial SW form in quadrisyllables and of 1.36 (instead of 1.19) for WSW words. As shown in Table 2.3, these differences are minimal and the general pattern across prosodic conditions resembles that of the monolinguals, in which ratios are lowest for phrase-final position and highest for WSW words. The only child who doesn't follow this trend is Simon who has a ratio of 1.0 rather than less than 1.0 for phrase-final trochees; however, a similar pattern was also seen in one of the monolinguals (María). A series of independent two-tailed t-tests based on mean ratios per child indicated no significant differences in the vowel ratios between monolinguals and bilinguals for any of the prosodic conditions [SW final: $t(4)=-1.09$, $p=0.34$; SW: $t(3)=-1.17$, $p=0.33$; SWSW: $t(4)=-1.48$, $p=0.21$; WSW: $t(3)=-0.92$, $p=0.43$].

Table 2.3. Duration ratios of stressed to unstressed Spanish vowels in three Spanish monolingual and three German-Spanish bilingual children, in phrase-final trochees (SW final), in phrase-medial trochees (SW), in WSW words (ratio of stressed vowel to initial unstressed) and in SWSW words (ratio of initial stressed vowel to the following unstressed).

Child		SW Final	SW	WSW	SWSW
José	M (SD)	0.74 (.41)	0.97 (.42)	1.38 (.54)	1.07 (.48)
	n	22	22	25	13
Maria	M (SD)	1.00 (.20)	1.02 (.20)	1.06 (.22)	1.06 (.20)
	n	17	29	35	7
Miguel	M (SD)	0.89 (.25)	1.01 (.27)	1.19 (.39)	0.96 (.24)
	n	19	30	14	19
Monolinguals	M (SD)	0.87 (.32)	1.00 (.29)	1.19 (.41)	1.01 (.33)
	n	58	81	74	39
Jens	M (SD)	0.94 (.42)	1.09 (.42)	1.64 (.63)	1.16 (.39)
	n	23	29	25	7
Simon	M (SD)	1.08 (.54)	1.02 (.31)	1.21 (.31)	1.04 (.40)
	n	22	26	23	10
Manuel	M (SD)	0.91 (.25)	1.00 (.42)	1.24 (.46)	1.11 (.34)
	n	25	26	32	16
Bilinguals	M (SD)	0.98 (.42)	1.04 (.38)	1.36 (.52)	1.10 (.36)
	n	69	80	80	33

German

Results of the acoustic analyses of duration for German are shown in Table 2.4. In contrast to the Spanish findings, the vowel ratios for the German monolinguals are all above 1.0, meaning that in all conditions the stressed vowel is longer than the schwa vowel. In phrase-final trochees, the differences are moderate (mean ratio of 1.37) but in phrase-medial trochees and in multisyllabic words, the differences are more extreme (mean ratios of 1.70 and 2.31 respectively). The vowel ratios for the bilinguals are all above 1.0; however, the magnitude of the ratio is smaller in phrase-medial trochees (i.e., 1.24 instead of 1.70) and in multisyllabic words (i.e., 1.74 instead of 2.31).[4] Whereas the ratios generally increased in the monolinguals when going from phrase-final to phrase-medial trochees and then on to multisyllabic words, the same was not true of the bilinguals. One bilingual child (Jens) had smaller ratios in phrase-medial as compared to phrase-final position (e.g. 1.18 vs 1.59) and one child (Simon) had similar vowel ratios in phrase-final position and in multisyllables. It also must be noted that the German data were characterized by standard deviations almost twice as large as the ones in the Spanish data.[5] Despite some apparent differences between monolingual and bilinguals, two-tailed t-tests based on mean vowel ratios per child indicated no significant differences between monolinguals and bilinguals for any of the prosodic conditions [SW final: $t(3)=0.33$, $p=0.76$; SW: $t(3)=2.52$, $p=0.086$; SWSW: $t(4)=0.77$, $p=0.48$].

German vs Spanish

The above analyses suggest differences in the stress-to-unstress vowel ratios between Spanish and German. The ratios for Spanish are less than or equal to 1.0 whereas the ratios for German are greater than 1.0. In order to determine whether these differences are statistically significant, we compared the

4 In general, there were no systematic differences between WSW and SWSW conditions in the German data. One of the reasons why the vowel ratios are large for SWSW words is that the first stressed syllable receives primary stress whereas in Spanish it receives secondary stress.

5 One factor which may explain the extreme variability observed in the German data was that vowel ratios may vary according to whether the stressed vowel is long or short. Due to space limitations, we have not been able to provide a systematic analysis of the effect of phonological vowel length on stress-to-unstress ratios.

Table 2.4. Duration ratios of stressed to unstressed (schwa) vowels in three German monolingual and three German-Spanish bilingual children in phrase-final trochees (SW final), in medial trochees (SW) and in WSW and SWSW words (ratio of stressed vowel to initial unstressed or ratio of initial stressed vowel to the following unstressed).

Child		SW Final	SW	WSW/SWSW
Britta	M (SD)	1.56 (0.95)	1.89 (0.84)	1.73 (0.70)
	n	20	19	8
Marion	M (SD)	1.28 (0.81)	1.41 (0.86)	3.07 (1.4)
	n	20	14	10
Thomas	M (SD)	1.28 (0.89)	1.73 (0.78)	1.89 (0.70)
	n	20	7	7
Monolinguals	M (SD)	1.37 (0.88)	1.70 (0.85)	2.31 (1.18)
	n	60	40	25
Jens	M (SD)	1.59 (0.68)	1.18 (0.50)	2.41 (1.67)
	n	17	18	7
Simon	M (SD)	1.29 (0.84)	1.34 (0.42)	1.20 (0.35)
	n	35	9	10
Manuel	M (SD)	1.06 (0.28)	1.36 (0.46)	1.81 (0.71)
	n	14	11	12
Bilinguals	M (SD)	1.32 (0.73)	1.24 (0.47)	1.74 (1.02)
	n	66	38	29

mean ratios for the German and Spanish monolingual children in two conditions, SW final and SW, the two prosodic conditions which were comparable across German and Spanish. The multisyllabic condition was not comparable since WSW and SWSW words were grouped together in German and separated out in Spanish. Results indicated that Spanish monolingual children displayed significantly lower vowel ratios than German monolingual children [SW final: $t(4)=-4.14$, $p=0.01$; SW: $t(2)=-4.9$, $p=0.04$]. The mean ratios in the German and Spanish of the bilingual children were not significantly different, however [SW final: $t(2)=-2.14$, $p=0.17$; SW: $t(2)=-2.72$, $p=0.11$]. In sum, although the stress-to-unstress vowel ratios of monolingual and bilingual children did not differ when separately comparing Spanish or German, bilingual children did not show as extreme differences between their two vowel systems as did the respective monolingual children, when comparisons were made between their two languages.

2.3.2 Quality of Unstressed Vowels in Monolinguals and Bilinguals

Spanish

Table 2.5 shows the mean vowel formant measures for stressed and unstressed /a/, /e/ and /o/ in the monolingual and bilingual children. To illustrate the vowel formant differences on an individual basis, we display formant values for ['a]–[a] and ['e]–[e] as produced by monolingual Miguel and bilingual Manuel (see Figures 2.2 to 2.5). In the monolingual data, there are certain trends consistent with the predictions made earlier: the mean F1 of /a/ decreases (by 49Hz), the mean F2 of /e/ decreases (by 78 Hz) and the mean F2 of /o/ increases (by 141 Hz) between stressed and unstressed position. In the bilingual data, the only vowel to evidence any major change between stressed and unstressed position is /e/ (F2 difference of 110 Hz), although on an individual basis some differences are observed for other vowels as suggested by the lowering of F1 in Manuel's production of ['a]–[a] (see Figure 2.4). Nevertheless, the magnitude of these changes is small when compared to the extreme variability present in the data. Paired t-tests indicated no significant differences between mean vowel formant measures for stressed and unstressed syllables in the monolingual and bilingual children.

Table 2.5. Means and standard deviations for vowel formants in stressed and unstressed syllables for the vowels /e/, /a/ and /o/ in the Spanish monolingual and bilingual children.

		Stressed		Unstressed	
	n	F1 M (SD)	F2 M(SD)	F1 M(SD)	F2 M (SD)
Monolinguals					
e-e	29	653 (149)	1431 (388)	710 (166)	1353 (434)
a-a	21	757 (162)	1343 (255)	708 (194)	1509 (381)
o-o	13	706 (136)	1238 (272)	783 (160)	1379 (354)
Bilinguals					
e-e	29	755 (94)	1503 (279)	697 (122)	1393 (329)
a-a	16	982 (186)	1485 (147)	959 (165)	1524 (202)
o-o	18	799 (95)	1280 (149)	802 (132)	1297 (259)

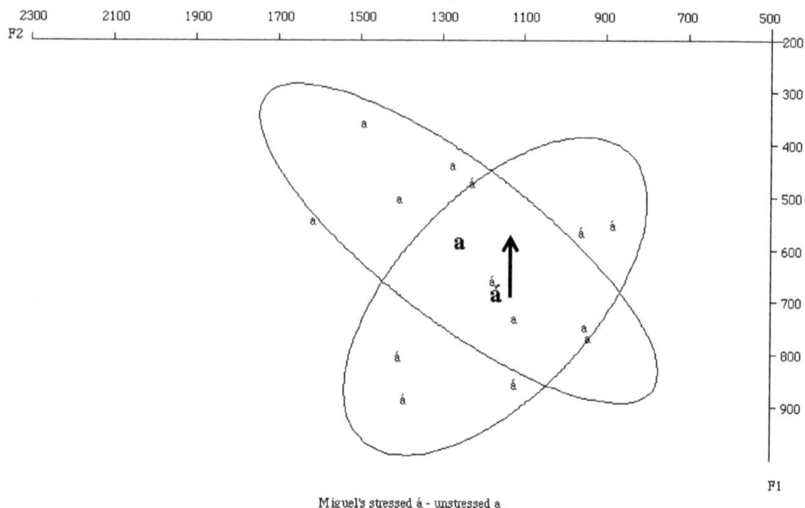

Figure 2.2. Vowel formants for individual productions of Spanish stressed [á] and unstressed [a] by monolingual Miguel. Mean values are indicated by the vowel symbols in the centre of the vowel space and the arrow shows the magnitude and direction of centralization.

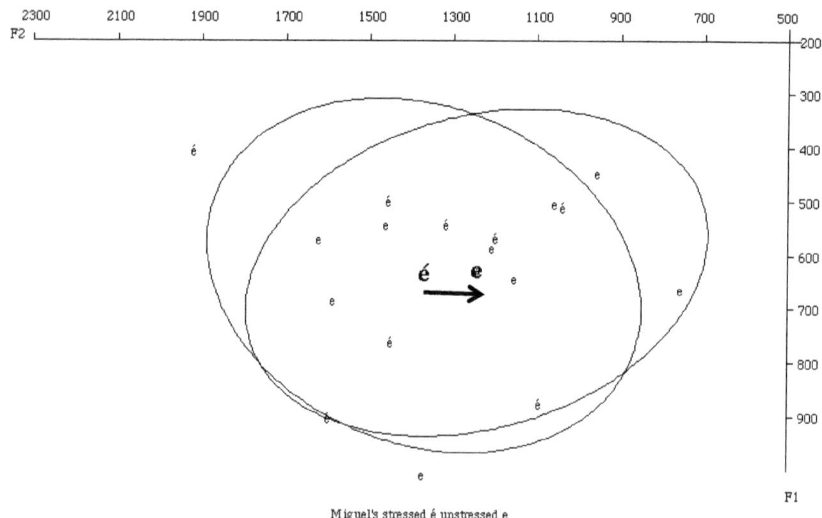

Figure 2.3. Vowel formants for individual productions of Spanish stressed [é] and unstressed [e] by monolingual Miguel.

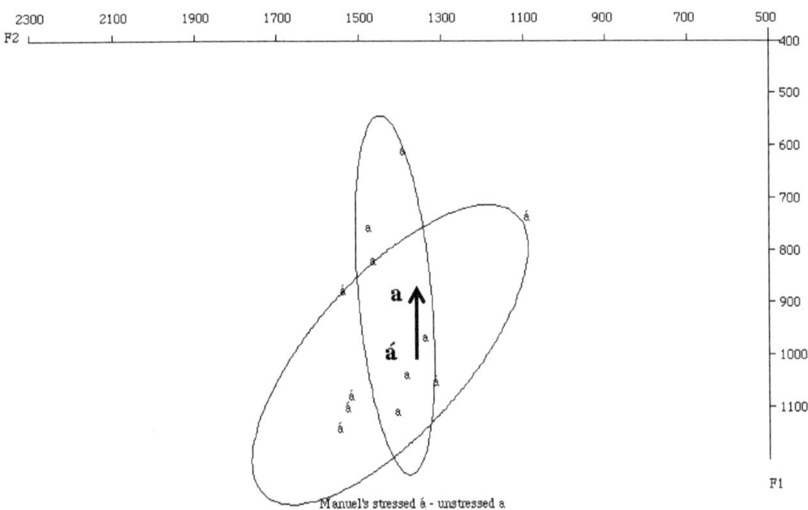

Figure 2.4. Vowel formants for individual productions of Spanish stressed [á] and unstressed [a] by bilingual Manuel.

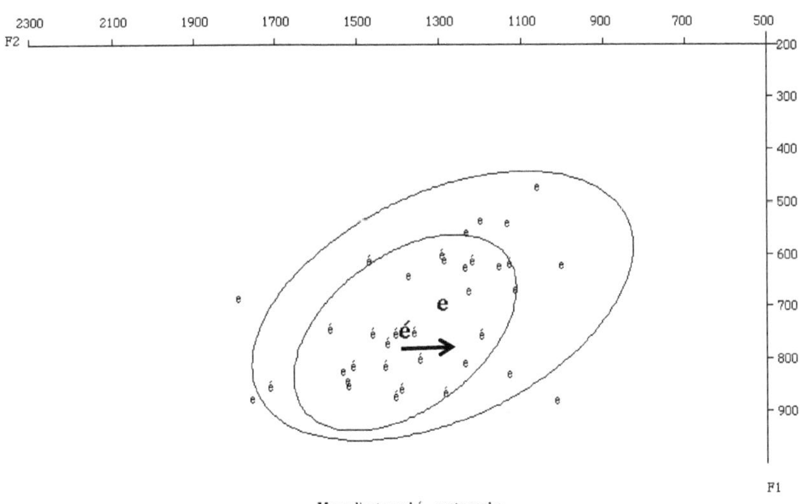

Figure 2.5. Vowel formants for individual productions of Spanish stressed [é] and unstressed [e] by bilingual Manuel.

German

Figures 2.6 to 2.8 display the schwa vowel spaces for the monolingual and bilingual children across the three prosodic conditions. The group means and standard deviations of F1s and F2s are given in Table 2.6. The schwa scatterplots attest to enormous acoustic variability in the realization of schwa; however, despite the variability, we observe that the vowel spaces of each group are not completely overlapping. In SW final, the bilinguals' F1s are slightly higher and their F2s are considerably higher than those of monolinguals; in SW position, there are few differences in F2 but more differences in F1 between monolinguals and bilinguals; in the multisyllabic words, there are differences in both the F1s and F2s of the monolinguals in comparison to the bilinguals. Independent two-tailed t-tests based on mean formant values per child indicated significant differences in some but not all of the formant values. Specifically, there were significant differences between the F2 values of monolinguals and bilinguals in the SW final condition [F2: $t(3)=-4.78$; $p=0.02$] and between the F1 values of monolinguals and bilinguals in the multisyllabic condition [F1: $t(4)=3.21$, $p=0.03$]. There were also marginally significant differences between F1 values of monolinguals and bilinguals in the SW condition [F1: $t(2)=-3.52$, $p=0.07$]. In sum, the acoustic quality of schwa was not the same in monolingual and bilingual children.

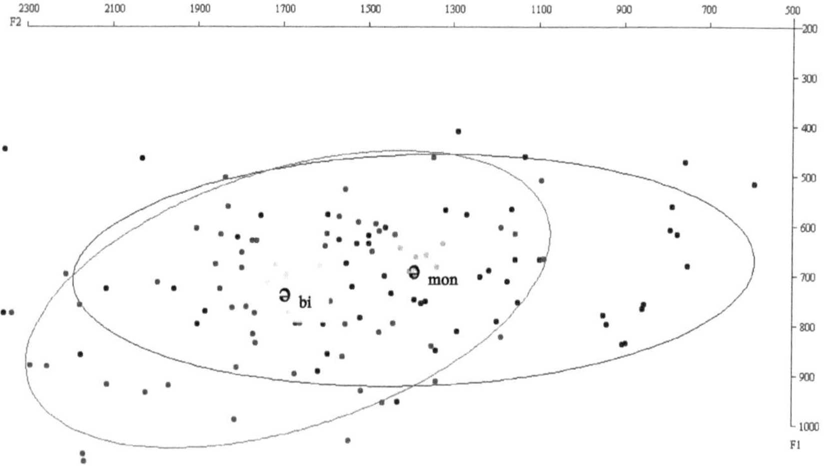

Figure 2.6. Vowel formants for individual productions of schwa in SW final condition by monolingual and bilingual German-speaking children. Mean values are indicated by the vowel symbols in the centre of the vowel space.

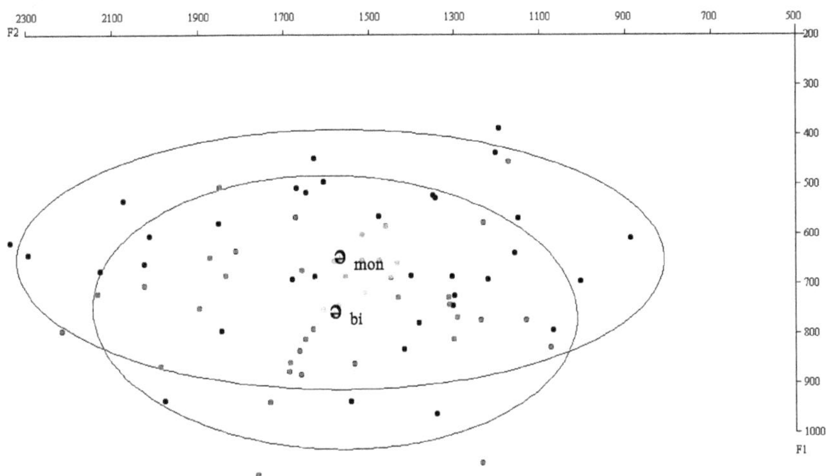

Figure 2.7. Vowel formants for individual productions of schwa in SW condition by monolingual and bilingual German-speaking children.

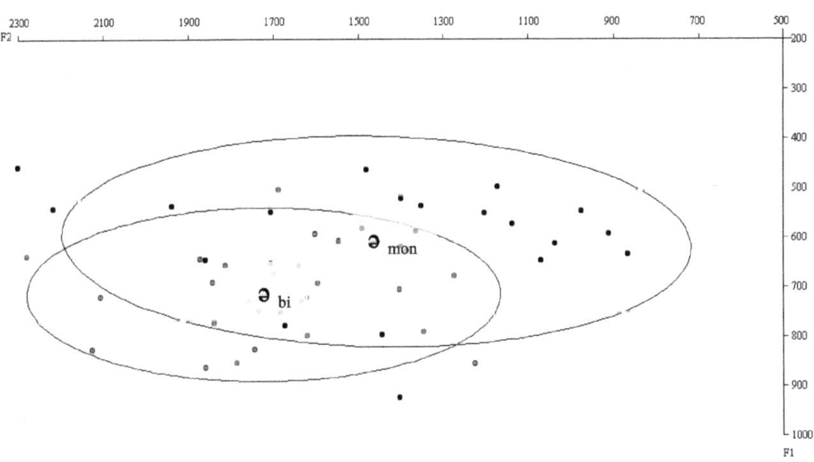

Figure 2.8. Vowel formants for individual productions of schwa in WSW/SWSW condition by monolingual and bilingual German-speaking children.

Table 2.6. Means and standard deviations for vowel formants in schwa syllables across the three prosodic conditions in the German monolingual and bilingual children.

	n	F1 M (SD)	F2 M (SD)
Monolinguals			
SW final	60	691 (118)	1392 (404)
SW	40	665 (171)	1609 (401)
WSW/SWSW	25	609 (109)	1459 (378)
Bilinguals			
SW final	66	761 (151)	1686 (309)
SW	38	760 (140)	1593 (302)
WSW/SWSW	30	722 (100)	1735 (272)

2.4 Discussion

This study has examined quantitative and qualitative vowel reduction in a group of monolingual and bilingual German-Spanish children, aged 2;6 to 3;0. We examined stress-to-unstress ratios across different prosodic conditions, and compared the vowel formants of stressed and unstressed vowels in Spanish as well as measured the vowel formants of schwa in German. Our results revealed that the stress-to-unstress ratios of the Spanish and German monolinguals were significantly different (in SW final and SW position) but not the ratios of the bilinguals. The bilinguals' ratios tended to be larger in Spanish than those of the Spanish monolinguals and smaller in German than those of the German monolinguals. Thus, the trends were consistent with bidirectional cross-linguistic interaction.[6]

The vowel formant findings in Spanish indicated minor quality differences between stressed and unstressed vowels in both the monolingual and bilingual populations. Such formant differences were in the right direction, although hardly noticeable when compared to the considerable overlap between stressed and unstressed vowel spaces. In German, however, there were some consistent vowel quality differences between the schwas produced by monolingual and bilingual children. The F1 and F2 values tended to be more extreme in the bilinguals and these differences

6 It does seem paradoxical that bilingual infants can make fine discrimination in perception of rhythm (Bosch and Sebastián-Gallés 2001) but not in production; it must be conceded that cross-lingusitic interaction may operate differently in perception versus production.

reached significance in certain prosodic conditions. In the remainder of this discussion, we will consider the findings in relation to previous work on vowel reduction and rhythm in second language and bilingual learners.

Many studies have shown that second language learners experience difficulties reducing or not reducing vowels to an appropriate extent (Bond and Fokes 1985; Flege and Bohn 1989; Kondo 2000). The same tendencies were present in our group of young simultaneous bilinguals; nevertheless, the differences between monolinguals and bilinguals were small and, for the most part, non-significant. One possibility is that vowel reduction is not a fragile domain for young simultaneous bilinguals as it is for second language learners. Byers and Yavaş (2014) found very few differences between adult monolinguals and early Spanish-English bilingual adults (i.e. bilinguals who had acquired English before the age of 10 years) in the duration of deletable and nondeletable schwa in English. This was in contrast to the findings of schwa production in a group of late Spanish-English bilinguals (i.e. bilinguals who had acquired English after the age of 10 years), who displayed significantly longer schwas than monolinguals and early bilinguals. Mastery of the phonetic cues of vowel reduction may be possible when bilingual input occurs early, as was the case for the young bilinguals in this study and the early adult bilinguals in Byers and Yavaş (2014). A second possibility is that vowel reduction *is* a fragile domain in bilingual learners but methodological factors such as the small subject numbers have obscured potential monolingual-bilingual differences. A study with increased subject numbers may have resulted in some of the apparent trends becoming significant.

The current findings on vowel reduction in young German- and Spanish-speaking children are consistent with rhythmic differences between the two languages. In Spanish we have some evidence for the rhythm category of syllable timing, in that duration ratios were close to 1.0 across all prosodic positions, meaning that stressed and unstressed vowels were of similar length. In German, duration ratios were greater than 1.0 and varied to a greater degree across prosodic condition, consistent with the stress-timed pattern of German. Previous studies on development of rhythm have shown that young bilingual children, aged around 3;0, are not yet distinguishing the rhythmic patterns of their two languages (Kehoe et al. 2011). The current study focusing on one aspect of rhythm is consistent with these prior studies. The differences in duration ratios between the two languages of the bilinguals were not as great as those of the monolingual children and did not reach statistical significance.

We observed some salient differences in the formant values of the schwas produced by the monolingual and bilingual children. It is interesting to relate these findings to those of Flemming (2009) who reported different values for schwa in word-final and non-final position. Flemming (2009) documented considerable variability in the F1s of schwa in final position and in the F2s of schwa in non-final position in English adults. In our study, we observed considerable variability in the F1s and F2s of schwas in both final and non-final position. Where we did observe some differences between the monolingual and bilingual children was in the F2 in (phrase)-final position and in the F1 in non-(phrase)-final position, which according to Flemming (2009) are the more stable formants.[7] We assume that, amongst all the variability present in the data, these are the formants in which significant differences are most likely to be detected. We do not have an explanation as to why F2 was more extreme in phrase-final position in the bilinguals; however, in non-final (phrase) position, the more extreme values of F1 suggest that the schwas produced by bilinguals are more open and resemble /a/-like productions, /a/ being considered the most unmarked vowel.[8] These are similar to the observations made by Kondo (2000) with Japanese-English bilinguals.

Interestingly, the main differences we observed between the monolingual and bilingual children pertained to German phonology. Few differences were observed in qualitative aspects of vowel reduction in Spanish. Why differences were more apparent in German than in Spanish may relate to the marked system of German vowels, which contains schwa as well as full vowels. Apart from its phonetic characteristics, schwa has phonological properties which make it a more complex vowel to acquire than a full unstressed vowel (Kehoe and Lleó 2003; Levelt 2008).

2.5 Conclusions

Our findings on the vowel reduction patterns of young German-Spanish bilinguals are consistent with mutual influence between the two languages.

7 Flemming (2009) distinguishes between word-final and word-medial schwa. Formant analyses on the child data showed differences between phrase-final and non-phrase-final schwa. It might be assumed that word-final (but phrase-medial) schwa may pattern with word-internal schwa in terms of coarticulatory effects in child speech.

8 It may be interesting to point out that the Catalan spoken in Barcelona has experienced a process of F1 raising of schwa, too, bringing this vowel very near to /a/.

The stress-to-unstress duration ratios of the bilingual children were not as extreme as those of their respective monolingual counterparts and the vowel quality of schwa was more open than in the monolingual German children. Differences between monolingual and bilingual groups were minimal, however, which may suggest that vowel reduction is not a fragile domain for young simultaneous bilinguals.

References

Allen, G. and Hawkins, S. (1978). The development of phonological rhythm. In A. Bell and J. Hooper (eds.), *Syllables and Segments*, 173–85. New York: North Holland Publishing Company.

Bartels, S., Darcy, I. and Höhle, B. (2009). Schwa syllables facilitate word segmentation by 9-month-old German-learning infants. In J. Chandlee, M. Franchini, S. Lord and G.-M. Rheiner (eds.), *Proceedings of the 33rd Annual Boston University Conference on Language Development*, 73–84. Somerville, MA: Cascadilla Press.

Boersma, P. and Weenink, D. (2007). Praat: Doing Phonetics by Computer. [Computer program]. Version 5.3.51, retrieved 2 June 2013 from http://www.praat.org/.

Bond, Z. and Fokes, J. (1985) Non-native patterns of English syllable timing. *Journal of Phonetics* 13: 407–20.

Bosch, L. and Sebastián-Gallés, N. (2001). Evidence of early language discrimination abilities in infants from bilingual environments. *Infancy* 2: 29–49.

Bunta, F. and Ingram, D. (2007). The acquisition of speech rhythm by bilingual Spanish- and English-speaking 4- and 5-year-old children. *Journal of Speech, Language, and Hearing Research* 50: 999–1014.

Bürki, A., Fougeron, C., Gendrot, C. and Frauenfelder, U. (2011). Phonetic reduction versus phonological deletion of French schwa: Some methodological issues. *Journal of Phonetics* 39: 279–88.

Byers, E. and Yavaş, M. (2014). Durational variability of schwa in early and late Spanish-English bilinguals. *International Journal of Bilingualism*. Early online, doi: 10.1177/1367006914547936.

Cambier-Langeveld, T., Nespor, M. and van Heuven, V. (1997). The domain of final lengthening in production and perception in Dutch. In *Proceedings of the Fifth European Conference on Speech Communication and Technology* (Eurospeech 1997), Vol. 2, Rhodes, 931–34.

Dasher, R. and Bolinger, D. (1982). On pre-accentual lengthening. *Journal of the International Phonetic Association* 12: 58–69.

Dauer, R. (1983). Stress-timing and syllable-timing reanalyzed. *Journal of Phonetics* 11: 51–62.

Delattre, P. (1969). An acoustic and articulatory study of vowel reduction in four languages. *International Review of Applied Linguistics in Language Teaching* 7(4): 295–325.

Flege, J. and Bohn, O. (1989). An instrumental study of vowel reduction and stress placement in Spanish accented English. *Studies in Second Language Acquisition* 11: 35–62.

Flemming, E. (2009). The phonetics of schwa vowels. In D. Minkova (ed.), *Phonological Weakness in English*, 78–95. Houndsmill, England: Palgrave Macmillan.

Flemming, E. and Johnson, S. (2007). Rosa's roses. Reduced vowels in American English. *International Phonetic Association* 37: 83–96.

Grabe, E. and Low, E. (2002). Durational variability in speech and the rhythm class hypothesis. In C. Gussenhoven and N. Warner (eds.), *Papers in Laboratory Phonology* 7: 515–46. Berlin: Mouton de Gruyter.

Gut, U. (2003). Non-native speech rhythm in German. In M.J. Solé and J. Romero (eds.), *Proceedings of 15th International Congress of Phonetic Sciences, ICPhS, Barcelona*, 2437–40.

Kaltenbacher, E. (1997). German speech rhythm in L2 acquisition. In J. Leather and A. James (eds.), *New Sounds 97. Proceedings of the Third Symposium on the Acquisition of Second Language Speech*, University of Klagenfurt.

Kehoe, M. (2002). The acquisition of unstressed syllables in bilingual children with a particular focus on vowel reduction. Paper presented at the Deutsche Gesellschaft für Sprachwissenschaft (DGfS) Mannheim.

Kehoe, M. and Lleó, C. (2003). A phonological analysis of schwa in German first language acquisition. *Canadian Journal of Linguistics* 48: 289–327.

Kehoe, M., Lleó, C. and Rakow, M. (2011). Speech rhythm in the pronunciation of German and Spanish monolingual and German-Spanish bilingual 3-year-olds. *Linguistische Berichte* 227: 323–51.

Kondo, Y. (2000). Production of schwa by Japanese speakers of English: An acoustic study of shifts in coarticulatory strategies from L1 to L2. In M. Broe and J. Pierrehumbert (eds.), *Papers in Laboratory Phonology 5. Acquisition and the Lexicon*, 29–39. Cambridge, UK: Cambridge University Press.

Koopmans-van Beinum, F. (1994). What's in a schwa? Durational and spectral analysis of natural continuous speech and diphones in Dutch. *Phonetica* 51: 68–79.

Lehiste, I. (1972). The timing of utterances and linguistic boundaries. *Journal of the Acoustical Society of America* 51: 2018–24.

Levelt, C. (2008). Phonology and phonetics in the development of schwa in Dutch child language. *Lingua* 118: 1344–61.

Lleó, C. (2012). Monolingual and bilingual phonoprosodic corpora of child German and child Spanish. In T. Schmidt and K. Wörner (eds.), *Multilingual Corpora and Multilingual Corpus Analysis. Hamburger Studies on Multilingualism 14*, 107–22. Amsterdam/Philadelphia: John Benjamins.

Martínez Celdrán, E. (1995). En torno a las vocales del español: Análisis y reconocimiento. *Estudios de Fonética Experimental* 7: 197–218.

Menke, M. (2010). Examination of the Spanish vowels produced by Spanish-English bilingual children. *Southwest Journal of Linguistics* 28: 98–135.
Menke, M. and Face, T. (2010). Second language Spanish vowel production. An acoustic analysis. *Studies in Hispanic and Lusophone Linguistics* 3: 181–214.
Mok, P. (2011). The acquisition of rhythm by three-year-old bilingual and monolingual children. *Bilingualism: Language and Cognition* 14: 458–72.
Mok, P. (2013). Speech rhythm of monolingual and bilingual children at age 2;6: Cantonese and English. *Bilingualism: Language and Cognition* 16: 693–703.
Navarro Tomás, T. (1916). Cantidad de las vocales acentuadas. *Revista de Filología Española* 3: 387–408.
Navarro Tomás, T. (1917). Cantidad de las vocales inacentuadas. *Revista de Filología Española* 4: 371–88.
Navarro Tomás, T. (1918). *Manual de pronunciación española.* Madrid: Imprenta de los sucesores de Hernando.
Payne, E., Post, B., Astruc, L., Prieto, P. and Vanrell, M. (2012). Measuring child rhythm. *Language and Speech* 55 (2): 202–28.
Pike, K. (1945). *The Intonation of American English.* Ann Arbor, MI: University of Michigan Press.
Quilis, A. and Esgueva, M. (1983). Realización de los fonemas vocálicos españoles en posición fonética normal. In M. Esgueva and M. Cantarero (eds.), *Estudios de Fonética*, 159–251. Madrid: Consejo Superior de Investigaciones Científicas.
Ramus, F., Nespor, M. and Mehler, J. (1999). Correlates of linguistic rhythm in the speech signal. *Cognition* 73: 265–92.
Ronquest, R.E. (2013). An acoustic examination of unstressed vowel reduction. In C. Howe, S. Blackwell and M. Lubbers Quesada (eds.), *Heritage Spanish. Selected Proceedings of the 15th Hispanic Linguistics Symposium*, 157–71. Somerville, MA: Cascadilla Proceedings Project.
Schmidt, E. and Post, B. (2015a). The development of prosodic features and their contribution to rhythm production in simultaneous bilinguals. *Language and Speech* 58: 24–47.
Schmidt, E. and Post, B. (2015b). Language interaction in the development of speech rhythm in simultaneous bilinguals. In E. Delais-Roussarie, M. Avanzi and S. Herment (eds.), *Prosody and Language in Contact*, 271–91. New York: Springer.
Simonet, M. and Cobb, K. (2015). Adult second language learning of Spanish vowels. *Hispania* 98: 47–60.

Margaret Kehoe lectures at the University of Geneva and works as a speech-language pathologist with bilingual children.

Conxita Lleó, now retired, was Professor of Romance Linguistics at the University of Hamburg, Germany.

3 Cross-Language Influence in the Productions of French-English Bilingual Children: Separation or Interaction?

Christelle Dodane and Ranka Bijeljac-Babic

3.1 Introduction

When two languages are learned simultaneously, in balanced quantities, and the bilingualism is socially accepted, it is assumed that each language will be learned like a native language. While adult bilinguals can reach native-like levels of lexical, syntactic and semantic skills, the prosody and especially the rhythm of their spoken language appears to be resistant to native-like acquisition (Abrahamsson and Hyltenstam 2009; Birdsong 2006). If adult bilinguals never achieve full separation of their systems at the phonological/prosodic level, can we expect bilingual children to be able to do so? In this study, we try to answer the question of whether simultaneous bilingual French-English children produce words in each language with a native-like stress or accent or whether they speak both languages in ways that reflect the reciprocal influences between the two systems. Only a handful of bilingual phonology studies have compared phonetic and/or phonological inventories (Ingram 1981/82; Schnitzer and Krasinski 1994, 1996; Zlatic, McNeilage, Matyear and Davis 1997), phonotactic structures (Johnson and Lancaster 1998; Paradis 1996) or the acoustic characteristics of phonemes (Deuchar and Clark 1996; Deuchar and Quay 2000; Kehoe, Lléo and Rakow 2004) in infants learning different pairs of languages. The results of these studies suggest that separation occurs at a very early stage (for a review, see Bhatia and Ritchie 1999) and that the phonologies show two 'independent systems'.

More recently, researchers have moved away from investigating whether there are one or two phonological systems and accept that there are two systems that interact. Thus, the phonological development of children who are exposed to two or more languages may always be different from that of monolingual children and rather than separation, there is interaction between the two prosodic systems. For example, in a study of truncation patterns (reduction of word duration) in French and/or English at age 2;6, Paradis (2001) found that the bilinguals' patterns were similar but not identical to those of the monolinguals in each language, leading to the conclusion that the bilinguals had separate but not autonomous phonological systems. Lleó (2002) studied the development of prosodic patterns in another pair of languages, in a longitudinal study of German-Spanish bilingual and monolingual children between the ages of 1;5 and 2;4 years. Prosodic patterns were found to interact, suggesting either acceleration or delay in the course of acquisition. Gawlitzek-Maiwald and Tracy (1996) argue in favour of acceleration only, asserting that one system may exert a positive influence on the other ('bilingual bootstrapping'), whereas Paradis and Genesee (1996: 4) suggest the possibility of three outcomes – acceleration, transfer and delay (deceleration) – in the 'overall rate of acquisition' due to the 'burden of acquiring two languages'. Other studies which provide evidence for early differentiation as well as interaction between phonological systems include Fabiano-Smith and Goldstein's (2010) study of Spanish-English 3–4-year-old bilinguals, Kehoe's (2015) study of the early productions of one-year-old Spanish-German bilinguals and Vihman's (2016) study of prosodic templates in English-speaking bilinguals (English-Estonian; English-German; English-Spanish).

The following question therefore remains unanswered: do children acquiring two languages from birth develop the specific prosodic structures of each language and separate the two languages at an early stage of production? Or, do the developing systems interact, with the prosodic properties of one language dominating early productions in both languages, due to the fact that they are perceptually more salient and/or easier to reproduce? From this perspective, the simultaneous acquisition of French and English is particularly interesting as these languages are rhythmically distinct (Abercrombie 1967; Ladefoged 1975; Pike 1946) leading to processing differences in adults (Cutler, Mehler, Norris and Segui 1983, 1989) and infants (Nazzi, Iakimova, Bertoncini, Frédonie and Alcantara 2006). Contrary to English, French does not have stress at the word level, but at the phrase level (Féry, Hörnig and Pahaut 2011). Whereas in English, lexical stress has a tendency to affect the first syllable of lexical words, primary stress in French has a fixed position on the final full syllable of the last lexical item of a stress group (Di Cristo 1998: 196) and thus is completely predictable (Delattre 1965). For that reason, stress cannot play a distinctive role at the lexical level as in English, but rather plays a demarcative function at the utterance level. Concerning the acoustic correlates of stress, primary stress in French is created mainly through temporal cues, the final syllable being approximately two times longer than the unstressed syllables, with no increase in fundamental frequency f0 or intensity (Rossi 1980; Vaissière 1991). In English by contrast, lexical stress is made salient by the use of higher f0, greater intensity and longer duration, which makes it more salient than in French. Gleitman and Wanner (1982) assume that stressed syllables could play a major role in bootstrapping learning. Because of their perceptive salience, stressed syllables are probably easier to localize. This information in syllable stress could help the child in lexical categorization (Dominey and Dodane 2004). In fact, for English children, the learning of non-stressed syllables is slower than the learning of stressed syllables (Brown 1973; Gerken 1996). Given the prosodic differences between French and English, we may expect these differences to manifest early in the speech of French and English monolingual children.

In a study comparing the acoustic realization of stress in the vocalizations of nine English and five French monolingual children between 13 and 20 months, Vihman, DePaolis and Davis (1998) showed that English-learning toddlers produced almost the same proportion of trochaic (strong-weak) and iambic (weak-strong) stress structure in disyllabic words, while the large majority of early words by the French toddlers were produced following an iambic pattern. Furthermore, they showed that production in these two languages differed significantly in terms of the acoustic realization of stress, f0, intensity and duration. First, French toddlers displayed higher f0 on the second, 'stressed' syllable in iambic words but also greater f0 variability on the stressed syllable, while the second-to-first vowel duration ratios (1.62) were stable and adult-like. Second, English toddlers showed only slight second syllable lengthening, higher f0 on the first syllable and greater differences in intensity between stressed and unstressed syllables when compared to the French toddlers. The authors concluded that in their production of disyllabic words, English and French monolinguals displayed the characteristics of their respective languages. More recently, DePaolis, Vihman and Kunnari (2008) extended the investigation of the acoustic correlates of lexical stress in disyllabic vocalizations to American English, Finnish, French and Welsh infants at the onset of word use (10–18 months). For all four languages, they found evidence of final syllable lengthening, but with smaller and less variable duration ratios for Finnish and Welsh than for either American English or French, and a great degree of variability for intensity and f0. While Finnish and Welsh infants produced proportionally more trochaic and iambic patterns, respectively, French and

American infants produced multiple stress or accentual patterns (acoustic iambs and trochees), which is consistent with other studies (Vihman and DePaolis 1998; Vihman et al. 1998; Vihman, Nakai and DePaolis 2006). It seems that the complete integration of lexical stress requires lexical knowledge or experience.

What about the productions of bilingual children? Those children are faced with a wide range of competing and sometimes even contradictory phonological input. They have to master a complex task that includes learning to make simultaneous adjustments to languages with contrasting features at many levels, including stress. Unfortunately, there are fewer studies with bilingual than with monolingual children, notably with respect to the acoustic characteristics of stress. Two studies have been conducted with French-English bilingual children, but with relatively contradictory results. LaBelle (2000) argued for a trochaic bias in the English and French productions of a young English-French bilingual learner (1;6–2;4), while on the basis of data from another English-French bilingual child (2;0–4;2), Rose and Champdoizeau (2008) showed that this child mastered the basic metrical properties and acoustic correlates of stress for each of the target languages. However, both studies are limited to a single subject, and include no comparisons with monolingual children of the same age.

Bunta and Ingram (2007) performed a larger-scale study with 4- to 5-year-old English-Spanish bilingual children (10 subjects) and compared their productions to those of monolingual children and bilingual adults. Focusing on the acquisition of speech rhythm, and not on the acoustic correlates of stress, they showed that while the youngest bilinguals (3;9–4;5) produced distinct rhythmic patterns in each of the two languages, their productions were different from those of monolinguals, a difference that disappeared in the older bilinguals (4;6–5;2). These results thus seem to confirm the hypothesis of increasing rhythmic differentiation between the two languages with age.

The purpose of the present study is to investigate the acquisition of lexical stress in the disyllabic words of French-English bilingual children by measuring the acoustic correlates of stress (f0, duration and intensity) and to compare the performance of these children with French and English monolingual peers of the same age (3;6–6;0). We hypothesize that the productions of the bilingual children will be different from those of the monolingual children because of possible influence from the specific accentual characteristics of each of the two languages: on one hand, the perceptual salience of stress in English (presence of higher pitch and greater intensity which tends to be localized on the first syllable in disyllabic words), and on the other, the complete predictability of final lengthening in French.

3.2 Method

3.2.1 Participants

Three groups of eight children each participated in the study (mean age: 4;6, range: 3;3–6;0), making 24 participants in total. The first group was made up of eight French-English bilingual children born and living in Paris or the surrounding region (four girls and four boys, mean age: 4;8, range: 3;5–6;0). Bilingual families were recruited through associations of American women living in Paris. These children had been regularly exposed to each of the two languages, their mothers being native speakers of American English, and their fathers, native French speakers. The second group consisted of eight monolingual French children born and living in Poitiers, France, all with monolingual parents (four girls and four boys, mean age: 4;5, range: 3;3–6;0). The children were recruited from the same primary school. The third group consisted of eight monolingual English children born and living in Baltimore, USA (five girls and three boys, mean age: 4;6, range: 3;7–5;5).

The children who participated in the study lived in equivalent socio-economic environments and presented no history of auditory deficiency. There was no significant age difference between the groups ($p=0.2$). Although we did not administer any hearing tests, there was no participant who had any known physical, psychological or cognitive problem, and they all displayed typical language development.

3.2.2 Procedure

Task

The children were recorded either at home or at school while interacting with an experimenter and in the presence of one or both of their parents. For the American monolingual children, the experimenter was anglophone and for the French monolingual children, he was francophone. Bilingual children were recorded over two separate sessions – one in each language. The order of presentation of each language was counterbalanced. A single language was spoken in each session in order to avoid the effects of code switching or code mixing amongst the two languages.

During the word elicitation task, the children had to produce 40/32 disyllabic words in French/English while looking at a picture book. The left-hand page presented a familiar context (kitchen, house, bedroom, bathroom, park, zoo), and the right-hand page showed isolated images corresponding to each of the words that the child had to produce.[1] The experimenter and the parents were asked to encourage the children to produce the words, without producing the target words themselves, so that the child would not be able to imitate them. Each recording session lasted between 15 and 30 minutes, depending on the child.

Materials

We analysed only the words produced in isolation (80% of all productions), excluding the words produced in imitation (4.8%). Out of the 40 disyllabic words in French and 32 in English, bilingual children produced 16 to 23 words (mean: 19.2) in French and 13 to 27 words (mean: 18.9) in English. The French monolinguals produced 24 to 39 words (mean: 29.2) and the English monolinguals produced 12 to 22 words (mean: 14.3). Overall, 359 words were analysed. The difference in words produced across groups can be explained by the fact that children were free to comment on the images and they did not all produce the same number of words. Also, certain children were shyer or more restless than others. In addition, some parents could not refrain from answering before the children's response or from speaking at the same time as the child.

Recordings

The children were videotaped using a Sony PD150 DVCAM digital video recorder. Adults' voices were recorded using a miniature AKG C 420 electrostatic microphone attached to a band worn around the neck. The children's voices were recorded using a Sennheiser ME3 super-cardioid wireless microphone mounted on a helmet, and a Sennheiser SK100 transmitter. A Sennheiser EM 100 receiver was mounted on the camera to capture the audio signal. This system not only allowed the child complete freedom of movement, but it also ensured interference-free transmission.

1 To estimate the vocabulary of bilingual children, we asked parents (or teachers for the French monolingual group) to complete the CDI (Communicative Development Inventory) for English (Fenson, Dale, Reznick, Thal, Bates, Hartung, Pethick and Reilly 1993) and a version of the same questionnaire adapted to the vocabulary of French children (Bassano, Labrell, Champaud, Lemétayer and Bonnet 2005) in order to be certain that the children knew the words that we included in the picture book.

Acoustic Measurements

Each disyllabic word was manually segmented with the Praat software (Boersma and Weenink 2009), using the simultaneous display of the sound waveform and a wideband spectrogram (frequency range: 0–8000 Hz, analysis bandwidth: 260 Hz, pre-emphasis: 6dB/octave, dynamic range: 50 dB). The quality of the f0 detection was checked in adjusting the analysis bandwidth (43 Hz, narrow-band spectrogram) and the frequency range of the spectrogram (0–500 Hz) to compare the automatic f0 detection to the evolution of the first harmonic in the spectrogram. A two-level annotation sheet was created, with one level for the phonetic segmentation and one level for the syllabic segmentation (see Figure 3.1 for an example).

(a)

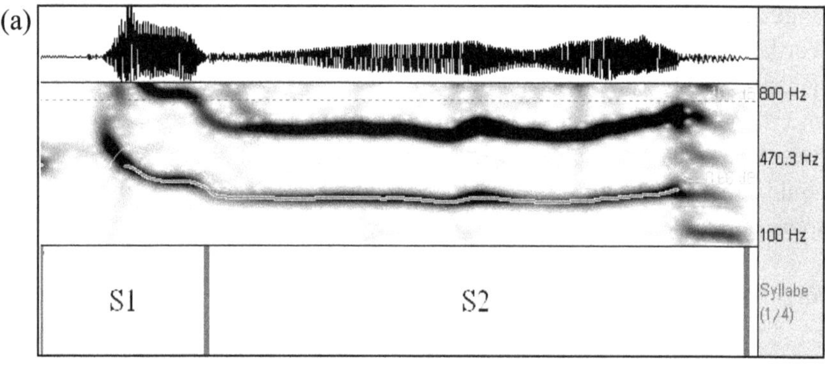

(b)

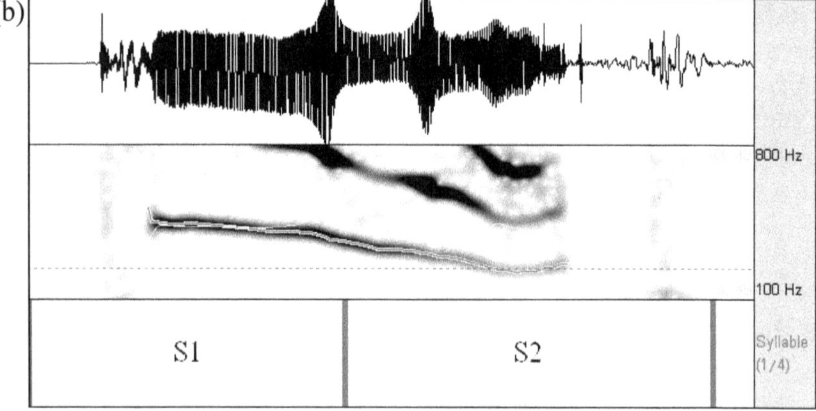

Figure 3.1. Waveforms (upper panels) and spectrograms (lower panels) of disyllabic words: (a) 'carotte' produced by a bilingual child in French and (b) 'carrot' produced by a bilingual child in English, with f0 contour (in Hz, scale 100–800 Hz) indicated by the bold line and intensity contour (in dB) indicated by the line in light grey.

Phonetic segmentation was performed according to principles of phonetic labelling based on a survey of previous work using speech segmentation (Peterson and Lehiste 1960). The acoustic analyses were based upon the segmented syllables and included measures of duration (in ms), fundamental frequency (f0 in Hz) and intensity (in dB) for a total of 359 words and 619 syllables. (1) Duration was extracted for all syllables. Then, we calculated the syllabic duration ratio (duration of syllable 1 divided by duration of syllable 2) to determine the presence of final lengthening on syllable 2 (S2) or, on the contrary, a lengthening on syllable 1 (S1). (2) Mean f0 was extracted for all syllables and subsequently, we computed the f0 differences between S1 and S2 in semitones, using the following equation: Semitone = 39.86 log10 (f0 S1/f0 S2). (3) Intensity values were extracted for all syllables (in dB) and for each word, the relative intensity was determined by computing the ratio of the Root-Mean Square energy (RMS in dB) of the selected syllable to the RMS energy of the loudest point in the selected word. For both intensity and f0 differences, a negative value indicated higher intensity or f0 on the second syllable, but the most important fact was the value of the interval: the higher the value, the greater the perceptual distance between syllables.

Measures of reliability were carried out to evaluate the segmentation made by the two authors for 10% of the words chosen randomly (50 words in French and 50 words in English). The percentage of exact agreement between the authors was 89.5%.

3.3 Results

In order to analyse variations of prosodic cues (duration, f0 and intensity) between S1 and S2 in disyllabic words, paired t-tests were carried out between French and English for each parameter. We predicted that if the productions of French-English-speaking children displayed cross-linguistic influence, fewer differences would be expected between French and English in bilinguals than between French and English in monolinguals. We also predicted a stronger influence of French on English, rather than the other way around, because the bilingual children being tested were living in France. Thus:

1. For duration, it was expected that second syllable lengthening, which characterizes French more than English, would occur in both

languages and more in the bilinguals' French than in the bilinguals' English due to the influence of French in the environment.

2. As stress is much more salient in English than in French and much more frequently localized on the first syllable of disyllabic words, it was expected that bilingual children would produce disyllabic words with a higher f0 and intensity on the first syllable in both languages.

Given that the age range for child participants was large (3;6 to 6:0), we first separated them in two groups: the younger (3;6 to 4;7) and the older children (5;0 to 6;0) (Bunta and Ingram 2007). We used a multivariate ANOVA (analysis of variance) with two independent variables and one dependent variable per analysis for each acoustic parameter. The independent variables were (a) age (two levels: younger vs older) and (b) language (monolingual English, bilingual English, bilingual French and monolingual French). The dependent variables were mean (a) duration ratios S2/S1, (b) f0 differences between S1 and S2, and (c) relative intensity differences between S1and S2.

For duration ratio S2/S1, there was a significant effect of language [F(1,3)=16,14, p<0.0001] and of age [F(1,1)=4,39, p=0.049], but there was no interaction between language and age (F<1). For mean f0 differences between S1 and S2, there was no effect of language [F(1,3)<1] or of age [F(1,1)=2.66, p=0.11], nor of an interaction language x age [F(1,3)=1.39, p=0.11]. There was an effect of language close to significance for relative intensity [F(1,3)=2.48, p=0.085], but no effect of age [F(1,1)<1] and no interaction between these two factors [F(1,3)<1]. Due to the lack of age-related effects, we did not separate younger and older children in the following analysis.

3.3.1 Comparison between Monolinguals and Bilinguals in French

With respect to duration, S2 was longer than S1 for both monolinguals (S2: 429 ms > S1: 248 ms) and bilinguals (S2: 488 ms > S1: 213 ms), but the S2/S1 ratio was significantly greater for bilinguals (2.29) than for monolinguals (1.73) [t(14)=2.89, p <0.02] (see Table 3.1). As for f0, higher mean f0 values were found in S1 than in S2 only in the bilingual group [S1: 312 Hz; S2: 285 Hz, t(14)=1.79, p=0.095], and this difference was close to significance. Concomitantly, there were greater f0 differences between S1 and S2 for bilinguals (1.33 semitones) than for monolinguals (0.22 semitones), but this difference was not significant [t(14)=1.71, p=0.10]. In the analysis of relative intensity, higher values were found in S1 than in S2 for both

Table 3.1. Mean values for duration (in ms), duration ratio, f0 (in Hz), f0 difference (S1–S2; in semitones) and relative intensity (in dB) in disyllabic words produced by monolingual and bilingual children in French and in English (with S1=syllable 1, S2=syllable 2 and the standard deviation indicated in parentheses).

Parameters	Syllable	Monolingual French	Monolingual English	Bilingual French	Bilingual English
Duration (ms)	S1	248 (35)	382 (76)	213 (18)	314 (57)
	S2	429 (83)	547 (120)	488 (104)	412 (81)
Duration ratio	S2/S1	1,73 (0,22)	1,73(0,18)	2,29(0,49)	1,30 (0,17)
f0 (Hz)	S1	327 (25)	262 (36)	312 (70)	277 (42)
	S2	323 (32)	251 (40)	285 (44)	270 (45)
f0 difference (S1–S2; semitones)	S1–S2	0,22 (1,46)	0,98 (2,47)	1,33 (1,89)	0,21(0,57)
Relative intensity (dB)	S1	0,90 (0,01)	0.92 (0,02)	0.89 (0,01)	0.88 (0,02)
	S2	0,88 (00,1)	0.83 (0,03)	0.85 (0,02)	0.83 (0,05)

groups, but were more marked for bilinguals (S1: 0.89; S2: 0.85) than for monolinguals (S1:0.90; S2: 0.88), [$t(14)=1.77$, $p=0.097$]. These results suggest that in French, bilingual children exaggerate the difference in duration between the first and second syllable. Moreover, they produce S1 louder and with a higher f0 than S2. Their French is thus different from the monolinguals' French, showing an influence of their other language, English (see Table 3.1).

3.3.2 Comparison between Monolinguals and Bilinguals in English

With respect to duration, S2 was longer than S1 for monolingual (S2: 547 ms > S1: 382 ms) and bilingual children (S2: 412 ms > S1: 314 ms) in English, but with a significantly greater S2/S1 ratio for monolinguals than for bilinguals (1.73 in monolinguals vs 1.3 in bilinguals) [$t(14)=4.92$, $p<0.001$]. Thus, bilingual children produced only a slight final lengthening in English compared to monolingual children, increasing the difference between their two languages. There were surprisingly only slightly higher f0 values in S1 than in S2 for monolinguals (S1: 262 Hz; S2: 251 Hz) and bilinguals (S1: 277 Hz; S2: 270 Hz) and the f0 differences between S1 and S2 were not significant [$t(14)<1$]. Finally, for relative intensity, we noticed higher values in S1 than in S2 for both groups, more marked for monolinguals (S1: 0.92;

S2: 0.83) than for bilinguals (S1: 0.88; S2: 0.83), the difference between the two groups being close to significance [t(14)=201, p=0.061].

The very small f0 differences between S1 and S2 in English monolinguals are quite surprising and inconsistent with the results obtained in other studies (Kehoe, Stoel-Gammon and Buder 1995; Vihman et al. 1998). One explanation could be that the monolingual children in our study mark stress more by intensity than by f0. We could also explain these results by the fact that the children were intimidated by our presence and the camera, leading to reduced pitch variation. We will discuss this point later, in Section 3.4.

3.3.3 Comparison between English and French in Bilingual Children

Primary stress in French is made salient by the use of final syllable lengthening (S2 in disyllabic words). If we compare the English and French productions of the bilingual children, a lengthening of the second syllable in comparison to the first was found in French (S2: 488 ms > S1: 213 ms) and in English (S2: 412 ms > S1: 314 ms), but the contrast in duration between the two was more marked in French. This difference is reflected in the ratio S2/S1 which is significantly greater in French (2.29) than in English (1.30) [t(14)=5.39, p<0.001]. When the duration ratio is equal or above 1.2, which corresponds to a lengthening of 20%, a listener can detect a difference of duration between the two syllables (Rossi 1980). This final lengthening was accompanied by a greater standard deviation on S2 than on S1 in both languages, more marked in French (S1: 18 ms; S2: 104 ms) than in English (S1: 81 ms; S2: 57 ms). Bilingual children evidence final lengthening in both languages, but they exaggerate it more in French than in English, which increases the difference between their two languages. The analysis of various measures of f0 differences showed the influence of English lexical stress on French in the bilinguals' productions. In both languages, bilinguals showed higher values in S1 than in S2 [in French, S1: 312 Hz; S2: 285 Hz; t(7)=1.96, p=0.097; in English, S1: 277 Hz; S2: 270 Hz; t(7)<1]. When we examined the f0 differences between S1 and S2, we noticed that they were bigger for French (1.33 semitones) than for English (0.21 semitones), but this difference was not significant [t(14)=1.27, p=0.22] and none of the other measures of f0 were significant. For relative intensity, we observed significantly higher values in S1 than in S2 in bilinguals in French [S1: 0.89 > S2: 0.85; t(7)=4.17, p=0.004] and in English [S1: 0.88 > S2: 0.83; t(7)=4.39, p=0.003], but there was no significant difference between the two languages [t(14)<1] for this parameter. Taken together, we observed a reciprocal influence of both languages in the productions of the bilingual children. Final lengthening, which is typical of the French language, is produced in both languages, with a S2/S1 ratio larger in French than in English. Moreover, S1 is produced with a higher f0 and intensity than S2.

3.4 Discussion

In this study, we tried to answer the question of whether simultaneous bilingual French-English children produce words in each language with a native-like accent or whether they speak both languages in ways that reflect the reciprocal influences between the two systems. Our analyses were based on the acoustic correlates of lexical stress (f0, duration and relative intensity) in disyllabic French and English words produced by monolingual and bilingual children aged between 3;6 and 6;0. Our results support our hypothesis that French-English-speaking children show cross-linguistic influence in their productions, and that, in each language, lexical stress patterns are different from those of their monolingual peers.

In the case of duration, we found a lengthening of the second syllable in all conditions, but the duration ratio (S2/S1) was greater in French for bilinguals than for monolinguals, while in English the ratio of monolinguals was greater than in bilinguals. French bilinguals exaggerated this feature and produced overly lengthened second syllables (2.29 in French vs 1.30 in English). We suggest that exaggeration of final-syllable lengthening in French allowed them to forcefully exhibit the prominence of this dimension in French as compared to English. In doing so, their productions were not similar to those of their monolingual peers. As far as f0 variations are concerned, we observed weaker evidence for cross-language influence in bilinguals and relative differences between monolinguals and bilinguals in French and English. While there was surprisingly little f0 difference in English between S1 and S2 in monolingual children, f0 on S1 was higher than that of S2 in bilingual children in French, reflecting the English trochaic f0 pattern. Finally, in the case of intensity, we observed that bilinguals used intensity to mark stress in S1 in a similar way in their both languages. Doing that, they over-generalized to French the use of increased loudness in S1 to mark lexical stress in English.

So, bilingual children in our study seem to perfectly capture the accentual characteristics of each of their two languages and they even tend to exaggerate them (exaggeration of final lengthening in French and transfer of the initial accent in English to French, especially for the parameter of intensity). These findings confirm data obtained from bilingual children showing that the phonological development of children who are exposed to two or more languages is consistently different from that of monolingual children (Lleó 2002; Paradis 2007). In the present study, we take this claim further by showing that the production of French lexical stress in bilinguals is at some point influenced by the properties of English.

Even if language discrimination abilities develop very early in bilingual infants (Bosch and Sebastián-Gallés 2001; Werker and Byers-Heinlein 2008) and rhythmical cues help the bilingual infant keep her two languages apart and facilitate the acquisition of syntax, bilingual children cannot avoid some interference between their two languages. Recently, Höhle, Bijeljac-Babic, Herold, Weissenborn and Nazzi (2009) found that German 6-month-olds showed a listening preference for a language-typical trochaic (strong-weak) pattern relative to an iambic (weak-strong) pattern while French 6-month-old infants did not show any preference at all. Further experiments revealed that French-German bilingual 6-month-olds show preference for the trochaic pattern. This suggests that bilingual infants' exposure to one language with lexical stress provides them with a basis for learning its predominant prosodic pattern without any delay compared to monolinguals (Bijeljac-Babic, Höhle and Nazzi 2016).

What are the acoustic correlates of lexical stress, which receive more influence from French and/or English in the productions of bilinguals? Whereas duration on its own appears to offer 'a reasonable acoustic correlate of rhythm in French', 'duration is not sufficient' in English 'and intensity and pitch movement appear to make more important contributions to rhythmic patterns' (Grabe, Post and Watson 1999: 1201). The bilingual children in the current study adopted lengthening of the second syllable more than has been observed in French adult speakers. Bilinguals appear to learn rapidly that duration offers an important acoustic correlate of rhythm and accent in French (Grabe et al. 1999). It seems that in our study, the exaggeration of final-syllable lengthening allowed bilingual children to make this dimension more salient in French compared to English. Dodane (2003) showed such an effect of exaggeration in a study conducted with 27 French children learning English, who produced intonation contours in English with an expanded pitch range and over-generalized the use of these contours to contexts where they should not have appeared. Doing that, their productions sounded more native-like.

Moreover, bilingual children produced disyllabic words with higher f0 and intensity on the first than the second syllable, tending to reproduce in French the lexical stress of English. We did not find significant f0 differences between S1 and S2 in English in either monolinguals or bilinguals. These results are surprising compared to previous findings (Kehoe et al. 1995; Vihman et al. 1998). For example, Kehoe et al. (1995) showed that American children between 18 and 30 months of age marked differences in stress, with a higher f0 on S1 in disyllabic words, much more than using duration and intensity. In contrast, adults made less use of f0 but greater use of intensity and duration to create stress contrast in their two-syllable productions. In our study, monolingual children used intensity and duration more to mark stress on S1 in disyllabic words, maybe because they were older (3;6 to 6;0) than the children in the study of Kehoe et al. (1995). One possible explanation may be that the acquisition of lexical stress patterns in French-English bilingual children follows a principle of 'simplicity' (Konopczynski 1991) according to which the acquisition of stress patterns in languages with fixed stress such as French is generally faster than in languages where the placement of stress is less predictable, such as English. Thus, the lengthening of the second syllable, rapidly stabilized in the course of language development, would come to dominate the other language and induce minor variations compared to the speech of monolingual children. However, the pitch contrast between S1 and S2, observed in adult production in English, could take place over several years, even in the case of monolingual speakers. Indeed, in a study conducted by Whitworth (2002) on the acquisition of speech rhythm in English-German bilingual children, bilinguals distinguished the speech rhythm of both languages at 9;11, although adult-like rhythm was not completely acquired in German- and English-speaking monolingual children until 11 years of age. In another study, which examined how the productions of monolingual and bilingual children were evaluated by native monolingual adults in French and in English (Bijeljac-Babic and Dodane 2009), older monolingual children were more accurately identified as monolingual speakers than the younger ones, whereas the percentage of bilinguals identified as monolinguals remained the same regardless of their age.

Future research should explore whether the speed at which bilinguals are able to acquire the accent of each language depends on the age of acquisition (Flege 1995) and the proximity/distance between the two languages in acquisition. Recent studies have pointed to delays or differences in bilingual children relative to monolinguals in the acquisition of VOT (Deuchar and Clark 1996; Johnson and Wilson 2002; Kehoe et al. 2004) or speech rhythm (Bunta and Ingram 2007) in different language pairs. Furthermore, longitudinal studies in the period between the onset of first words and the first school years will tell us more about eventual changes in the nature of cross-linguistic interference, as bilinguals gradually improve their command of each language.

References

Abercombie, D. (1967). *Elements of General Phonetics*. Edinburgh: University Press.

Abrahamsson, N. and Hyltenstam, K. (2009) Age of onset and nativelikeness in a second language: Listener perception versus linguistic scrutiny. *Language Learning* 59: 249–306.

Bassano, D., Labrell, F., Champaud, C., Lemétayer, F. and Bonnet, P. (2005). Le DLPF: Un nouvel outil pour l'évaluation du Développement du Langage de Production en Français. *Enfance* 2: 171–208.

Bhatia T.K. and Ritchie, W. (1999). Language mixing and second language acquisition. In C.K. Elaine. and G. Martohardjono (eds.), *The Development of Second Language Grammars*, 241–67. Amsterdam: John Benjamins.

Bijeljac-Babic, R. and Dodane, C. (2009). Perception of native vs. foreign accent: Is the accent in the words or in the listener's head? *Speech and Language*, 3rd International conference on fundamental and applied aspects of speech and language, Belgrade, 13–14 November 2009.

Bijeljac-Babic, R., Höhle, B. and Nazzi, T. (2016). Early prosodic acquisition in bilingual infants: The case of the perceptual trochaic bias. *Frontiers in Psychology* 7: 210.

Birdsong, D. (2006). Age and second language acquisition and processing: A selective overview. *Language Learning:* 56: 9–49.

Boersma, P. and Weenink, D. (2009). Praat: Doing phonetics by computer (version 5.0), Retrieved on 10 November 2009 from http://www.praat.org

Bosch, L. and Sebastián-Gallés, N. (2001). Evidence of early language discrimination abilities in infants from bilingual environments. *Infancy* 2: 29–49.

Brown, R. (1973). *A First Language*. Cambridge: Harvard University Press.

Bunta, F. and Ingram, D. (2007). The acquisition of speech rhythm by bilingual Spanish-and English-speaking 4- and 5-year old children. *Journal of Speech, Language, and Hearing Research* 50: 999–1014.

Cutler, A., Mehler, J., Norris, D.G. and Segui, J. (1983). A language-specific comprehension strategy. *Nature* 304: 159–60.

Cutler, A., Mehler, J., Norris, D.G. and Segui, J. (1989). Limits on bilingualism. *Nature* 340: 141–77.

Delattre, P. (1965). *Comparing the Phonetic Features of English, French, German and Spanish*. Heidelberg: Julius Gross Verlag.

DePaolis, R.A., Vihman, M.M. and Kunnari, S. (2008). Prosody in production at the onset of word use: A cross-linguistic study. *Journal of Phonetics* 36: 406–22.

Deuchar, M. and Clark, A. (1996). Early bilingual acquisition of the voicing contrast in English and Spanish. *Journal of Phonetics* 24: 351–65.

Deuchar, M. and Quay, S. (2000). *Bilingual Acquisition: Theoretical Implications of a Case Study*. Oxford, New York: Oxford University Press.

Di Cristo, A. (1998). Intonation in French. In D. Hirst and A. Di Cristo (eds.), *Intonation Systems: A Survey of Twenty Languages*, 195–218. Cambridge: Cambridge University Press.

Dodane, C. (2003). *La Langue en Harmonie: Influences de la Formation Musicale sur l'Apprentissage Précoce d'une Langue Etrangère.* Doctoral Thesis, Université de Franche-Comté.

Dominey, P.F. and Dodane, C. (2004). Indeterminacy in language acquisition: The role of child directed speech and joint attention. *Journal of Neurolinguistics* 17: 121–45.

Fabiano-Smith, L. and Goldstein, B.A. (2010). Phonological acquisition in bilingual Spanish-English speaking children. *Journal of Speech, Language and Hearing Research* 53: 160–78.

Fenson, L., Dale, P., Reznick, S., Thal, D., Bates, E., Hartung, J., Pethick, S. and Reilly, J. (1993). *MacArthur Communicative Development Inventories: User's Guide and Technical Manual.* San Diego, CA: Singular Publishing.

Féry, C., Hörnig, R. and Pahaut, S. (2011). Correlates of phrasing in French and German from an experiment with semi-spontaneous speech. In C. Gabriel and C. Lleó (eds.), *Intonational Phrasing in Romance and Germanic: Cross-Linguistic and Bilingual Studies 10,* 11–42. Amsterdam: John Benjamins Publishing Company.

Flege, J.E. (1995). Second-language speech learning: Theory, findings, and problems. In W. Strange (ed.), *Speech Perception and Linguistic Experience: Issues in Cross-Language Research,* 233–73. Timonium, MD: York Press.

Gawlitzek-Maiwald, I. and Tracy, R. (1996). Bilingual bootstrapping. *Linguistics* 34: 901–26.

Gerken, L.A. (1996). Sentential processes in early child language: Evidence from the perception and production of function morphemes. In J. Morgan and K. Demuth (eds.), *From Signal to Syntax,* 411–25. Mahwah, NJ: Erlbaum.

Gleitman, L.R., and Wanner, E. (1982). *Language Acquisition: The State of the Art.* Cambridge: Cambridge University Press.

Grabe, E., Post, B., and Watson, I. (1999). The acquisition of rhythmic patterns in English and French. *Proceedings of the 14th International Congress of Phonetic Sciences,* 1201–4.

Höhle, B., Bijeljac-Babic, R., Herold, B., Weissenborn, J. and Nazzi, T. (2009). Language specific prosodic preferences during the first half year of life: Evidence from German and French infants. *Infant Behavior and Development* 32(3): 262–74.

Ingram, D. (1981/82). The emerging phonological system of an Italian-English bilingual child. *Journal of Italian Linguistics* 2: 95–113.

Johnson, C.E. and Lancaster, P. (1998). The development of more than one phonology: A case study of a Norwegian-English bilingual child. *The International Journal of Bilingualism* 2: 265–300.

Johnson, C.E. and Wilson, I.L. (2002). Phonetic evidence for early language differentiation: Research issues and some preliminary data. *The International Journal of Bilingualism* 6: 271–89.

Kehoe, M.M. (2015). Lexical-phonological interactions in bilingual children. *First Language* 35(2): 93–125.

Kehoe, M.M., Lleó, C. and Rakow, M. (2004). Voice onset time in bilingual German-Spanish children. *Bilingualism: Language and Cognition* 7: 71–88.

Kehoe, M.M., Stoel-Gammon, C. and Buder, E.H. (1995). Acoustic correlates of stress in young children's speech. *Journal of Speech and Hearing Research* 38: 338–50.

Konopczynski, G. (1991). Le Langage Emergent II: Aspects Vocaux et Mélodiques. Hambourg : Buske Verlag.

LaBelle, C. (2000). A longitudinal study of lexical and prosodic differentiation by simultaneous French/English bilingual child (1;5–2;3). In C. Howell, S. Fish and T. Keith-Lucas (eds.), *Proceedings of the 24th Annual Boston University Conference on Language Development*, 474–85. Somerville, MA: Cascadilla Press.

Ladefoged, P. (1975). *A Course in Phonetics*. New York: Harcourt Brace Jovanovich.

Lleó, C. (2002). The role of markedness in the acquisition of complex prosodic structures by German-Spanish bilinguals. *The International Journal of Bilingualism* 6: 291–313.

Nazzi, T., Iakimova, G., Bertoncini, J., Frédonie, S. and Alcantara, C. (2006). Early segmentation of fluent speech by infants acquiring French: Emerging evidence for crosslinguistic differences. *Journal of Memory and Language* 54: 283–99.

Paradis, J. (1996). Phonological differentiation in a bilingual child: Hildegard revisited. In A. Stringfellow, D. Cahana-Amitay, E. Hughes and A. Zukowski (eds.), *Proceedings of the 20th Annual Boston University Conference on Language Development*, 528–39. Somerville, MA: Cascadilla Press.

Paradis, J. (2001). Do bilingual two-year-olds have separate phonological systems? *International Journal of Bilingualism* 5: 19–38.

Paradis, J. (2007). Second language acquisition in childhood. In E. Hoff and M. Shatz (eds.), *Handbook of Language Development*, 387–406. Oxford: Blackwell.

Paradis, J. and Genesee, F. (1996). Syntactic acquisition in bilingual children: Autonomous or interdependent? *Studies in Second Language Acquisition* 18: 1–25.

Peterson, G. E., and Lehiste, I. (1960). Duration of syllabic nuclei in English. *Journal of the Acoustical Society of America* 32: 693–703.

Pike, K.L. (1946). *The Intonation of American English*. Ann-Arbor: University of Michigan Press.

Rose, Y. and Champdoizeau, C. (2008). There is no trochaic bias: Acoustic evidence in favor of the neutral start hypothesis. In A. Gavarro and M.J. Frietas (eds.), *Language Acquisition and Development: Proceedings of GALA 2007*, 359–69. Newcastle: Cambridge Scholars Publishing.

Rossi, M. (1980). Le français, langue sans accent? [French: A non-stressed language?]. In I. Fonagy and P. Léon (eds.), *L'accent en Français Contemporain* [Stress in modern French], 13–51. Paris: Didier.

Schnitzer, M.L. and Krasinski, E. (1994). The development of segmental phonological production in bilingual child. *Journal of Child Language* 21: 585–622.

Schnitzer, M.L. and Krasinski, E. (1996). The development of segmental phonological production in bilingual child: A contrasting second case. *Journal of Child Language* 23: 547–71.

Vaissière, J. (1991). Rhythm, accentuation and final lengthening in French. In J. Sundberg, L. Nord and R. Carlson (eds.), *Music, Language, Speech and Brain*, 108–20. Macmillan Press.

Vihman, M.M. (2016). Prosodic structure and templates in bilingual phonological development. *Bilingualism: Language and Cognition* 19(1): 69–20.

Vihman, M.M., and DePaolis, R.A. (1998). Perception and production in early vocal development: Evidence from the acquisition of accent. In M.C. Gruber, D. Higgins, K.S. Olson and T. Wysocki (eds.), *Chicago Linguistic Society 34, Part 2: Papers from the panels*, 373–86. Chicago, IL: CLS.

Vihman, M.M., DePaolis, R.A. and Davis, B.L. (1998). Is there a 'Trochaic Bias' in early word learning? Evidence from infant production in English and French. *Child Development* 69: 933–47.

Vihman, M.M., Nakai, S. and DePaolis, R.A. (2006). Getting the rhythm right: A cross-linguistic study of segmental duration in babbling and first words. In L. Goldstein, C. Best and D. Whalen (eds.), *Laboratory phonology 8*, 341–66. Cambridge: Cambridge University Press.

Werker, J. F. and Byers-Heinlein, K (2008). Bilingualism in infancy: First steps in perception and comprehension. *Trends in Cognitive Sciences* 12: 144–51.

Whitworth, N. (2002). Speech rhythm production in three German-English bilingual families, In D. Nelson (ed.), *Leeds Working Papers in Linguistics* 9: 175–205.

Zlatic, L., MacNeilage, P.F., Matyear, C.L. and Davis, B.L. (1997). Babbling of twins in a bilingual environment. *Applied Psycholinguistics* 18: 453–69.

Christelle Dodane is a lecturer at the Université Paul Valéry, Montpellier, France.

Ranka Bijeljac-Babic is a lecturer in the Department of Psychology at the University of Poitiers and assistant professor and researcher in the 'Laboratoire Psychologie de la Perception' at the Paris Descartes Univeristy, France.

4
The Initial Development of Voice Onset Time in Early Successive French-Swedish Bilinguals

Frida Splendido

4.1 Introduction

This study takes as its starting point differences between first language (L1) and second language (L2) phonology and the explanations provided for these differences. Previous studies have typically attributed such differences to a sensitive period for language learning or to L1 influence (Ioup 2008). It has generally been suggested that L2 acquisition needs to start before the age of 5–6 years in order for L2 phonology to develop as in an L1 (Flege 1999; Long 1990). However, recent extensive studies in morpho-syntax have suggested that L2 acquisition needs to start already at the age of 3–4 for the L2 to fully develop (Granfeldt 2012; Meisel 2008; Schwartz 2004). Moreover, it has been suggested that language acquisition with an age of onset of 4–8 years constitutes a separate mode of acquisition: child second language acquisition (cL2 – Meisel 2009; Schwartz 2004), sometimes also referred to as early successive bilingualism. Development under this mode of acquisition presents similarities with both bilingual L1 development and adult L2 acquisition (aL2). Such results have been attributed to a combination of a sensitive period and the level of L1 development at onset (Granfeldt 2012; Schlyter and Thomas 2012). However, the phonology of early successive bilinguals is relatively under-researched (Anderson 2004). Consequently, evidence for or against a cL2 mode of acquisition in phonology is scarce, despite suggestions that phonological development might need to start at a younger age than that of morpho-syntax (Meisel 2008).

One phenomenon that has been studied in both simultaneous bilinguals and L2 learners is voice onset time (VOT). VOT is the time from the burst of a stop consonant to the onset of vocal cord vibration for the subsequent vowel. Three categories of VOT are traditionally distinguished: long lag (>40 ms), short lag (0–40 ms) and lead or negative VOT (<0 ms) (Lisker and Abramson 1964). Languages use these categories differently to distinguish between series of stop consonants. In Zampini's words, 'languages may have the same *phonemic* distinction (e.g. voiceless /p t k/ vs. voiced /b d g/), but differ with respect to the phonetic realization of those phonemes' (2008: 217). Acoustic cues other than VOT are also involved in distinguishing stop series (see e.g. Stölten 2013 and Watson 1990 for Swedish and French respectively). However, according to a literature review by Auzou, Ozsancak, Morris, Jan, Eustache and Hannequin (2000) VOT is considered the most reliable of the cues.

Given that VOT can be used to contrast two different stop series within a given language and the same stop series in two different languages, bilingual speakers' use of this acoustic cue has received a lot of attention from researchers in language acquisition and bilingualism.

4.1.1 VOT in Swedish and French

Swedish and French differ in the VOT categories used to differentiate voiced stops from voiceless ones, as illustrated in Figure 4.1. Swedish uses long lag for voiceless stops and short lag or lead for voiced stops (Helgasson and Ringen 2008; Sundberg and Lacerda 1999). Averages for Swedish long lag stops fall within the range of 46–78 ms (Helgasson and Ringen 2008; Larsson and Wiman 2011). French uses short lag for voiceless stops and lead for voiced ones (Serniclaes, D'Alimonte and Alegria 1984; Kessinger and Blumstein 1997). Reported averages for the individual voiceless stops vary from 15 to 49 ms (Birdsong 2003; Caramazza, Yeni-Komshian, Zurif and Carbone 1973; Carter, Leblanc, Olsen, Sigouin and Tremblay 2012; Fowler, Sramko, Ostry, Rowland and Hallé 2008; Serniclaes 1987).

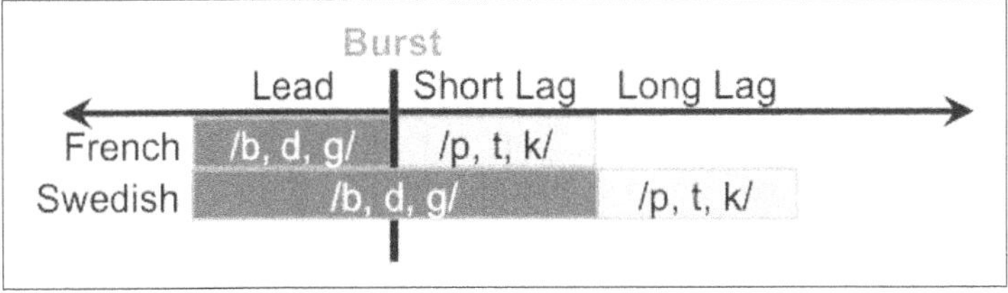

Figure 4.1. Simplified comparison of VOT categories in Swedish and French.

There is one exception to the Swedish categorization: voiceless stops in branching onsets with /s/ (e.g. *spotta* [spɔtːa] 'to spit'). Unlike word-initial stops, when preceded by /s/ stops are not aspirated and are thus produced with short lag VOT (cf. *potta* [pʰɔtːa] 'potty', *spotta* [spɔtːa] 'to spit').

Other phonetically contextual factors influencing VOT in adult native speakers include the place of articulation for the stop (bilabial stops are produced with shorter VOT than velar ones) and the height of the following vowel (the more open the vowel the shorter the VOT) (Berns 2013; Lisker and Abramson 1964; Serniclaes 1987; Sundberg and Lacerda 1999). For Swedish VOT, stress is also a factor: stops in stressed syllables are produced with a longer VOT than in unstressed ones (Sundberg and Lacerda 1999).

Considering that voiced stops can be pronounced with the same voicing lag in Swedish and French, this study will examine the development of word-initial voiceless stops. As mentioned above, /p, t, k/ are produced with short lag in French and long lag in Swedish. This means that Swedish learners of French will need to learn to produce a VOT category that their L1 primarily associates with a different stop series when pronouncing French voiceless stops. The following sections will focus on voiceless stops in different modes of acquisition.

4.1.2 Monolingual and Bilingual Development of VOT

There are only a small number of studies on the monolingual acquisition of VOT in Swedish and French, and no previous studies on the VOT of Swedish and French in bilinguals or L2 learners. Part of this section will therefore be based on other languages and language combinations.

Development of VOT in Monolingual L1 Acquisition (1L1)

Studies on monolingual development of VOT for voiceless stops in Swedish and French have observed an initial stage where both voiced and voiceless stops are primarily produced with short lag VOT (Allen 1985; Karlsson 2006). For both languages a period of overshooting or extreme VOT has been reported, i.e. a phase when child VOT is (much) longer than the adult target. Following this phase VOT approaches target-like VOT. Whereas Swedish children arrive at adult-like averages sometime around the age of 6, French monolinguals overshoot for a substantially longer period of time, probably even after the age of 10, at least for /k/ and /t/. Nevertheless, for both languages children produce progressively longer VOT for voiceless stops before voicing lag is reduced and starts approaching adult VOT values. (Larsson and Wiman 2010; Watson 1990)

Karlsson (2006) shows that Swedish children start out with short lag VOT also for /p, t, k/: the children aged 1;6–2;0 produced 84.7% of voiced stops and 72.5% of voiceless stops with short lag. The proportion of long lag gradually increases and children aged 2;6–4;0 produce approximately 75% of word-initial voiceless stops with long lag. At 4;0–4;6 children produce 63:5% of voiceless stops with long lag. This decrease indicates that overshooting is less frequent. Larsson and Wiman (2010: 13) report similar results with VOT averages peaking at age three: 83.6 ms for /p/, 82.37 ms for /t/ and 100.57 ms for /k/. As mentioned above, averages are close to target VOT at age 6 but child data are still characterized by more variation than adult productions. VOT is fully adult-like (i.e. both in terms of averages and variation) at approximately age 9 (Larsson and Wiman 2011).

French-speaking monolinguals are expected to produce adult-like short lag VOT significantly later. As mentioned above, overshooting lasts for a longer period of time compared to Swedish monolinguals. According to Allen (1985), monolinguals produce mostly short VOTs (median 8 ms) around age 2. For children aged 6–10, VOT averages of around 60 ms have been reported for /t/ and /k/ (individual children's averages ranging from 39 to 105 ms – Ryalls and Larouche 1992; Watson 1990). Ryalls and Larouche (1992) report shorter averages for /p/: 32 ms (individual averages ranging from 16 to 58 ms). So far no study has investigated VOT in French adolescents and we therefore do not know exactly when voiceless stops are produced with adult-like VOT in French-speaking monolinguals.

Given the developmental paths of monolinguals it appears important to make a distinction between monolingual-like and target-like VOT. Indeed, monolingual-like VOT for Swedish at age 6 also implies target-like averages. For French, monolingual-like VOT at age 6 implies that VOT is longer than target-like values. For the age range that is of interest in this study, 4–6 years, monolingual-like in Swedish means that VOT is progressively shortened to approach target-like values. What is monolingual-like for French has not yet been described in the literature for the entire age range. It is thus not known whether the development is linear from short lag to long lag, before decreasing back to short lag.

VOT in Simultaneous Bilinguals (2L1)

Previous studies show that adult simultaneous bilinguals separate VOT for the two languages' stop series (Fowler et al. 2008; MacLeod and Stoel-Gammon 2005; Sundara, Polka and Baum 2006) but that the average VOT values typically differ from those of monolingual adults for at least one of the series. Two types of results can be observed: assimilation and overlapping categories.

Some studies have reported on a type of assimilation effect where the two languages' VOT productions are closer together in the bilingual adults than in two monolingual speakers (Fowler et al. 2008; Kupisch et al. 2014). Both studies attribute this to 'equivalence classification' from Flege's Speech Learning Model (Flege 1995), that is, the bilingual adults do not perceive the stop series of their two languages as different.

Other studies report overlapping VOT for the voiced series (MacLeod and Stoel-Gammon 2005; Sundara et al. 2006). The English-French bilingual adults in these studies behave as monolinguals when producing voiceless stops, but produce voiced stops with lead voicing in both languages. MacLeod and Stoel-Gammon (2005) explain that '[p]erception studies have demonstrated that monolingual [Canadian English] speakers do not distinguish between stops produced with lead voicing and stops produced with short lag voicing (Caramazza et al. 1973)'. It is thus possible that the informants differ acoustically from monolingual speakers without their interlocutors noticing. The authors interpret the overlapping category as a strategy to reduce processing load while maintaining only essential phonetic contrasts.

Several studies on simultaneous bilingual children report separation for at least some of the informants and one of the stop series (Deuchar and Clark 1996; Kehoe, Lleó, and Rakow 2004; Khattab 2000; Watson 1990). However, only some report a complete separation of the two languages, that is, a separation of both voiced and voiceless stops (Deuchar and Clark 1996; Watson 1990). Moreover, only some of the children who separate the languages (partially or completely) produce monolingual-like VOT. In a case study by Kehoe et al. (2004) two of the four German-Spanish bilinguals show separation. Both children produce monolingual-like VOT but only in German. Watson (1990) presents results on English-French bilinguals at 6, 8 and 10 years of age. Their VOT mainly differs from the monolinguals for the voiceless stops. Much like some of the adults in the studies mentioned above, the bilingual children produce slightly longer French VOT than their age-matched monolinguals. The author interprets this effect as a compromise between the two systems and stresses that these are minor differences that might go unnoticed (Watson 1990). In summary, studies on simultaneous bilinguals indicate that even though the languages might be separate, there is still influence between the two languages.

4.1.3 Modelling Bilingual Phonological Acquisition (Lleó and Cortés 2013)

Lleó and Cortés (2013) present a model for the outcome of bilingual acquisition based on four facilitating factors:

1. *Frequency* in the bilingual context, i.e. how frequent a phenomenon or feature is when both languages are considered.
2. *Additive*, i.e. if there is an identical equivalent in the other language.
3. *Unmarkedness*, i.e. if the phenomenon, in comparison to related ones, is learnt first in monolingual acquisition, and is the more common in the world's languages.
4. *Uniformity*, i.e. if the same form is used in all contexts.

Applied to the acquisition of VOT, the model would imply the following: Short lag VOT is present in both languages (Frequency++), it is used differently in the two languages (Additive–), it is unmarked (Unmarkedness+), and it does not vary in French (Uniformity+). Long lag VOT is present only in Swedish, but relatively frequent in this language (Frequency+; Additive–), it is marked (Unmarkedness–), and it varies depending on the context (cf. [pʰɔtːa] ≠ [spɔtːa]; Uniformity–). According to the model short lag recruits more facilitating factors and would be acquired without delay in bilingual children. Long lag, on the other hand, would potentially be delayed.

4.1.4 VOT in L2 Acquisition

Previous studies on VOT in L2 learners mainly focus on adult learners, even if some studies include children. A few rare studies have reported transfer from the learner's L1 VOT to stops in the L2 (Flege 1980; Flege and Port, 1981). Other studies have found monolingual-like VOT for some of the participants (Birdsong 2003; Flege 1987, 1991). However, the majority of previous studies have found 'compromise VOT', i.e. VOT in the L2 that is neither monolingual-like nor a transfer from the learner's L1. Such results have been observed both for young L2 learners (Caramazza et al. 1973; Flege and Eefting, 1987; Fowler et al. 2008) and adult learners (Flege 1987, 1991; Flege and Eefting 1987) independently of the VOT category of the L2. In other words, there does not seem to be an advantage for learners whose L1 uses short lag-long lag and who need to learn to produce lead-short lag (e.g. English-speaking learners of French) compared to learners in the opposite situation (e.g. Spanish-speaking learners of English).

4.1.5 Research Questions

In light of previous research, a developmental perspective on early successive bilingualism would help clarify some of the observations regarding phonology in successive bilinguals in general and VOT in L2 acquisition in specific. The present study aims to answer the following questions:

1. Do early successive bilinguals separate their two languages? If so, at what point in their development?
2. How does Swedish long lag and French short lag VOT develop over the first years of successive bilingualism?
3. Do early successive bilinguals develop VOT similarly to simultaneous bilinguals?

4.2 Method

4.2.1 Participants

Eight age-matched children participated in this study: three successive bilinguals (Fia, Isa and Naomi), three simultaneous bilinguals (Évita, Liam and Yann) and two monolingual French-speaking children (Anne and Linda). All eight children attended the same *école maternelle* (nursery class) at a French school in Stockholm, Sweden. The successive bilingual group is the main focus of this chapter and the other two serve as controls, given that no French reference VOT for the entire age range (3;7–6;5) is available in the literature. Table 4.1 presents each child's age at the respective recordings.

Table 4.1. Each child's age of onset of acquisition (AOA) and age at the respective recordings.

			Recording		
			(1)	(2)	(3)
	Name	AOA	2010	2011	2010
cL2	Fia	3;0	3;9	4;9	5;9
	Isa	3;5	4;2	5;2	6;2
	Naomi	3;4	4;2	5;1	6;1
2L1	Évita	0;	4;5	5;5	6;5
	Liam	0;	4;2	5;1	6;2
	Yann	0;	3;9	4;9	5;9
1L1	Anne	0;	3;7	4;6	5;6
	Linda	0;	4;0	5;0	6;0

The simultaneous bilinguals had one Swedish-speaking and one French-speaking parent. They had all been exposed to both languages since birth. The successive bilinguals had Swedish-speaking parents and had started learning French (through immersion) when they were enrolled in the school, at 3;0–3;5. The French-speaking monolinguals' parents were both native speakers of French. The two children lived in Sweden at the time and had obviously been exposed to Swedish. However, their school and families, i.e. their main social contexts, were French-speaking and the children therefore did not speak any Swedish.[1]

4.2.2 Material

The children were recorded at the end of each school year, i.e. three times over a period of two years, corresponding to 10, 19 and 29 months of exposure for the successive bilinguals. All recordings were made in a quiet room at the participants' school using a Marantz Solid State Recorder PMD660.

Word-initial stops were elicited through a picture-naming task, disguised as a memory game. Each of the picture pairs in the game illustrated a stop-initial word: *piscine, pomme, papillon, tigre, tomate, table, quiche, collier* and *carotte* for French, and *pil, potta, panda, tio, tomte, tand, kiwi, korv* and *kam* for Swedish. All three voiceless stops occurred in three different vowel contexts: followed by /i, ɔ, a/. However, in the first recording, only the /i/ and /ɔ/ contexts were elicited.

Each participant played the game with a native speaker of the target language. Every time one of the players turned a card over the child named the object in the picture. Each word was produced approximately 8 times per recording. In all a total of 3,085 items were recorded, 2,378 of which were measured. The remaining 707 items were excluded for reasons such as simultaneous noise, failure to produce the target word and substitution or omission of the stop.[2]

1 At the end of the observation period, the French children's knowledge of Swedish was limited to a small number of frequent words like *hello* and names of colours. They were not able to communicate in Swedish.

2 Reasons for exclusion were noise (n=345), devoicing of the following vowel (n=139), substitution or omission of the stop (n=98), atypical pronunciation (e.g. if the children were laughing or speaking with their hands over the mouth, n=80), nonproduction of the target word (n=32) or other (n=13).

4.2.3 Measurements

VOT was measured in Praat (Boersma and Weenink 2015) as illustrated in Figures 4.2 and 4.3. VOT was identified on the waveform of a 200-millisecond window and confirmed with the spectrogram. VOT was measured from the first peak indicating the burst of the stop to the last extreme spike in the waveform preceding regular voiced pulsation.

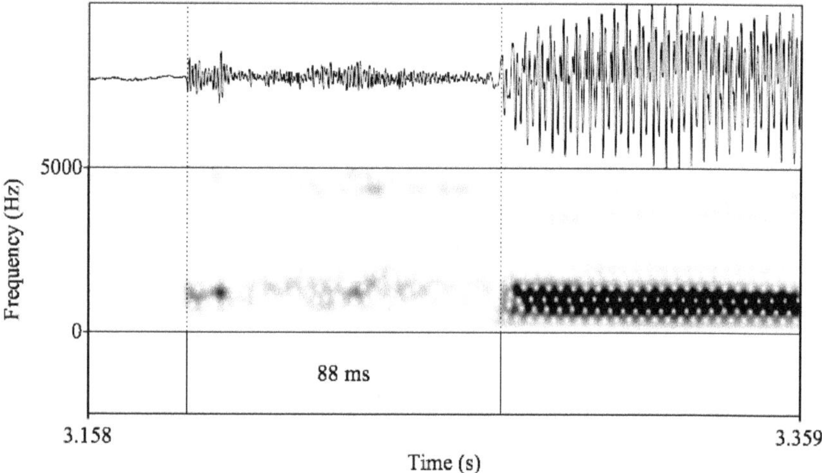

Figure 4.2. Long lag VOT for the Swedish word *korv* produced by one of the 2L1 children.

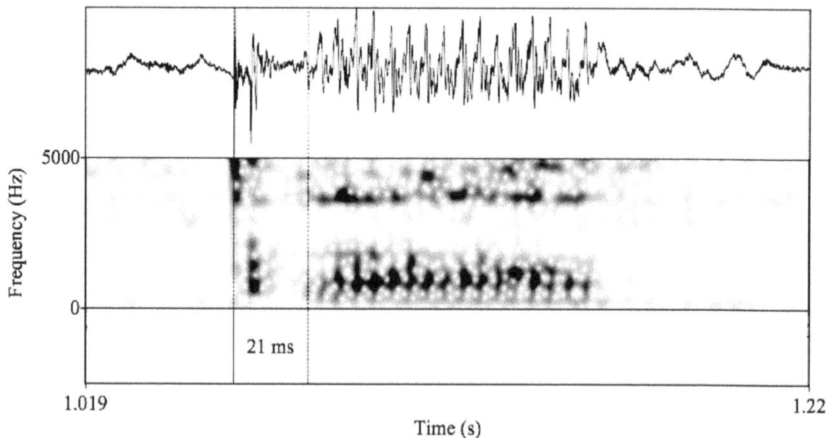

Figure 4.3. Short lag VOT for the French word *papillon* produced by one of the cL2 children.

To ensure inter-rater reliability, a second researcher measured a subset of the material (n=50). Inter-rater reliability was calculated through a Pearson correlation coefficient yielding a strong correlation: $r(50)=0.941$, $p<0.001$.

4.3 Results

A first result concerns the impact of place of articulation for the stop and height of the following vowel on VOT in child data. For the material as a whole, a mixed effects regression analysis with VOT in milliseconds as the dependent variable revealed significantly shorter VOT for /p/ compared to /t/ and /k/ respectively, but no significant difference between /t/ and /k/. Similarly, there was a statistically significant relationship between VOT and the subsequent vowel: the more open the vowel, the shorter the VOT, i.e. /a/</ɔ/</i/. These two principles, influence from consonant and the subsequent vowel, hold for both languages and for all informant groups. As mentioned above, similar observations have previously been made for adult native speakers but not for French- or Swedish-speaking children.

This section will first present the results from the controls in box plots. The results for the successive bilinguals will be described in more detail, presented both as box plots and in tables with mean values.

4.3.1 Results for Monolingual and Bilingual Controls

Figure 4.4 indicates that the 1L1 children's VOT development is compatible with previous accounts for monolingual French-speaking children. Linda and Anne produce somewhat longer VOT in recordings 2 and 3, as can be seen in the increasing median. It is also clear that there is still a lot of variation, especially in Anne's productions. For the final recording the two children's averages (Anne: 77 ms, Linda: 52 ms) are comparable to observations from 6- and 7-year-olds in the literature, i.e. short lag for /p/ and overshooting for /t/ and /k/ yielding averages in the long lag range (Ryalls and Larouche 1992; Watson 1990).

The 2L1 children's French productions only differ slightly from the 1L1 data (Figure 4.5). Evita and Liam appear to produce somewhat shorter VOT over time, but some of this effect might be due to the addition of /a/ in

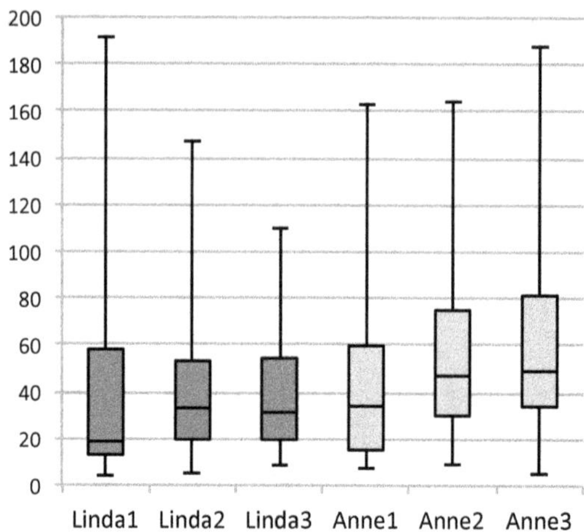

Figure 4.4. Box plots showing the distribution of all 1L1 French productions in milliseconds for the three recordings.

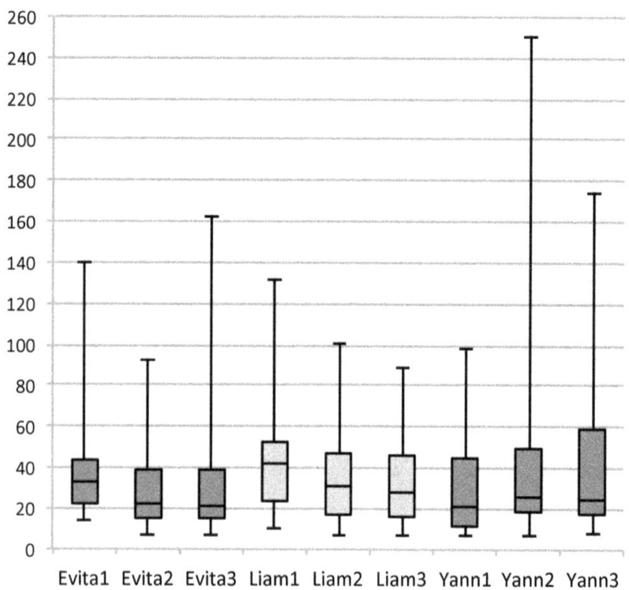

Figure 4.5. Box plots showing the distribution of all 2L1 French productions in milliseconds for the three recordings.

recording 2. Yann's medians remain relatively stable over time, but there is more variation in his productions from recordings 2 and 3. Even though 2L1 children do not appear to follow the exact same developmental pattern as the monolinguals over time, these differences are only trends and no statistically significant difference was found between monolingual and bilingual VOT.

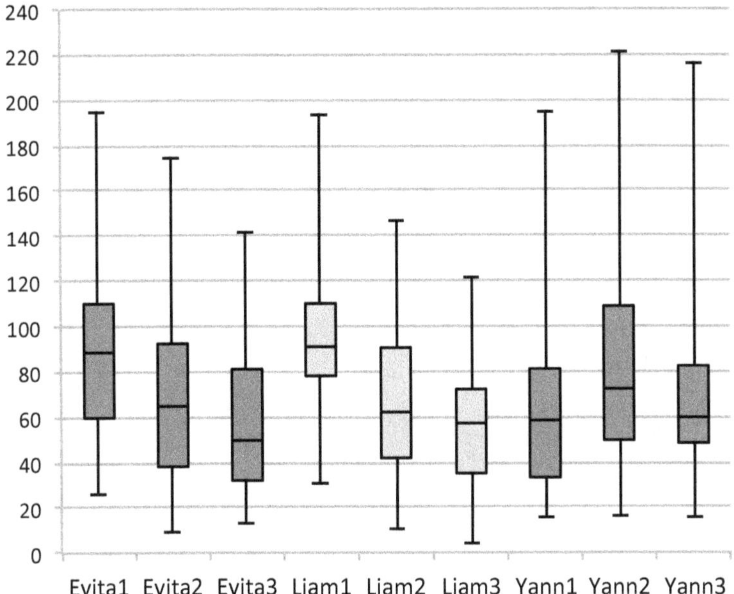

Figure 4.6. Box plots showing the distribution of all 2L1 Swedish productions in milliseconds for the three recordings.

Figure 4.6 shows that Evita's and Liam's Swedish productions get shorter over time, whereas Yann produces longer VOT in the second recording. The pattern observed in Evita's and Liam's productions is expected, but the children still produce overshooting and their averages are not consistently comparable to those of age-matched monolinguals. Some target syllables are produced with longer VOT; others with much shorter. These children's VOT development thus differs from age-matched monolinguals. Yann's development over the three recordings, with overshooting peaking at recording 2 (at 4;9) indicates a delay compared to monolinguals.

For the monolingual and bilingual controls, there was no statistically significant difference between the three recordings. In other words, there was no clear development over time for the monolingual and simultaneous bilingual children.

4.3.2 Results for the Early Successive Bilinguals

The early successive bilinguals differ from the controls in that the contrast between their first and second French recording is statistically significant. As Figure 4.7 shows, this development is particularly clear in Isa's and

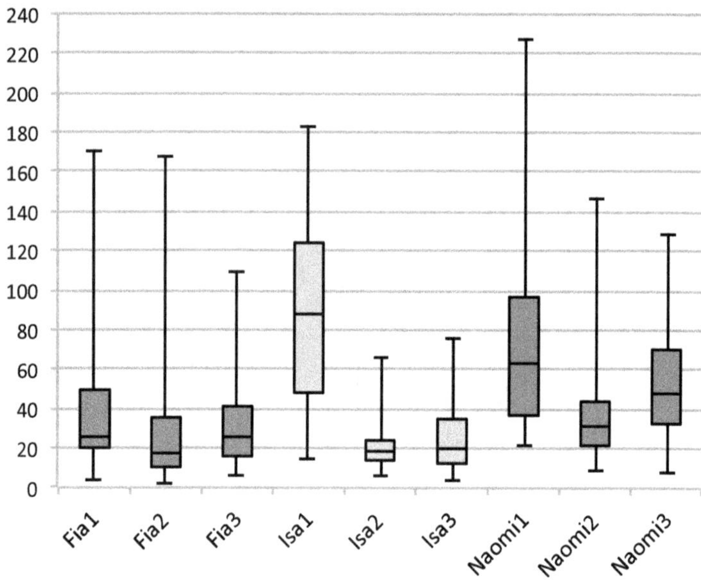

Figure 4.7. Box plots showing the distribution of all cL2 French productions in milliseconds for the three recordings.

Naomi's VOT. However, even in recording 1, they all produce at least some VOT in the short lag range. Moreover, when taking the three recordings as a whole and VOT in milliseconds as the dependent variable, a mixed effects regression analysis yielded no significant difference between the early successive bilinguals and the monolingual children, $t(5.16)=-0.46$, $p=0.667$.

The children's Swedish development appears delayed compared to previous studies on Swedish-speaking monolinguals. Indeed, Figure 4.8 shows that both Fia and Naomi produce their longest VOT in recording 2 (at 4;9 and 5;1). Moreover, all three children produce some very long VOT throughout the observation period.

Despite the probable influence from Swedish on French VOT in recording 1, the three early successive bilinguals in this study separate VOT for the two languages already in the first recording, i.e. after only 10 months of exposure to French. Indeed, the mixed effects regression analysis found a significant effect of language, $t(11.79)=5.24$, $p<0.001$. Furthermore, when looking at Figures 4.7 and 4.8 together, it seems that the long VOT in recording 2 may be a dissimilation effect. In fact, for both Fia and Naomi, the long Swedish productions are parallel to shorter VOTs for French. The figures also show differences between the children's development over time. The following discussion will look closer at each child's VOT in French and Swedish.

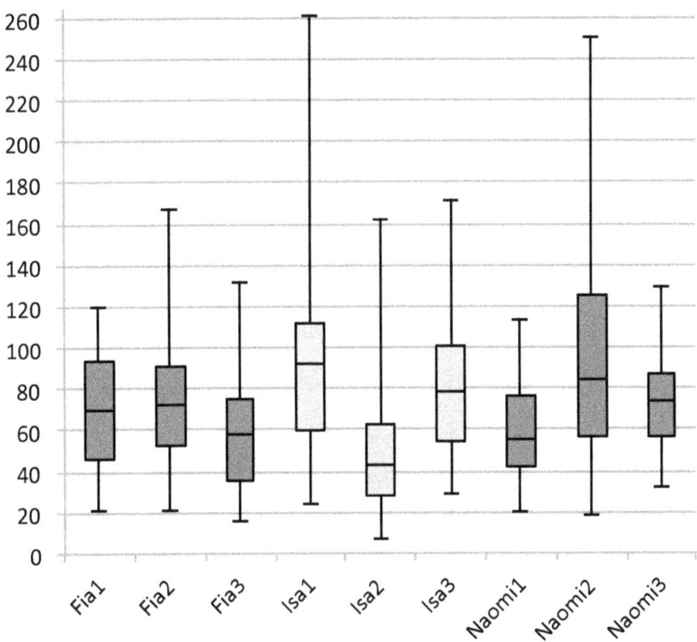

Figure 4.8. Box plots showing the distribution of all cL2 Swedish productions in milliseconds for the three recordings.

Fia's averages for each target syllable show that the separation of the two languages does not exclude some cross-linguistic influence. Interestingly, whereas her French VOT seems unaffected by Swedish, Fia's L1 (i.e. Swedish) productions appear influenced by the French short lag.

Fia's French productions indicate that short lag VOT for voiceless stops is not a difficulty for her. Table 4.2 shows that most of her averages fall within the short lag range. The exceptions are associated with syllables that would yield longer VOT in adult native speakers: /ti/, /kɔ/ and /ki/. Fia produces short lag VOT in the first recording, which means that her averages are not Swedish-like even after only 10 months of exposure to French. In fact, Fia's averages for the three recordings are shorter, and thus more target-like, than the ones observed for the two monolingual children.

Fia's Swedish VOT appears influenced by her French productions. Her longest averages correspond to recording 2 (at 4;9) and, as mentioned, this could indicate a delay compared to monolinguals in the literature who produce their longest VOT around the age of 3. Nevertheless, given that this development is parallel to a shortening of her French VOT, it is possible that she is merely exaggerating the distinction between the two languages. In other words, the longer VOT is not necessarily a sign of articulatory

Table 4.2. Mean VOT (roman type) and standard deviation (italics) for the three target syllables in Fia's three recordings.

		/pa/	/pɔ/	/pi/	/ta/	/tɔ/	/ti/	/ka/	/kɔ/	/ki/		
French	1	–	23.8	30.3	–	37.6	–	–	–	–	1	French
		–	*17.5*	*7.6*	–	*20.6*	–	–	–	–		
	2	8.0	12.8	20.5	13.5	22.5	119.2	17.4	36.0	77.1	2	
		4.1	*7.6*	*4.9*	*5.3*	*19.6*	*40.1*	*3.6*	*13.5*	*33.0*		
	3	15.0	14.5	27.7	17.7	26.4	79.4	29.3	44.0	56.1	3	
		6.6	*5.7*	*10.2*	*6.0*	*10.9*	*21.6*	*6.5*	*23.5*	*16.6*		
			/p/			/t/			/k/			
Swedish	1	–	53.0	69.8	–	46.0	77.7	–	99.0	67.3	1	Swedish
		–	*20.6*	*26.4*	–	*28.6*	*21.0*	–	*14.6*	*26.5*		
	2	78.7	76.3	68.1	81.6	–	119.4	87.0	97.7	103.6	2	
		48.4	*29.6*	*36.3*	*29.5*	–	*29.3*	*32.0*	*31.7*	*18.6*		
	3	36.6	39.8	63.1	40.7	58.9	98.7	69.4	73.4	74.5	3	
		11.9	*14.9*	*23.4*	*13.7*	*23.1*	*17.3*	*30.5*	*30.3*	*15.5*		
		/pa/	/pɔ/	/pi/	/ta/	/tɔ/	/ti/	/ka/	/kɔ/	/ki/		

immaturity but rather a dissimilation effect. Moreover, in recording 3 the averages approach target VOT for the respective consonants. Some are even shorter than the averages reported for adult speakers. It thus seems that, whereas there is no apparent L1 effect on her L2 productions, Fia's L1 VOT displays signs of possible influence from French.

Isa's averages indicate cross-linguistic influence in both directions. Indeed, as shown in Table 4.3, the two languages seem to follow the same trend through the first two recordings.

The three recordings appear to illustrate three stages in Isa's development. In recording 1, Isa generally produces very long VOT in both languages, with some French averages exceeding the Swedish ones. In recording 2, she produces much shorter VOT in both Swedish and French. As a consequence Swedish averages are shorter than the adult target but at the same time consistently longer than the French ones. In recording 3, French VOT is still short but the Swedish averages are generally longer than in recording 2. At this point there appears to be a clearer distinction between the two languages' VOT. Some of the very long averages (e.g. for /ka/) could indicate a dissimilation effect.

Isa's development over time differs slightly from that of age-matched monolinguals for both languages. As of recording 2, her French averages are generally shorter than those observed for the monolingual children

Table 4.3. Mean VOT (roman type) and standard deviation (italics) for the target syllables in Isa's three recordings.

		/pa/	/pɔ/	/pi/	/ta/	/tɔ/	/ti/	/ka/	/kɔ/	/ki/		
French	1	–	114.8	40.2	–	34.2	148.0	–	99.1	96.6	1	French
		–	*33.4*	*14.4*	–	*13.9*	*25.2*	–	*30.4*	*23.5*		
	2	11.2	16.1	19.7	20.9	17.6	18.0	22.4	32.8	–	2	
		5.6	*5.4*	*11.8*	*5.6*	*8.8*	*6.7*	*4.1*	*12.5*	–		
	3	21.5	14.0	15.0	15.2	14.0	13.7	34.6	34.6	60.2	3	
		10.7	*10.3*	*7.6*	*5.4*	*6.0*	*6.2*	*10.1*	*13.1*	*13.0*		
			/p/			/t/			/k/			
Swedish	1	–	83.0	137.4	–	40.7	83.5	–	114.1	106.0	1	Swedish
		–	*30.7*	*62.2*	–	*15.1*	*40.5*	–	*54.7*	*43.8*		
	2	32.1	38.3	56.6	49.1	30.9	52.3	48.2	64.1	99.6	2	
		30.0	*16.4*	*28.6*	*33.7*	*14.3*	*39.0*	*11.2*	*31.7*	*31.5*		
	3	44.7	86.0	–	81.3	36.4	88.0	113.0	63.2	93.4	3	
		12.4	*19.5*	–	*17.8*	*5.9*	*16.8*	*46.1*	*8.7*	*21.3*		
		/pa/	/pɔ/	/pi/	/ta/	/tɔ/	/ti/	/ka/	/kɔ/	/ki/		

in this study. Many of them fall within the lower range for adult VOT. In recordings 2 and 3, Isa's French productions are thus more target-like than those of the monolingual controls. The overshooting in Isa's first Swedish recording is expected at this age but her averages for recording 2 are much shorter than those of monolinguals in the literature. Averages for recording 3 are predominantly longer than for age-matched monolinguals and adults. As mentioned above, this could be a dissimilation effect but it could also indicate a delay in her Swedish development.

Table 4.4 shows the development of Naomi's averages over the three recordings. Just like Isa, Naomi initially produces very long VOT in French, a possible influence from Swedish even though most of her averages are longer in French than in Swedish. In recording 2, her averages are shorter and most fall within the short lag range. For recording 3, Naomi's averages have become longer again, although not as long as in recording 1.

Naomi's Swedish averages are relatively short in recording 1, even for syllables, like /ki/, that are typically associated with longer VOT. In recording 2, there is clear overshooting, with several averages above 100 ms. Naomi's VOT is the longest at 5;1 (compared to the age of 3 for monolinguals). This could indicate a delay in Naomi's Swedish development. From recordings 2 to 3, averages drop and so do standard deviations, indicating a more mature VOT that is closer to target and more stable.

Table 4.4. Mean VOT (roman type) and standard deviation (italics) for the target syllables in Naomi's three recordings.

		/pa/	/pɔ/	/pi/	/ta/	/tɔ/	/ti/	/ka/	/kɔ/	/ki/		
French	1	–	55.2	37.0	–	40.4	107.0	–	112.3	136.7	1	French
		–	*24.7*	*15.0*	–	*13.4*	*33.5*	–	*66.3*	*0.5*		
	2	29.3	31.3	21.0	18.9	31.3	60.8	27.7	40.8	56.4	2	
		23.6	*16.7*	*12.4*	*6.0*	*12.3*	*32.3*	*7.9*	*9.5*	*17.3*		
	3	44.9	32.7	24.8	54.3	60.3	59.6	31.9	82.2	94.6	3	
		12.7	*8.5*	*11.3*	*16.5*	*12.4*	*36.4*	*7.3*	*8.8*	*21.1*		
			/p/			/t/			/k/			
Swedish	1	–	35.3	43.6	–	52.3	74.0	–	61.2	65.2	1	Swedish
		–	*5.2*	*18.7*	–	*15.7*	*11.7*	–	*26.4*	*16.3*		
	2	85.8	99.2	77.8	101.6	79.0	87.5	102.8	119.5	129.8	2	
		23.7	*55.2*	*49.7*	*51.6*	*58.3*	*27.1*	*68.1*	*69.1*	*58.2*		
	3	67.3	49.6	59.8	69.3	75.1	79.9	89.3	74.7	87.7	3	
		14.9	*11.6*	*22.1*	*21.8*	*18.9*	*15.3*	*21.2*	*13.4*	*19.9*		
		/pa/	/pɔ/	/pi/	/ta/	/tɔ/	/ti/	/ka/	/kɔ/	/ki/		

Naomi's VOT seems to differ more from monolingual development in Swedish than in French. Her French averages are longer than those of the monolinguals for recording 1 but are monolingual-like in recordings 2 and 3. This means that, contrary to the other cL2 learners, her averages generally overshoot the adult target. Compared to Swedish monolinguals, Naomi's averages are shorter in recording 1, longer in recording 2 and finally monolingual-like in recording 3. As mentioned above, the overshooting in recording two could be due to a delay in her Swedish development. It could also be a dissimilation effect. This latter possibility seems more probable given that her French VOT is shortened in the same recording and her productions are monolingual-like in recording three.

The successive bilinguals all separate the two languages throughout the observation period. However the separation does not exclude influence from one language on the other. Swedish influence on French can be seen by the very long VOT in Isa's and Naomi's first recordings. Despite this, the cL2 learners' French VOT did not differ significantly from that of the monolinguals. Moreover, there seem to be indications of French influence on the three children's Swedish, i.e. an L2 influence on the L1. In Isa's productions the two languages seem to develop together in recording 1 and 2 before developing more independently in recording 3. In recording 2, Fia and Naomi produce shorter VOT for French than previously and longer

VOT for Swedish. This could be interpreted either as a delay compared to monolinguals in the literature or as a dissimilation effect, but in both cases it is the effect of French influence on Swedish.

4.4 Discussion

This study set out to explore the development of VOT in early successive bilinguals, but the findings also include new information about child VOT in general and L1 development of French VOT in particular. First, statistical analyses showed influence from place of articulation of the stop as well as from the following vowel on VOT in child productions for both Swedish and French. Such influence has previously only been reported for adults. Future research on VOT in children thus needs to control not only for place of articulation but also for the height of the vowel in the experimental design. Second, the results from the monolingual French children aligned with previous reports indicating a longer period of overshooting compared to languages that use long lag. Indeed, at the end of the observation period (at approximate age 6), the monolinguals' averages were still within the long lag range for /t/ and /k/, just like the 6- and 7-year-olds in previous studies (Ryalls and Larouche 1992; Watson 1990). At that age, Swedish-speaking children's averages are expected to be adult-like. However, this is only a small case study and more research is needed to explore the monolingual acquisition of (short lag) VOT in French.

The Lleó and Cortés (2013) model was developed to explain and predict the outcomes of simultaneous bilingualism. However, given the similarities between the simultaneous and successive bilinguals in this study, this section will discuss the successive bilinguals' French VOT and all six bilinguals' Swedish VOT with respect to the model.

Unlike several previous studies on adult L2 acquisition, the three cL2 learners in this study produce monolingual-like VOT in their L2 (French). As previously mentioned, monolingual-like, in this case, does not equal adult-like. More specifically, even though short lag is the target, the monolingual controls produce a relatively large proportion of long lag productions (over 50% for Anne in recording 2 and 3). Nevertheless, the cL2 learners separate the two languages' VOT from recording 1 and produce VOT within the short lag range, in some cases to a greater extent than the monolinguals. This means that their monolingual-like productions in French are not transferred from Swedish even when they include productions in the long lag.

According to the Lleó and Cortés model, short lag VOT recruits several facilitating factors: frequency, unmarkedness and uniformity. Other aspects may also favour the acquisition of short lag: it is the default VOT (Serniclaes et al. 1984), it is the least 'demanding' category from an articulatory point of view, and short lag is used in Swedish for voiced stops and voiceless stops preceded by /s/. In other words, the actual phonetic realization of the phonemes is relatively unproblematic and should already be acquired in the L1 at the participants' age (Karlsson 2006). However, these facilitating factors appear to play out differently for the cL2 learners in this study compared to adult learners in the literature. Indeed like Swedish, English also uses short lag with voiced stops (Lisker and Abramson 1964). The facilitating factors would thus be similar for English-speaking learners of French. Yet previous studies have primarily reported 'compromise VOT' for this population (e.g. Birdsong 2003; Flege 1987). To further explore this potential difference between adult and child L2 learners, more research is needed on the acquisition of short lag VOT in early successive bilinguals but also in children in the reverse situation, e.g. French-speaking children learning Swedish as an L2.

The bilinguals' Swedish development differs from monolingual development. This could be interpreted as a delay but also, in some cases, as a dissimilation effect. Delay was observed for some of the children in the study by Kehoe et al. (2004). Such results correspond to the predictions made by the Lleó and Cortés (2013) model. According to Kehoe et al. (2004), the delay is due to the markedness of long lag VOT. The simultaneous bilinguals in this study appeared slightly delayed, except for Yann whose overshooting clearly peaked in recording 2 (at age 4;9), indicating a more pronounced delay. The cL2 learners, Fia and Isa also produced very long Swedish VOT in recording 2. However, contrary to Yann's overshooting, the cL2 learners' productions coincide with shorter VOT for French, compared to recording 1. This might mean that the overshooting is a dissimilation effect. In other words, Fia and Isa exaggerate the contrast between French and Swedish. Independently of whether these divergences are due to delays or dissimilations, it appears obvious that they are connected to the children's bilingualism. With regard to the cL2 learners, this means that their L2 (French) has an impact on their L1 (Swedish) even after a relatively short period of exposure to the language.

This chapter took as its starting point the idea of a possible cL2 mode of acquisition for phonology. For VOT, it seems that there might be an initial stage in which the cL2 learners behave more like adult L2 learners, but their productions quickly align with those of simultaneous bilinguals and monolinguals. Similar results were observed for the same children with regard to the acquisition of French *liaison* (Splendido 2014). This would be in line with a cL2 mode of acquisition also for phonology. Moreover, it would seem that acquisition must start before the age of 3 for the development to unfold as in simultaneous bilinguals.

References

Allen, G.D. (1985). How the young French child avoids the pre-voicing problem for word-initial voiced stops. *Journal of Child Language* 12: 37–46.

Anderson, R. (2004). Phonological acquisition in preschoolers learning a second language via immersion: A longitudinal study. *Clinical Linguistics and Phonetics* 18(3): 183–210.

Auzou, P., Ozsancak, C., Morris, R.J., Jan, M., Eustache, F. and Hannequin, D. (2000). Voice onset time in aphasia, apraxia of speech and dysarthria: A review. *Clinical Linguistics and Phonetics* 14(2): 131–50.

Berns, J.K.M. (2013). *Friction between Phonetics and Phonology: The Status of Affricates.* Doctoral Thesis, Radboud Universiteit, Nijmegen. Retrieved on 28 May 2014 from http://repository.ubn.ru.nl/handle/2066/119022

Birdsong, D. (2003). Authenticité de pronconciation en français L2 chez des apprenants tardifs anglophones: Analyses segmentales et globales. *Aile* 20: 17–36.

Boersma, P. and Weenink, D. (2015). *Praat: Doing Phonetics by Computer.* Available from http://www.praat.org

Caramazza, A., Yeni-Komshian, G., Zurif, E. and Carbone, E. (1973). The acquisition of a new phonological contrast: The case of stop consonants in French-English bilinguals. *The Journal of the Acoustical Society of America* 54(2): 421–28.

Carter, N., Leblanc, C., Olsen, M.-J., Sigouin, C. and Tremblay, V. (2012). Un potentiel effet de l'origine géographique sur le délai d'établissement du voisement en français. *Communication, lettres et sciences du langage* 6(1): 41–56.

Deuchar, M. and Clark, A. (1996). Early bilingual acquisition of the voicing contrast in English and Spanish. *Journal of Phonetics* 24(3): 351–65.

Flege, J.E. (1980). Phonetic approximation in second language acquisition. *Language Learning* 30: 117–34.

Flege, J.E. (1987). The production of 'new' and 'similar' phones in a foreign language: Evidence for the effect of equivalence classification. *Journal of Phonetics* 15: 47–65.

Flege, J.E. (1991). Age of learning affects the authenticity of voice-onset time (VOT) in stop consonants produced in a second language. *The Journal of the Acoustical Society of America* 89(1): 395–411.

Flege, J.E. (1995). Second language speech learning: Theory, findings, and problems. In W. Strange (ed.), *Speech Perception and Linguistic Experience: Issues in Cross-Language Research*, 233–77. Timonium, MD: York Press.

Flege, J.E. (1999). Age of learning and second language speech. In D. Birdsong (ed.), *Second Language Acquisition and the Critical Period Hypothesis*, 101–32. Hillsdale: Lawrence Elbaum.

Flege, J.E. and Eefting, W. (1987). Production and perception of English stops by native Spanish speakers. *Journal of Phonetics* 15: 67–83.

Flege, J.E. and Port, R. (1981). Cross-language phonetic interference: Arabic to English. *Language and Speech* 24.2: 125–46.

Fowler, C.A., Sramko, V., Ostry, D.J., Rowland, S.A. and Hallé, P. (2008). Cross language phonetic influences on the speech of French-English bilinguals. *Journal of Phonetics* 36: 649–63.

Granfeldt, J. (2012). Development of object clitics in child L2 French: A comparison of developmental sequences in different modes of acquisition. *Language, Interaction and Acquisition / Langage, Interaction et Acquisition* 3(1): 140–62.

Helgasson, P. and Ringen, C. (2008). Voicing and aspiration in Swedish stops. *Journal of Phonetics* 36: 607–28.

Ioup, G. (2008). Exploring the role of age in the acquisition of a second language phonology. In J.G.H. Edwards and M.L. Zampini (eds.), *Phonology and Second Language Acquisition*, 41–62. Amsterdam/Philadelphia: John Benjamins Publishing Company.

Karlsson, F. (2006). *The Acquisition of Contrast: A Longitudinal Investigation of Initial s+plosive Cluster Development in Swedish Children*. Umeå: Umeå Studies in Linguistics.

Kehoe, M.M., Lleó, C. and Rakow, M. (2004). Voice onset time in bilingual German-Spanish children. *Bilingualism: Language and Cognition* 7(1): 71–88.

Kessinger, R.H. and Blumstein, S.E. (1997). Effects of speaking rate on voice-onset time in Thai, French, and English. *Journal of Phonetics* 25: 143–68.

Khattab, G. (2000). VOT production in English and Arabic bilingual and monolingual children. In D. Nelson and P. Foulkes (eds.), *Leeds Working Papers in Linguistics 8*, 95–122. Retreived on 16 May 2014 from: http://www.leeds.ac.uk/arts/download/1332/ khattab2000

Kupisch, T. Lein, T., Barton, D., Schröder, D.J., Stangen, I. and Stoehr, A. (2014). Acquisition outcomes across domains in adult simultaneous bilinguals with French as weaker and stronger language. *Journal of French Language Studies* 24(3): 1–30.

Larsson, M. and Wiman, S. (2010). *Voice onset time hos svenska förskolebarn: Ett utvecklingsperspektiv*. Bachelor's Thesis, Linköping University. Retreived on 16 May 2014 from http://liu.diva-portal.org/smash/ record.jsf?pid=diva2:318601

Larsson, M. and Wiman, S. (2011). *Voice onset time hos svenska barn och vuxna : Ett utvecklingsperspektiv*. Master's Thesis, Linköping University. Retreived on 16 May 2014 from: http://liu.diva-portal.org/smash/ record.jsf?pid=diva2:421461

Lisker, L. and Abramson, A.S. (1964). A cross-language study of voicing in initial stops: Acoustical measurements. *Word* 20(3): 384–422.

Lleó, C. and Cortés, S. (2013). Modeling the outcome of language contact in the speech of German-Spanish and Catalan-Spanish bilingual children. *International Journal of the Sociology of Language* 221: 101–25.

Long, M.H. (1990). Maturational constraints on language development. *Studies in Second Language Acquisition* 12: 251–85.

MacLeod, A.A. and Stoel-Gammon, C. (2005). Are bilinguals different? What VOT tells us about simultaneous bilinguals. *Journal of Multilingual Communication Disorders* 3: 118–27.

Meisel, J.M. (2008). Child second language acquisition or successive first language acquisition. In B. Haznedar and E. Gavruseva (eds.), *Current Trends in Child Second Language Acquisition: A Generative Perspective*, 55–80. Amsterdam; Philadelphia: John Benjamins Publishing.

Meisel, J.M. (2009). Second language acquisition in early childhood. *Zeitschrift für Sprachwissenschaft* 28(1): 5–34.

Ryalls, J. and Larouche, A. (1992). Acoustic integrity of speech production in children with moderate and severe hearing impairment. *Journal of Speech and Hearing Research* 35: 88–95.

Schlyter, S. and Thomas, A. (2012). L1 or L2 acquisition? Finiteness in child second language learners (cL2), compared to adult L2 learners (aL2) and young bilingual children (2L1). In M. Watorek, S. Benazzo and M. Hickmann (eds.), *Comparative Perspectives on Language Acquisition: A Tribute to Clive Perdue*, 282–302. Bristol: Multilingual Matters Limited.

Schwartz, B. (2004). Why child L2 acquisition? In J. van Kampen and S. Baauw (eds.), *Proceedings of GALA 2003*, 47–66. Utrecht: Netherlands Graduate School of Linguistics (LOT).

Serniclaes, W. (1987). *Étude expérimentale de la perception du trait de voisement des occlusives du français.* Doctoral Thesis, Université libre de Bruxelles, Institut de phonétique. Retreived on 15 May 2014 from http://lpp.psycho.univ-paris5.fr/pdf/2554.pdf

Serniclaes, W., D'Alimonte, G. and Alegria, J. (1984). Production and perception of French stops by moderately deaf subjects. *Speech Communication* 3: 185–98.

Splendido, F. (2014). *Le développement d'aspects phonético-phonologiques du français chez des enfants bilinguals simultanés et successifs: Le VOT et la liaison dans une étude de cas multiples.* Doctoral Thesis, Lund University.

Stölten, K. (2013). *The Effects of Age of Onset on VOT in L2 Aquisition and L1 Attrition: A Study of the Speech Production and Perception of Advanced Spanish-Swedish Bilinguals.* Doctoral Thesis, Stockholm University.

Sundara, M., Polka, L. and Baum, S. (2006). Production of coronal stops by simultaneous bilingual adults. *Bilingualism: Language and Cognition* 9: 97–114.

Sundberg, U. and Lacerda, F. (1999). Voice onset time in speech to infants and adults. *Phonetica* 56: 186–99.

Watson, I. (1990). Acquiring the voicing contrast in French: A comparative study of monolingual and bilingual children. In J.N. Green and W. Ayres-Bennett (eds.), *Variation and Change in French: Essays Presented to Rebecca Posner on the Occasion of Her Sixtieth Birthday*, 37–60. London; New York: Routledge.

Zampini, M.L. (2008). L2 speech production research: Findings, issues, and advances. In J.G.H. Edwards and M.L. Zampini (eds.), *Phonology and Second Language Acquisition*, 219–49. Amsterdam; Philadelphia: John Benjamins Publishing Company.

Frida Splendido is a senior lecturer of French and Swedish as a second language at the Centre for Languages and Literature, Lund University.

5
Voice Onset Time in German-Italian Simultaneous Bilinguals: Evidence on Cross-Language Influence and Markedness

Tanja Kupisch and Conxita Lleó

5.1 Introduction

This chapter examines voice onset time (VOT) in the two languages of adult bilingual speakers of Italian and German with exposure to both languages from birth, i.e. simultaneous bilinguals (henceforth 2L1s).[1] More specifically, we compare German-Italian 2L1s who grew up in Italy with German as their minority language, to German-Italian 2L1s who grew up in Germany with Italian as their minority language. Our main purpose is to investigate potential effects of dual language exposure. We assume that early simultaneous bilinguals are a subgroup of heritage speakers. This entails that those early bilinguals who grew up in Italy are heritage speakers of German, whereas those who grew up in Germany are heritage speakers of Italian.

Despite a few early studies (Au, Knightly, Jun and Oh 2002; Oh, Jun, Knightly and Au 2003), phonology has been an understudied domain in the field of heritage language research, as noted by Benmamoun, Montrul and Polinsky (2013). Since then, there have been only a few more studies on this topic. These mostly focus on global accent and VOT and generally find that heritage speakers are perceived to sound different from monolinguals, while having advantages over late L2 learners (Kupisch, Barton, Hailer, Lein, Kostogryz, Stangen and van de Weijer 2014; Chang, Yao, Haynes and Rhodes 2011). Another general finding is that although heritage speakers

1 Many thanks to Miriam Geiss, Bee Mitchell Harms and Simone Waitz for assisting with the data analysis.

tend to be (mis)taken for non-native speakers of their heritage language, they are often within the range of monolingual native speakers with regard to VOT (see Au et al. 2002 on Spanish; Lein, Kupisch and van de Weijer, forthcoming on French and German; Oh et al. 2003 on Korean).

Most of these studies of adult heritage speakers have focused on *successive* bilinguals, for whom the heritage language was the only language at home. However, the disadvantage of studying these populations is that they differ in terms of when they were first exposed to the majority language, and these differences in age of onset (AoO) may result in different acquisition outcomes with respect to both the minority language and the majority language. Specifically, earlier exposure to the majority language could have a negative effect on minority language development (Montrul 2008), while later exposure to the majority language might have a negative effect on the majority language. This means that once such speakers reach adulthood, it is unclear to what extent deviances from monolinguals are due to (i) AoO, (ii) diminished input, (iii) the interaction of their two languages, or a combination thereof. It is equally unclear whether they are the result of arrested development during childhood ('incomplete acquisition') or the loss of previously acquired properties ('attrition') during adulthood.

As mentioned in the previous paragraph, studies on heritage speakers have typically focused on the acquisition outcomes of *successive* bilinguals, but rarely on those of bilinguals with exposure to two languages from birth. However, there are advantages in studying simultaneous bilingual heritage speakers. First, potential AoO effects are minimized both (i) when comparing the bilinguals' two languages, and (ii) when comparing across bilingual individuals, because AoO coincides with birth. Second, 2L1s tend to be the focus of developmental studies (e.g. Deuchar and Clark 1996; Kehoe, Lleó and Rakow 2004). Consequently, we already know a lot about their development and are thus in a good position to speculate about the causes of acquisition outcomes, i.e. incomplete acquisition or attrition. More specifically, if a property is typically acquired early in life (when heritage speakers still have a lot of input in the heritage language), while being absent during adulthood, arrested development is not a plausible explanation. Finally, the amount of exposure during the early years is generally considered to be crucial. Thus, simultaneous bilinguals could be seen as facing the greatest challenge when acquiring the heritage language, since their heritage language develops under the influence of the dominant language of the environment from birth.

The following section provides an overview of VOT in acquisition, focusing on learners who acquire a Germanic language and a Romance language and comparing studies on child development with studies on acquisition outcomes in adults. Section 5.3 summarizes our study of VOT in adult simultaneous bilinguals. We discuss our results in Section 5.4 and conclude in Section 5.5.

5.2 Acquisition of VOT

VOT is considered to be the most salient cue differentiating the language-specific realizations of voiced (/b, d, g/) and voiceless (/p, t, k/) plosives. It refers to the interval between the release of the stop and the onset of voicing (Lisker and Abramson 1964: 389). There exist three different types of VOT: (i) 'voicing lead' (voicing starts before the release), (ii) 'short voicing lag' (voicing begins with the release or shortly after it), (iii) 'long voicing lag' (voicing starts late after the release). Many of the world's languages distinguish two categories of stops, voiced and voiceless, which, depending on the language, are associated with different types of VOT. In Italian (i) voicing lead with negative VOTs characterizes voiced stops, and (ii) short voicing lag (with VOT values defined as <30 ms) characterizes voiceless stops. In German, (i) voiced stops are produced with a short voicing lag, while (ii) voiceless stops are produced with a long lag. German voiceless stops have much longer VOTs than Italian ones.

In this study, we focus on the VOT of /k/. There are comparatively few studies on Italian VOT. For Calabrese, Sorianello (1996) found that /k/ is produced with an average VOT of 24 ms when the dialect was spoken, and 29 ms when people from Calabria spoke Standard Italian. The data is based on a reading task and the VOTs have been measured in pretonic intervocalic syllables. Table 5.1 summarizes findings for /k/ in German from various studies.

Table 5.1. VOT in German.

Study	No. of Subjects	Type of Data Collection	VOT for /k/
Stock 1971	6	Reading the news (word-medial stops)	37
Fischer-Jørgensen 1976	2	Reading word lists	59.73
Haag 1979	1	Reading sentences	66.5
Lein et al. forthcoming	5	Spontaneous story-telling	78.47

There are several factors that influence VOT. Place of articulation is the most important one, with a hierarchy of shorter to longer VOTs ranging from /p/ over /t/ to /k/ (e.g. Lisker and Abramson 1964). VOT can further be influenced by syllable stress, speech rate (Kessinger and Blumstein 1997), word length (e.g. Lisker and Abramson 1964) and the quality of the following vowel (e.g. Fischer-Jørgensen 1979: 98). There is also regional variation in German (Braun 1996: 25) and possibly in Italian. Finally, stops in isolated words are said to have longer VOTs than those in spoken sentences and spontaneous speech (e.g. Baran, Laufer and Daniloff 1977).

This variety of factors contributes to considerable variation of VOT within and across speakers and across studies. Despite variation, VOT is traditionally considered as the categorical unit par excellence: a sound is voiceless, for example, if it has a certain VOT range, but if it crosses the relevant threshold, it is automatically perceived as voiced (see Eimas, Siqueland, Jusczyk and Vigorito 1971, who showed that babies, even at one month of age, can classify stops as discrete phonemic categories on this basis). Finally, despite variation, it is safe to assume that the VOT of German voiceless stops is noticeably longer than the VOT of Italian voiceless stops, which leads to the prediction that a German influence on Italian will result in relatively long VOTs compared to those of monolingual Italian speakers. Conversely, an Italian influence on German will result in relatively short VOTs compared to monolingual German speakers (i.e. resulting in short lag, similar to the VOT of German voiced stops /b, d, g/).

5.2.1 VOT in Bilingual Development

VOT is a well-studied phenomenon in the speech of bilingual children and adults who have one Germanic and one Romance language. As outlined above, the two language families at the same time differ and overlap in terms of their VOT realizations, which makes VOT a potentially vulnerable category. As for language development, Jong Kong, Beckman and Edwards (2012: 742) report that the short lag VOT category appears first in children's productions, the long lag VOT category appears next, and the lead VOT category appears last, often after the age of 5 years. With regard to language contact, phonological categories have been argued to be subtractive if (i) they are present only in one of the two languages of the bilingual, and (ii) they alternate with a category also belonging to the other language (Lleó 2008). For example, a phenomenon like spirantization in Spanish, by which voiced stops alternate with approximants or so-called *spirants*, depending on the phonetic context, could be considered a subtractive category if Spanish is in contact with German because (i) spirants are only present in Spanish but hardly in German (Kohler 1995: 204, 209), and (ii) spirants alternate with voiced stops, which are present in German as well. Similarly, bilingual German-Romance children might have difficulties with voiced stops (but not with voiceless ones) in their Romance language, and with voiceless stops (but not voiced ones) in their Germanic language, because those two categories are only present in one of their languages.

There have been a few studies on developing bilingual children, focusing on VOT. Deuchar and Clark (1996) studied an English-Spanish 2L1 child (aged 1;7–2;3) raised in England. They found that the VOT contrast between voiced and voiceless stops in English was acquired at age 2;3, and the child started distinguishing the Spanish stops just like monolingual children, suggesting language separation and monolingual-like development in her two languages. Similarly, Lee and Iverson (2012) showed that Korean-English 2L1s living in the USA (15 children at age 5, and 15 children at age 10) acquired distinct VOTs in both languages.

Kehoe et. al. (2004) studied the VOT of four simultaneous German-Spanish 2- to 3-year-old bilinguals, who grew up in Germany. Table 5.2 shows the VOTs for /k/ measured for the four children in their two languages at different stages.[2] The VOTs of the monolingual German controls were 88.9 ms and 76.1 ms at age 1;9–2;0, that is, quite similar to those reported for adults in spontaneous speech (cf. Table 5.1). Given the monolingual German children's reference values, none of the bilinguals had monolingual-like VOTs during the first recording period, while Spanish VOTs were within the target-range (there were no monolingual Spanish controls but the bilinguals' productions correspond to those reported for L1 adult Spanish speakers). During the earliest stage in German, the bilinguals' long lag VOT category might still have been in the process of developing, or there was influence from Spanish to German. At the age between 2;3 and 2;6, two children, Simon and Nils, display target-like long lag VOTs in German. Simon also produces target-like VOTs in Spanish, while Nils' Spanish VOT is comparatively long, arguably due to influence from German. Stefan, on the other hand, produces comparatively short VOTs in German and only slightly shorter ones in Spanish, and the values produced in the two languages become even more similar at a later age (2;9–3;0), suggesting that his German undergoes influence from Spanish or that his phonological development is still ongoing (cf. Nils at age 2;0–2;3). Overall, Kehoe et al's results indicate slight delays in the formation

2 We concentrate on /k/ here because that is the focus of our own study. The stages in the study by Kehoe et. al. (2004) are not exactly the same for all children, and one child was studied only during one stage.

Table 5.2. VOT in ms for /k/ in 2L1 children in German (Ge.) and Spanish (Sp.) (adapted from Kehoe et al. 2004).

	Robert	Stefan	Simon	Nils
2;0-2;3	(2;0–2;4)			
Mean Ge. VOT (Range)	28.8 (14–64)		23.8 (9–43)	39.3 (14–67)
Mean Sp. VOT (Range)	36.6 (17–115)		41.22 (17–112)	33.5 (18–75)
2;3-2;6				
Mean Ge. VOT (Range)		50.6 (24–80)	83.4 (23–123)	76.1 (45–134)
Mean Sp. VOT (Range)		39.5 (20–67)	26.1 (13–76)	59 (20–91)
2;9-3;0	–			
Mean Ge. VOT (Range)		33.9 (21–53)		
Mean Sp. VOT (Range)		40.6 (17–95)		

of age-appropriate VOT categories, but at the same time clear cases of language separation (Simon) and bidirectional influence (Stefan: Spanish to German, Nils: German to Spanish).

Splendido (2014) studied three French-Swedish 2L1 children in a semi-longitudinal fashion, i.e. recording them several times between 3;7 and 6;3. Overall, the children did not seem to differ from monolinguals and separated the two languages. However, Swedish long lag VOT was potentially delayed. Normally, Swedish-learning children go through a period of VOT overshoots (VOT>100 ms). Splendido's 2L1 children also go through such a stage, but they dwell in that stage longer than monolinguals (see Chapter 4, this volume). The 2L1s' prolonged phase of long lag overshoots suggest that bilingual children may show delays independently of the properties of their other language, possibly due to their relatively reduced input in each of their two languages.

Fabiano-Smith and Bunta (2012) showed that the /p/ and /k/ productions of eight Spanish-English 2L1s (aged 3;0–4;0) did not differ from those of Spanish monolinguals, while they did differ from those of English monolinguals, suggesting influence from Spanish to English. Watson (1990), by contrast, found that the VOT development of 15 English-French 2L1s (aged 6, 8 and 10 years) was similar to that of monolinguals in both languages. Comparing these studies, one might assume that 3–4-year-olds are still in the process of developing their systems, but they may perform monolingual-like a few years later.

In summary, studies on early developing bilingual children have come to various results including very early language separation, bidirectional cross-linguistic influence, or even delays, which cannot be traced back to a direct influence of the other language.

5.2.2 VOT in Adult Bilinguals

As for adults, Fowler, Sramko, Ostry, Rowland and Hallé (2008) set out to extend previous VOT investigations of voiceless stops to a larger sample of participants (n=78): monolingual English, monolingual French, French-English bilinguals from birth (2L1s), French-English bilinguals with English as L1 and French as L2 (they learned French at primary school, at around 4–5 years), and vice versa, French as L1 and English as L2 (they learned English at school, at around 9–10 years). They focused on the production of /p/, /t/ and /k/ by simultaneous bilinguals, the main research question being whether simultaneous bilinguals are affected by cross-linguistic influence. Results showed that simultaneous bilinguals produced long-lag VOTs in English shorter than those of monolingual English speakers; their short-lag VOTs in French were longer than those of monolingual French speakers. For sequential bilinguals long lag was shorter in L2 English and short lag was longer in L2 French, suggesting cross-linguistic influence.

However, not all researchers find cross-language influence in simultaneous bilingual production. Sundara, Polka and Baum (2006) analysed the production of word-initial /t/ and /d/ by Canadian English-French simultaneous bilinguals and by monolingual adults in each language, based on the VOT differences (long lag vs short lag in English, and short lag vs lead in French). Articulation place was also considered, because coronal sounds are alveolar in English and dental in French. The main inquiry was whether simultaneous bilingual adults produce such language-specific differences. This is indeed the case, according to the results, although monolinguals differentiated more phonetic cues in their productions of /t/ and /d/ than bilinguals. Note that both studies (Fowler et al. 2008 and Sundara et al. 2006) were carried out in Canada, where French and English are official languages. Although official bilingualism in Canada does not imply that each individual region is bilingual and that bilinguals speak the two languages in an accent-free manner, access to both languages is greatly facilitated through TV and other media, as well as the presence of fluent bilinguals. The question is to what extent these results are mirrored in European countries, which are not officially bilingual, though often de facto multilingual.

Lein et. al. (forthcoming) studied the VOT of /k/ in simultaneous bilinguals during adulthood. Their participants had been exposed to German and French from birth and had grown up in either Germany or France. Most bilinguals produced VOTs in different ranges in their two languages. Comparison of French-dominant bilinguals (who had grown up in France) and German-dominant bilinguals (who had grown up in Germany) further revealed that the French VOTs of the German-dominant speakers were monolingual-like in both languages, while the French-dominant speakers were less target-like in German, although they had been living in Germany at the time of testing. Since most German-dominant speakers had attended a French school throughout childhood, the study leaves open whether this group had an advantage in their minority language through intensive exposure during their school years. Alternatively, French /k/ might be easier to produce than German /k/ due to aspiration of the latter.

As for Italian, Nagy and Kochetov (2013) compared the VOT of Italian, Ukrainian and Russian heritage speakers in the English-speaking part of Canada across three to five generations. Their results indicated that Italian heritage speakers were more resilient than the other bilingual groups to influence from English in their VOTs. While the Ukrainian and Russian speakers' VOTs drifted towards more English-like long lag VOTs over the generations, the Italian heritage speakers' VOTs remained in the short lag range.

One aspect recently reported in bilingual studies relates to the malleability of segmental production, which can show accommodation to various idiolectal characteristics of the interlocutor and thus to cross-linguistic influence (e.g. see Street 1983 on speech rate, turn duration and vocalization duration, as well as Kessinger and Blumstein 1997 on the effects of speaking rate on VOT, specially on long lag and pre-voicing). Sancier and Fowler (1997) report the case of a bilingual speaker with L1 Portuguese and with AoO for English being 15 years. Her VOT values changed significantly as a function of the ambient language. After staying a few months in a monolingual English context, her VOTs for voiceless stops (short lag in Portuguese and long lag in English) became longer in both languages, and after staying two months in Brazil, her VOTs became shorter. As Fowler et al. (2008) comment, 'this suggests a psychological link between similar categories.' Such a link has been proposed in Flege's Speech Learning Model (SLM), according to which categories of an L2 with a certain similarity to categories of L1 are classified as 'equivalent categories' (1995). The SLM can explain in the Sancier and Fowler (1997) case that voiceless stops were treated in a parallel fashion in the two languages, in spite of a different phonetic implementation in the two target systems. Such findings have important consequences with regard to development, as the order of acquisition is partly dependent on markedness and on the system's layout.

5.2.3 Summary

Bilingual children may show delays in acquiring target-like VOT categories, possibly due to cross-linguistic influence, especially with respect to the more marked VOT categories, i.e. long lag and especially voicing lead (Davis 1995).[3] Studies on adult and child bilinguals indicate that VOT categories are not stable, neither during childhood, nor during adulthood. This raises the question whether in simultaneous bilingualism monolingual-like development is guaranteed at least in one language, and whether this one language is always the majority language. Moreover, if we find gradual differences, based on few milliseconds, between the various participant groups analysed, can we still maintain that VOT is categorical?

This study will add new data from 12 simultaneous bilinguals, who grew up hearing and speaking Italian and German from birth. We compare speakers in different countries (Italy and Germany), and we investigate VOT in the (dominant) majority language and in the (weaker) minority language. The main goal is to find out whether monolingual-like VOTs can be attained and maintained in both languages, or, if not, whether only the heritage language is affected by language influence. Our research questions are:

(i) Is there evidence for cross-linguistic influence (CLI)?
(ii) If there is CLI, is it *bi*directional or *uni*directional?
(iii) If CLI is unidirectional, does it mean that VOT in one language is monolingual-like?

Furthermore, in research on heritage speakers there is an ongoing discussion about whether differences between monolinguals and bilinguals during adulthood are due to incomplete acquisition or attrition – a question that is hard to answer in the absence of longitudinal data. Since it is typical for early bilinguals to have comparatively more input in the heritage/minority language *before* entering school, one might assume early-acquired categories to be acquired and to stabilize before input in the majority language becomes predominant. We might therefore hypothesize that phenomena in the speech of adult bilinguals that deviates from monolingual-like behaviour are (i) the result of attrition

3 Davis (1995) has proposed an innovative explanation for the most marked status of voicing lead which appeals to the fact that lead voicing would enhance the perception of lead plosives, as the latter, besides having lead, would also have a very short lag between the release of the plosive and the beginning of sonority.

if typically acquired early and (ii) the result of incomplete acquisition if typically acquired late. In both cases, it is important to control whether such effects are restricted to the heritage language. If not, more general mechanisms of cross-linguistic influence could be at play.

5.3 VOT Study

5.3.1 Participants

Data for this study were taken from the HABLA corpus, a publicly available corpus of interviews with bilingual speakers (Kupisch, Barton, Bianchi and Stangen 2012; http://www1.uni-hamburg.de/exmaralda/files/e11-korpus/public/index.html). The recording sessions consisted of loosely prestructured interviews of 20–30 minute duration in a relaxed atmosphere. The speakers selected for the present study were recruited in Hamburg, Rome and Milan. In the following analysis, we examine the speech of German-Italian bilinguals who are second-generation speakers of German (2L1s from Italy) and have one parent born in Germany, as well as German-Italian bilinguals who are second-generation speakers of Italian (2L1s from Germany) and have one parent born in Italy. All were exposed to both languages at home when they were children. Most of the 2L1s from Italy (n=6) had attended German schools in Milan or Rome. None of the 2L1s from Germany (n=6) attended Italian schools, but two of them studied Italian in the context of a Bachelor's programme at the University of Hamburg. Table 5.3 provides an overview of the bilingual participants; with respect to their heritage language, we indicate the parents' place of origin.

Table 5.3. Overview of bilingual participants.

	2L1s from Germany	2L1s from Italy	L1 German	L1 Italian
No. of participants	6	6	5	5
Male/female	2/4	4/2	2/3	4/1
Age range	20–40	20–40	20–60	22–35
Place of origin	Hamburg	Milan, Rome	Hamburg, Bochum	Liguria, Veneto, Sicily
Parents' place of origin in heritage country	Calabria, Tuscany, Liguria, Piemonte, Veneto	Hamburg, Erfurt, Frankfurt, Munich	–	–

The monolingual data was collected later in a picture-based storytelling task, in which the depicted objects started with a voiceless stop. The speakers' task was to invent stories that included all depicted characters and objects.

5.3.2 Methods

VOT of /k/ was acoustically analysed, using Praat (Boersma and Weenink 2013). Following Lisker and Abramson (1964: 422), we identified the 'time interval between the burst that marks release [of the stop] and the onset of periodicity that reflects laryngeal vibration', with reference to the waveform. We focused on the velar stop /k/, analysing only words with initial stress and with /k/ in word-onset prevocalic position. Since in Italian, words with more than two syllables carry stress on the penultimate syllable and since monosyllabic words are rare, the analysis in this language is restricted to disyllabic words, all of them being trochaic, i.e. stressed on the first syllable. In German, by contrast, besides disyllables, we included monosyllabic words, because disyllabic ones are comparatively less frequent and monosyllables were necessary to outbalance the total number of items in the two languages. Each /k/-word was coded for number of syllables and quality of the following vowel (high-medium-low, front-back). Cases in which /k/ was produced as /g/ were excluded from the analysis (this only happened in the group of 2L1s from Italy).

We had two reasons for choosing /k/ as the focus sound of our study: (i) stops produced at the velum have the longest VOT values, the large area involved in velar production should facilitate the characterization of such segments; (ii) /k/ is acquired later than other consonants (Macken and Barton 1979; Bortolini, Zmarich, Fior and Bonifacio 1995), thus being potentially more vulnerable in bilingual development.

5.3.3 Results

Monolingual Data

As shown in Table 5.4, the monolingual Italian speakers produced VOTs between 35.5 and 46 ms (individual means), and the monolingual German speakers between 65.1 and 93.9 ms (individual means). For both languages, the values are higher than those previously reported in the literature (cf. Table 5.1), suggesting an effect of methodology. Recall that the monolingual

Table 5.4. VOT (in ms) in monolingual Italian and monolingual German adult speakers (German data from Lein et al. forthcoming).

Italian				German			
	Mean (range)	SD	N		Mean (range)	SD	N
CAR	35.7 (8.3–63.7)	11.8	36	*MAR*	72.6 (39.6–107.8)	16.8	39
MAT	35.5 (20.1–54.6)	8.6	35	*MAT*	79.9 (46.3–110.9)	16	49
ANT	33.8 (16.3–71.6)	14.2	48	*ROS*	93.9 (35.7–171.8)	24.6	64
SAN	46.0 (26.8–73.1)	11.4	32	*FRA*	65.1 (20.4–121.5)	22.3	43
MAR	40.8 (15.9–60.8)	11.6	38	*JAN*	73.7 (33.8–163.9)	24.8	61
Mean	38.4				77.04		

data reported in the literature are mostly based on list readings and that VOTs are said to be longer in isolated words than in spoken sentences and spontaneous speech (e.g. Lisker and Abramson 1964: 514), contrary to what we found. We suspect that our data display an effect of story-telling. Specifically, words that constitute the focus of the story, made up by the participants, have been emphasized. Interestingly, there is also a difference in SDs between the two languages: the monolingual Italian speakers tend to show lower standard deviations, thus deviating less from the mean than the monolingual German speakers. The reason for this difference might be related to /k/'s VOT being short lag in Italian and long lag in German, thus offering a much longer time span in German than in Italian.

Bilingual Data

The highest VOTs were produced by the 2L1s from Germany in German (mean 59.3 ms), and the lowest VOTs were produced by the 2L1s from Italy in Italian (mean 36.5 ms). The 2L1s from Germany produced higher VOTs in Italian (mean 43.8 ms) than the 2L1s from Italy, as expected under the influence from German; the 2L1s from Italy produced lower VOTs in German (mean 52.5 ms) than the 2L1s from Germany, as expected under influence from Italian. Table 5.5 shows mean values and ranges for each individual speaker (top to bottom) in each language (Italian on the left, German on the right).

Table 5.5 further shows a comparatively high degree of variation in both mean VOTs and VOT differences between the two languages (right-most column). Although all speakers have lower VOTs in Italian, the VOT differences between their two languages vary considerably: there are *short differences* of less than 10 ms (COR, LUC, JON, ALE), *intermediate differences* between 10 and 20 ms (DAR, PAT, DOM, LUI) and *long differences*

Table 5.5. VOT (in ms) in bilingual German-Italian speakers from Germany.

		Italian VOT			German VOT			***Diff.***
		Mean (range)	SD	N	Mean (range)	SD	N	
2L1s from Italy	*COR*	32.6 (20–47)	6.8	35	39.8 (23–60)	8.4	36	***7.2***
	CLF	30.8 (17–49)	8.0	20	62.1 (26–143)	28	19	***31.3***
	FRA	35.7 (6–74)	13.7	31	60.3 (11–81)	15.7	22	***24.6***
	LUC	43.5 (2–108)	19.4	25	49.0 (29–79)	13.1	30	***5.5***
	VAL	39.6 (21–64)*	15.8	14	58.8 (33–95)	17.3	19	***19.2***
	JON	36.7 (19–55)	10.3	19	45.1 (25–65)	11.9	19	***8.4***
Mean (range)		36.5 (2–108)			52.5 (11–143)		145	***16***
2L1s from Germany	*GIU*	44.4 (36–60)	9.7	10	66.1 (35–112)	21.6	25	***21.7***
	DAR	39.0 (26–62)	9.2	20	55.2 (28–146)	31.7	19	***16.2***
	PAT	48.4 (29–83)	19	8	64.6 (37–106)	15.8	49	***16.2***
	DOM	33.3 (24–66)	9.6	21	48.8 (14–109)	17.3	56	***15.1***
	ALE	43.8 (21–80)	14.2	32	53.1 (31–92)	13.2	40	***9.3***
	LUI	53.9 (38–99)	17.3	11	68.0 (47–107)	16.1	17	***14.1***
Mean (range)		43.8 (21–99)			59.3 (14–146)		206	***15.4***

* Produced many instances of /k/ as Italian /g/, i.e. with a perceived voicing lead.

above 20 ms (VAL, CLF, FRA, GIU).[4] Given that the difference between our two monolingual groups amounts to almost 40 ms, only those speakers with VOT differences around and above 20 ms (VAL, CLF, FRA, GIU) are arguably resilient to cross-linguistic influence.

5.4 Discussion

5.4.1 Cross-Linguistic Influence

Going back to the reports from the literature, it is safe to expect cross-language effects in the case of simultaneous bilinguals. On this basis, we

4 We excluded some instances of Italian /k/ from the data of the speaker VAL from Rome, since they were produced as /g/. The phenomenon is consistent with Hualde and Nadeu's (2011) report on lenition in Rome Italian. Including these lenited consonants in the analysis would have decreased the VOT means for VAL, thus leading to a more pronounced difference between his Italian and German productions.

have hypothesized that German influence on Italian should result in relatively long VOTs for /k/ compared to those of monolingual Italian speakers. Conversely, an Italian influence on German should result in relatively short VOTs for /k/ compared to those of monolingual German speakers (i.e. resulting in short lag, similar to the VOT of German voiced stop /g/). An alternative hypothesis is based on markedness: since short lag is the least marked of VOT categories, German long lag VOT might be more vulnerable than Italian short lag VOT (Kehoe et al. 2004).

The group means seem to confirm the first hypothesis: the German VOTs of 2L1s from Italy are 'too short' (compared to German monolinguals), while the Italian VOTs of the 2L1s from Germany are 'too long' (compared to Italian monolinguals). However, a closer look at the 2L1s from Italy with short VOT differences indicates that two of them (JON, COR) lean towards Italian-like VOTs when speaking German, while one speaker (LUC) produces VOTs that are neither clearly German-like nor clearly Italian-like. Interestingly, these three speakers also have comparatively low SDs when producing German VOTs, a property that seems typical of Italian monolinguals (cf. Table 5.5). This could suggest that Italian affects their German productions.

A closer look at the six 2L1s from Germany shows a large VOT difference only for GIU. Most others have intermediate or short VOT differences. Two speakers (LUI, PAT) lean towards German-like VOTs in Italian, which indicates influence from stronger to heritage language. ALE, DOM, DAR, by contrast, produce comparatively short VOTs in German and quasi Italian-like VOTs in Italian. These findings for the latter three speakers are unexpected under the assumption that cross-linguistic influence is unidirectional from stronger to heritage language, but they make sense once markedness is taken into consideration, because long lag is more marked than short lag. The assumption of Italian-like VOTs for ALE, DOM and DAR is supported by their comparatively low SDs, with the exception of DAR, typical of Italian monolinguals.

Returning to our research questions, in our study, only LUC (and possibly ALE) seems to represent such a case. The more common pattern is a *uni*directional influence from Italian to German for speakers in Italy (JON, COR) and from German to Italian (LUI, PAT) for speakers in Germany. For these speakers, *uni*directional influence also means that the stronger (i.e. societal) language tends to display monolingual-like values. By contrast, ALE, DOM and DAR seem to be affected in their *dominant* language as well (though not to the extent the values are completely off the monolingual range). Interestingly though, this only happens in German but not in

Italian. Put differently, in the stronger language, *long* lag may be affected while *short* lag is never affected.

In summary, our data confirm an existing interaction between the two languages of bilinguals, including adult speakers with exposure to both languages from birth. Most of the time, the majority language influences the heritage language: Italian is heritage in Germany, but in Italy, German is heritage. This answers the second question we posed, namely whether in simultaneous bilingualism monolingual-like development is guaranteed at least in one language, and whether this one language is always the majority language. According to our results, monolingual-like VOTs are *mostly* found in the majority language. However, some speakers do not conform to such a pattern, which seems to allocate an additional role to markedness. Short lag has often been described as being less marked than long lag, which is the reason why children begin producing short lag, irrespective of the VOT categories of their target language. These observations seem to be mirrored in our data: cross-linguistic influence can easily bring the values down (long lag becoming shorter), *while it seems to resist a large increase* in the sense of short lag becoming slightly longer, but not much. Moreover, the likelihood that German-dominant bilinguals deviate from monolingual-like productions in their German VOTs is higher than the likelihood that Italian-dominant speakers deviate from monolinguals in their Italian VOTs. We attribute this pattern to short lag being unmarked in relation to long lag.

5.4.2 Is VOT Gradient or Categorical?

A final issue relates to whether VOT is comprised of discrete categories or whether it is a gradual reality. As discussed in Section 5.2, VOT is considered to be categorical par excellence, as it corresponds to categories like phonologically voiced and voiceless. Since Lisker and Abramson's (1964) seminal paper, such categories are clearly quantifiable, and classifiable into long lag, short lag and voicing lead. However, these three categories are applied to a continuum, and arrangements are possible: for instance, a new category has been proposed, with intermediate values between long lag and short lag (Jong Kong et al. 2012) for certain dialects of Japanese, for Canadian French and Hebrew. This poses the question whether we can still consider VOT to be categorical. We believe that the creation of an intermediate category does not affect the categorical status of VOT, if overlap does not exceedingly increase. It just shows that between short and long lag there is unused space.

Another objection to the categorical status of VOT is related to the results of the present study. Under certain circumstances in-between category values are found: long lag and short lag vary from speaker to speaker, especially in bilinguals (e.g. LUC and ALE in Table 5.5). Here, the edges of the relevant category are moved up and down the continuum. The divisibility of the VOT continuum might be seen as comparable to the partition of the colour spectrum, which is divided differently depending on the language. Such categories built on continua tend to be variable towards the edges and, as proposed by the Speech Learning Model (Flege 1995) and by the Magnet Model (Kuhl and Iverson 1995), they can increase their range and become more encompassing, while not necessarily losing their categorical status. It would seem that some of the speakers we investigated have in-between categories, while others have clearly distinct ones. However, even for the speakers who produce VOTs at the edges between short and long lag in both languages, we cannot conclude that they have no separate categories for short versus long lag, because their intermediate VOTs may simply be a strategy to facilitate production, which is not necessarily mirrored in perception. A decisive way of finding out whether bilingual speakers abide by discrete categories would be to carry out a perception test.

5.4.3 Incomplete Acquisition or Attrition

One of our motivations for studying simultaneous bilinguals was that previous research on adult heritage speakers often included populations with different AoOs in the majority language, while studies on developing bilinguals are often based on simultaneous bilinguals. In this study, we have focused on simultaneous bilinguals, knowing that they may show delays in their VOT development. Ideally, determining whether target-deviant production during adulthood is due to loss or to incomplete acquisition would require longitudinal data. But even in the absence of such data, our knowledge about 2L1 development allows us to speculate which of the two possibilities is more reasonable. Since short lag VOT is acquired very early, one might speculate that speakers who produce long lag instead of short lag may have acquired the short lag category, but subsequently lost it under the impact of the majority language. For our case, this is not plausible because short lag still exists in the other language, though it is associated with a different phonemic value. Similarly, one might speculate that speakers who produce short lag instead of long lag have lost the long lag category or never acquired long lag because it is acquired rather late. Again, we do not find this plausible because even the 2L1s with the lowest VOTs in German manage to produce values up to at least 60 ms, i.e. within the range of monolingual German productions. Finally, restricting the discussion of heritage language competencies to incomplete acquisition and attrition might be inept. Although influence is often unidirectional from stronger to weaker language, it may also occur for reasons such as markedness. In the latter case, the stronger language may be affected too.

5.5 Conclusion

This study has confirmed that the two languages of adult bilingual speakers interact, leading to VOT values differing from those of monolingual speakers, even if they had been exposed to both languages from birth. Despite having the same age of onset, there is noticeable variation regarding the speakers' influence patterns, including *bi*directional, but mostly *uni*directional influence, going predominantly (though not exclusively) from stronger to weaker (i.e. heritage) language. The fact that influence is sometimes bidirectional indicates that more than one factor is at play. The stronger language, if affected, is comparatively more vulnerable in the case of long lag VOT, suggesting that markedness has a prominent role to play. Although these findings are robust, the study is limited in scope, because it has focused on the short lag of /k/ in Italian and its long lag counterpart in German. However, the story does not end here, because Italian also has voicing lead. Voicing lead is the most marked VOT, acquired late by monolinguals, 'often after the age of 5 years' (Jong Kong et al. 2012: 742). Studies including lead voicing are urgently required.

An open question remains why we found smaller SDs in Italian. One reason could be that we excluded productions of /k/ as /g/, but since this only happened in the 2L1s from Rome, it cannot be the only explanation. Another reason might be the one adduced in Section 5.3, namely that there is a higher probability of hitting the right value if the time span is short (as in Italian) than if it is long (as in German). In other words, there is a higher probability of overshooting into the long lag direction than into the short lag direction, which would again be consistent with markedness considerations, as the least marked of the VOTs, i.e. short lag, is also the shortest one. The idea that markedness can determine the direction of cross-linguistic influence receives support from previous research in segmental bilingual acquisition, e.g. Lleó (2002) on truncation, and Lleó and Rakow (2005) on spirantization.

References

Au, T.K., Knightly, L.M., Jun, S.-A. and Oh, J.S. (2002). Overhearing a language during childhood. *Psychological Science* 13: 238–43.

Baran, J.A., Laufer, M.Z. and Daniloff, R. (1977). Phonological contrastivity in conversation: A comparative study of voice onset time. *Journal of Phonetics* 5: 339–50.

Benmamoun, E., Montrul, S. and Polinsky, M. (2013). Heritage languages and their speakers: Opportunities and challenges for linguistics. *Theoretical Linguistics* 39: 129–81.

Boersma, P. and Weenik, D. (2013). Praat: doing phonetics by computer [Computer program]. Version 5.3.52. Retrieved from http://www.praat.org/

Bortolini U., Zmarich, C., Fior, R. and Bonifacio, S. (1995). Word-initial voicing in the productions of stops in normal and preterm Italian infants. *International Journal of Pediatric Otorhinolaryngology* 31: 191–206.

Braun, A. (1996). Zur regionalen Distribution von VOT im Deutschen. In A. Braun (ed.), *Untersuchungen zu Stimme und Sprache/Papers on Speech and Voice*, 19–32. Stuttgart: Steiner.

Chang, C.B., Yao, Y., Haynes, E.F. and Rhodes, R. (2011). Production of phonetic and phonological contrast by heritage speakers of Mandarin. *Journal of the Acoustical Society of America* 129: 3964–80.

Davis, K. (1995). Phonetic and phonological contrasts in the acquisition of voicing: Voice onset time production in the acquisition of Hindi and English. *Journal of Child Language* 22: 275–305.

Deuchar, M. and Clark, A. (1996). Early bilingual acquisition of the voicing contrast in English and Spanish. *Journal of Phonetics* 24: 351–65.

Eimas, P.D., Siqueland, E.R., Jusczyk, P. and Vigorito, J. (1971). Speech perception in infants. *Science*, New Series 172 (3968): 303–6.

Fabiano-Smith, L. and Bunta, F. (2012). Voice onset time of voiceless bilabial and velar stops in 3-year-old bilingual children and their age-matched monolingual peers. *Clinical Linguistics and Phonetics* 26: 148–63.

Fischer-Jørgensen, E. (1976). Some data on North German stops and affricates. *Annual Report of the Institute of Phonetics of the University of Copenhagen* 10: 149–200.

Fischer-Jørgensen, E. (1979). Zu den deutschen Verschlußlauten und Affrikaten. In K. Ezawa and K.H. Rensch (eds.), *Sprache und Sprechen. Festschrift für Eberhard Zwirner zum 80. Geburtstag*, 149–200. Tübingen, Germany: Max Niemeyer.

Flege, J.E. (1995). Second language speech learning. Theory, findings, and problems. In W. Strange (ed.), *Speech Perception and Linguistic Experience: Issues in Cross-Language Research*, 233–77. Timonium, MD: York Press.

Fowler, A.C., Sramko, V., Ostry, D.J., Rowland, S.A. and Hallé, P. (2008). Cross language phonetic influences on the speech of French-English bilinguals. *Journal of Phonetics* 3: 649–63.

Haag, W.K. (1979). An articulatory experiment on voice onset time in German stop consonants. *Phonetica: International Journal of Speech Science* 36: 169–81.

Hualde, J.I. and Nadeu, M.M. (2011). Lenition and phonetic overlap in Rome Italian. *Phonetica* 68: 215–42.

Jong Kong, E., Beckman, M.E. and Edwards, J. (2012). Voice onset time is necessary but not always sufficient to describe acquisition of voiced stops: The cases of Greek and Japanese. *The Journal of Phonetics* 40: 725–44.

Kehoe, M.M., Lleó, C. and Rakow, M. (2004). Voice onset time in bilingual German-Spanish children. *Bilingualism: Language and Cognition* 7: 71–88.

Kessinger, R.H. and Blumstein, Sh.E. (1997). Effects of speaking rate on voice-onset time in Thai, French and English. *Journal of Phonetics* 25: 143–68.

Kohler, K.J. (1995). *Einfuhrung in die Phonetic des Deutschen*. 2nd edn. Berlin: Schmidt.

Kuhl, P.K. and Iverson, P. (1995). Linguistic experience and the 'Perceptual Magnet Effect'. In W. Strange (ed.), *Speech Perception and Linguistic Experience: Issues in Cross-Language Research*, 121–54. York Press.

Kupisch, T., Barton, D., Bianchi, G. and Stangen, I. (2012). The E11-corpus of adult bilinguals (German-French and German-Italian). In T. Schmid and K. Wörner (eds.), *Multilingual Corpora and Multilingual Corpus Analysis: Hamburg Studies in Multilingualism 14*, 163–79. Amsterdam: John Benjamins.

Kupisch, T., Barton, D., Hailer, K., Lein, T., Kostogryz, T., Stangen, I. and van de Weijer, J. (2014). Foreign accent in adult simultaneous bilinguals? *Heritage Language Journal* 11(2): 123–50.

Lee, S. and Iverson, G.K. (2012). Stop consonant productions of Korean-English bilingual children. *Bilingualism: Language and Cognition* 15: 275–87.

Lein, T., Kupisch, T. and van de Weijer, J. (forthcoming). VOT and global foreign accent in German-French simultaneous bilinguals during adulthood. *International Journal of Bilingualism*.

Lisker, L. and Abramson, A. (1964). A cross-language study of voicing in initial stops: Acoustical measurements. *Word* 20: 384–422.

Lleó, C. (2002). The role of markedness in the acquisition of complex prosodic structures by German-Spanish Bilinguals. *International Journal of Bilingualism* 6: 291–313.

Lleó, C. (2008). Interacció dels dos sistemes fonològics en el marc de l'adquisició fonològica bilingüe. *Estudis Romànics* XXX: 103–26.

Lleó, C. and Rakow, M. (2005). Markedness effects in voiced stop spirantization in bilingual German-Spanish children. In J. Cohen, K.T. McAlister, K. Rolstad and J. MacSwan (eds.), *Proceedings of the 4th International Symposium on Bilingualism (ISB4)*, 1353–71. CD Rom. Somerville, MA: Cascadilla Press.

Macken, M.A. and Barton, D. (1979). The acquisition of the voicing contrast in English: A study of voice onset time in word-initial stop consonants. *Journal of Child Language* 7: 41–74.

Montrul, S. (2008). *Incomplete Acquisition in Bilingualism*. Amsterdam: John Benjamins.

Nagy, N. and Kochetov, A. (2013). Voice onset time across the generations: A cross-linguistic study of contact-induced change. In P. Siemund, I. Gogolin, M. Schulz and J. Davydova (eds.), *Multilingualism and Language Contact in Urban Areas*, 19–38. Amsterdam: John Benjamins.

Oh, J., Jun, S., Knightly, L. and Au, T. (2003). Holding on to childhood language memory. *Cognition* 86: 53–64.

Sancier, M.L. and Fowler, C.A. (1997). Gestural drift in a bilingual speaker of Brazilian Portuguese and English. *Journal of Phonetics* 25: 421–36.

Sorianello, P. (1996). Indici fonetici delle occlusive sorde nel cosentino. *Rivista Italiana di Dialettologia* 20: 123–59.

Splendido, F. (2014). *Le développement d'aspects phonético-phonologiques du français chez des enfants bilingues simultanés et successifs. Le VOT et la liaison dans un eétude de cas multiples.* PhD Thesis, Lund University, Sweden.

Stock, D. (1971). *Untersuchungen zur Stimmhaftigkeit hochdeutscher Phonem-realisationen*. Hamburg: Helmut Buske.

Street, R.L. (1983). Noncontent speech convergence in adult-child interactions. In R.N. Bostrom (ed.), *Communication Yearbook 7*, 369–95. Beverly Hills, CA: Sage.

Sundara, M., Polka, L. and Baum, S. (2006). Production of coronal stops by simultaneous bilingual adults. *Bilingualism: Language and Cognition* 9: 97–114.

Watson, I. (1990) Acquiring the voicing contrast in French: A comparative study of monolingual and bilingual children. In J.N. Green and W. Ayers-Bennet (eds.), *Variation and Change in French: Essays Presented to Rebecca Posner on the Occasion of Her Sixtieth Birthday*, 37–60. London: Routledge.

Tanja Kupisch is Professor of Romance Linguistics in the Department of General Linguistics at the University of Konstanz, Germany, and Professor II at the Arctic University of Norway.

Conxita Lleó, now retired, was Professor of Romance Linguistics at the University of Hamburg, Germany.

6
Production of English Laterals by Early Sequential Spanish-English Bilinguals

Mehmet Yavaş

6.1 Introduction

It is a prevailing view in second language acquisition (especially in phonology) that 'earlier is better', and 'age of acquisition' (hereafter AOA) has been treated as the most important variable with regard to the native-like performance in bilingual speech. As seen in many immigrant families, although the parents can become very fluent in their L2, their phonologies are always non-native. Children, on the other hand, with the same length of residency, can sound native-like if their AOA is early. There are several large-scale studies that have supported the importance of age of learning in L2 phonology (Asher and Garcia 1969; Oyama 1976; Flege and Fletcher 1992; Flege, Munro and MacKay 1995; Flege, Yeni-Komshian and Liu 1999; Thompson 1991; Darcy and Kruger 2012; Oh, Guion-Anderson, Aoyama, Flege, Akahane-Yamada and Yamada 2011; Aoyama, Flege, Guion, Yamada and Akahane-Yamada 2004). These findings led some researchers to suggest a biological/neurological-based critical age for learning L2 pronunciation. Those who defend the Critical Age Hypothesis (Scovel 1988, 2000; Patkowski 1990, 1993) argue for the existence of a sensitive period for the acquisition of phonology in a second language, in that humans' abilities become limited for successful acquisition due to maturational constraints as the AOA increases. Simply put, it is suggested that there is a sensitive period from birth to puberty in which it is possible to acquire second language phonology in a native-like manner. This capacity seems to deteriorate after puberty and consequently, the L2 pronunciation of a post-puberty learner will not be accent-free. Thus, a person who acquires a second language before the end of this critical period will have a marked phonological advantage over a later learner.

There are, on the other hand, other scholars who question the Critical Period Hypothesis, and for various reasons, do not accept the neurological/biological-based argument. Some (Bongaerts 1999; Bongaerts, Mennen and van der Slik 2000) claim that there is evidence that some adults are successful in learning an L2 phonology. Others (Flege 1987a, 2002; Flege, MacKay and Piske 2002; Moyer 2004) state that while there are advantages of earlier acquisition of an L2, this is not uniquely because of AOA, as it is frequently confounded with other factors such as 'amount of L1 use', 'amount of native speaker input', 'length of residency', 'aptitude', 'motivation' and 'language dominance', and these are expected to influence performance. Thus, it is unclear to what extent deviances from monolinguals are due to AOA or a combination of a variety of other factors. In any case, regardless of the reasons, there seems to be overwhelming agreement that 'earlier is better' has been demonstrated convincingly during the last 3–4 decades. It is, however, important to point out that 'how early' the acquisition needs to be is still in dispute.

Several studies have shown that a lag of even a few years in acquiring an L2 tends to have dramatic consequences on both speech production and perception (Flege et. al. 1999; Fowler, Sramko, Ostry, Rowland and Halle 2008; Flege and MacKay 2004; Sebastian-Galles and Soto-Faraco 1999). Also, recent comprehensive and detailed linguistic analyses of early learners have revealed that even very low AOAs do not automatically result in completely native-like L2 proficiency (Abrahamsson 2012; Bylund, Abrahamsson and Hyltenstam 2012; Stölten, Abrahamsson and Hyltenstam 2014).

One of the most influential models of explanation regarding the ultimate attainment in L2 phonological acquisition is the 'Speech Learning Model' (hereafter SLM) (Flege 2002, 2003, 2007, 2009). SLM treats phonological acquisition with a view of phonetic approximation and interference based on perceptual judgements. The model is concerned with 'ultimate attainment', and thus focuses on long-term bilinguals. SLM holds the view that there is no critical period after which the learner will be unable to acquire an L2 sound system. However, it is also stated that L2 development is constrained by age of learning. It is predicted that learners are more likely to have native-like perception with early age of learning. The later the age of learning, the less likely a learner is to hear the differences between L1 and L2 sounds, because the learner's L1 categories will be more developed and are likely to impede the formation of new categories for L2 sounds of L1. In other words, as L1 categories become more robust through childhood, they become more powerful 'attractors' for L2 speech sounds (Baker, Trofimovich, Mack and Flege 2002). SLM is built on the ideas of categorical perception and equivalence classification in the determination of how a learner will react to, and ultimately acquire, sounds in an L2. In the interaction of L1 and L2 phonetic subsystems, SLM proposes two specific mechanisms: 'category assimilation' and 'category dissimilation'. Category assimilation will occur when category formation for an L2 sound has been blocked. This happens when the L2 learner judges the instances of an L2 category to be instances of an L1 category. That is, if L2 sounds are categorized as 'similar', their assimilation to the existing L1 phonetic categories will be through a process of equivalence classification. The investigation of Italian-English bilinguals' productions of /b, d, g/ by MacKay, Flege, Piske and Schirru (2001) provides evidence for category assimilation. While English has short lag and Italian has pre-voiced (voice lead) /b, d, g/ in monolinguals, Italian-English bilinguals produced fully pre-voiced English /b, d, g/ (their L1 like). These results were consistent with the view that they had not established separate phonetic categories for English /b, d, g/.[1]

If, on the other hand, there is great dissimilarity between L2 and L1 sounds, the sound will be judged 'new' and it will not be assimilated to any L1 category (category dissimilation); that is, a new phonetic category will be formed for an L2 speech sound. For example, English speakers learning French as a second language could produce French /y/ (a 'new' vowel for English speakers) more accurately than French /u/, because French /y/ is perceptually more distant from the closest English vowel than is French /u/, which has a near (but not identical) counterpart in English /u/.

Simply put, SLM's 'equivalence classification' states that similar sounds are difficult to acquire because of their assimilation to an existing L1 sound; new (dissimilar) sounds are easier to acquire because there are salient differences. The idea that L2 sounds, which are different from those in L1, may be easier to acquire than those that are similar is also expressed by the Similarity Differential Rate Hypothesis, hereafter SDRH (Major and Kim 1999).

The study reported in this chapter investigates the production of American English laterals by early sequential Spanish-English bilinguals. The central question is whether early sequential bilinguals are able to develop native-like phonological patterns and maintain separate phonetic categories for the sounds of their second language (English) when

1 Since 1994, the SLM has treated L1-L2 phonetic dis/similarity as a continuum, not as tripartite 'identical-similar-new', as specified by the SLM of 1984–93.

these sounds closely resemble phonetic categories of their first language (Spanish),[2] or if starting a few years late will create impediments in the formation of new categories. This question is motivated by the idea that sequential bilinguals, unlike simultaneous bilinguals, may not be able to be balanced bilinguals because their initial 4–5 years are spent in a primarily monolingual environment. Consequently, they will not be able to form their two phonetic systems separately and comparable to those of monolingual speakers of the two languages.[3]

6.1.1 English and Spanish Laterals

English and Spanish laterals are both coronals in their place of articulation, in that the tip of the tongue is raised towards the alveolar ridge. However, the similarity between them ends there. Spanish /l/ is always 'clear', while English lateral is described as having both 'clear' and 'dark' variants. Dark laterals have a dorsal approximation at the velar region as well as some pre-dorsal lowering (Narayanan, Alwan and Haker 1997; Recasens and Espinosa 2005). Also, the point of contact is said to be more front (dento-alveolar) in 'dark' laterals, whereas it is plain alveolar in 'clear' laterals (Ladefoged and Maddieson 1996). The distribution of English laterals is said to be determined by their position in the syllable: syllable-initially 'clear', and syllable-finally 'dark'. While this account is valid for British English, the picture for most American English speakers is more like a continuum, in the form of the 'degrees of dark'. In other words, even in syllable-initial position, the lateral is not as 'clear' as the one you find in British English; rather, it is 'less dark' (compare the onset lateral in the word 'law' in British English and American English). It has also been shown that the adjacent vowel (following vowel in onset laterals and preceding vowel in coda laterals) has an effect on the degree of darkness of the lateral. Adjacent to a front vowel, especially high front, 'dark' lateral becomes less dark, and adjacent to a back vowel, especially high back, 'clear' lateral becomes less clear. Putting all these together, we tend to observe the least dark in syllable-initial position before a high front vowel (e.g. lead), a little darker in syllable-initial position

2 The terms 'first language' and 'second language' refer to the order in which these languages are acquired and have nothing to do with the language dominance. As a matter of fact, almost all of the participants' dominant language is their chronological second language English.

3 It should be pointed out that bilingual speakers rarely attain balanced bilingualism, even if both of the languages are acquired simultaneously, since the variation of the language input is influenced by the mother's native language (Mack, Bott and Boronat 1995; Sebastian-Galles, Echeverria and Bosch 2005).

before a high back vowel (e.g. Luke), followed by yet darker in syllable-final position before a high front vowel (e.g. feel), and finally the darkest in syllable-final position before a high back vowel (e.g. fool).[4]

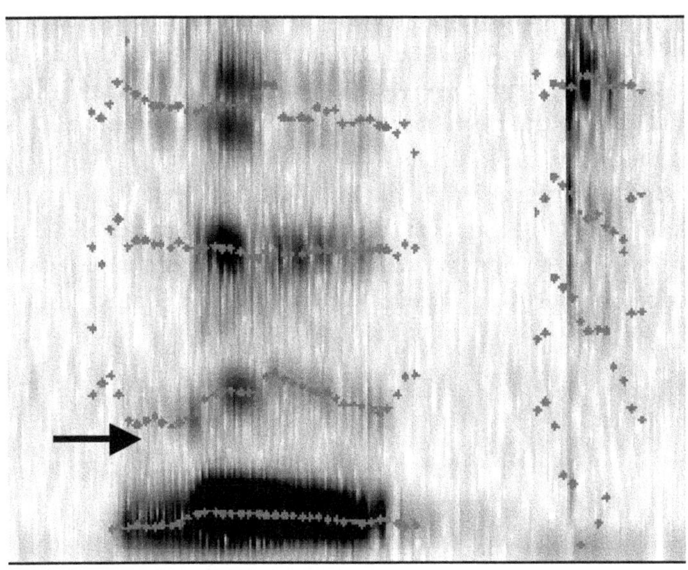

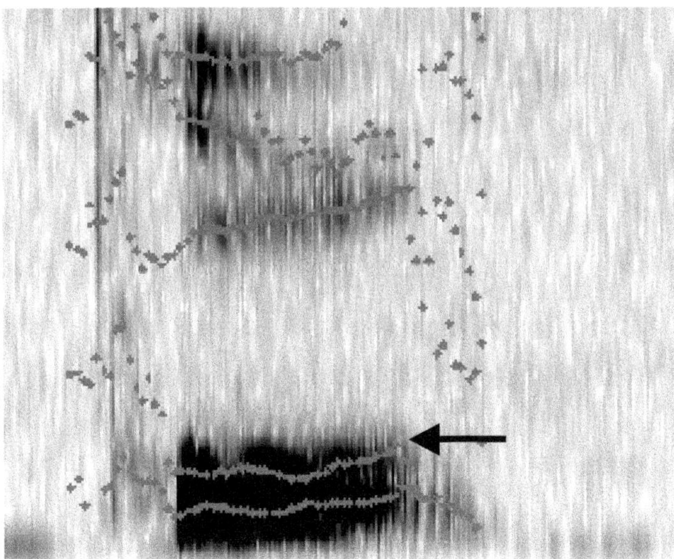

Figure 6.1. Onset and coda laterals in American English (F2 marked with an arrow).

4 Dialects may gradually vary according to the degree of darkness (Carter and Local 2007).

In acoustic terms, cross-linguistically, the frequencies of the first two formants – especially F2 – are correlated with the degree of velarization (darkness) of /l/. Dorsal backing and lowering of 'dark' laterals triggers a significant lowering of F2 (and some raising of F1). The resulting narrowed space between F2 and F1 is a typical sign of a more back (velarized) articulation. Laterals with F2 frequencies higher than 1200 Hz are generally perceived as 'clear', and those with lower than that as 'dark' (Fant 1960; Recasens 2004). Figure 6.1 shows the difference between the onset and coda laterals in American English.

As stated earlier, the Spanish lateral is always 'clear'; it is characterized by a relatively high second formant (F2) frequency. Studies of laterals from a variety of different Spanish dialects report F2 frequencies above 1400 Hz even before a high back vowel /u/, which is the context for lowest F2

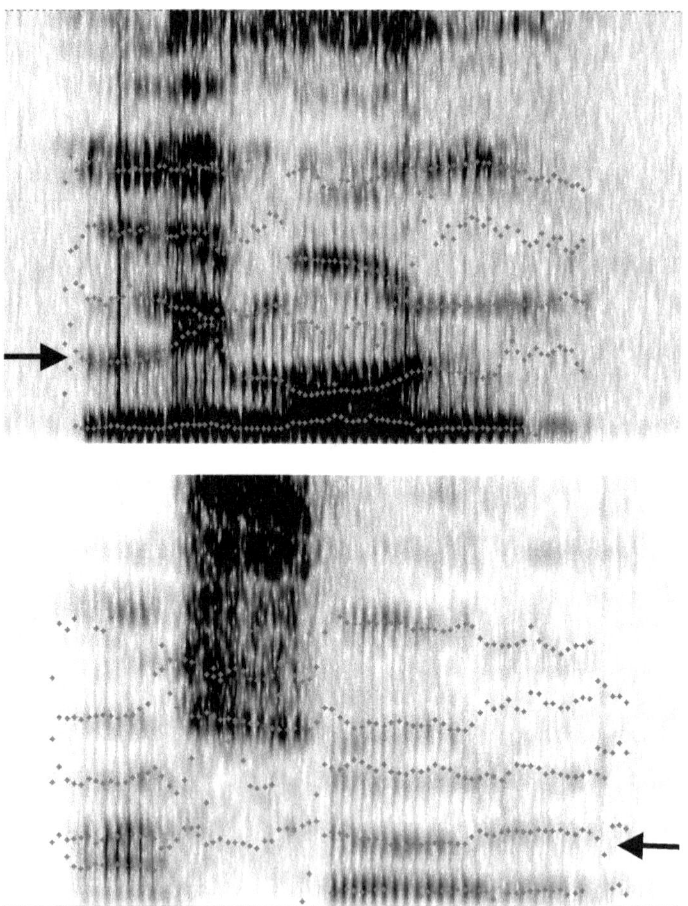

Figure 6.2. Onset and coda laterals in Spanish (F2 marked with an arrow).

frequencies in syllable-initial position (Chafcouloff 1972; Quilis, Esgueva, Gutierrez-Araus and Cantarero 1979; Hualde 2005). Figure 6.2 shows the onset and coda laterals of Spanish.

As seen in Figure 6.2, Spanish laterals show more or less identical formant structure in both the onset and the coda positions. In other words, the obvious lowering of the F2 in English coda laterals is never the case in Spanish.

One of the very rare acoustic investigations of laterals in Spanish-English bilinguals is of Barlow, Branson and Nip (2013) which examined the acquisition of /l/ by 7 Spanish-English bilingual children (mean age 4;7) and compared them with monolingual children in respective languages. Bilingual data showed merged phonetic categories for pre-vocalic (onset) [l] for the two languages, but separate phonetic categories for post-vocalic [l]; velarized (dark) [l] was present in English, but not Spanish. This was explained through sufficient distinctness of the post-vocalic (dark) laterals in English.

6.2 The Study

The present study investigates the patterns of production of American English laterals by early sequential Spanish-English bilinguals. It addresses the question of whether early bilinguals have been able to develop a different acoustic distribution for a novel L2 sound (phonologically the same, but phonetically different) and whether new category formation, if found, led to a dissimilation of the similar L1 and L2 sounds in these speakers. It is important to emphasize the one-to-one phonological correspondences and yet the existence of phonetic differences in the laterals of the two languages involved. Since these phonetically different sounds do not involve any phonemic separation, they may not force the learner to learn these just for phonetic differences even with early bilingualism.

In examining the bilinguals' production, the following research questions are considered:

1. Do productions of early sequential bilinguals acoustically match those of monolinguals with respect to American English laterals?
2. If not, are the differences due to different syllabic and/or vocalic environments?
3. Does AOA explain the different performances of individual subjects?
4. Is the frequency of target words influential for the subjects' performances?

6.2.1 Method

Participants

The participants of this study were 25 monolingual American English speakers and 25 Spanish-English bilinguals. The speakers of the first group came from the students and faculty of the Florida International University. The age range was between 23 and 45. They may have had some limited foreign language classes in their secondary education, but none claimed to have functional knowledge of any foreign language, Spanish or otherwise. The second group comprised 25 early sequential Spanish-English bilinguals. Most participants were undergraduate students from Florida International University. The group consisted of 9 males and 16 females whose ages ranged from 18 to 27. Within this group, the average age of L2 (English) acquisition was 4;9. As a group, the average length of residence in the United States was 19 years. However, the majority of the participants in this group were born in the United States. The non-US-born participants came from Cuba (2), Colombia (1), and Peru (1); their age of arrival in the USA was not later than 9;0. All the students who reported being born in the United States were either natives of Miami, Florida, or had moved to Miami from New York City during infancy and did not begin learning English from their parents. In other words, they belonged to the very typical local pattern whereby the children are in a Spanish-speaking environment until they begin their education. Although they are typically Spanish monolinguals until they start kindergarten, the language dominance shifts to English through the elementary education, and strengthens more thereafter. At the time of our data collection, from their self-reporting, which is confirmed by our own perception, they were all English dominant. While the use of English was proportionally higher in their daily lives, their contact with Spanish was not negligible, which was made quite clear by the lengthy language history questionnaire they completed prior to their participation. In almost all cases, their home language continued to be Spanish with their relatives, parents and grandparents. They also reported frequent code switching in their interactions with siblings and among bilingual friends. At this point, it is also relevant to mention the predominance and prestige of Spanish in South Florida. Unlike in other parts of the United States (e.g. Texas, Arizona, New Mexico, Southern California), Spanish does not have a secondary status; rather it enjoys equal footing with English.

Materials

The experimental stimuli, which consisted of English sentences containing laterals in different syllable positions, were presented in randomized blocks. There were 16 target words with the following distribution: four syllable-initial before high front vowels, four syllable-initial with high back vowels, four syllable-final after high front vowels, and four syllable-final after high back vowels. There were also 16 sentences, as distractors, with no target words with laterals. (See Appendix A for the complete list.)

Procedures

Participants were told that the study involved reading sentences on a computer screen and that their speech would be recorded for later analysis. They were situated in a quiet room. After signing the consent form, they sat in front of a laptop, and the procedure was explained to them in English. They were instructed to read each individual sentence from a PowerPoint presentation, as it appeared on the screen, and to also self-advance the slides, as the experiment was not timed. Participants were prompted to read the sentences aloud, and their productions were recorded digitally. Recordings were saved at 44100 Hz sampling rate and at 16 bit resolution. The recordings were segmented and labelled using Praat speech analysis software version 5.4.10 manually (Boersma and Weenink 2013).

6.2.2 Analysis

A total of 800 tokens were analysed (16 targets x 25 monolinguals = 400, and 16 targets x 25 bilinguals = 400). Formant frequencies (F1 and F2) were obtained from spectrograms. The middle of the steady-state portion of each lateral production was identified perceptually and visually. Lateral targets in onsets were further confirmed by waveform where the following vowels show a clear increase in amplitude. In the analyses, F2 frequencies were the focus of attention. Twelve tokens (less than 2% of the total) could not be measured and were discarded. Randomly chosen, 96 spectrograms (12% of the total) were re-measured and the inter-judge reliability was over 93%.

6.2.3 Results and Discussion

We start off by examining F2 frequencies of laterals in the four different positions; these are (a) onsets before front vowels (hereafter OF), (b) onsets before back vowels (hereafter OB), (c) codas after front vowels (hereafter CF) and (d) codas after back vowels (hereafter CB). First of all, we examine the pair-wise differences between adjacent positions in the continuum within each group of participants. These comparisons include the two onset positions (OF and OB), followed by the comparison of OB and CF, and finally the two coda positions, CF and CB. These can be seen in the following displays. We first give the monolingual results with F2 means:

OF: 1260 Hz. OB: 1166 Hz. p<0.001
OB: 1166 Hz. CF: 967 Hz. p<0.001
CF: 967 Hz. CB: 802 Hz. p<0.001

The values in the bilingual productions are as follows:

OF: 1761 Hz. OB: 1530 Hz. p<0.001
OB: 1530 Hz. CF: 1188 Hz. p<0.001
CF: 1188 Hz. CB: 901 Hz. p<0.001

As can be seen clearly, the comparisons of the different environments within each group result in significant differences. We next present the monolingual-bilingual comparisons in each of the four different positions; in every one of these four positions, the differences between the two groups are found to be significantly different.

Monolingual-Bilingual

OF 1260 Hz. 1761 Hz. p<0.001
OB 1166 Hz. 1530 Hz. p<0.001
CF 967 Hz. 1188 Hz. p<0.001
CB 802 Hz. 901 Hz. p<0.001

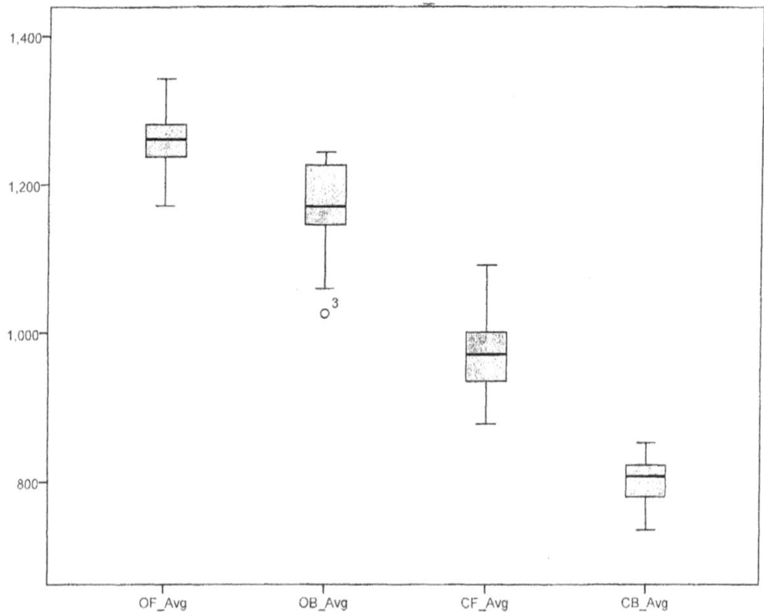

Figure 6.3. F2 frequencies in monolinguals' laterals.

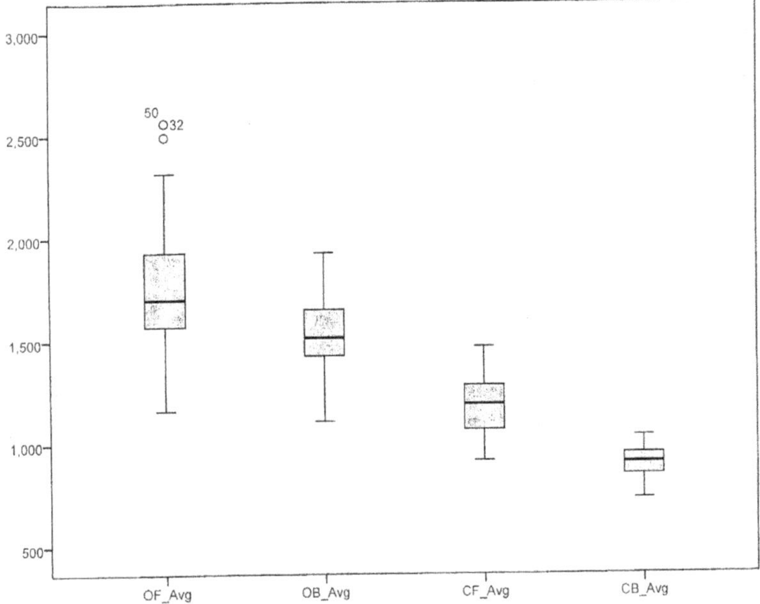

Figure 6.4. F2 frequencies in bilinguals' American English laterals.

Figures 6.3 and 6.4, with box plots, display the measures of central tendency for F2 frequencies illustrating the means as well as minimum and maximum values, in monolinguals and bilinguals, respectively.

The significant differences that are found between the two groups with respect to the four different positions are not due to the combined averages of the four targets in each position; rather they are seen in each of the sixteen individual targets in these different positions. Means of fourteen out of sixteen targets display the same significance (p<0.001). The two targets that display different degrees of significance are 'pull' (p<0.004), and 'pool' (p<0.003). The individual targets with their central tendencies for F2 frequencies illustrating the means, as well as minimum and maximum values, are shown in Figure 6.5 for monolinguals, and Figure 6.6 for bilinguals.

Although in each of the four positions, and also in each target of these positions, there are significant differences between monolinguals and bilinguals, our findings also point to a fact clearly observable among these syllable positions with different adjacent vowels. This is related to the number of productions that are within the range of the monolingual productions. We calculate these by looking at the minimum and maximum F2 values in Hz found in different positions. For the general onset position, 'clear [l]', we find the range 1020–1390 Hz, which is quite similar to the values

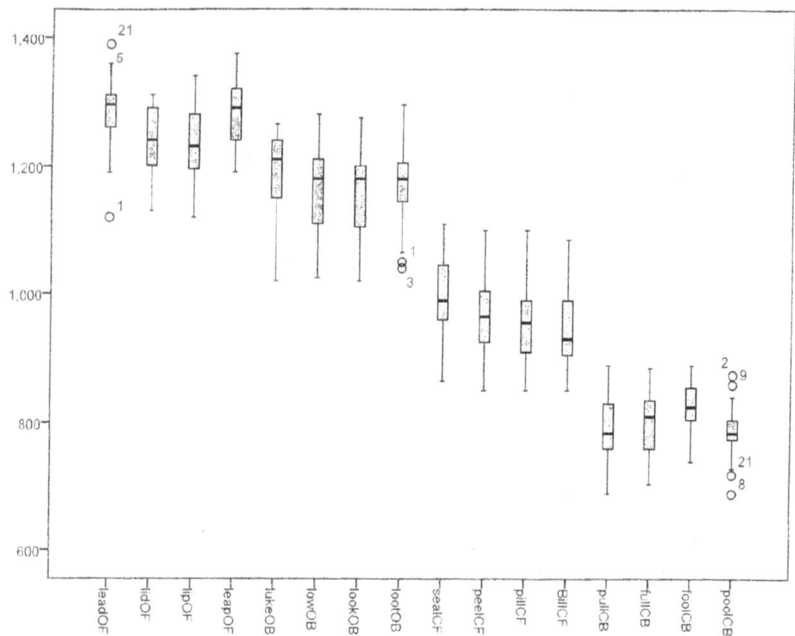

Figure 6.5. F2 frequencies of individual targets in monolinguals' laterals.

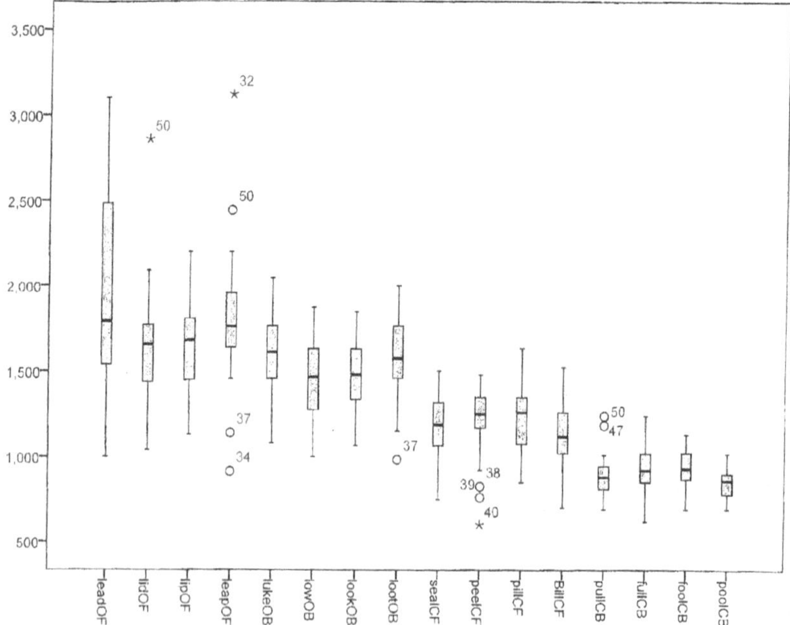

Figure 6.6. F2 frequencies of individual targets in bilinguals' American English laterals.

reported in the literature (1000–1400 Hz). For the coda position ('dark [l]'), our range is 700–1050 Hz, which again, is not far from the values reported in the literature (below 1000 Hz: Proctor 2010; Recasens 2004). Since we examined the laterals in four different environments, we give our monolingual control ranges accordingly, in the following:

OF	OB	CF	CB
1120–1390	1020–1295	850–1050	700–890

The productions of the bilinguals that are found within monolingual range in these four environments are given in Appendix B. The list also shows the individually different performances by these bilinguals. For example, while participant 11 is quite successful in monolingual range (with 13 out of 16 targets), participant 20 is extremely weak in this respect (only 1 out of 16 targets in monolingual range). The inventory presented in Appendix B is much more revealing in the patterns it shows. There seems to be an undeniable gradation in terms of the bilingual participants un/successful productions (with respect to reaching the monolingual range) when results are analysed through the four different environments. Overall, the OF environment is the least successful (greatest difficulty, with the least number of in-range productions) and CB is the most successful (least difficulty, with the highest number of in-range productions). Although onset environments (OF and OB) present greater difficulty than the coda environments (CF and CB), it is important to point out that there are obvious gradations with the 'onset' and 'coda' laterals. Thus, it looks like the continuum formed above, among the four different environments, is well justified. More specifically, we have 13 out of 100 in-range productions in OF, which goes up to 18 out of 100 in OB, which in turn is followed by a more successful CF environment (46 out of 100), and finally the most successful CB with 69 out of 100 in-range productions. A close examination of the results will also show a support for an implicational hierarchy of the 'in-range' productions by our bilingual subjects. In other words, with few exceptions, the following holds: whoever has in-range productions in the least successful environment also has in-range productions in the environments that are deemed more favourable. However, the reverse does not hold.

These results give support to the view expressed by SLM. As stated earlier, learning success is predicted to be a function of the phonetic dis/similarity of the sounds of the L1 and L2, and thus the task will be easier with dissimilar sounds than with similar sounds. Since the dis/similarity is considered as a continuum in SLM, the gradation in the success rate we see in different environments with the target laterals is in agreement with this situation. Note that the gradual dissimilarity continuum with L1 (Spanish) starts with OF environment and ends with CB environment, with OB and CF in between. This is exactly the opposite tendency in our participants' performance whereby the most dissimilar CB was the most successful and the least dissimilar (most similar) OF was the least successful. This is exactly what is predicted by SLM, and SDRH. Finally, this is similar to the findings reported by Barlow et al. (2013), in that the postvocalic (coda) [l]s are sufficiently distinct in the two languages so that the bilinguals are able to form separate categories.[5]

We also examined the word frequencies of the targets, which may have been responsible for the observed patterns. To do this, we have consulted Kucera and Francis' (1967) Word Pool (http://memory.psych.upenn.edu/wordpools.php) and the frequencies noted there do not seem in any way suggestive of the differences we have seen in our data. For example, the very frequently found 'look' (OB) or 'full' (CB) were not significantly different from less frequently found 'loot' and 'fool', respectively.

The results given in Appendix B also give us the opportunity to examine the question regarding the AOA and the possible relationship with the participants' performance. Here, again, we do not seem to go very far in explaining the differences among the participants. For example, despite the adverse time line, participant 21 (AOA=7;9, the age of arrival from Colombia) has a far superior performance with respect to in-range productions than participant 22 (AOA=4;1). Also, participants 12 and 20 who have almost identical AOAs – 4;5 and 4;4 respectively – show remarkable differences. Also, from the Language Background Questionnaires I obtained from the participants, it was not possible to find an explanation for the individual differences through the amount of daily L1 use. If the length of residences, the amount of L1 use and the amount of input are comparable among the participants, then one possible variable remaining would be the nature (quality) of the input, which may be responsible for the individual differences. Needless to say, however, this is extremely difficult to quantify. Although I have conducted lengthy individual interviews regarding the quality of the input with our participants, I have concluded that accounting for the facts going back 15 to 22 years would be speculative at best.

5 Simonet (2010) studied the lateral productions of Spanish-Catalan bilinguals (Catalan has 'dark' laterals). Although the productions of bilinguals were unlike those of monolinguals of the respective languages, the productions of Catalan-dominant bilinguals influenced their Spanish laterals in relative darkness of /l/.

The 'clear' and 'dark' variation, or rather, gradual darkening of the English laterals, and our speakers' gradient success rate with the target words, also has certain implications with regard to markedness. It is usually assumed that the onset-coda positional variation is not universal. Besides Spanish, other languages such as German and Arabic lack such variation. However, where it does occur, as in Dutch or Portuguese, the variation always seems to be in the same direction ('clear' in onset and 'dark' in coda position). Thus, the patterns found in English, although they do not have the status of 'universal', follow robust phonetic tendencies. Our bilinguals' in-range productions with respect to greater ease (or, less difficulty) in coda position, despite the obvious conflict with the patterns of L1, might be interpreted as an enhancement via markedness. As such, this situation is relatable to the Markedness Differential Hypothesis (MDH) and its further modification, Structural Conformity Hypothesis (SCH) advanced by Eckman (1977 and 1991, respectively). According to MDH, areas of the target language that are different from, but not more marked than, the native language will not be difficult. SCH, on the other hand, extends the principle beyond the relationship between L1 and L2 and states that the structure of an interlanguage will conform to the universal typological principals found in primary languages. Thus, our participants' interlanguage productions through their gradient success give support to these principles by matching the robust phonetic tendencies found in primary languages.

6.3 Conclusions

In this chapter, we have examined the L2 acquisition data from early sequential Spanish-English bilinguals regarding the American English laterals. We found that sequential learning has an effect on speech production even in cases in which speakers have acquired their L2 in early childhood and have subsequently had ample opportunities to learn the speech patterns of their L2 and even become L2 dominant. However, it was not possible to explain the differential performances of the participants through AOA, or the amount of L1 use. These findings are in agreement with other studies (Bosch, Costa and Sebastian-Galles 2000; Dupoux, Peperkamp and Sebastian-Galles 2010), in that even early exposure to L2 may not be enough for bilinguals to acquire native-like phonetic patterns in their L2. It is very difficult at this point to explain the reason(s) for the non-nativeness of the productions by our early bilinguals. While one can advance the idea that the speech patterns attuned to the native language act as a filter that interferes with the way the L2 can be acquired (Flege 2007; Iverson, Kuhl, Yamada, Diesch, Tohkura and Ketterman 2003; Kuhl, Conboy, Coffey-Corina, Padden, Rivera-Gaxiola and Nelson 2008), it is equally viable to point at the quality of input the subjects received in their early stages of English acquisition, which may have been predominantly by non-monolingual agents. Overall, the results are in support of the principles of SLM (dissimilar sounds are easier to acquire because there are salient differences) and SDRH (dissimilar phenomena are acquired at faster rates than similar phenomena).[6] They also lend support to the MDH, which states that the areas of the target language that are different from but not more marked than the native language will not be difficult, and the SCH, which predicts that the interlanguages follow the typological principles found in primary languages. Our data do not suggest any influence of word frequency or AOA as determinants of differential success rate among the participants.

6.4 Future Directions

Although we compared bilinguals' production of L2 laterals with the monolingual norms and found significant differences, it is worthwhile to compare bilinguals' L1 speech with that of monolinguals, as there have been several studies revealing non-monolingual-like L1 productions among bilinguals. Evidence for such phonetic drift was provided by Flege (1987b) regarding VOTs in English-French bilinguals, Major (1992, 1996) in English-Portuguese bilinguals, Harada (2003) in early Japanese-English bilinguals, and Kang and Guion (2006) in late Korean-English bilinguals. The occurrence of phonetic drift is not restricted to temporal aspects and can also be found in spectral aspects of consonant production (Peng 1993), in intonational properties (Mennen 2004) and in vowel production (Baker and Trofimovich 2005; Guion 2003). Thus, it will be interesting to compare our bilinguals' production of Spanish laterals to those of monolingual Spanish speakers. This is the next project I would like to engage in.

6 It should be pointed out that the non-native productions do not necessarily claim inaccurate perception of these targets in SLM. While the model postulates inaccurate perception will lead to problems in production, it does not predict that *all* production errors are perceptually based.

Acknowledgements

I am grateful to the participants who gave their time generously to the study. Thanks are also due to research volunteers Gabriela Perez, Melanie Fernandez and Eric Torres for their help in recordings and measurements, and to Tyler Stout for the statistical analyses.

Appendix A: Sentences Presented for Participants to Read (target words italicized)

1. Don't be a *fool,* save your money.
2. Don't use that bib; use that one instead.
3. His second name is *Luke*; the same with that of his nephew.
4. She is the primary caregiver for her parents.
5. It has a good *seal*; don't worry about it.
6. It was very decent of you to help in time of trouble.
7. He finally took the *lead*; we can breathe easily now.
8. The citizens of each state vote to elect two senators.
9. You need a strong *pull*; only then will it open.
10. Use the back entrance for deliveries.
11. It wasn't this *low*; the next one is better.
12. The governor's speech enunciated new programs of reforms.
13. Watch out for that banana *peel*; you can break your leg.
14. The weather governs the success or failure of crops.
15. Don't close the *lid*; we need to wait longer.
16. Insects often cause great harm to crops.
17. The fridge is *full*; you can't put it there.
18. Don't be so harsh with him; he is only 10.
19. Don't give me that *look*; why are you so surprised?
20. The theft must have been the work of an insider.
21. There is a cut on his lower *lip*; we need to put a bandage on it.
22. This is a critical moment; we shouldn't hurry our decision.
23. You can't take your *pill* now; you need to wait one more hour.
24. Please get rid of this box of old newspapers.
25. The thieves escaped with the *loot*; it was too late for the police.
26. Don't rely on her judgment; she is not very experienced.
27. This is our new *pool*; it was constructed last year.
28. We have always worked in a careful manner.

29. Don't pay that *bill*; we need to dispute that first.
30. New prescription drug will be made by a 3-D printer.
31. That was a huge *leap*; not one that many people dare to accept.
32. She gave her employer two-weeks' notice before leaving,

Appendix B: Number of In-Range Productions by Bilinguals

Participants	OF	OB	CF	CB
1	0/4	2/4	1/4	3/4
2	0/4	0/4	0/4	2/4
3	0/4	0/4	1/4	3/4
4	0/4	0/4	0/4	3/4
5	0/1	1/4	2/4	2/4
6	1/4	0/4	2/4	2/4
7	0/4	0/4	2/4	2/4
8	0/4	0/4	2/4	3/4
9	1/4	1/4	2/4	3/4
10	0/4	0/4	2/4	3/4
11	3/4	2/4	4/4	4/4
12	3/4	3/4	2/4	3/4
13	0/4	0/4	3/4	3/4
14	0/4	1/4	3/4	4/4
15	0/4	1/4	3/4	3/4
16	0/4	0/4	0/4	2/4
17	0/4	1/4	1/4	2/4
18	0/4	0/4	4/4	4/4
19	2/4	2/4	2/4	2/4
20	0/4	0/4	0/4	¼
21	3/4	4/4	2/4	2/4
22	0/4	0/4	0/4	¼
23	0/4	0/4	2/4	4/4
24	0/4	0/4	3/4	4/4
25	0/4	0/4	3/4	4/4
Total	13/100	18/100	46/100	69/100

References

Abrahamsson, N. (2012). Age of onset and ultimate attainment of L2 phonetic and grammatical intuition. In N. Abrahamsson and K. Hyltenstam (eds.), *High-Level L2 Acquisition, Learning and Use* [*Studies in Second Language Acquisition* 32(2), thematic issue]. Cambridge: Cambridge University Press.

Aoyama, K., Flege, J.E., Guion, S.G., Yamada, T. and Akahane-Yamada, R. (2004). Perceived phonetic dissimilarity and L2 speech learning: The case of Japanese /r/ and English /l/ and /r/. *Journal of Phonetics* 32: 233–50.

Asher, J. and Garcia, R. (1969). The optimal age to learn a language. *Modern Language Journal* 53: 1219–27.

Baker, W. and Trofimovich, P. (2005). Interaction of native and second language vowel systems in early and late bilinguals. *Language and Speech* 48(1): 1–27.

Baker, W., Trofimovich, P., Mack, M. and Flege, J.E. (2002). The effect of perceived phonetic similarity on non-native sound learning by children and adults. In B. Skarabela and S. Do (eds.), *Proceedings of the 26th Annual Boston University Conference on Language Development*, pp. 36–47. Somerville, MA: Cascadilla Press.

Barlow, J.A., Branson, P.E. and Nip, I.S.B. (2013). Phonetic equivalence in the acquisition of /l/ by Spanish-English bilingual children. *Bilingualism: Language and Cognition* 16(1): 68–85.

Boersma, P. and Weenink, D. (2013). *Praat: Doing Phonetics by Computer.* [Computer program] Version 5.3.52. Retrieved from http://www.praat.org/

Bongaerts, T. (1999). Ultimate attainment in L2 pronunciation: The case of very advanced late learners. In D. Birdsong (ed.), *Second Language Acquisition and the Critical Period Hypothesis*, 133–60. Mahwah, NJ: Lawrence Erlbaum Associates.

Bongaerts, T., Mennen, S. and van der Slik, F. (2000). Authenticity of pronunciation in naturalistic second language acquisition: The case of very advanced late learners of Dutch as a second language. *Studia Linguistica* 54: 298–308.

Bosch, L., Costa, A. and Sebastian-Galles, N. (2000). First and second language vowel perception in early bilinguals. *European Journal of Cognitive Psychology* 12: 189–221.

Bylund, E., Abrahamsson, N. and Hyltenstam, K. (2012). Does first language maintenance hamper nativelikeness in a second language? A study of ultimate attainment in early bilinguals. In N. Abrahamsson and K. Hyltenstam (eds.), *High-level L2 Acquisition, Learning and Use* [*Studies in Second Language Acquisition* 32(2), thematic issue]. Cambridge: Cambridge University Press.

Carter, P. and Local, J. (2007). F2 variation in Newcastle and Leeds English liquid systems. *Journal of the International Phonetic Association* 37: 183–99.

Chafcouloff, M. (1972). Recherches sur la structure acoustique de /l/ et ses correlations articulatoires. *Travaux de l'Institut de Phonetique d'Aix* 1: 101–10.

Darcy, I. and Kruger, F. (2012). Vowel perception and production in Turkish children acquiring L2 German. *Journal of Phonetics* 40: 568–81.

Dupoux, E., Peperkamp, S. and Sebastian-Galles, N. (2010). Limits on bilingualism revisited: Stress 'deafness' in simultaneous French-Spanish bilinguals. *Cognition* 114: 266–75.

Eckman, F. (1977). Markedness and the contrastive analysis hypothesis. *Language Learning* 27: 315–30.

Eckman, F. (1991). The Structural Conformity Hypothesis and the acquisition of consonant clusters in the interlanguage of ESL learners. *Studies in Second Language Acquisition* 13: 23–41.

Fant, G. (1960). *Acoustic Theory of Speech Production.* The Hague: Mouton.

Flege, J.E. (1987a). A critical period for learning to pronounce foreign languages? *Applied Linguistics* 8: 162–77.

Flege, J.E. (1987b). The production of 'new' and 'similar' phones in a foreign accent: Evidence for the effect of equivalence classification. *Journal of Phonetics* 15: 47–65.

Flege, J.E. (2002). Interactions between the native and second language phonetic systems. In P. Burmeister et al. (eds.), *An Integrated View of Language Development: Papers in Honor of Henning Wode*, 217–44. Trier: Wissenschaftlicher.

Flege, J.E. (2003). Assessing constraints on second-language segmental production and perception. In N.S. Meyer (ed.), *Phonetics and Phonology in Language Comprehension and Production*, 319–55. Berlin: Mouton.

Flege, J.E. (2007). Language contact in bilingualism: Phonetic system interactions. In J. Cole and J.I. Hualde (eds.), *Laboratory Phonology* 9: 353–81. Berlin: Mouton de Gruyter.

Flege, J.E. (2009). Give input a chance! In T. Piske and M. Young-Scholten (eds.), *Input Matters in SLA*, 175–90. Bristol: Multilingual Matters.

Flege, J.E. and Fletcher, K. (1992). Talker and listener effects on degree of perceived foreign accent. *Journal of the Acoustical Society of America* 91: 370–89.

Flege, J.E. and MacKay, I. (2004). Perceiving vowels in a second language. *Studies in Second Language Acquisition* 26: 1–34.

Flege, J.E., MacKay, I. and Piske, T. (2002). Assessing bilingual dominance. *Applied Psycho-linguistics,* 23: 567–98.

Flege, J. E., Munro, M. and MacKay, I. (1995). Factors affecting strength of perceived foreign accent in a second language. *Journal of the Acoustical Society of America,* 97: 3125–34.

Flege, J. E., Yeni-Komshian, G. and Liu, S. (1999). Age constraints on second language acquisition. *Journal of Memory and Language* 41: 78–104.

Fowler, C., Sramko, V. Ostry, D., Rowland, S. and Halle, P. (2008). Cross language phonetic influences on the speech of French-English bilinguals. *Journal of Phonetics* 36: 649–63.

Guion, S.G. (2003). The vowel systems of Quichua-Spanish bilinguals: Age of acquisition effects on the mutual influence of the first and second languages. *Phonetica* 60(2): 98–128.

Harada, T. (2003). L2 influence on L1 speech in the production of VOT. In M.J. Sole, D. Recasens and J. Romero (eds.), *Proceedings of the 15th International Congress of Phonetic Sciences*, 1085–8. Barcelona: Causal Productions.

Hualde, J.I. (2005). *The Sounds of Spanish*. New York: Cambridge University Press.

Iverson, P., Kuhl, P., Yamada, R., Diesch, E., Tohkura, Y. and Ketterman, A. (2003). A perceptual interference account of acquisition difficulties for non-native phonemes. *Cognition* 87: B47–57.

Kang, K-H. and Guion, S.G. (2006). Phonological systems in bilinguals: Age of learning effects on the stop consonant systems of Korean-English bilinguals. *Journal of the Acoustical Society of America* 119(3): 1672–83.

Kucera, H. and Francis, W.N. (1967). *Computational Analysis of Present-Day American English.* Providence, RI: Brown University Press.

Kuhl, P., Conboy, B., Coffey-Corina, S., Padden, D., Rivera-Gaxiola, M. and Nelson, T. (2008). Phonetic learning as a pathway to language; new data and native language magnet theory expanded. *Philosophical Transactions of the Royal Society, B* 636: 979–1000.

Ladefoged, P. and Maddieson, I. (1996). *The Sounds of the World's Languages.* London: Blackwell.

Mack, M., Bott, S. and Boronat, C. (1995). Mother, I'd rather do it myself, maybe: An analysis of voice onset time produced by early French-English bilinguals. *Idea* 8: 23–55.

MacKay, I., Flege, J.E., Piske, T. and Schirru, C. (2001). Category restructuring during second-language (L2) speech acquisition. *Journal of the Acoustical Society of America* 110: 516–28.

Major, R. (1992). Losing English as a first language. *The Modern Language Journal* 76(2): 190–208.

Major, R. (1996). L2 acquisition, L1 loss, and the critical period hypothesis. In A. James and J. Leather (eds.), *Second Language Speech: Structure and Process*, 147–59. Berlin: Mouton De Gruyter.

Major, R. and Kim, E. (1999). The similarity differential rate hypothesis. *Language Learning* 46: 465–96.

Mennen, I. (2004). Bi-directional interference in the intonation of Dutch speakers of Greek. *Journal of Phonetics* 32(4): 543–63.

Moyer, A. (2004). *Age, Accent and Experience in Second Language Acquisition.* Clevedon: Multilingual Matters.

Narayanan, S., Alwan, A. and Haker, K. (1997). Toward articulatory-acoustic models for liquid approximants based on MRI and EPG data, Part 1: The laterals. *Journal of the Acoustical Society of America* 101: 1064–77.

Oh, G. E., Guion-Anderson, S., Aoyama, K., Flege, J.E., Akahane-Yamada, R. and Yamada, T. (2011). A one-year longitudinal study of English and Japanese vowel production by Japanese adults and children in an English-speaking setting. *Journal of Phonetics* 39: 156–67.

Oyama, S. (1976). A sensitive period of the acquisition of a nonnative phonological system. *Journal of Psycholinguistic Research* 5: 261–83.

Patkowski, M. (1990). Age and accent in a second language: A reply to James Emil Flege. *Applied Linguistics* 11: 73–89.

Patkowski, M. (1993). The critical age hypothesis and interlanguage phonology. In M. Yavaş (ed.), *First and Second Language Phonology*, 205–22. San Diego, CA: Singular Publishing Group.

Peng, S. (1993). Cross-language influence on the production of Mandarin /f/ and /x/ and Taiwanese /h/ by native speakers of Taiwanese Amoy. *Phonetica* 50(4): 245–60.

Proctor, M. (2010). *Gestural Characterization of a Phonological Class: The Liquids.* PhD Dissertation, Yale University.

Quilis, A., Esgueva, M., Gutierrez-Araus, M. and Cantarero, M. (1979). Caracteristicas Acusticas de las consonants laterals espanolas. *Linguistica espanola actual* 1: 233–43.

Recasens, D. (2004). Darkness in [l] as a scalar phonetic property: Implications for phonology and articulatory control. *Clinical Linguistics and Phonetics* 18: 593–603.

Recasens, D. and Espinosa, A. (2005). Articulatory, positional and coarticulatory characteristics for clear /l/ and dark /l/: Evidence from two Catalan dialects. *Journal of the International Phonetic Association* 35: 1–25.

Sebastian-Galles, N., Echeverria, S. and Bosch, L. (2005). The influence of initial exposure on lexical represention: Comparing early and simultaneous bilinguals. *Journal of Memory and Language* 37: 159–73.

Sebastian-Galles, N. and Soto-Faraco, S. (1999). Online processing of native and non-native phonemic contrasts in early bilinguals. *Cognition* 72: 111–23.

Scovel, T. (1988). *A Time to Speak: A Psycholinguistic Inquiry into the Critical Period for Human Speech.* Cambridge, MA: Newbury House Publishers.

Scovel, T. (2000). A critical review of critical period research. *Annual Review of Applied Linguistics* 20: 213–23.

Simonet, M. (2010). Dark and clear laterals in Catalan and Spanish: Interaction of phonetic categories in early bilinguals. *Journal of Phonetics* 38: 663–78.

Stölten, K., Abrahamsson, N. and Hyltenstam, K. (2014). Effects of age of learning on voice onset time: Categorical perception of Swedish stops by near-native L2 speakers. *Language and Speech* 57(4): 425–50.

Thompson, I. (1991). Foreign accents revisited: The English pronunciation of Russian immigrants. *Language Learning* 41: 177–204.

Mehmet Yavaş is a professor of linguistics at Florida International University.

7 Production and Perception of Danish Front Rounded /y/: A Comparison of Ultimate Attainment in Native Spanish and Native English Speakers

Camila Linn Garibaldi and Ocke-Schwen Bohn

7.1 Introduction

Front rounded vowels are quite rare among the languages of the world (Maddieson 2013). These vowels are not part of the inventory of most Romance languages, whereas most Germanic languages do have front rounded vowels. The primary motivation for the present study was to explore whether native speakers of Spanish, which has no front rounded vowels, would be able to produce the close front rounded vowel /y/ of Danish correctly after many years of naturalistic exposure to Danish, i.e. at or near a stage of their second language acquisition of Danish which would be close to their ultimate level of attainment. We contextualized the acquisition of Danish /y/ by highly experienced native Spanish speakers in two ways: first, by examining the production and the perception of not just Danish /y/, but also the other close vowels /i/ and /u/, which Spanish and Danish share; and second, by comparing native Spanish speakers' perception and production of Danish /y/ to that of native speakers of English, which also lacks /y/.

Previous studies of L2 speech learning (e.g. Bohn and Flege 1990, 1992; Flege, Bohn and Jang 1997) have shown that experienced learners' production and perception accuracy largely depend on the phonetic relation between segments in the target language (L2) and the native language (L1). These studies have generally confirmed the predictions of the two most widely used models of L2 speech learning – Flege's (1995: 237) Speech Learning Model (SLM) and Best's (1995: 193) Perceptual Assimilation Model (PAM, and its extension to L2 learning, PAM-L2, Best and Tyler

2007: 24). The SLM and PAM-L2 differ in a number of ways (for discussions, see Best and Tyler 2007: 20; Bohn 2016), and they may generate different predictions (e.g. Bohn and Best 2012), but they agree in that ultimate learning success is predicted to be a function of the phonetic similarity of the sounds of the L1 and the L2. Similar sounds of the L2 (in SLM terms), or L2 contrasts that are perceived as equally good exemplars of an L1 category (Single-Category assimilation in PAM terms) are unlikely to be produced and perceived accurately, even after years of L2 experience. However, the more phonetically dissimilar the sounds of the L2 are, the more likely it is for experienced L2 learners to accurately perceive and produce these sounds. Specifically, the SLM predicts that 'new' sounds, which do not have an easily identifiable acoustic or articulatory counterpart in the L1, are learnable, given sufficient and extended L2 experience. PAM-L2 predicts that ultimate learning success depends on how non-native contrasts are assimilated to the native inventory; learning success is most likely for two of PAM's assimilation types – Two-Category assimilation, in which the members of a non-native contrast are assimilated as exemplars of two different native categories, and Uncategorized-Categorized assimilation, in which one member of the non-native contrast is uncategorizable in terms of native categories, whereas the other member has a native counterpart. Learning success is still possible, but somewhat less likely, for non-native contrasts which are assimilated as differing in Category-Goodness, i.e. as exemplars of a single native category differing in goodness of fit.

No previous study has examined the production or perception of Danish /y/ by non-native speakers, which makes it necessary to include a brief review of the perception and production of this vowel, as it occurs in other languages, by non-native speakers. Several previous studies have examined how native speakers of Spanish, or of English, perceive and/or produce the [y] vowel of various languages such as French, German and Dutch.[1] Regarding the assimilation of [y] by native Spanish speakers, Escudero and Willams (2011) reported that naïve L1 Spanish listeners classified isolated tokens of Dutch [i] and [u] as instances of Spanish /i/ and /u/, respectively, in more than 90% of the instances. Dutch [y] tokens, however, were variously assimilated to either Spanish /i/ (in 59% of the instances) or to Spanish /u/ (in 32% of the instances).[2] This suggests that [y] is an uncategorized vowel (in terms of PAM) for native Spanish listeners, and that it is

1 A cursory investigation of published acoustic measurements and of plots of /y/ as realized in French, Dutch and German in the F1/F2 space (e.g. Escudero and Williams 2011, 2012; Flege 1987; Steinlen 2005; Polka and Bohn 1996) suggests that the realization of /y/ does not differ much across these languages.

2 Escudero and Williams (2011) did not obtain ratings of goodness of fit.

perceived to be quite dissimilar from any native category. Regarding native Spanish speakers' production of /y/, we are aware of only one study on this topic, namely Burgos, Jani, Cucchiarini, van Hout and Strik (2014), who examined Spanish speakers' production of Dutch vowels. The participants in that study were very heterogeneous in terms of L2 Dutch experience (range: 1 month to 20 years), which makes it difficult to conclude more than that /y/ may represent a production problem for native Spanish speakers.

The perception and/or production of [y] by native English speakers has been examined in several detailed studies. Overall, studies of the assimilation of either French [u] and [y] or German [u] and [y] to English vowels reveal that both non-native vowels are categorized as English /u/, but with a clear difference in goodness of fit, such that French or German [u] is perceived to be a moderately good example of English /u/, whereas [y] is perceived to be a less good example of English /u/ (Polka, Escudero and Matchett 2002; Mayr and Escudero 2010; Polka and Bohn 1996; Polka 1995; Strange, Bohn, Trent and Nishi 2004; Strange, Bohn, Nishi and Trent 2005; Strange, Levy and Law 2009; Williams and Escudero 2014). In terms of PAM, then, these studies suggest that L1 English listeners assimilate the non-native [u]–[y] contrast as differing in Category-Goodness. In terms of SLM, L1 English listeners perceive both [u] and [y] to be similar to L1 /u/, with [u] being more similar to L1 /u/ than [y]. Regarding native English speakers' production accuracy for /y/, two studies have examined the production of French /y/ (among other vowels) by L1 English speakers: Flege (1987) and Levy and Law (2010). These studies can be summarized by stating that experienced L1 English speakers of French produce French /u/ and /y/ as distinct vowels, but they do not produce either vowel in a French-like manner. That is, their French /u/ productions are produced with higher F2 values (more fronted) than native French /u/, and their /y/ productions have lower F2 values (are less fronted) than native French /y/ (Flege 1987: 57).

The brief review of the literature above indicates that the perception and/or production of L2 /y/ by L1 Spanish speakers with extended L2 experience has not been examined, and that it could be interesting to compare the production and perception of /y/ by highly experienced L1 speakers of Spanish and of English. The present study explores the role of the phonetic relation between L1 and L2 sounds for the production accuracy of highly experienced L2 learners who are likely to be close to their ultimate level of attainment. Specifically, we examined the production of L2 Danish (DK) /i, y, u/ by speakers with Spanish (SP) and English (EN) as their L1. From a phonological viewpoint, the learning task for SP and for EN learners appears to be the same: Both EN and SP have /i/ and /u/, and both EN and SP lack front rounded vowels like DK /y/. However, a review of the literature suggests that /u/ is implemented differently in EN and SP: EN /u/ can be quite fronted with a high F2 frequency, whereas SP /u/ is a true back vowel with a low F2 (see Bradlow 1995; Bohn and Steinlen 2003: 2290). Thus, previous acoustic comparisons suggest that Danish /y/ is unlike any Spanish vowel, whereas English /u/, realized as [ʉ], is similar to Danish /y/. We hypothesized, based on PAM and SLM, that the different phonetic relation between the Spanish close vowels /i, u/ and Danish /y/ on the one hand, and English /i, u/ and Danish /y/ on the other, would make it easier for native Spanish speakers than for native English speakers to produce Danish /y/ correctly. We first examined the phonetic relation between Danish /i, y, u/ on the one hand and Spanish /i, u/ and English /i, u/ on the other, in two experiments. Experiment 1 compared the production of /i, u/ by L1 speakers of SP, EN and DK, and of /y/ by L1 DK speakers. We focused on the most important acoustic correlate of tongue position (front–back), F2, for productions of the close vowels /i, y, u/. Experiment 2 examined the perceptual assimilation of DK /i, y, u/ to the SP and EN close vowels /i, u/. The non-native listeners first categorized DK [i, y, u] tokens as native /i/ or /u/, and then rated the goodness of this fit. The results of the production experiment and of the cross-language perception experiment were then used to predict production accuracy for DK /i, y, u/ by highly experienced learners of DK with L1 SP and L1 EN, which was examined in Experiment 3.

7.2 Experiment 1

7.2.1 Methods

Participants were 10 L1 SP speakers (5 f, 5 m; M_{age}=43;4), 10 L1 EN speakers (4 f, 6 m; M_{age}=48;8), and 3 L1 DK speakers (2 f, 1 m; M_{age}=41;0). DK language experience was comparable for the SP and EN participants with a mean length of residence in Denmark of 14.4 years (SD=8.7) for the SP group, and 15.7 years (SD=9.1) for the EN group. Participants volunteered to take part in this and the following experiments, without any form of compensation.

Digital recordings were obtained from the participants reading target $C_1V_1C_2(V_2)$ words from their L1 in L1 carrier sentences. The SP speakers read *Digo la palabra* __ *otra vez,* the EN speakers read *I say the word* __ *again,* and the DK speakers read *Jeg siger ordet* __ *igen.* In the $C_1V_1C_2(V_2)$

words, C_1 was /t/ or /d/, V_1 was the segment of interest (/i, u/, and /y/ for the L1 DK speakers), C_2 was an obstruent and V_2 could be any vowel. Each speaker produced 3 randomly arranged repetitions of each of the 16 (EN and SP) or 15 (DK) target words. Acoustic measurements were conducted using Praat (Boersma and Weenink 2013). F2 frequency was measured near the temporal centre of the vowel, where formant frequencies appeared most stable in the spectral display.

7.2.2 Results

We compared the F2 values for natively produced /i, y, u/ across the three groups using one-way ANOVAs. Significant results were further explored using post-hoc pair-wise multiple comparisons (Holm-Sidak method). Statistical comparisons were conducted on both Hertz values for F2 and on Bark-transformed Hertz values, because of the unequal gender composition of the three groups. The results did not differ for the Bark-transformed or untransformed Hertz values. For ease of reference, Hertz values will be reported.

Figure 7.1 presents the F2 values for natively produced /i, y, u/ in Spanish, English and Danish. Separate ANOVAs for the F2 of /i, y, u/ revealed that

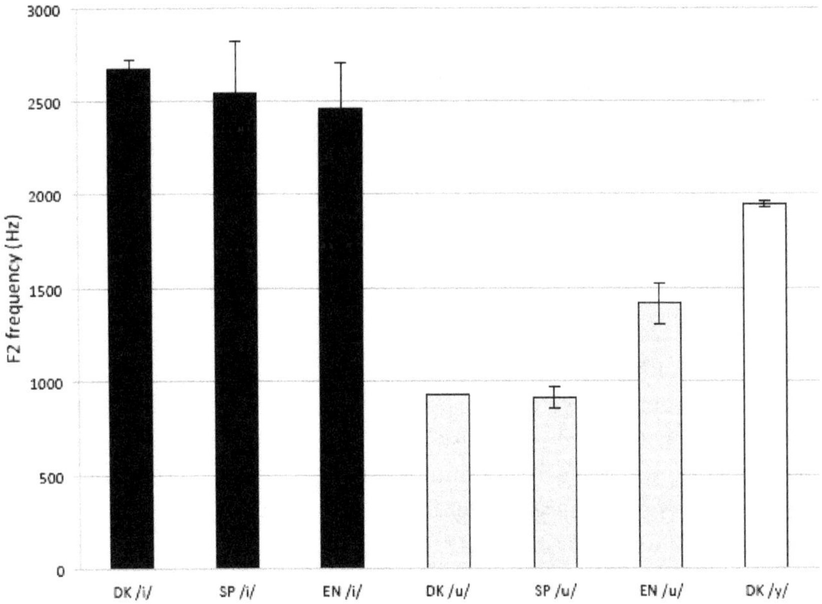

Figure 7.1. F2 values for natively produced /i, y, u/ by Danish (DK), Spanish (SP) and English (EN) speakers.

the mean F2 of /i/ as produced by the three language groups (DK: 2668 Hz, EN: 2458 Hz, SP: 2540 Hz) did not differ significantly, $p=0.418$. However, the mean F2 was higher for EN /u/ (1416 Hz) than for both SP /u/ (911 Hz) and DK /u/ (932 Hz), [$F(2,20)=100.29$, $p<0.001$], whose F2 did not differ significantly. This suggests a more anterior tongue position for EN /u/ than for SP and DK /u/. The mean F2 of DK /y/ (1943 Hz) differed significantly from the F2 values of DK, EN and SP /i/ as well as /u/.

7.2.3 Conclusions and Predictions

The present results are very much in line with the results of previous studies (e.g. Bradlow 1995; Flege 1987; Polka and Bohn 1996; Steinlen 2005; Strange et al. 2004, 2005) which examined, among other things, F2 values for /i/ and /u/ in DK, SP and EN, and for /y/ in DK, German and French. Our comparison of the F2 of /i, y, u/ suggests that, in terms of tongue position, /i/ is an identical vowel in DK, EN and SP, whereas DK /u/ is an identical vowel only for SP learners of DK. EN /u/ is considerably more fronted than both SP and DK /u/. This leads to the expectation that, because the two Spanish close vowels /i/ and /u/ are acoustically (in terms of F2) quite distinct from DK /y/, whereas EN /u/ is acoustically almost exactly halfway between DK /y/ and /u/, SP speakers will be more successful at producing the very different ('new' in terms of SLM) DK /y/, whereas EN speakers will be less successful at producing DK /y/. We also expect that EN speakers will not produce a DK-like /u/ but rather a compromise between the similar (in SLM terms) back DK /u/ and fronted EN /u/.

7.3 Experiment 2

Experiment 2 examined the perceptual assimilation of DK [i, y, u] tokens to L1 /i, u/ by L1 EN and SP participants, who first categorized the DK tokens as exemplars of native categories, and then rated the goodness of fit of this categorization. Based on the results of Experiment 1, we expected that DK [i] and [u] would be consistently assimilated to SP and EN /i/ and /u/, respectively. The goodness ratings for the match of DK [i] to native /i/ provided a baseline for the goodness ratings for DK [y, u], because Experiment 1 revealed that the DK, SP and EN realizations of /i/ were identical (in terms of F2). The focus of interest in Experiment 2 was the assimilation of DK [y] to either native /i/ or /u/ by the EN and SP listeners. The results of

Experiment 1 led us to expect that the SP listeners would inconsistently assimilate the acoustically distinct DK [y] to both SP /i/ and /u/, whereas the EN listeners would consistently assimilate DK [y] to EN /u/, whose realization (fronted/high F2) is similar to DK [y]. We were also interested in whether the SP and the EN listeners would show different assimilation patterns for DK [u], which is realized identically to SP /u/, but is realized with a lower F2 than EN /u/.

7.3.1 Methods

Participants were 8 L1 SP speakers (4 f, 4 m) and 8 L1 EN speakers (3 f, 5 m), who had also participated in Experiment 1. Using the Praat (Boersma and Weenink 2013) stimulus presentation module, the participants individually first identified tokens of DK /di, dy, du/ as EN <dee> or <doo> (EN listeners) or as SP <di> or <du> (SP listeners).[3] Three tokens each of DK /di, dy, du/ as produced by a male native DK speaker were selected from a corpus of DK vowels (see Polka and Bohn 2011), normalized for peak intensity and presented five times each in random order. Immediately after labelling, the listeners rated the goodness of fit on a scale from 1 (*bad*) to 5 (*perfect*). Instructions were given orally and presented on the screen in the L1 of the participants.

7.3.2 Results

Table 7.1 shows how DK [i, y, u] were assimilated to native /i, u/ by the SP listeners (left panel) and the EN listeners (right panel). DK [i] was consistently assimilated to L1 /i/ by all SP and EN listeners, as was DK [u] to L1 /u/. However, the SP and the EN listeners differed considerably in how they assimilated DK [y], both in terms of the native category chosen, and in terms of their goodness ratings for DK [y]. Whereas the EN listeners classified all DK [y] tokens as EN /u/, the SP listeners as a group used both

3 We did not include additional response alternatives beyond the close vowels /i/ and /u/ because previous studies suggested that both native English and native Spanish speakers would not assimilate the close Danish vowels [i, y, u] to more open vowels (e.g. Spanish /o, e/, English /ɪ, ʊ/). Additionally, English lax vowels like /ɪ, ʊ/ would be invalid response alternatives in the present task because the stimulus syllables are open CV syllables, whereas lax vowel can only occur in closed syllables. This also makes it impossible to provide an orthographic response alternative involving lax vowels in an open syllable.

Table 7.1. Mean percent identification and goodness rating (in parentheses) of DK [i, y, u] in terms of SP and EN categories.

Danish Stimuli	Spanish Response		English Response	
	/i/	/u/	/i/	/u/
[i]	100 (3.7)		100 (3.3)	
[y]	33.3 (2.1)	66.7 (2.0)		100 (2.4)
[u]		100 (3.6)		100 (3.2)

SP /i/ and SP /u/ as labels for DK [y]. Specifically, five of the eight SP listeners assimilated DK [y] variously to both SP /i/ and /u/, one SP listener assimilated DK [y] to only SP /i/, and two SP listeners assimilated DK [y] to only SP /u/.

To explore the results of Experiment 2 in more detail, we conducted a series of ANOVAs on the goodness ratings. The goodness ratings of the SP listeners (for DK [i] as SP /i/, DK [y] as SP /i/, DK [y] as SP /u/, and DK [u] as SP /u/) differed significantly [$F(3,18.052)=14.346$, $p<0.001$]. Post-hoc tests (Holm-Sidak) revealed that the SP listeners' goodness ratings for DK [i] ($M=3.7$) and for DK [u] ($M=3.6$) did not differ significantly ($p=0.942$), and that the goodness ratings for DK [y] as SP /i/ ($M=2.1$) or /u/ ($M=2.0$) did not differ significantly ($p=0.814$). However, and importantly, the overall goodness ratings for DK [y] were significantly lower than for DK [i] and DK [u] ($p>0.001$). These results are very much in line with the results of Experiment 1: the /i/ and the /u/ productions do not differ between SP and DK, resulting in equivalent goodness ratings for Danish tokens of these vowels as exemplars of SP categories, whereas [y], which is absent from the SP vowel inventory, receives significantly lower goodness ratings. In contrast to the SP listeners, the goodness ratings of the EN listeners for all three DK vowels (DK [i] as EN /i/, DK [y] as EN [u], and DK [u] as EN /u/) did not differ significantly [$F(3,3.803)=3.393$, $p=0.053$]. Because the ANOVA narrowly missed significance, we explored this result through pair-wise comparisons, which revealed that the goodness ratings for DK [i] as EN /i/ ($M=3.3$) and DK [u] as EN /u/ ($M=3.2$) did not differ significantly ($p=0.760$). This is interesting because it indicates that the EN listeners perceive DK [u] tokens to be as good exemplars of EN /u/ as DK [i] tokens of EN /i/, in spite of the fact that Experiment 1 revealed that the /u/ vowels were implemented differently in EN and DK, but not the /i/ vowels. The post-hoc comparisons further revealed that the EN listeners' goodness ratings for DK [y] as EN /u/ ($M=2.4$) were significantly lower than those for DK [i] and DK [u] [$F(1,2.403)=4.92$, $p=0.044$], which suggests that the EN listeners are sensitive to the acoustic difference between DK [y] and [u].

7.3.3 Discussion

The results from the perceptual assimilation experiment reflect the results of the acoustic comparisons of Experiment 1. The F2 for DK and SP /i/, and DK and SP /u/, did not differ significantly, which is reflected in the goodness ratings by the SP listeners which were much the same for the DK [i] and [u] tokens. However, for DK and EN, F2 differed for /u/, but not for /i/, which is not reflected in lower goodness ratings for DK [u] than for DK [i] tokens. This suggests that EN listeners may not be aware of the different realizations of /u/ (in terms of F2) in DK and in EN. The relatively low goodness ratings on a scale of 1 to 5 (3.3 for DK [i], 3.2 for DK [u]) could reflect L1 English listeners' expectations of vowel inherent spectral change, which is typical of many EN accents, but absent from languages such as DK (e.g. Bohn and Polka 2001; Strange and Bohn 1998).

DK [y] is not a good match to two different SP categories, suggesting that [y] is so different as to be 'new' (SLM) or Uncategorized (PAM), so that it is ultimately learnable. Our result for the L1 Spanish listeners' perceptual assimilation of DK [i, y, u] is similar to Escudero and Williams' (2011) for the assimilation of Dutch [i, y, u], except that Dutch [y] was more often assimilated to SP /i/ than to SP /u/, whereas DK [y] was more often assimilated to SP /u/ than to /i/. There could be two reasons for this discrepancy: First, the realization of Dutch /y/ and DK /y/ could differ such that Dutch /y/ is more fronted (i.e. more similar to /i/ realizations) than DK /y/. This appears unlikely given the very similar F2 values for DK /y/ in the present study and the F2 values for Dutch (gleaned from visual inspection of figure 1 in the Escudero and Williams study). Second, the discrepancy could be due to differences in L2 experience between the participants of the present study and those of Escudero and Williams. Our participants were highly experienced with DK (with a mean length of residence in DK of 14.4 years), whereas the participants in the Escudero and Williams study apparently had no or very limited experience with languages that have front rounded vowels.[4]

Regarding the EN listeners, their goodness ratings for [y] suggest that they are aware of the less than perfect match between DK [y] and EN /u/, indicating that this is a 'similar' (SLM) vowel which is CG-assimilated (PAM). The present results are in agreement with those of previous studies,

4 Of Escudero and Williams' (2011) 40 monolingual SP participants 'none reported knowledge of any other language greater than 2 on a scale from 0 to 7 (0=no knowledge, 7=native-like knowledge)' (Escudero and Williams 2011: EL2).

which examined L1 EN listeners' assimilation of non-native [u] and [y] tokens (see Section 7.1), and they echo the results of Terbeek's (1977) pioneering study on cross-language vowel perception, in which he reported that several of his L1 EN listeners referred to [y] 'as a kind of "u"' (Terbeek 1977: 199).

Overall, the predictions derived from Experiment 2 are the same as those derived from Experiment 1 (see Section 7.2.3 above): SP speakers will be more successful at producing /y/ and /u/ correctly in DK than EN speakers because DK [y] is 'uncategorized' (PAM) or 'new' for SP listeners, whereas for EN listeners, DK [y] is a 'similar' (SLM) vowel, which differs in category goodness (PAM) from [u]. Additionally, the realization of /u/ in DK and EN, but not in DK and SP, differs, which EN listeners do not seem to be aware of.

7.4 Experiment 3

Experiment 3 tested the predictions derived from Experiment 1 and Experiment 2 by examining the production of DK /i, y, u/ by the same L1 SP and L1 EN speakers as in Experiment 1. Specifically, we compared the non-native speakers' F2 for DK /i, y, u/ to the L1 DK speakers' values, and to the corresponding values for /i, u/ as produced by the same speakers in their respective L1.

7.4.1 Methods

The methods as well as the participants were the same as in Experiment 1, except that the SP and the EN speakers now read the DK word list. Acoustic analyses were conducted using the same software and criteria as for Experiment 1.

7.4.2 Results

We used the same statistical procedures as for Experiment 1 (one-way ANOVAs with post-hoc pair-wise multiple comparisons [Holm-Sidak method]). As for Experiment 1, Hertz values are reported for /i, y, u/ because comparisons did not differ when conducted on the Bark-transformed or untransformed Hertz values of F2.

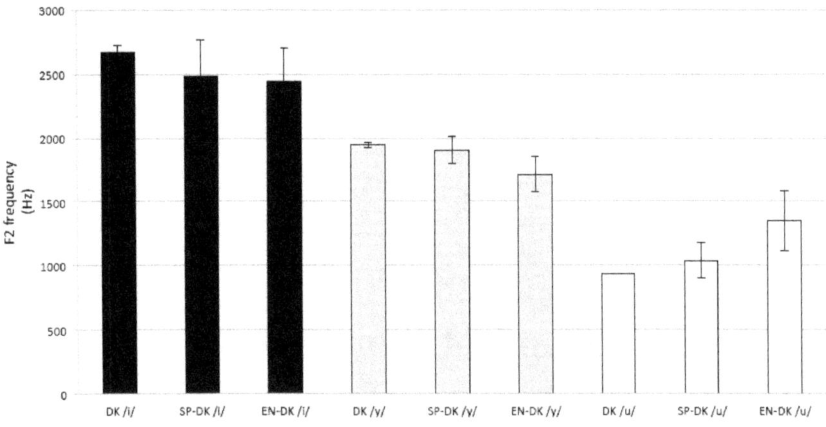

Figure 7.2. F2 values for Danish /i, y, u/ as produced by native Danish (DK), native Spanish (SP) and native English (EN) speakers.

Figure 7.2 presents the F2 values for DK /i, y, u/ as produced by the native DK, SP and EN speakers. The F2 for /i/, which did not differ in the cross-language comparison (Experiment 1), did not differ when produced in DK by the DK, EN and SP speakers [F(2,20)=0.912, p=418]. However, the F2 for DK /u/ differed significantly [F(2,20)=100.299, p<0.001] because the EN speakers produced DK /u/ with a higher mean F2 (1350 Hz) than the DK and SP speakers, whose mean F2 for DK /u/ (DK speakers: 932 Hz; SP speakers: 1037 Hz) did not differ significantly. Paired t-tests revealed that the EN speakers did not produce a significant difference between the F2 for EN /u/ (M=1416 Hz) and DK /u/ (M=1350 Hz), p=0.296. Surprisingly, the SP speakers produced DK /u/ with a higher F2 (M=1037 Hz) than SP /u/ (M=911 Hz), p<0.05. Finally, the ANOVA revealed a significant difference between the F2 for DK /y/ [F(2,20)=8.01, p=0.003] because the EN speakers produced DK /y/ with a lower F2 (M =1712 Hz) than the DK (M = 1943 Hz) and the SP (M=1902 Hz) speakers. The difference in F2 between DK /u/ and DK /y/ as produced by the EN group was significant, p<0.001.

7.4.3 Conclusions

Experiment 3 revealed that the SP speakers produced a DK-like /y/, whereas the EN speakers did not produce /y/ correctly. This was expected based on the acoustic comparisons of natively produced DK /i, y, u/ and SP and EN /i, u/ in Experiment 1, and based on the perceptual assimilation patterns found in Experiment 2. Experiment 3 also showed that both non-native groups produced DK /u/ with higher F2 values than the L1 DK speakers. This was expected for the EN speakers, whose natively-produced /u/ was more fronted (had a higher F2) than DK /u/, and whose goodness ratings for DK /u/ did not indicate an awareness of this difference. However, the moderate fronting of the SP speakers' DK /u/ came as a surprise because their natively produced /u/ was produced as far back as the DK speakers' /u/.

7.5 Discussion and Conclusion

The primary aim of the present study was to compare native SP speakers' and native EN speakers' ultimate attainment with regard to the perception and production of DK /y/. This vowel, as well as other front rounded vowels, is typically not part of the inventory of Romance languages, and it is also absent from EN. No previous study has examined both the perception and the production of /y/ by native speakers of SP, and no previous study has examined both SP and EN speakers for their ultimate attainment with regard to a front rounded vowel.

We conducted two experiments which generated predictions, based on Flege's (1995: 234) SLM and on Best's (1995: 193) PAM and PAM-L2 (Best and Tyler 2007: 24), regarding the accuracy of DK /y/ productions by highly experienced native speakers of SP and of EN. The acoustic Experiment 1 compared the second formant frequency (F2, as an index of the position of vowels on the front-back dimension) of natively produced SP and EN /i, u/ and Danish /i, y, u/. The results of Experiment 1 revealed that DK /y/ is acoustically roughly equidistant from SP and EN /i/, and that it is acoustically closer to the fronted EN /u/ than to the back SP /u/. This led to the SLM-based prediction that SP speakers will be more successful than EN speakers at producing DK /y/, because DK /y/ is more dissimilar from native categories for SP than for EN speakers.

Experiment 2 examined the perceptual assimilation of DK [i, y, u] tokens to native /i, u/ by a subset (16/20) of the participants in Experiment 1. This experiment revealed that SP listeners assimilated DK [y] to both SP /i/ and /u/, which is consistent with results of Escudero and Williams (2011) on the assimilation of Dutch [y] to SP vowels. The EN participants, however, assimilated DK [y] exclusively to EN /u/, which is also consistent with previous studies that examined the assimilation of, for instance, German [y] to EN vowels (e.g. Strange et al. 2004, 2005). In terms of PAM, the uncategorized nature of DK [y] for SP speakers makes learning success more likely than for EN listeners, who detected a category difference between DK [y] and [u] tokens.

The predictions generated from the acoustic data in Experiment 1 and the perceptual data in Experiment 2 were confirmed by the results of Experiment 3, in which the SP speakers produced a DK-like /y/, whereas the EN speakers did not produce /y/ correctly. We are confident that the present results for SP speakers' ultimately correct [y] productions can be extended to native speakers of other languages with just two close vowels (/i, u/), if these vowels are located near the extreme front and back of the vowel space, as are SP /i/ and /u/. Examples could be native speakers of Italian (e.g. Flege, MacKay and Meador 1999) or Brazilian and European Portuguese (e.g. Escudero, Boersma, Rauber and Bion 2009) whose L1 has /i/ and /u/ vowels which are close to the periphery (front vs back) of the vowel space. We predict that native speakers of these and other languages with similar vowel properties will ultimately be similarly successful at producing a non-native /y/ correctly.

An important limitation of the present study is that we examined the production and perception of /i, y, u/ in only one consonantal context. It is well known from several previous studies that flanking consonants can exert very different, language-specific, influences on the acoustic realization of vowels (e.g. Strange et al. 2004, 2005; Bohn 2004). The potential effect of consonant context could perhaps account for the surprising fronting of DK /u/ by the SP speakers vis-à-vis their native SP (back) /u/. We can currently offer no explanation for why the production of SP /u/ in the first open syllable of SP /CuCV$_2$/ would be more likely to result in a native back /u/ than the production of a DK /u/ in closed DK /CuC/ syllables.

An important open question that could not be addressed in the present study is how much L2 experience is required to enable the production of a DK-like /y/ by native SP speakers (or native speakers of any language with two peripheral close vowels). Flege's (1987) study compared the production accuracy of French /y/ and /u/ by EN speakers differing in French language experience. His results for Americans who had lived in France for a mean length of 11.7 years mirror the results of the present study, in which English speakers who had lived in DK for a mean length of 15.7 years produced neither L2 /u/ nor /y/ correctly (i.e. produced a fronted /u/ and an /y/ that was not front enough). Another group of subjects in the Flege (1987) study, who each held an advanced degree in French, taught French at a university, and had spent a mean total of 1.3 years in France, produced distinct French /u/ and /y/, but the acoustic difference (in terms of F2) between these French vowels was considerably smaller than for the more experienced group. Flege's results can be interpreted to mean that

L2 speech learning extends over the whole first decade of L2 exposure. It would be interesting to examine the nature of the learning curve during this decade, in particular, how steep it is initially, when it asymptotes, and whether the nature of this curve differs for learners who ultimately produce /y/ correctly (as the SP speakers in our study) and learners who do not (as the EN speakers in the current study).

References

Best, C.T. (1995). A direct realist perspective on cross-language speech perception. In W. Strange (ed.), *Speech Perception and Linguistic Experience: Issues in Cross-language Research* 167–200. Timonium MD: York Press.

Best, C.T. and Tyler, M.D. (2007). Nonnative and second-language speech perception: Commonalities and complementarities. In O.-S. Bohn and M.J. Munro (eds.), *Language Experience in Second Language Speech Learning: In Honor of James Emil Flege*, 13–34. Amsterdam: John Benjamins.

Boersma, P. and Weenink, D. (2013). *Praat version 5.3.56*. Retrieved on 20 September 2013 from http://www.fon.hum.uva.nl/ praat/download_win.html

Bohn, O.-S. (2004). How to organize a fairly large vowel inventory: The vowels of Fering (North Frisian). *Journal of the International Phonetics Association* 34: 161–73.

Bohn, O.-S. (2016). Cross-language and second language speech perception. In E. Fernandez and H. Cairns (eds.), *Handbook of Psycholinguistics* (in press). Hoboken, NJ: Wiley.

Bohn, O.-S. and Best, C.T. (2012). Native-language phonetic and phonological influences on perception of American English approximants by Danish and German listeners. *Journal of Phonetics* 40: 109–28.

Bohn, O.-S. and Flege, J.E. (1990). Interlingual identification and the role of foreign language experience in L2 vowel perception. *Applied Psycholinguistics* 11: 303–28.

Bohn, O.-S. and Flege, J.E. (1992). The production of new and similar vowels by adult German learners of English. *Studies in Second Language Acquisition* 14: 131–58.

Bohn, O.-S. and Polka, L. (2001). Target spectral, dynamic spectral, and duration cues in infant perception of German vowels. *Journal of the Acoustical Society of America* 110: 504–15.

Bohn, O.-S. and Steinlen, A.K. (2003). Consonantal context affects cross-language perception of vowels. *Proceedings of the 15th International Congress of Phonetic Sciences*: 2289–92.

Bradlow, A.R. (1995). A comparative acoustic study of English and Spanish vowels. *Journal of the Acoustical Society of America* 97: 1916–24.

Burgos, P., Jani, M., Cucchiarini, C., van Hout, R. and Strik, H. (2014). Dutch vowel production by Spanish learners: Duration and spectral features. *Interspeech* 15: 529–33.

Escudero, P., Boersma, P., Rauber, A.S. and Bion, R.A.H. (2009). A cross-dialect acoustic description of vowels: Brazilian and European Portuguese. *Journal of the Acoustical Society of America* 126: 1379–93.

Escudero, P. and Williams, D. (2011). Perceptual assimilation of Dutch vowels by Peruvian Spanish listeners. *Journal of the Acoustical Society of America* 129: EL1–7.

Escudero, P. and Williams, D. (2012). Native dialect influences second-language vowel perception: Peruvian versus Iberian Spanish learners of Dutch. *Journal of the Acoustical Society of America* 131: EL406–12.

Flege, J.E. (1987). The production of 'new' and 'similar' phones in a foreign language: Evidence for the effect of equivalence classification. *Journal of Phonetics* 15: 47–65.

Flege, J.E. (1995). Second language speech learning: Theory, findings, and problems. In W. Strange (ed.), *Speech Perception and Linguistic Experience: Issues in Cross-language Research*, 233–77. Timonium MD: York Press.

Flege, J.E., Bohn, O.-S. and Jang, S. (1997). Effects of experience on non-native speakers' production and perception of English vowels. *Journal of Phonetics* 25: 437–70.

Flege, J.E., MacKay, I.R.A. and Meador, D. (1999). Native Italian speakers' perception and production of English vowels. *Journal of the Acoustical Society of America* 106: 2973–87.

Levy, E.S. and Law, F.F. (2010). Production of French vowels by American-English learners of French: Language experience, consonantal context, and the perception-production relationship. *Journal of the Acoustical Society of America* 128: 1290–1305.

Maddieson, I. (2013). Front rounded vowels. In M.S. Dryer and M. Haspelmath (eds.), *The World Atlas of Language Structures Online*. Leipzig: Max Planck Institute for Evolutionary Anthropology. Retrieved on 25 May 2015 from http://wals.info/chapter/11

Mayr, R. and Escudero, P. (2010). Explaining individual variation in L2 perception: Rounded vowels in English learners of German. *Bilingualism: Language and Cognition* 13: 279–97.

Polka, L. (1995). Linguistic influences in adult perception of non-native vowel contrasts. *Journal of the Acoustical Society of America* 95: 1286–96.

Polka, L. and Bohn, O.-S. (1996). A cross-language comparison of vowel perception in English-learning and German-learning infants. *Journal of the Acoustical Society of America* 100: 577–92.

Polka, L. and Bohn, O.-S. (2011). Natural Referent Vowel (NRV) framework: An emerging view of early phonetic development. *Journal of Phonetics* 39: 467–78.

Polka, L., Escudero, P. and Matchett, S. (2002). Assimilation and discrimination of Canadian French vowels by English-speaking adults. *Journal of the Acoustical Society of America* 112: 2250.

Steinlen, A.K. (2005). The influence of consonants on native and non-native vowel perception. Tübingen: G. Narr.

Strange, W. and Bohn, O.-S. (1998). Dynamic specification of coarticulated German vowels: Perceptual and acoustical studies. *Journal of the Acoustical Society of America* 104: 488–504.

Strange, W., Bohn, O.-S., Nishi, K. and Trent, S.A. (2005). Contextual variation in the acoustic and perceptual similarity of North German and American English vowels. *Journal of the Acoustical Society of America* 118: 1751–62.

Strange, W., Bohn, O.-S., Trent, S.A. and Nishi, K. (2004). Acoustic and perceptual similarity of North German and American English vowels. *Journal of the Acoustical Society of America* 115: 1791–1807.

Strange, W., Levy, E. and Law, F. (2009). Cross-language categorization of French and German vowels by naïve American listeners. *Journal of the Acoustical Society of America* 126: 1461–76.

Terbeek, D. (1977). A cross-language multidimensional scaling study of vowel perception. UCLA Working Papers in *Phonetics* 37.

Williams, D. and Escudero, P. (2014). Influences of listeners' native and other dialects on cross-language vowel perception. *Frontiers in Psychology* 5: 1065.

Camila Linn Garibaldi is a graduate student at Aarhus University.

Ocke-Schwen Bohn is Professor of English Linguistics at Aarhus University.

8
Interactions between Native and Non-Native Vowels in French-Danish Contact: Production Training Study

Natalia Kartushina

8.1 Introduction

Speakers who acquire a foreign language (L2) in adolescence or later often experience major difficulties in the production of non-native speech sounds, a phenomenon commonly known as having a foreign accent. These difficulties in non-native phonetic production are generally attributed to difficulties in discriminating between native and non-native sounds which are similar to them. Consequently, native sounds are used to produce similar non-native ones. Production training techniques whereby speakers receive feedback that compares their production to that of native speakers have been shown to remediate these accents. In this study, monolingual French speakers were trained to produce the Danish /ɔ/ vowel quality that is similar to the French /o/ vowel. First, it explores the relationship between individual differences in the production of the French /o/ vowel before training and the production of the Danish /ɔ/ vowel before and during training. Second, it examines the effects of training with the Danish /ɔ/ on the production of the Danish /ɔ/ and the French /o/ vowel.

This chapter focuses on mutual influences between native and non-native (L2) vowels in production. It is divided into three parts. This first part provides a survey of literature on the role of native phonology in L2 production and on how L2 production difficulties can be remediated by training. The second part focuses on the effects of L2 use/experience on the production of native sounds. Finally, the third part presents an experimental longitudinal study that examines the relationship between the production of native French /o/ and non-native Danish /ɔ/ vowels before and after production training with the Danish /ɔ/ vowel quality in monolingual French speakers with no experience in Danish.

8.1.1 Native Accent in the Production of Non-Native Sounds

Learning a foreign language is highly promoted in modern society. More than half of Europeans (54%), for example, are able to maintain a conversation in a language that is not their native language and half of them estimate that their foreign language abilities are very good.

In practice, however, even those L2 speakers who have achieved native-like proficiency at lexical and grammatical levels experience persistent difficulties in mastering the pronunciation of foreign sounds. This phenomenon is commonly known as having a foreign accent. According to Scovel, 'foreign accents are ... phonological cues, either segmental or suprasegmental, which identify the speaker as a non-native user of the language' (1969: 38). In the current work, I focus on difficulties that L2 speakers experience in the production of non-native isolated segments. For instance, native Spanish speakers are easily identified by their accent when producing the English /i/-/ɪ/ vowels, whereas native Italian speakers are known for their difficulty with the English /ɚ/-/ʌ/ contrast (Flege 2003).

Difficulties that L2 speakers experience in the production of non-native sounds are generally attributed to a bias in L2 perception stemming from the native phonology (Best and Tyler 2007; Flege 1995). Non-native sounds are perceived through a native phonological 'sieve' as being similar to or dissimilar from the native categories. Similar L2 sounds, those that are difficult to distinguish perceptually from native categories, assimilate to them. For example, native Spanish speakers misidentify the French /e/ and /ɛ/ vowels since they assimilate both of them to the Spanish /e/ vowel (Kartushina and Frauenfelder 2013). This assimilation blocks novel category formation for L2 similar sounds. Dissimilar L2 sounds, i.e. those that are sufficiently different phonetically from native categories, do not assimilate. Novel categories are, therefore, expected to be established for dissimilar L2 sounds. For instance, Japanese speakers perceive the English /æ/ vowel accurately, since it is phonetically distinct from the closest native /e/ category to be assimilated to it (Ingram and Park 1997). Categories, established for L2 perception, are expected to guide L2 production (Flege 1995). Analogously to the perception results, Spanish speakers do not distinguish the French /e/ and /ɛ/ vowels in production (Kartushina and Frauenfelder

2014), whereas Japanese speakers produce the English /æ/ and the Japanese /e/ vowels contrastively (Ingram and Park 1997).

Inaccurate pronunciation of L2 sounds can be partly remediated by training. Either perception or production ability can be trained. Traditionally, training experiments are composed of three phases: pre-test, training and post-test. Pre-test and post-test phases are generally identical. They aim at assessing training-related improvements in L2 speakers' abilities to perceive and/or to produce target L2 sounds. During training, L2 speakers receive corrective feedback on their perception or production, on a trial-by-trial basis.

In perception training, for instance, participants perform identification or discrimination tasks and receive feedback on their accuracy ('correct' versus 'incorrect') (Bradlow, Pisoni, Akahane-Yamada and Tohkura 1997; Lively, Logan and Pisoni 1993). Perception training has been shown to improve L2 speakers' perception by 10–20% (Bradlow et al. 1997; Lopez-Soto and Kewley-Port 2009; Wong 2013). For instance, Japanese L2 speakers' perception of the English /r/-/l/ contrast (e.g. 'rock' versus 'lock') improved by 16% after a three-and-a-half-week identification training with English /r/-/l/ minimal words (Bradlow et al. 1997). Interestingly, the production of the /r/-/l/ consonants also improved, but only by 7%. A more recent perception training study, however, has shown that a three-hour identification training improved Spanish L2 speakers' ability to identify English codas by 11%, with no improvement in production (Lopez-Soto and Kewley-Port 2009). These results suggest that training is domain-specific: it improves the trained modality with little or no transfer to the other modality.

Pure production training has been shown to be more effective in improving L2 speakers' pronunciation. During production training, participants produce one target L2 sound and receive immediate, typically visual, feedback that compares their production of this sound to that of a native speaker. Feedback can be provided directly from the articulators, as, for example, via ultra-sound (Pillot-Loiseau, Kocjančič Antolík and Kamiyama 2013; Wilson and Gick 2006) or electropalatography imaging (Dagenais 1995), or indirectly, via the acoustic analysis of the produced sounds (Akahane-Yamada, McDermott, Adachi, Kawahara and Pruitt 1998; Carey 2004; Dowd, Smith and Wolfe 1998; Leather 1997). Due, principally, to their costs and difficulties in implementation, direct feedback techniques are almost exclusively reserved for clinical practice. Indirect feedback techniques, on the other hand, present a good trade-off between the ease and cost of implementation and the observed production benefits for L2 learners.

A graphic representation of acoustic information about L2 learners' production compared to that of a native speaker is one of the most frequently used indirect feedback techniques. This representation contains generally the acoustic properties that are crucial to discriminating difficult L2 sounds. For example, the English /r/-/l/ consonants differ principally with respect to their third formant frequency (F3): F3 is low for /r/ and high for /l/. Akahane-Yamada and colleagues (1998) used spectrographic representations (i.e. spectrograms) that showed the formant tracks of the English /r/ and /l/ consonants produced by Japanese participants compared to those of native speakers. Although all three formants (i.e. F1, F2 and F3) were displayed in the feedback, participants' attention was brought, principally, to the F3. After five hours of training, Japanese learners' production of the English /r/-/l/ contrast improved by 22%. Other studies have used oscillograms, on which contrastive visual patterns representing the presence or absence of voicing were coloured (e.g. to distinguish Swedish voiced 'buss' versus unvoiced 'puss' contrasts, in Öster 1997) or acoustic two-dimensional spaces, on which the F1 (on the y-axis) and the F2 (on the x-axis) of the contrastive vowels were displayed (Carey 2004). These studies have revealed that L2 speakers' production improved after training. However, the results of these studies are neither comparable nor conclusive, mainly because control groups have rarely been included, and if they have, control participants have not undergone training. As a result, improvements observed in the experimental group may have resulted from articulatory practice (i.e. repetition), and not from the feedback itself.

A recent study addressed the above-raised issue and assessed the efficacy of indirect feedback training on the production of non-native sounds in speakers with no experience with the L2 (Kartushina, Hervais-Adelman, Frauenfelder and Golestani 2015). Two groups of monolingual French native speakers were trained for five days (45 minutes per day) to produce four front Danish vowels: unrounded raised close-mid /e/ (as in *mele*, 'meal'), unrounded close-mid /ɛ/ (as in *mæle*, 'speak'), rounded close /y/ (as in *lyse*, 'shine') and rounded close-mid /ø/ (as in *løse*, 'loosen'). These vowels form two height contrasts, /e/-/ɛ/ and /y/-/ø/. These Danish vowel contrasts are poorly discriminated by French speakers due to their similarity to the French vowels: the Danish /e/-/ɛ/ contrast assimilates to the French unrounded close-mid /e/ vowel, whereas the Danish /y/-/ø/ contrast assimilates to the French rounded close /y/ vowel (Kartushina et al. 2015). During training, on each trial, participants of both groups heard one target sound, repeated it and received visual feedback. Participants of the experimental group received feedback in the form of a two-dimensional acoustic space in which Danish vowels produced by themselves and by the native speakers of Danish were displayed simultaneously. Participants of the control group received a similar image with one exception: it did not include information about their own production (see Figure 8.1). In order to keep them motivated and engaged in performing the task, they received an aggregate score of accuracy (expressed as a percentage), presented at the end of each block of 21 trials. As can be seen from the figure, visual feedback provides information about F1 and F2, which are crucial to distinguish the target vowels within each contrast. The F1 (on the y-axis) reflects the degree of vowel openness: a vowel that is produced with a tongue positioned lower in the mouth (e.g. /a/) has a higher F1, whereas a vowel that is produced with a tongue positioned higher (e.g. /i/) has a lower F1 (Ladefoged 1962). The F2 (on the x-axis) reflects the back-to-front position of vowel articulation: a vowel that is produced with the tongue positioned more at the back (e.g. /u/) has a lower F2, and one produced with the tongue positioned more at the front (e.g. /i/) has a higher F2.

Training with indirect feedback which provides acoustic information about the position of the learner's articulators (i.e. tongue height and frontness) compared to that of a native speaker improved the production of non-native vowels by an average of 17%. The production of the control group that received feedback on the position of the target Danish vowel only did not improve (Kartushina et al. 2015). These results suggest that training-related improvements observed in the experimental group are specifically due to trial-by-trial feedback that compares the learner's production to the target and not to articulatory practice with non-native sounds.

To conclude, production training studies suggest that the production of similar L2 sounds, which are known to be difficult to acquire in natural learning conditions, can be improved by undergoing a brief (1–5 hours) laboratory training where corrective fine-grained feedback on their

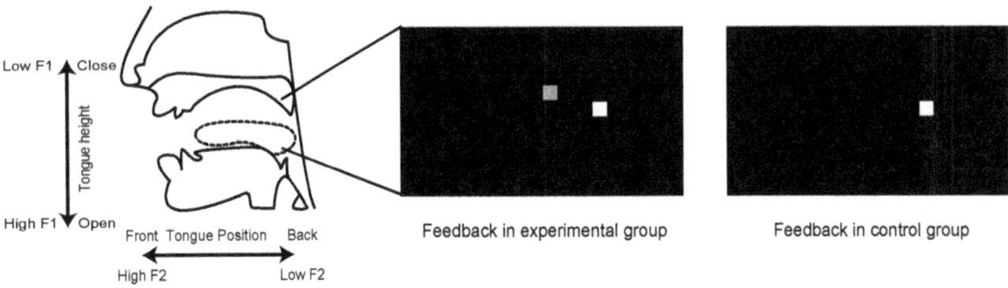

Figure 8.1. Example of visual feedback provided to participants of the experimental and control groups on their vowel production during training in Kartushina et al. (2015). The grey square corresponds to the participant's production and the white square corresponds to the target vowel (the control group only saw the white squares).

production is provided. One may ask, then, what happens to native categories that were presumably used to produce similar L2 sounds before training, once the production of L2 sounds improves. Will they drift toward newly established non-native sounds? Will they deflect from them? Or, else, will they remain unchanged? To date, no study has examined the effects of improved L2 sound production resulting from training on the production of native sounds in novice learners. The experimental study presented in this chapter addresses this issue by examining the production of the French /o/ vowel before and after visual feedback production training with a similar non-native Danish vowel, /ɔ/, in native French speakers with no experience with Danish. Before presenting this study, I will survey briefly previous studies on the effects of L2 on the production of native sounds in bilinguals and L2 speakers who have been immersed in an L2-speaking country.

8.1.2 Foreign Accent in the Production of Native Sounds

According to the Speech Learning Model (SLM), 'phonetic categories established in childhood for L1 sounds evolve over the lifespan to reflect the properties of all L1 or L2 phones identified as a realization of each category' (Flege 1995: 239). While simultaneous bilinguals produce similar cross-language sounds distinctly and similarly to monolingual speakers of their respective languages (Fowler, Sramko, Ostry, Rowland and Hallé 2008; Guion 2003; MacLeod, Stoel-Gammon and Wassink 2009; see, however, Sundara, Polka and Baum 2006 for contradictory results), consecutive (or sequential) bilinguals and late L2 speakers experience difficulties in maintaining their native categories unchanged when in contact with L2 (Chang 2012, 2013; Flege 1987; Flege and Eefting 1987a, 1987b; Major 1992; Mora, Keidel and Flege 2015; Sancier and Fowler 1997). Their native categories can drift toward or deflect away from similar L2 sounds.

Drift of native categories toward similar L2 sounds has been reported in those L2 speakers who have been immersed in an L2-speaking country (Chang 2012; Flege 1987; Major 1992; Sancier and Fowler 1997). For instance, Major (1992) examined the production of the voiceless /p/, /t/ and /k/ stops in native American English (AE) speakers who had been living in Brazil for an average of 23 years; their age at the time of arrival was 22–36 years. The amount of aspiration in the production of the voiceless /p, t, k/ stops, referred to as voice-onset time (VOT), is small in Portuguese (about 20 ms) and large in AE (about 85 ms). Native AE speakers immersed in Brazil were shown to shorten their VOT in the production of AE stops to approach that of Portuguese stops.

Other studies have shown a drift in the production of native sounds toward the phonetic properties of similar L2 sounds even after a brief period of immersion in an L2-speaking country (Chang 2012; Sancier and Fowler 1997). For example, the productions of native AE speakers became more Korean-like after a 5-week learning course of Korean in Korea (Chang 2012). Mora and colleagues have shown that the drift in the production of native categories toward the non-native ones depends on the frequency of L2 use. Catalan-Spanish early bilinguals who used their Spanish more frequently than Catalan showed a drift in their production of the Catalan /ɛ/ vowel toward the similar Spanish /e/ vowel (Mora et al. 2015; Mora and Nadeu 2012). The results of the above-mentioned studies suggest that native categories are sensitive to L2 exposure and the frequency of L2 use. Prolonged and/or frequent contact with L2 sounds leads to a drift of native productions toward the phonetic properties of similar L2 sounds.

Deflection of native categories away from similar L2 sounds has been reported in proficient L2 speakers who discerned the phonetic differences between similar L1 and L2 sounds (Flege and Eefting 1987a, 1987b). Flege and Eefting (1987b) examined the production of the Dutch voiceless /t/ stop in Dutch speakers of English. In Dutch, voiceless stops are produced with short VOT (about 23 ms) whereas in English they are produced with long (about 85 ms). Only those Dutch speakers who were proficient in English, i.e. those whose accents in English were judged by native speakers as more native-like, produced the Dutch /t/ stop with shorter VOT (17 ms) than in prototypical Dutch /t/. Similarly, Flege and Eefting (1987a) showed that Spanish speakers of English who started learning English at the age of 5–6 years produced Spanish voiceless consonants with shorter VOT (18 ms) than in prototypical Spanish voiceless stops (23 ms). Analogously, Quichua speakers who acquired Spanish early in their childhood produced native Quichua vowels with the tongue raised higher than prototypically in Quichua (Guion 2003). The deflection of native categories reported in these studies was attributed to the need to exaggerate the phonetic difference between similar L1 and L2 sounds in proficient L2 speakers (who are not immersed into an L2-speaking environment) and in L2 speakers who started to learn L2 early.

The experimental study presented in this chapter assesses the effects of visual feedback phonetic training with a non-native Danish /ɔ/ vowel on the production of the (similar) French /o/ vowel in native French speakers with no experience with Danish. Both 'drift' and 'deflection' hypotheses are considered (see below). Although, other aspects of the Danish phonology are more likely to be difficult to acquire by the French speakers (e.g. stressed versus unstressed syllables, long-short vowel distinction, syllable structures), this study is limited to the acquisition of an individual vowel, i.e. the Danish /ɔ/ vowel, and to the effects it has on the production of the French /o/ vowel.

8.2 Experimental Study

Danish and French vowel inventories differ considerably. First, the Danish inventory is larger: Danish contains 16 monophthongal vowel qualities (Basbøll, 2005; Steinlen 2005), whereas French contains 10 vowels (Vaissière 2007). Second, Danish vowels are unevenly distributed across the acoustic space with almost all Danish vowels placed in the upper third of the vowel space, whereas French vowels are distributed evenly. Third, most Danish vowels occur in both short and long forms, whereas vowel length is not contrastive in French.

The Danish /ɔ/ vowel quality (as in *måle* 'measure', *skåle* 'cheer') was selected as a target non-native vowel. It is characterized as an advanced raised open-mid back rounded vowel (Basbøll 2005). It is similar to the French /o/ vowel (as in *eau,* 'water') which is an open-mid back rounded vowel (Georgeton, Paillereau, Landron, Jiayin and Kamiyama 2012), see Figure 8.2. A separate experimental study established that native French speakers categorize the Danish /ɔ/ vowel as a French /o/ vowel (Kartushina, Hervais-Adelman, Frauenfelder, and Golestani 2016). The average

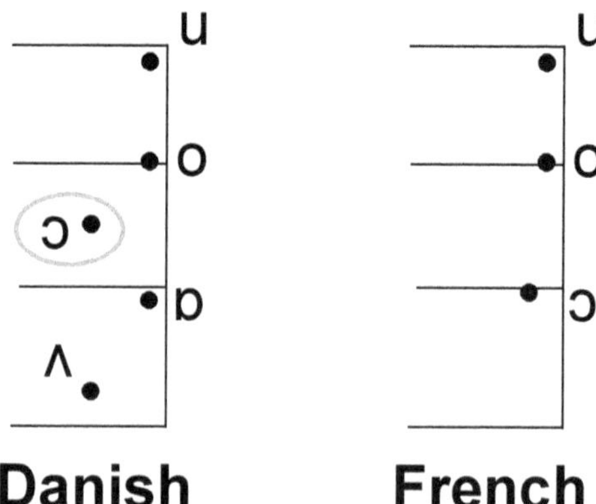

Figure 8.2. Danish and French spaces for back vowels; the Danish vowel quality used for training is circled.

acceptability rating on a scale from 1 to 10 (where 10 was 'strongly agree that the vowel is French-like') was 7.03, suggesting that this vowel was perceived with a moderately high degree of certainty as being a relatively good example of the French /o/ vowel. Acoustical analyses of the French /o/ and Danish /ɔ/ vowels produced by native speakers confirmed the perception results: the Danish /ɔ/ vowel quality is acoustically very close to the French /o/ vowel (Kartushina et al. 2016).

The first question posed in this study was *whether the production of the Danish /ɔ/ vowel would be related to individual differences in the production of the French /o/ vowel before training.* Two hypotheses were tested.

(1) It was expected, that due to assimilation mechanisms, French speakers would use their native French /o/ category to produce the Danish /ɔ/ vowel before training. So, those French speakers whose native French /o/ category was closer to the Danish /ɔ/ vowel in F1/F2 space were predicted to produce the Danish /ɔ/ vowel more accurately before training.

According to the SLM, L1 and L2 sounds coexist in a common space. The likelihood of establishing a phonetic category for an L2 sound increases with decreasing similarity between L2 and L1 sounds. Recently, it has been shown that L2 speakers whose native vowels are compactly distributed in acoustic space produce similar L2 sounds better than L2 speakers whose native vowels are more variably distributed. These individual differences in L2 production are likely due to individual differences in similarity between the L1 and L2 categories which is greater in 'uncompact' L1 speakers than compact L1 speakers (Kartushina and Frauenfelder 2014).

(2) It was predicted that those French speakers whose French vowel was more variably distributed in F1/F2 space would produce the Danish /ɔ/ vowel less accurately before training and would benefit from the training more (more room for improvement) in terms of training-related gains (pre minus post) than those whose French vowel was distributed compactly before training.

The second question was *whether the production of the French /o/ vowel would be modified by training with the Danish /ɔ/ vowel,* and, if so, *what would be the nature of this change: a drift toward or a deflection away from the Danish vowel*? The 'drift' hypothesis stems from previous L2 studies showing that late novice learners drift native sounds toward similar L2 ones after a short period of L2 learning (e.g. Chang 2012). The 'deflection' hypothesis is supported by studies showing that L1 categories deflect away from similar L2 sounds in those speakers who discern the phonetic difference between L1 and L2 sounds, that is, in those listeners who establish a novel L2 category (e.g. Flege and Eefting 1987a). Since French participants will receive feedback that will help them (among others) to distinguish the

Danish /ɔ/ from the similar French /o/ vowel and to create a novel L2 category, this might lead to the need to enhance the distance between these two vowels in production.

8.2.1 Materials and Methods

In order to answer these questions, 20 native monolingual French speakers (18 female and 2 male, mean age = 21;9) with no experience of Danish were trained with visual feedback about articulation to produce the Danish /ɔ/ vowel over three training sessions that were administered on alternating days (see Figure 8.3 for a schema of experimental design). Feedback provided to participants was similar to that used in Kartushina and colleagues' study (2016). It consisted of a two-dimensional visual display showing F1–F0 (F1 minus the fundamental frequency) and F2–F0 along the y- and x-axes, respectively. The former corresponds to tongue height and the latter to its front-back position. A participant's production of the Danish /ɔ/ vowel was represented on this display in the form of a square in F1–F0/F2–F0 space alongside the target trained vowel (see Figure 8.1). This time, in contrast to the above-mentioned study, the target vowel (i.e. Danish /ɔ/) was represented by a target sex-matching acoustic space (rather than by a target example) that derived from the productions of native Danish speakers (see below for details and Figure 8.4). Participants were trained and tested using stimuli recorded by a speaker of the same sex as themselves.

In order to assess the effects of training on the production of the Danish /ɔ/ and the French /o/ vowels, participants performed two vowel repetition tasks that were administered separately for each language, on the first (before training) and last (after training) session. On each trial, participants heard an auditory stimulus and repeated it as accurately as possible.

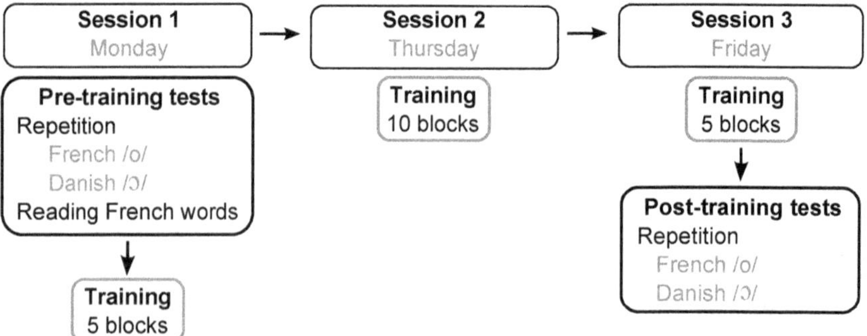

Figure 8.3. Experimental design.

To create the Danish auditory stimuli, two female and two male native speakers of Danish were recorded while reading the sentence 'Jeg siger måle, håde*, skåle' ('I say measure, pseudo-word*, cheer') that contained the Danish /ɔ/ vowel embedded in two words and in one pseudo-word. The sentences were repeated five times. The vowels that were produced in the pseudo-words were extracted, resulting in 10 exemplars of the Danish /ɔ/ vowel for each sex. Analogously, two female and two male native speakers of French were recorded in order to obtain 10 exemplars of the French /o/ vowel for each sex (for details, see Kartushina et al. 2016). In each repetition task, participants produced three times each of the 10 sex-matching exemplars, for a total of 30 production trials per language. The productions were recorded on a hard-disk and analysed acoustically in Matlab. Adapted scripts from the COLEA toolbox were used to calculate the F0, F1 and F2 of the produced vowels (see Kartushina et al. 2015 for details on the acoustic analyses applied).

The formant values for the Danish /ɔ/ tokens, produced by French speakers in the repetition task, were used to compute the Mahalanobis acoustic distances in F1–F0/F2–F0 space between each token and a representative sex-matching acoustic space for the Danish /ɔ/ vowel, before and after training. This space (hereafter called 'target space'), was composed of the vowels that were produced by native Danish speakers in words (10 exemplars x 2 speakers) and in pseudo-words (5 exemplars x 2 speakers), for a total of 30 vowel tokens. The Mahalanobis distance is a joint F1–F2 measure of distance that takes into account the natural variability present in the speech signal. The distance of '1' between a token and the target space corresponds to one standard deviation from this token to the mean of the target space; the distance increases as tokens move away from this mean. Also, the formant values were used to compute the compactness (i.e. acoustic stability between realizations) of the Danish vowel in F1–F0/F2–F0 space for each participant, before and after training. A compactness score (CS) was calculated as the area of an ellipse having major and minor axes with a length of one standard deviation of the mean along the given axis. It was then scaled as a proportion of the compactness of the target space. Thus, a lower CS corresponds to less variable productions, with a CS of 1 being equal to the CS of a native Danish speaker.

The formant values for the French /o/ tokens were used to compute analogous distances between the French /o/ vowel, produced in the repetition task, and the target space, before and after training. The compactness of the French /o/ vowel was computed for each participant, before and after training, using a similar procedure as for the Danish /ɔ/ vowel.

In order to test whether the production of the Danish vowel was related to individual differences in L1 production (the first question), a word reading task was administered before training. On each trial, participants saw a word on a screen and were asked to read it aloud as naturally as possible at a moderate tempo. Each word was presented twice. There were 15 [CV], [CVC] and [CVCV] French words containing the French /o/ vowel in the first (for the CVs and CVCs) or in the first or second syllable (for the CVCVs). In total, 30 words were recorded. The French /o/ tokens were extracted and analysed acoustically in Matlab using the above-mentioned procedure. Two properties in individuals' production of the French /o/ vowel in the reading task were considered: its acoustic (Mahalanobis) distance (distance score, DS) to the Danish /ɔ/ vowel and its compactness.

At the beginning of the first session, after completing the pre-training tasks (i.e. repetition of the French /o/ and Danish /ɔ/ vowels and reading), participants passed to training. They received, first, basic instructions explaining the nature of the feedback and its correspondence to the articulators (i.e. tongue position with respect to the y-axis [vowel height], and to the x-axis [vowel backness]) during production. Participants were familiarized with this feedback using a task involving reading the French vowels /i/, /e/, /a/, /o/ and /u/. The familiarization phase lasted 5 minutes and was immediately followed by the training.

Training was composed of 20 blocks. Within each block, 10 same-sex tokens extracted from Danish pseudo-words were presented 3 times each, resulting in 30 production trials per block. On each trial, participants heard an example of the Danish /ɔ/ vowel, repeated it and received immediate visual feedback on their production. On the second and each consequent trial, the visual feedback also included information about the position of the produced non-native vowel on the previous trial (see Figure 8.4). The

Figure 8.4. Visual feedback provided to participants on the first and second (and subsequent) training trials (white square=participant's production, white ellipse=Danish target, grey square=vowel produced on preceding trial).

produced vowels were analysed online acoustically in Matlab using the same procedure as the one that was used to analyse participants' productions in the repetition task. The F1–F0 and F2–F0 values obtained for each production trial were displayed on a window, the values of which ranged from 2500 Hz to 400 Hz on the x-axis and from 500 Hz to 50 Hz on the y-axis. There were pauses between blocks, the duration of which was controlled by the participants. In total, participants produced each vowel 600 times.

8.3 Results

The effects of training on the production of the Danish /ɔ/ and French /o/ vowels were assessed for each vowel separately.

General linear mixed-effects model analyses with crossed random effects for subjects and items were applied to the DSs for the Danish /ɔ/ vowel (Baayen 2008). The R software package was used. There was a significant effect of time (β=−0.41, SE=0.16, t=−2.56), indicating that productions after training were more accurate (i.e. closer to the Danish target space) than before training with an overall improvement of 18% (see Figure 8.5A).

Training-related changes in the compactness of the Danish /ɔ/ vowel productions were analysed using ANOVA. The logarithm transformation was applied to the CSs. There was a significant effect of time on the CS ($t_{(1,19)}$−1.86, p−0.038), indicating that the Danish /ɔ/ vowel was produced less variably after training as compared to before. There was an overall improvement of 25% in its compactness (see Figure 8.5B).

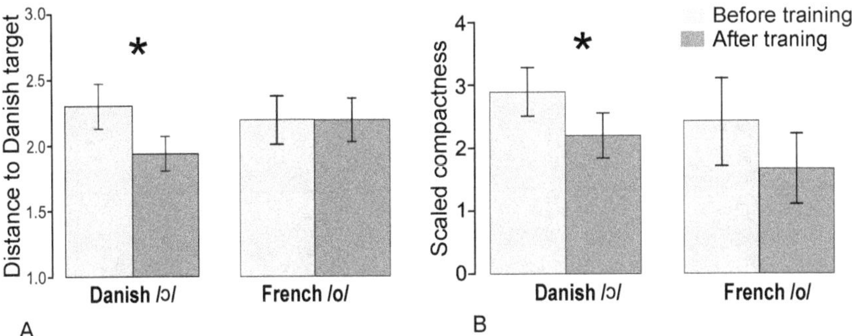

Figure 8.5. Effect of training on the production of the Danish /ɔ/ and French /o/ vowels. A. Mean distance scores to the target before and after training. B. Mean compactness scores before and after training. Error bars represent ±1 standard error of the mean.

Analogous analyses were applied to the French /o/ vowel. There was no effect of time either on the DS ($t<2$) or on the CS ($p>0.1$), suggesting that the French /o/ vowel did not become closer to the Danish /ɔ/ vowel, nor less variable in its production after training (see Figure 8.5).

In order to explore whether there was a relationship between training-related changes in the acoustic location of the Danish /ɔ/ and French /o/ vowels within individuals, the differences between pre- and post-training formant values in F1 ($F1_{POST}-F1_{PRE}$) and F2 ($F2_{POST}-F2_{PRE}$) were computed for each vowel and subject and then correlated. There were significant, strong positive correlations in the changes in F1 ($r=0.68$, $p<0.01$) and F2 ($r=0.61$, $p<0.01$) between the Danish /ɔ/ and the French /o/ vowels, showing that participants who obtained a larger, negative pre-/post-training difference score for the Danish /ɔ/ also obtained a larger, negative pre-/post-training difference score for the French /o/ (and vice versa for positive difference scores). In other words, the results show that, for each participant, the formants tend to move in the same direction for the French and Danish vowels (see Figure 8.6).

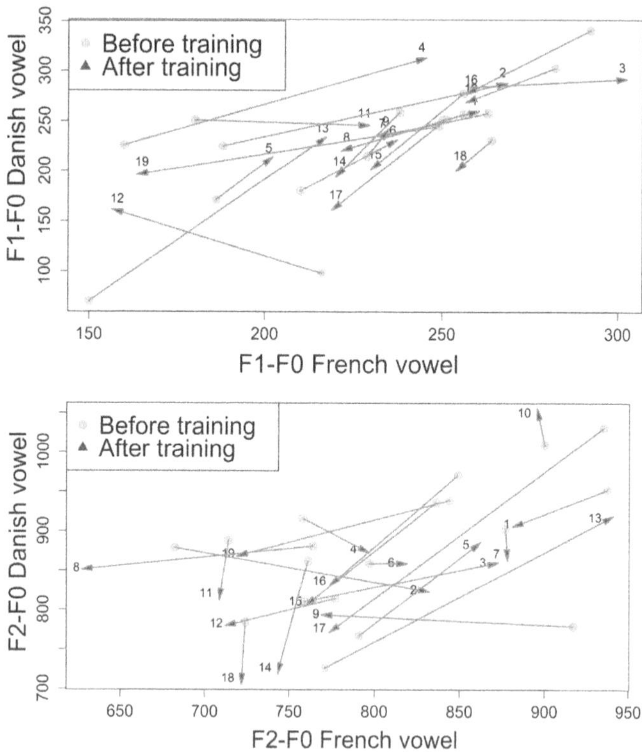

Figure 8.6. F1 and F2 values for the Danish /ɔ/ and the French /o/ vowels before and after training.

In order to test for relationships between individual differences in the production of the French /o/ vowel (i.e. its position and compactness) and the production accuracy of the Danish /ɔ/ vowel before training and training-related gains, correlation analyses were applied. They revealed a significant correlation between the production of the French /o/ and the Danish /ɔ/ vowels before training: those French speakers whose native French /o/ category was closer to the Danish /ɔ/ vowel produced the Danish /ɔ/ vowel more accurately ($r=0.51$, $p=0.03$). There was a significant correlation between the compactness of the French /o/ vowel and non-native production accuracy before training: those French speakers whose native productions of the French /o/ vowel were compact produced the Danish /ɔ/ vowel more accurately ($r=0.49$, $p=0.03$). Finally, there was a significant correlation between the compactness of the French /o/ category before training and training-related gains for the Danish /ɔ/ vowel ($r=0.63$, $p=0.007$): those French speakers whose French vowel was more variably distributed benefited more from the training.

8.4 Discussion

The results will be discussed in relation to the research questions. The first question was *whether the production of the Danish /ɔ/ vowel before training and training-related gains would be related to individual differences in the production of the French /o/ vowel.* Productions of the French /o/ vowel were analysed acoustically in terms of their position and compactness (inverse of variability) in the acoustic space. Results revealed that the position of the French /o/ vowel was related to accuracy in the production of the non-native Danish /ɔ/ vowel before training. Those French speakers whose native French /o/ category was closer to the Danish /ɔ/ vowel produced the Danish /ɔ/ vowel more accurately before training. These results suggest that the closest native vowel category was used to produce a non-native similar vowel. Previous studies have shown that acoustic differences in the production of native vowels affect perception (Escudero and Vasiliev 2011; Kartushina and Frauenfelder 2013) and production of similar non-native vowels (Kartushina and Frauenfelder 2014). The results of the current and previous studies support the hypothesis that there is phonetic transfer of the L1 system into the L2 (Flege 1995; Hallé, Best and Levitt 1999).

The compactness in the production of the French /o/ vowel was related to accuracy in the production of the Danish /ɔ/ vowel before training and training-related gains. Speakers whose native French vowel was realized compactly (less variably) produced a similar Danish vowel more accurately before training and benefited from training less than those whose French vowel was realized more variably. These results are consistent with the SLM postulate of a shared interspace between languages, according to which L1 and L2 sounds are related to each other at the acoustic-phonetic level (Flege 1995). Within this space, the likelihood of establishing a new category is greater with increased distance between L1 and L2 similar sounds. Since the compactness provides a measure of category 'size', it is likely that speakers with compact acoustic spaces are more likely to discern the phonetic differences between L1 and L2 similar sounds, and to establish L2 categories more accurately, than speakers whose productions are more dispersed. Consequently, since their productions were more accurate before training, they benefited from training less.

The second question was *whether the production of the French /o/ vowel would be modified by training with a similar Danish /ɔ/ vowel.* It is important to discuss, first, the efficacy of training. One hour of phonetic training with visual feedback that provided information about participants' production alongside that of the target-vowel space improved French participants' accuracy and stability in their production of the Danish /ɔ/ vowel by 18% and 25%, respectively. In line with previous L2/non-native training studies, these results show that L2 speakers can improve their production of non-native sounds which are similar to native ones if trial-by-trial visual feedback on their production is provided (Carey 2004; Kartushina et al. 2015; Öster 1997). With regard to the French /o/ vowel, the results showed that, overall, its production was not modified after training: (1) it had not become closer to or farther from the Danish /ɔ/ vowel, and (2) it had not changed in its compactness. An absence of changes in the production of native categories has been previously reported in late non-proficient L2 speakers. Due to assimilation mechanisms, they use their native categories to produce similar L2 sounds with no impact on the production of the former (Flege 1987; Flege and Eefting 1987a). However, when training-related changes in acoustic position were compared between the two vowels across speakers, high correlations were found. This indicates that the native and non-native categories underwent similar training-related changes with partial drift in the same direction after training across speakers: those speakers who produced the Danish /ɔ/ with higher openness after training produced the French /o/ with higher openness as well; the same relationship was obtained for tongue back-front position. These observed results on the F1 and F2 arising from laboratory training are similar to those reported in L2 speakers who are immersed in an L2 country (i.e. naturalistic learning): they drift native categories toward similar L2 sounds (Chang 2012, 2013; Major 1992). A recent L2 learning study suggests that drift is multifaceted (i.e. L1 assimilates to the phonetic properties of L2 at subsegmental, segmental and global levels) and is more important in novice learners than in experienced L2 speakers (Chang 2012). Other studies, however, suggest that more experience with L2 is associated with more L2-accented L1 speech (Major 1992; Flege 1987). More research is needed to examine the longevity of this effect and its dynamics. The results support the SLM postulate: L1 categories are not fossilized but continue to develop over the lifespan 'to reflect the properties of all L1 or L2 phones identified as a realization of each category' (Flege 1995: 239). Moreover, they extend it to novice speakers showing that even brief experience with non-native sounds affects the production of similar native categories at the early stages of L2 learning.

To conclude, this study suggests that native and non-native vowels interact with each other in a common (acoustic) space from very early steps of learning. Before training, the production of non-native vowels is related to individual differences in the position of similar native vowels. Training-related gains are related to the compactness of native similar vowels. In its turn, as much as one hour of training with a non-native vowel induces partial drift in the production of a native similar vowel: it drifts in the same F1/F2 direction as the trained vowel after training. It remains to be tested whether more training would result in a bigger drift in the production of native vowels or whether a deflection mechanism occurs once native-like proficiency is achieved.

References

Akahane-Yamada, R., McDermott, E., Adachi, T., Kawahara, H. and Pruitt, J.-S. (1998). Computer-based second language production training by using spectrographic representation and HMM-based speech recognition scores. In *Proceedings of Interspeech* (paper 0429 1–4).

Baayen, R.H. (2008). *Analyzing Linguistic Data: A Practical Introduction to Statistics Using R*. New York: Cambridge University Press.

Basbøll, H. (2005). *The Phonology of Danish: The Phonology of the World's Languages.* Oxford: Oxford University Press.

Best, C.T. and Tyler, M. (2007). Non-native and second-language speech perception: Commonalities and complementarities. In M.J. Munro and O.-S. Bohn (eds.). *Second Language Speech Learning: The Role of Language Experience in Speech Perception and Production*, 13–34. Amsterdam: John Benjamins.

Bradlow, A.R., Pisoni, D.B., Akahane-Yamada, R. and Tohkura, Y. (1997). Training Japanese listeners to identify English/r/and/l: IV. Some effects of perceptual learning on speech production. *The Journal of the Acoustical Society of America* 101(4): 2299–310.

Carey, M. (2004). CALL visual feedback for pronunciation of vowels: Kay Sona-Match. *CALICO Journal* 21(3): 571–601.

Chang, C.B. (2012). Rapid and multifaceted effects of second-language learning on first-language speech production. *Journal of Phonetics* 40(2): 249–68.

Chang, C.B. (2013). A novelty effect in phonetic drift of the native language. *Journal of Phonetics* 41(6): 520–33.

Dagenais, P.A. (1995). Electropalatography in the treatment of articulation/phonological disorders. *Journal of Communication Disorders* 28: 303–29.

Dowd, A., Smith, J. and Wolfe, J. (1998). Learning to pronounce vowel sounds in a foreign language using acoustic measurements of the vocal tract as feedback in real time. *Language and Speech* 41(1): 1–20.

Escudero, P. and Vasiliev, P. (2011). Cross-language acoustic similarity predicts perceptual assimilation of Canadian English and Canadian French vowels. *The Journal of the Acoustical Society of America* 130(5): EL277–83.

Flege, J.E. (1987). The production of 'new' and 'similar' phones in a foreign language: Evidence for the effect of equivalence classification. *Journal of Phonetics* 15(1): 47–65.

Flege, J.E. (1995). Second language speech learning theory: Findings, and problems. In W. Strange (ed.), *Speech Perception and Linguistic Experience: Issues in Cross-Language Research*, 233–77. Timonium, MD: York Press.

Flege, J.E. (2003). Assessing constraints on second-language segmental production and perception. In N.O. Schiller and A.S. Meyer (eds.), *Phonetics and Phonology in Language Comprehension and Production: Differences and Similarities*, Vol. 6, 319–55. Berlin: Walter de Gruyter.

Flege, J.E. and Eefting, W. (1987a). Cross-language switching in stop consonant perception and production by Dutch speakers of English. *Speech Communication* 6: 185–202.

Flege, J.E. and Eefting, W. (1987b). Production and perception of English stops by native Spanish speakers. *Journal of Phonetics* 15: 67–83.

Fowler, C.A., Sramko, V., Ostry, D.J., Rowland, S.A. and Hallé, P. (2008). Cross language phonetic influences on the speech of French–English bilinguals. *Journal of Phonetics* 36(4): 649–63.

Georgeton, L., Paillereau, N., Landron, S., Jiayin, G. and Kamiyama, T. (2012). Analyse formantique des voyelles orales du français en contexte isolé: à la recherche d'une référence pour les apprenants de FLE. In *JEP-TALN-RECITAL*, Vol. 1, 145–52. University of Grenoble.

Guion, S.G. (2003). The vowel systems of Quichua-Spanish bilinguals: Age of acquisition effects on the mutual influence of the first and second languages. *Phonetica* 60(2): 98–128.

Hallé, P.A., Best, C.T. and Levitt, A. (1999). Phonetic vs. phonological influences on French listeners' perception of American English approximants. *Journal of Phonetics* 27(3): 281–306.

Ingram, J.C. and Park, S.-G. (1997). Cross-language vowel perception and production by Japanese and Korean learners of English. *Journal of Phonetics* 25(3): 343–70.

Kartushina, N. and Frauenfelder, U.H. (2013). On the role of L1 speech production in L2 perception: Evidence from Spanish learners of French. In *Proceedings of Interspeech*, 2118–22. Baixas, France: ISCA.

Kartushina, N. and Frauenfelder, U.H. (2014). On the effects of L2 perception and of individual differences in L1 production on L2 pronunciation. *Frontiers in Psychology* 5. doi.org/10.3389/fpsyg.2014.01246

Kartushina, N., Hervais-Adelman, A., Frauenfelder, U.H. and Golestani, N. (2015). The effect of phonetic production training with visual feedback on the perception and production of foreign speech sounds. *The Journal of the Acoustical Society of America* 138(2): 817–32.

Kartushina, N., Hervais-Adelman, A., Frauenfelder, U.H. and Golestani, N. (2016). Mutual influences between native and non-native vowels in production: Evidence from short-term visual articulatory feedback training. *Journal of Phonetics* 57: 21–39.

Ladefoged, P. (1962). *Elements of Acoustic Phonetics.* Chicago: University of Chicago Press.

Leather, J. (1997. Interrelation of perceptual and productive learning in the initial acquisition of second-language tone. In A.R. James and J. Leather (eds.), *Second-Language Speech: Structure and Process*, 75–101. Berlin: Mouton de Gruyter.

Lively, S.E., Logan, J.S. and Pisoni, D.B. (1993). Training Japanese listeners to identify English /r/ and /l/. II: The role of phonetic environment and talker variability in learning new perceptual categories. *The Journal of the Acoustical Society of America* 94(3 Pt 1): 1242–55.

Lopez-Soto, T. and Kewley-Port, D. (2009). Relation of perception training to production of codas in English as a second language. *The Journal of the Acoustical Society of America* 125(4): 2756.

MacLeod, A.A.N., Stoel-Gammon, C. and Wassink, A.B. (2009). Production of high vowels in Canadian English and Canadian French: A comparison of early bilingual and monolingual speakers. *Journal of Phonetics* 37(4): 374–87.

Major, R.C. (1992). Losing English as a first language. *The Modern Language Journal* 76(2), 190–208.

Mora, J.C., Keidel, J.L. and Flege, J.E. (2015). Effects of Spanish use on the production of Catalan vowels by early Spanish-Catalan bilinguals. In J. Romero and M. Riera (eds.), *The Phonetics-Phonology Interface: Representations and Methodologies*, 33–53. Amsterdam: John Benjamins.

Mora, J.C., and Nadeu, M. (2012). L2 effects on the perception and production of a native vowel contrast in early bilinguals. *International Journal of Bilingualism* 16(4): 484–500.

Öster, A.-M. (1997). Auditory and visual feedback in spoken L2 teaching. *Reports from the Department of Phonetics, Umeå University, PHONUM* 4: 145–8.

Pillot-Loiseau, C., Kocjančič Antolík, T. and Kamiyama, T. (2013). Contribution of ultrasound visualisation to improving the production of the French /y/-/u/ contrast by four Japanese learners. In *PPLC13: Phonetics, Phonology, Languages in Contact: Varieties, Multilingualism, Second Language Learning*, 86–9. Paris, France.

Sancier, M.L. and Fowler, C.A. (1997). Gestural drift in a bilingual speaker of Brazilian Portuguese and English. *Journal of Phonetics* 25(4): 421–36.

Scovel, T. (1969). Foreign accents, language acquisition, and cerebral dominance. *Language Learning* 19(3–4): 245–53.

Steinlen, A.K. (2005). *The Influence of Consonants on Native and Non-native Vowel Production: A Cross-linguistic Study*. Tübingen: Gunter Narr Verlag.

Sundara, M., Polka, L. and Baum, S. (2006). Production of coronal stops by simultaneous bilingual adults. *Bilingualism* 9(1): 97.

Vaissière, J. (2007). *La phonétique*. Paris: Presses Universitaires de France.

Wilson, I. and Gick, B. (2006). Ultrasound technology and second language acquisition research. In *Proceedings of the 8th Generative Approaches to Second Language Acquisition Conference (GASLA 2006)*, 148–52.

Wong, J.W.S. (2013). The effects of perceptual and/or productive training on the perception and production of English vowels /ɪ/ and /iː/ by Cantonese ESL learners. In *Proceedings of Interspeech*, 2113–17. Baixas, France: ISCA.

Natalia Kartushina is a postdoctoral researcher at the Basque Centre on Cognition, Brain and Language, Donostia-San Sebastián, Spain.

9
Environmental Markedness in Portuguese-English Contact

Robert Carlisle

9.1 Introduction

Researchers investigating phonological variables in both primary languages and second languages have long recognized the importance of phonological environments in inducing the frequencies with which the variants of a variable occur. One finding in SLA research, which closely agreed with that in primary language research, was that the frequencies with which the variants of word-initial and word-final variables occurred were determined by whether the word-final environment before a word-initial variable or a word-initial environment before a word-final variable consisted of a consonant or a vowel.

Starting in the 1980s, research interest turned to variables that were in a markedness relationship, research that greatly focused on margins: word-final codas and word-initial onsets. With great consistency, results revealed that less marked margins were modified significantly less frequently than more marked margins. For example, longer margins, which are more marked, were simplified significantly more frequently than were shorter margins, which are less marked (Abrahamsson 1999, 2003; Anderson 1987; Carlisle 1997, 1998, 2002). Many of these studies also examined the role of phonological environment, finding that, regardless of their degree of markedness, word-initial onsets were modified significantly less frequently after word-final vowels than after word-final consonants (Abrahamsson 1999; Carlisle 1991a, 1992, 1997; Rauber 2006). Similarly, word-final codas, regardless of their degree of markedness, were simplified significantly less frequently before word-initial vowels than before word-initial consonants (Abrahamsson 2003; Bayley 1996; Wolfram 1985).

Based on a study with word-initial sC onsets, Carlisle suggested that 'the frequency of epenthesis may be inversely proportional to the sonority of the preceding environment' (1991a: 90). In other words, the constraints for determining the frequency of prothesis were more numerous than just the dichotomous distinction between consonants and vowels. Carlisle (2010) refined his earlier suggestion by hypothesizing that the frequency of prothesis before sC(C) onsets would be determined by the markedness relationships among word-final demisyllables (Clements 1990): the less marked the demisyllable the lower the frequency of prothesis. Carlisle asserted that just as variables can be in markedness relationships so can the environments that determine the frequency with which variants occur. As noted by Clements (1990), all syllables have two demisyllables. The initial demisyllable consists of the nucleus and the onset, and the final demisyllable consists of the nucleus and the coda. As will be discussed in a later section, Clements documented markedness hierarchies among demisyllables based on their length and sonority profiles.

The following study tests the hypothesis first put forth by Carlisle (2010) and is divided into two parts. The first part examines the hypothesis that native speakers of Portuguese will use prothesis before English sC(C) onsets significantly more frequently after word-final consonants than after word-final vowels, a pattern that has been found in at least seven studies with native Spanish speakers learning Swedish (Abrahamsson 1999) and English (Carlisle 1991a, 1991b, 1992, 1997, 2006; Rauber 2006), but never with Portuguese speakers (Rauber 2006; Rebello and Baptista 2006). The second part of the study tests the more complex hypothesis that different word final demisyllables in a markedness relationship will induce different frequencies of prothesis before sC(C) onsets, a pattern that has again been documented for native Spanish speakers learning English, but not for native Portuguese speakers. Accurately identifying the environments that induce different frequencies of variants is important because environment has consistently been shown to be the primary variable constraint in accounting for the frequency of variants, even more powerful than the markedness relationships among variables (Carlisle 1991b, 1992, 1997).

9.2 Part 1

9.2.1 Background

Phonological Environment in Variation Analyses

Even from the first studies in variation analysis (Labov 1966, 1969; Wolfram 1969), researchers recognized the importance of linguistic environment in inducing the frequencies with which the variants of a variable occur. Statistical findings from these studies especially revealed the consistent strength of phonological environment on deletion and insertion processes at word boundaries.

Wolfram (1969) examined the simplification of word-final clusters by upper middle class whites and African Americans from four socio-economic classes from Detroit. Examining both monomorphemic clusters as in *mist* and bimorphemic clusters as in *missed*, he found that all five groups simplified the clusters significantly more frequently before word-initial consonants than before word-initial vowels (see Table 9.1).[1] Examining the simplification of the same type of clusters by speakers of Appalachian English, Wolfram and Christian (1976) found the same pattern of results obtained in the Detroit study (see Table 9.2).

Table 9.1. Percentage of correct production of word-final obstruent clusters ending in an alveolar stop before consonantal and non-consonantal environments by upper middle class whites (UMW), upper middle class African-Americans (UMA), lower middle class African Americans (LMA), upper working class African Americans (UWA), and lower working class African Americans (LWA) (based on data from Wolfram 1969).

	Type of Cluster			
	Bimorphemic		Monomorphemic	
Environment	#C	#–C	#C	#–C
Participants				
UMW	63.8	97.2	33.6	88.5
UMA	50.8	93.2	21.1	77.4
LMA	38.3	86.7	13.3	56.7
UWA	27.5	75.7	6.5	34.6
LWA	24.0	66.1	2.7	17.9

Table 9.2. Percentage of correct production of word-final obstruent clusters ending in an alveolar stop before word-initial consonants and word-initial vowels by speakers of Appalachian English (based on data from Wolfram and Christian 1976).

	Type of Cluster			
	Bimorphemic		Monomorphemic	
Environment	##C	##V	##C	##V
	68.5	94.6	24.7	82.1

1 Wolfram used the term 'non-consonantal' because he found that pauses tended to behave in the same manner as vowels in inducing simplification.

Table 9.3. Percentage of (r) retention before consonantal and vocalic environments by upper middle class African-Americans (UMA), lower middle class African Americans (LMA), upper working class African Americans (UWA), and lower working class African Americans (LWA) (based on data from Wolfram 1969).

Environment	#C	#V
Participants		
UMA	74.7	89.2
LMA	59.2	65.9
UWA	29.8	42.5
LWA	20.9	34.3

A comparison of the results in Tables 9.1 and 9.2 reveals that all six groups of participants followed the same pattern of simplifying word-final clusters: monomorphemic clusters were simplified more frequently than bimorphemic clusters, and deletion of the final consonant in both types of clusters occurred much more frequently before a word-initial consonant than before a word-initial vowel.

For the upper middle class white and upper middle class African American participants, Wolfram (1969) further subdivided the consonantal group into two categories, resonant consonants and non-resonant consonants, finding that the participants deleted 87.5% of final consonants before non-resonant consonants and 42.4% of final consonants before resonant consonants. Consequently, this study provided some evidence that the frequency of deletion may be related to the sonority of the environment, though Wolfram did not specifically mention the possible role of sonority in the findings.

Studies examining the deletion of /r/ in word-final position have also found that deletion occurred more frequently before consonants than before vowels. Wolfram (1969) found that all four groups of African Americans from different socio-economic classes living in Detroit deleted word-final /r/ more frequently before a word-initial consonant than before a word-initial vowel (see Table 9.3). In addition, Wolfram and Christian (1976) found that speakers of Appalachian English deleted 38.7% of /r/s when they occurred in word-final position in unstressed syllables before a word-initial consonant; however, the frequency of deletion was only 14% when /r/s in the same types of syllables were followed by a word-initial vowel.

A number of studies examining the deletion of word-initial variables have documented that word-final consonants and vowels induce different frequencies of deletion. An example again comes from Appalachian

Table 9.4. Percentage of retention of word-initial unstressed syllables after word-final consonants and word-final vowels by speakers of Appalachian English (based on data from Wolfram and Christian 1976).

	Type of Unstressed Syllable			
	V		CV	
Environment	C#	V#	C#	V#
	64.8	36.0	71.4	61.2

English (Wolfram and Christian 1976). In that dialect, word-initial unstressed syllables are deleted more frequently after word-final vowels than after word-final consonants (see Table 9.4). The same study found that word-initial voiced interdental fricatives are more frequently deleted after a word-final consonant than after a word-final vowel.

Phonological Environment in SLA Research

Influenced by the methodologies of variation analysis and their findings, a few SLA researchers in the 1970s began examining variation in interlanguage phonology. The earliest studies dealt with feature changing processes (L. Dickerson 1975; W. Dickerson 1976; Dickerson and Dickerson 1977) and uniformly found that all variables had several variants and that the differing frequencies with which the variants occurred crucially depended on phonological environment. In the first of these studies, L. Dickerson (1975) examined the production of the variable (z) in English by native Japanese speakers and found that the target variant [z] occurred more frequently before a vowel than before a consonant. In another study of adult Japanese speakers learning English, Dickerson and Dickerson (1977) examined (r) in prevocalic position and found that the occurrence of the target variant [r] depended on the height of the following vowel: the lower the vowel, the higher the frequency of the target variant.

Later studies investigated the influence of environment on the production of onsets in word-initial position and codas in word-final position. Because many of the studies investigating the modification of complex onsets in word-final position were primarily concerned with the question of whether more marked codas would be modified more frequently than would less marked codas, environment was not strictly controlled or it was held constant by examining codas only in utterance-final position (Anderson 1987; Benson 1988; Tarone 1980). However, a small number of studies investigating word-final codas have controlled for environment. Wolfram (1985) examined monomorphemic and bimorphemic word-final codas, finding that the frequency of the simplification of both depended on whether the following environment was a consonant or vowel, Final clusters were simplified more frequently before word-initial consonants than before word-initial vowels, a finding consistent with variation analyses in L1s (Labov 1969; Wolfram 1969, 1973; Wolfram and Christian 1976). Bayley (1996) investigated the deletion of word-final /t/ and /d/ by native speakers of Mandarin learning English, finding that deletion occurred most frequently before word-initial obstruents or liquids, less frequently before glides, and least frequently before vowels. These findings suggest that the different degrees of sonority of word-initial sounds may induce different frequencies of deletion of word-final consonants. Abrahamsson (2003) also investigated the modification of word-final singleton codas (either by deletion of epenthesis) by native speakers of Chinese, finding that word-initial consonants and vowels induce different frequencies of modification of word-final codas depending upon the sonority of the segment constituting the coda. If the coda consisted of a stop, modification frequencies were significantly higher before word-initial consonants than before word-initial vowels. If the coda consisted of a liquid, the same pattern was evident for two of the three participants. In contrast, if the coda consisted of a nasal, the opposite pattern occurred: modification frequencies were significantly higher before word-initial vowels than before word-initial consonants. Finally, meaningful results were not available for codas consisting of a fricative or glide because of the small number of occurrences produced by the participants.

More consistent results have been found in the substantial number of studies that have investigated the role of word-final environments on the variable production of sC(C) onsets (Abrahamsson 1999; Carlisle 1991a, 1991b, 1992, 1997, 2006; Rauber 2006; Rebello and Baptista 2006). Seven of the studies examined the production of native Spanish speakers learning either Swedish (Abrahamsson 1999) or English (Carlisle 1991a, 1991b, 1992, 1997, 2006; Rauber 2006) and were consistent in finding that prothesis occurred significantly less frequently after word-final vowels than after word-final consonants (see Table 9.5).

Two studies (Rauber 2006; Rebello and Baptista 2006) examined the production of native Portuguese speakers learning English, but the results were unexpected, at least when compared to the studies involving native Spanish speakers. Rebello and Baptista found that their participants actually used prothesis more frequently after vowels (58%) than after consonants (51%), though the difference did not reach significance. Rauber examined three environments – consonants, vowels and silence – finding that her participants used prothesis most frequently after vowels (40.7%), less frequently after consonants (32.1%) and least frequently after silence

Table 9.5. Percentage of the correct production of word-initial sC(C) onsets after word-final consonants and vowels.

		Environments		
Studies	N	-V##	-C##	p
*Abrahamsson 1999	1			
/sC(C)/		66	6	<0.01
Carlisle 1991a	9			
/st/		39	21	=0.001
/sp/		35	27	=0.05
/sk/		37	24	=0.001
Carlisle 1991b	11			
/sl/		82	71	<0.001
/st/		73	59	<0.001
Carlisle 1992	14			
/sl/		77	69	<0.004
/sN/		72	61	<0.004
Carlisle 1997	11			
/sC/		71	53	<0.001
/sCC/		58	45	<0.001
Carlisle 2006	17			
/sl/		74	55	<0.001
/sn/		65	48	<0.001
/st/		58	35	<0.001
*Rauber 2006	9			
/sC(C)/		77	60	<0.001
*Rauber 2006[a]	10			
/sC(C)/		59	68	<0.001
*Rebello and Baptista 2006[a] /sC(C)/	6	42	49	ns

/sN/ = /s/ followed by a nasal.
*These studies also examined the onsets in absolute word-initial position and/or after pauses.
[a]Studies of native Portuguese speakers learning English.

(21.8%), differences that reached statistical significance using a chi-square analysis. Rauber's finding is especially interesting because she used the same data-gathering instrument for her native Spanish-speaking participants and found that in accordance with previous studies, her participants used prothesis least frequently after silence (16.9%), less frequently after vowels (22.7%), and most frequently after consonants (39.6%), differences that again reached significance using a chi-square analysis.

Both Rauber (2006) and Rebello and Baptista (2006) offer a number of possible reasons for their apparently aberrant findings. Although Rebello and Baptista state that 'the reason for the discrepancy in the results... regarding vowels versus consonants is not exactly clear' (2006: 149), they suggest that 'it might have to do with the choice of vowels.' They used a restricted number of word-final vowels in the study. There were only seven, and none were lax. Consequently, their data-gathering instrument differed significantly from those used in the studies with native Spanish speakers, which used more simple vowels, including schwa. This may not seem like much of a problem but their study contained only 222 instances of vowels and 981 instances of consonants for statistical analysis. Rauber's (2006) study, which used many of the same sentences found in the other study, had an even smaller number of items for statistical analysis: 570 for vowels and 579 for consonants. If lax vowels had also been used in their studies, the results may have been different. Rebello and Baptista go on to state that the use of reduced vowels in the studies by Carlisle is a 'likely explanation for the differences in findings between this study and his' (2006: 150), a statement with which Rauber agrees (2006: 164). Rauber goes on to state that 'the context vowels in that study were all tense vowels in content words, which would have a tendency to take stress, thus favoring the insertion of a vowel for the double purpose of maintaining the alternation of strong and weak syllables and allowing the resyllabification of the cluster' (ibid.).

The purpose of Part 1 is to examine the influence of word-final consonants and vowels on the production of sC(C) onsets by native speakers of Portuguese by addressing the points by Rebello and Baptista (2006) and Rauber (2006) discussed above.

9.2.2 Methodology

Participants

The initial pool of participants consisted of 38 native Portuguese speakers enrolled at the Universidade Federal de Santa Catarina in Florianopolis, Brazil. However, because only intermediate learners were eligible for the study, only nine of the potential participants actually qualified. To be considered as intermediate learners of English, the participants had to produce at least 21% of the onsets correctly, but no more than 80%. Previous research has used 80% correct production of any particular structure as the criterion level for acquisition (Andersen 1978; Carlisle 1997, 2006; Carlisle and Cutillas Espinosa 2015).

As is true for Spanish (Harris 1983), the syllable structure conditions of Portuguese prohibit word-initial onsets of the form /sC(C)/. As has been documented in previous research, (Rauber 2006; Rebello and Baptista 2006), Portuguese speakers treat the initial /s/ of complex onsets as an extrasyllabic consonant, which they mostly modify by prothesis. They then resyllabify the extrasyllabic consonant with the prothetic vowel (Clements and Keyser 1983).

Though both native Spanish speakers and native Portuguese speakers use prothesis before /sC(C)/ onsets, the quality of the vowels is different. Sonograms of three examples of prothesis by native Spanish speakers revealed that the midpoints of the first and second formats were approximately 375 HZ and 1590 Hz, indicating that the prothetic vowel resembles English epsilon. In contrast, researchers working with native Portuguese speakers report that the prothetic vowel approximates English /i/ (Major 2001; Rauber 2006).

Instrumentation

The data-gathering instrument consisted of 336 sentences, each of which contained one instance of the target onsets: /st/, /sp/, /sk/, /str/, /spr/ and /skr/. Environment was controlled so that each of 28 word-final segments occurred exactly twice before the six target onsets. The environments before the onsets consisted of 14 obstruents, 3 nasals, 2 liquids, 3 diphthongs and 6 vowels, among them unstressed schwa.[2]

Procedure, Data Transcription and Analysis

The participants were individually audio-recorded in a quiet office on the campus of the Universidade Federal de Santa Catarina in Florianopolis with a high quality microphone and recorder.

Two faculty members, one from the Universidade Federal de Santa Catarina in Florianopolis and the other from California State University, Bakersfield, independently transcribed the 12 recordings. Both faculty

2 Four sentences accidentally contained an additional occurrence of an sC(C) onset, but they did not count in the statistical calculations.

members have degrees in linguistics and extensive experience in phonetic transcription. Three specific features were transcribed: the quality of the environment, the presence of the prothetic vowel, and the target onset. All items on which complete agreement was not reached were discarded from the study. However, items were eliminated for other reasons as well. First, they were eliminated if the participants changed the manner of articulation of the environment before the target onset. For example, one participant read the sentence 'Long speeches are boring' as 'The speeches are boring', which changed the environment from a consonant to a vowel. Items were not eliminated if participants devoiced an obstruent because the environment remained an obstruent. The second reason for removing items was if participants misread the word containing the target onset. For example, one participant read 'skate' as 'kate'. Third, items were eliminated if the participants paused before the target onsets. Finally, items were eliminated if the participants skipped them.

The inter-rater reliability coefficients calculated for all nine participants ranged between 0.848 and 0.931, the average being 0.912. All items on which the transcribers disagreed were eliminated as were those for the reasons discussed immediately above. Of the 3024 possible items produced by the nine intermediate learners, 528 were eliminated, leaving 2496 items for statistical analysis.[3]

Two t-tests were calculated to analyse the difference in correct production of sC and sCC onsets after consonants and vowels.

9.2.3 Results and Discussion

The frequency of correct production of sC onsets was 0.792 after vowels and 0.553 after consonants, a significant difference: $t(8)=6.486$, $p<0.0001$. In turn, the frequency of correct production of sCC onsets was 0.751 after vowels and 0.568 after consonants, also a significant difference: $t(8)=7.182$, $p<0.0001$.

As demonstrated in Figures 9.1 and 9.2, these statistical findings were not due to a few participants modifying an unusually larger percentage of target onsets after vowels than after consonants. On the contrary, both figures display that all participants followed the same pattern to a greater or lesser extent: a greater percentage of target onsets correctly produced after vowels than after consonants.

3 Of the 528 items that were eliminated, 53 were agreed upon pauses; 36 were misreadings; and the rest were disagreements.

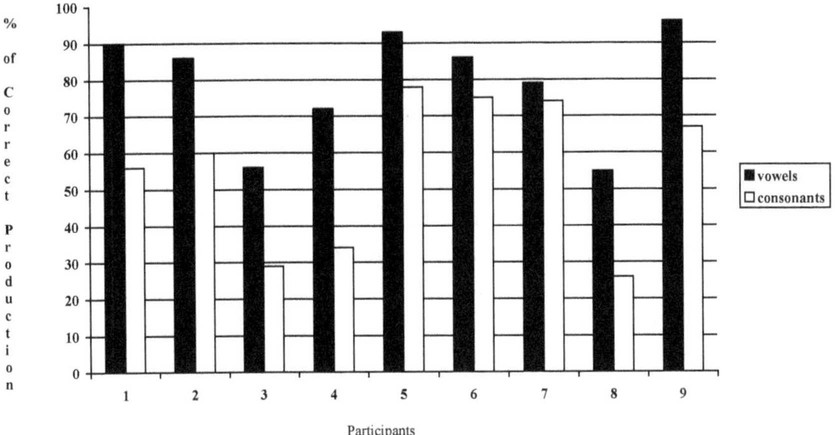

Figure 9.1. Percentage of sC onsets correctly produced after vowels and consonants.

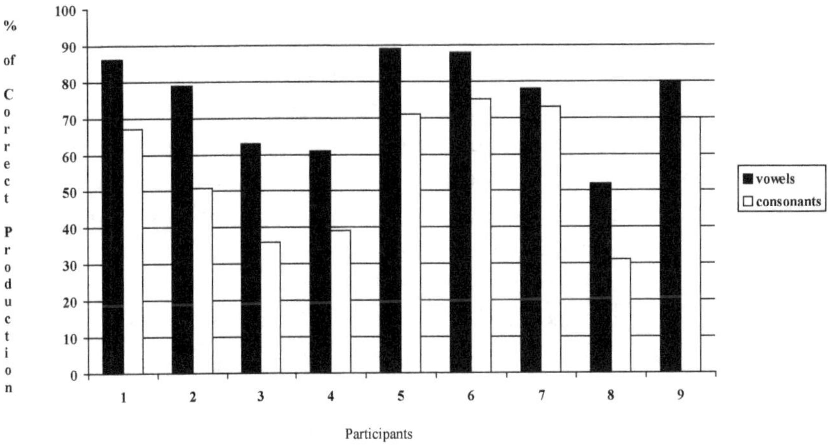

Figure 9.2. Percentage of sCC onsets correctly produced after vowels and consonants.

The results of this study are in accordance with those of the seven previous studies with native Spanish speakers learning either English or Swedish (Abrahamsson 1999; Carlisle 1991a, 1991b, 1992, 1997, 2006; Rauber 2006), but not with those examining the English onset production of native Portuguese speakers (Rebello and Baptista 2006; Rauber 2006). The results of the current study may differ from those of the two previous ones for a number of reasons. First, the data-gathering instrument was different in that it contained two vowels that did not occur in either of the two previous studies with native Portuguese speakers. One of the vowels was word-final schwa which did not induce a single instance of prothesis; the other vowel was /a/ as in the word *saw*, which induced very little prothesis. However, even if those two vowels were eliminated from the current study, consonants still induced a higher frequency of prothesis than did vowels, not the other way around, as was found in the two previous studies.

Another way in which these studies differ is how tightly the onsets were controlled and the amount of data gathered to test the hypotheses. The number of onsets in the current study was limited to six, and they were all highly marked. For example, of all the English sC onsets, /st/, /sp/ and /sk/, are the most marked because they are sonority plateaus (Clements 1990), and all sCC onsets are highly marked because of their length and because the first two consonants also constitute a sonority plateau. In addition, the three sC onsets are not in a markedness relationship to one another and therefore should induce the same frequency of prothesis; the same is true of the three different sCC onsets. Rebello and Baptista (2006) and Rauber (2006) had more goals in their studies and, consequently, used 12 more onsets, many of which are in a markedness relationship and therefore would have induced different frequencies of prothesis. For example, the studies not only tested for onsets by length, they also compared sC onsets whose second members were either obstruents or sonorants. Given the number of contrasts that the two studies examined, and the fact that combined they had little over 3100 items for statistical analysis (fewer than the current study), they may have been too ambitious for the amount of data that was obtained and used for statistical analysis.

Finally, both previous studies examined silence as an environment, which consisted of absolute word-initial position and agreed-upon pauses. The environment of silence accounted for about a quarter of the data used to investigate the influence of environment, which may account for the statistical differences observed. In contrast, the current study examined only word-final consonants and vowels, all instances of silence having been removed from the study.

9.3 Part 2

The results from the first part of this study as well as from the studies previously discussed with native Spanish speakers reveal that word-final vowels and consonants induce significantly different frequencies of prothesis before sC(C) onsets. However, as suggested by Carlisle (1991a) and documented in his 2010 study, the influence of environment is more complex. According to the Sonority Cycle (Clements 1990), word-final demisyllables are in markedness relationships based upon both their length and sonority profile, and as the markedness of the word-final environment decreases, the frequency of correct production increases.

9.3.1 Background

The Sonority Cycle

Clements' Sonority Cycle is a model that accounts for the sonority-based patterns of the syllable margins found in the world's languages. Syllable margins can differ from one another in two ways. The first is length. Descriptive studies of the syllable concur that the CV syllable is the one universally occurring syllable type in languages and consequently regarded as unmarked (Blevins 1995; Clements and Keyser 1983; Greenberg 1978), meaning that the optimal onset consists of a single C and the optimal coda is void. Increases in the length of either margin produce corresponding relative increases in markedness. Research reveals an implicational relationship of margins based on their length (Greenberg 1978). A margin of length n implies the presence of a margin of length n–1 as long as the basic CV pattern remains inviolate, given that the CV syllable is an absolute universal (Greenberg 1978).

Onsets and codas also differ in their sonority profiles, for even though margins may be equal in length, some orders of segments occur much more frequently than others and are therefore less marked; preferred onsets have a consistent rise in sonority from the most peripheral segmental member through the segmental member closest to the nucleus. In turn, preferred codas display a consistent fall in sonority from the segmental member closest to the nucleus through the most peripheral segmental member. Taken together these two patterns comprise the Sonority Sequencing Principle (SSP) (Blevins 1995; Clements 1990; Clements and Keyser 1983; Green 2003; Greenberg 1978; Morelli 2003). Consisting of two principles, Core Syllabification and Feature Dispersion, the Sonority Cycle ranks initial and final demisyllables based on the sonority relationships among their segmental members.

The Core Syllabification Principle (CSP) is essentially a formalized statement of the SSP: Those syllables are preferred that display a constant rise in sonority from the most peripheral member of the onset through the nucleus, and a constant fall in sonority from the nucleus through the most peripheral member of the coda. The CSP creates two broad categories of margins – those that adhere to the SSP and those that do not. Those that do not adhere to the principle consist of sonority plateaus or reversals. Margins violating the CSP are marked in relationship to those that do not, a point reinforced by the observation that all languages having sonority plateaus or reversals also have margins that adhere to the CSP. However, the converse is not true; languages may have only margins that adhere to the CSP – such as Chinese and Spanish. However, the ranking of syllables based upon preferred sonority profiles is much more complex than can be captured by the CSP. As mentioned previously, different margins may adhere to the CSP yet still be in markedness relationships to one another. For example, both glide+obstruent and glide+liquid codas abide by the CSP, yet universally the latter is preferred over the former (Greenberg 1978).

Feature Dispersion – the second principle of the Sonority Cycle – accounts for these preferences by applying only to those strings of segments that adhere to the CSP and ranking them according to preferred sonority profiles. As discussed by Clements (1990), the Feature Dispersion Principle (FDP) applies to demisyllables. Each syllable has two demisyllables, each of which shares the nucleus. The initial demisyllable consists of the onset and the nucleus, and the final demisyllable consists of the nucleus and the coda. Because the nucleus occurs in both demisyllables, the FDP expresses itself in terms of linear rises and falls in sonority. According to Clements (1990: 303), the optimal final demisyllable is one which minimizes the contrast in sonority among its members. In other words, of all the three-member final demisyllables, VGL would be optimal in the world's languages, as demonstrated by assigning a number to the five segmental classes in the sonority scale as shown in (1):

(1)	Classes:	obstruents	<	nasals	<	liquids	<	glides	<	vowels
	Values:	1		2		3		4		5

If the optimal three-member final demisyllable minimizes the contrast in sonority among its members, then it must begin with a vowel (a value of 5), be followed by a glide (a value of 4), and end with a liquid (a value of 3); the distance between each contiguous member is one. Final three-member demisyllables will be increasingly less preferred, the more that their sonority profiles differ from the optimal profile above. In the less preferred VNO demisyllable, the distance between V and N is 3 and the distance between N and O is 1, so the distance between one pair of segments is minimal, but not for the other; this demisyllable therefore has a less preferred sonority profile and consequently a lower value for dispersion. The least preferred final three-member demisyllable is the VLO, having a distance of two between V and L and between L and O. So even though the distance is equal between the two members of the two pairs, neither distance is minimal.

To rank all demisyllables that abide by the CSP, Clements incorporates a formula that assigns a value for dispersion to all margins. The formula considers the number of pairs of segments in each demisyllable and the sonority distance between each pair including all the non-adjacent ones. Clements' formula to calculate dispersion (D) produces rankings for final two-member, three-member and four-member demisyllables. Given that the current study is concerned only with final two-member demisyllables, only their rankings are displayed in (2).

(2) Rankings for final two-member demisyllables

VO	0.06
VN	0.11
VL	0.25
VG	1.00

As shown in (2), final two-member demisyllables are ranked according to their values for D; the higher the value of D the less marked the final demisyllable in each group. The higher the sonority value of the final segment, the more preferred the demisyllable. Thus a VG demisyllable is less marked than any of the other two-member demisyllables, because the distance is minimal between V and G and because G has a higher sonority value than do any of the other segmental categories. Note that a demisyllable consisting of just a V is not on the rankings presented above. Because the optimal syllable is a CV, a final demisyllable consisting of just a V is optimal and preferred over even the most preferred two-member demisyllable, VG.

Previous Research in SLA

Only one study (Carlisle 2010) has examined the idea that the sonority profile of the word-final demisyllable influences the frequency of prothesis before sC(C) onsets. The ordering prediction was that the highest frequency of correct production would occur after the least marked of the five demisyllable environments, V, and that the frequency of correct production would decrease linearly with the markedness of the demisyllables as determined by their D values.

Carlisle (2010) reanalysed data from his 1997 and 2006 studies. The first study originally found that native Spanish speakers used prothesis significantly more frequently after consonants than after vowels for both sC

Table 9.6. Mean correct production of sC and sCC onsets after five word-final demisyllables: VO, VN, VL, VG and V (based on Carlisle 1997).

	Target Onsets	
Environment	sC	sCC
VO	0.483	0.402
VN	0.600	0.455
VL	0.597	0.557
VG	0.670	0.523
V	0.729	0.619

onsets and sCC onsets. Table 9.6 displays the frequency with which the two target onsets were correctly produced after the five demisyllable environments. As displayed in the table, the frequencies of correct production triggered by the five environments before sC onsets were nearly perfectly linear, and their differences produced a significant main effect for environment. Before sCC onsets the mean frequencies of correct production triggered by the five environments displayed the same degree of linearity, and again their differences resulted in a significant main effect for environment.

To determine if the between mean differences were linear and significant, two contrast tests were calculated as a post hoc analysis. The prediction of linearity was violated once for each onset. Before the sC onsets VL (0.597) induced a lower amount of correct production than did VN (0.600). Before sCC onsets VG induced a lower amount of correct production than did VL, 0.523 to 0.557. In spite of these single violations of the predicted order, both contrast tests were significant.

Carlisle (2006) originally found that native Spanish speakers used prothesis significantly more frequently after consonants than after vowels before three sC onsets: sl-, sn- and st-. Table 9.7 indicates the frequencies with

Table 9.7. Correct production of sl-, sn- and st- after five word-final demisyllables: vO, VN, VL, VG and V (based on Carlisle 2006).

	Target Onsets		
Environment	sl-	sn-	st-
VO	0.511	0.446	0.314
VN	0.575	0.478	0.428
VL	0.704	0.655	0.411
VG	0.639	0.550	0.488
V	0.793	0.692	0.624

which the three onsets were correctly produced after the five demisyllable environments; in all three cases the differences among the means produced a significant main effect for environment.

Again, to test for the predicted linearity, three contrast tests were calculated. The expected linear order was violated once before sl-, where VG induced a lower frequency of correct production than did VL; the contrast test of linearity was significant. A single violation of the predicted linear pattern also occurred before sn-; again VG induced a lower frequency of correct production than did VL. Nevertheless, the result for the contrast test was significant. Finally, a single violation in linearity also occurred before st- where VL induced a lower frequency of correct production than did VN. Nevertheless, the contrast test was also significant.

Using the same data as discussed in Part 1, the following study specifically examines whether the frequency of prothesis before sC(C) onsets differs after four final two-member demisyllables that are ranked according to their D value from the least marked to the most marked: VG, VL, VN and VO [see (2)]. In addition, the study examines the frequency of prothesis after the one-member final demisyllable, V. The specific prediction is that as the markedness of the five word-final demisyllables increases, the frequency of the correct production of the target word-initial onsets decreases as measured by the amount of prothesis.

9.3.2 Analysis

The analysis began with the calculation of 5 x 1 ANOVAs with repeated measures, the five demisyllable environments being the independent variables, and the frequency of correct production being the dependent variable. Two ANOVAs were calculated, one for sC onsets and the other for sCC onsets. In addition, contrast tests for each of the target onsets were also calculated as a post hoc analysis.

Unlike most post hoc tests, contrast tests not only take the differences of means into account, but also any predicted ordering effects. The current study predicted a particular ordering effect: that for each onset the frequency of correct production would be determined by the sonority of the five preceding demisyllable environments. That is, for each onset the lowest frequency of correct production would occur after VO, followed by VN, VL, VG and V.

9.3.3 Results

Table 9.8 displays the frequency with which the two target onsets were correctly produced after the five demisyllable environments. For sC onsets the frequencies of correct production after VO, VN, VL, VG and V were 0.509, 0.670, 0.648, 0.798 and 0.800 respectively. These differences produced a significant main effect for environment: $F(4,32)=13.776$, $p<0.007$. For sCC onsets the mean frequencies of correct production from VO to V were 0.520, 0.702, 0.690, 0.733 and 0.756, differences resulting in a significant main effect: $F(4,32)=13.526$, $p<0.007$.

To determine if the between mean differences were linear and significant, two contrast tests were calculated as a post hoc analysis. The prediction of linearity was violated once for each onset. Before the sC onsets VL (0.648) induced a lower amount of correct production than did VN (0.670). Similarly, before sCC onsets VL induced a lower amount of correct production than did VN, 0.690 to 0.702. In spite of these single violations of the predicted order, both contrast tests were significant: $F(1,8)=26.754$, $p<0.001$ for sC onsets and $F(1,8)=34.586$, $p<0.0001$ for sCC onsets.

As was true with Part 1, the results for Part 2 of this study are in complete accordance with previous research, which found a significant linear relationship between the D values of word-final demisyllables and the frequency of the correct production of word-initial complex onsets (Carlisle 2010); as the markedness of environments increases as measured by D values, the frequency of correct production of the target onsets decreases. Ten different contrast tests (eight with data from native Spanish speakers and two with native Portuguese speakers) have produced significant results for the pattern described above and this substantiates the claim that environments can be in markedness relationships just as variables can, and less marked environments will induce a higher frequency of target variants than will more marked environments.

Table 9.8. Mean correct production of sC and sCC onsets after five word-final demisyllables: VO, VN, VL, VG and V.

	Target Onsets	
Environment	sC	sCC
VO	0.509	0.520
VN	0.670	0.702
VL	0.648	0.690
VG	0.798	0.733
V	0.800	0.756

9.3.4 Discussion

Carlisle (1997) suggested that the lower frequency of prosthesis after word-final vowels than after word-final consonants might be attributed to the resyllabification of the word-initial extrasyllabic consonant /s/ to the preceding word-final vowel as in (3).

(3) a. hi.#s.pok
    b. hi#s.pok (after resyllabification)

In (3a) *he spoke* contains an extrasyllabic consonant for native speakers of both Spanish and Portuguese. Because extrasyllabic consonants must be incorporated into a syllable, the L2 learners resyllabify them with the preceding word-final vowels, a process that must be variable because even after some vowels, native speakers of Spanish and Portuguese will sometimes use prothesis. Carlisle (1997) originally based this suggestion on the work of Harris (1983), which displayed that Spanish has prosodic resyllabification as in (4).

(4) a. los.#s.ku.dos
    b. los.#es.ku.dos (after prothesis and resyllabification)
    c. lo.s#es.ku.dos (after prosodic resyllabification)

As illustrated in (4a) the underlying representation of *los escudos* contains an extrasyllabic consonant, which triggers a prothetic vowel to which the extrasyllabic consonant resyllabifies as in (4b). Prosodic resyllabification may then apply, which results in the creation of a syllable (.s#es.), which crosses a word boundary (4c). This same process is also evident in Brazilian Portuguese.

If native Spanish speakers use prosodic resyllabification in their production of English, then a natural explanation occurs for the more frequent use of prothesis after consonants than after vowels as shown in (5) for *Mike spoke.*

(5) a. majk.#s.pok
    b. majk.#es.pok (after epenthesis and resyllabification)
    c. maj.k#es.pok (after prosodic resyllabification)

As thoroughly discussed by Carlisle (1997), the proposal that native speakers of Spanish are using prosodic resyllabification depends on the assumption that they are transferring that rule into the interlanguage. Fortunately, there is a lot of evidence that L2 learners transfer rules from the L1 into the interlanguage, especially rules that affect syllabification. Broselow (1984) found that native speakers of English learning Arabic resyllabified Arabic syllable structure so that it conformed to English syllable structure conditions. Broselow (1983) found the same tendency among native speakers of Arabic learning English. The tendency was so strong that Broselow proposed the Syllable Structure Transfer Hypothesis.

Further evidence for the transferring of rules that affect syllable structure come from all the studies that have examined the modification of SC(C) onsets by native speakers of Portuguese and Spanish. In both languages, SC(C) onsets are disallowed by syllable structure conditions, and speakers modify them by prothesis, which then induces resyllabification. When native speakers of Portuguese and Spanish learn a language that has SC(C) onsets such as English and Swedish, they transfer the same rule of prothesis into the interlanguage (Abrahamsson 1999; Carlisle, 1991a, 1991b, 1992, 1997, 1998, 2002, 2006; Carlisle and Cutillas Espinsa 2015; Major 1996, 2001; Rauber 2006; Rebello and Baptista 2006).

The above discussion may explain why prothesis occurs more frequently after word-final consonants than after word-final vowels. However, in addition to examining the influence of word-final vowels, the current study examined four word-final two-member demisyllables in a markedness relationship [see (2)]; each of the four ended in a segmental class that differed from the others in sonority, and the results showed a significant effect for these differences: the greater the sonority of the last segment in the two-member word-final demisyllable, the lower the frequency of prothesis. This difference in the frequency of prothesis may have been caused by the native speakers of Portuguese resyllabifying the extrasyllabic consonant to the last segment of the preceding word as shown in (6) for *boy spoke.*[4]

(6) a. boj.#s.pok
 b. boj#s.pok (resyllabification without prothesis)

The word *boy* ends in a glide which is highly sonorant, the most sonorant class after vowels. As seen in (6), the resyllabification eliminates the onset that violates Portuguese syllable structure conditions and creates a word-final demisyllable of VGO, which is tied with VNO as the least marked final three-member demisyllable ending in an obstruent [see (7)].

4 My appreciation to Niclas Abrahamsson for pointing out this possible explanation for the different frequencies of prothesis.

(7) Rankings for final three-member demisyllables ending in an obstruent
VLO 0.56
VNO, VGO 1.17

As displayed in (2), the other demisyllables in the markedness hierarchy end in a liquid, nasal and obstruent, each descending in sonority and becoming more marked; in fact, VOO is not even on Clements' scale because it contains a sonority plateau, making it more marked than any of the other three-member demisyllables ending in an obstruent. If the native Portuguese speakers were to resyllabify the extrasyllabic consonant to the preceding word-final sound, the resulting word-final demisyllables would be VLO, VNO and VOO, all of which (with the exception of VNO) are more marked than VGO.

However, even if the participants were not resyllabifying the word-initial /s/ with the last segment of the preceding word, the sonority profile of the word-final demisyllable may influence the production of the word-initial variable. Phonologists have long realized that the greater the sonority of the last segment of a word, the more preferred it is (Hooper 1976). With great consistency, languages display a preference for higher sonority in the word-final position than in word-initial position, resulting in a natural rhythm of higher to lower sonority across word boundaries. L2 learners are always caught between the tensions of language preferences, and the demands of the L2. If the L2 contains syllable structure conditions not found in the L1, it would be expected that the L2 learners would have greater facility producing the target structures in less marked environments. In the case of the current study, the word-initial variable was more successfully produced after less marked environments in a markedness hierarchy.

9.4 Conclusion

Germanic languages such as English, Swedish and German generally have sC(C) onsets. In contrast, the Romance languages, Spanish and Portuguese, do not. Given that sC(C) onsets are in a markedness hierarchy, the production of native speakers of Spanish and Portuguese learning Germanic languages provides the opportunity to examine the influence of syllable universals in SLA, and previous research with native Spanish speakers learning either English or Swedish has revealed that less marked onsets are modified significantly less frequently than are more marked onsets

(Abrahamsson 1999; Carlisle 1991b, 1992, 1997, 1998, 2002, 2006, 2010; Carlisle and Cutillas Espinsa 2015; Rauber 2006). In addition, word-final demisyllables are also in a markedness hierarchy, so again the influence of environments in markedness relationships on the production of sC(C) onsets can be examined with native speakers of Spanish and Portuguese learning a Germanic language. Results from this study and Carlisle (2010) have revealed that prothesis occurs less frequently after less marked word-final environments than those that are more marked. Markedness thus plays a crucial role in the acquisition of a second language phonology.

References

Abrahamsson, N. (1999). Vowel epenthesis of /sC(C)/ onsets in Spanish/Swedish interphonology: A longitudinal study. *Language Learning* 49: 473–508.

Abrahamsson, N. (2003). Universal constraints on L2 coda production: The case of Chinese/Swedish interphonology. In S. Giannini and L. Costamagna (eds.), *Interlanguage Phonology: Strategies and Tactics*, 131–62. Milan, Italy: Franco Angeli.

Anderson, J. (1987). The markedness differential hypothesis and syllable structure difficulty. In G. Ioup and S. Weinberger (eds.), *Interlanguage Phonology: The Acquisition of a Second Language Sound System*, 279–91. Cambridge, MA: Newbury House.

Andersen, R. (1978). An implicational model for second language research. *Language Learning* 28: 221–81.

Bayley, R. (1996). Competing constraints on variation in the speech of Chinese learners of English. In R. Bayley and D. Preston (eds.), *Second Language Acquisition and Linguistic Variation*, 97–120. Amsterdam: John Benjamins.

Benson, B. (1988). Universal preference for the open syllable as an independent process in interlanguage phonology. *Language Learning* 38: 221–42.

Blevins, J. (1995). The syllable in phonological theory. In J. Goldsmith (ed.), *The Handbook of Phonological Theory*, 206–44. Cambridge, MA: Blackwell.

Broselow, E. (1983). Non-obvious transfer: On predicting epenthesis errors. In S. Gass and L. Selinker (eds.), *Language Transfer in Language Learning*, 269–80. Rowley, MA: Newbury House.

Broselow, E. (1984). An investigation of transfer in second language phonology. *International Review of Applied Linguistics* 22: 253–69.

Carlisle, R. (1991a). The influence of environment on vowel epenthesis in Spanish/English interphonology. *Applied Linguistics* 12: 76–95.

Carlisle, R. (1991b). The influence of syllable structure universals on the variability of interlanguage phonology. In A.D. Volpe (ed.), *The Seventeenth LACUS Forum 1990*, 135–45. Lake Bluff, IL: Linguistic Association of Canada and the United States.

Carlisle, R. (1992). Environment and markedness as interacting constraints on vowel epenthesis. In J. Leather and A. James (eds.), *New Sounds 92*, 64–75. Amsterdam: University of Amsterdam Press.

Carlisle, R. (1997). The modification of onsets in a markedness relationship: Testing the interlanguage structural conformity hypothesis. *Language Learning* 47: 327–61.

Carlisle, R. (1998). The acquisition of onsets in a markedness relationship: A longitudinal study. *Studies in Second Language Acquisition* 20: 245–60.

Carlisle, R. (2002). The acquisition of two and three member onsets: Time III of a longitudinal study. In A. James and J. Leather (eds.), *New Sounds 2000*, 42–7. Klagenfurt, Austria: University of Klagenfurt Press.

Carlisle, R. (2006). The sonority cycle and the acquisition of complex onsets. In B. Baptista and A. Watkins (eds.), *English with a Latin Beat: Studies in Portuguese/Spanish-English Interphonology*, 105–37. Amsterdam: John Benjamins.

Carlisle, R. (2010). Word-final sonority as an environmental constraint on prothesis. In A. Rauber, M. Watkins, R. Silveira and R. Koerich (eds.), *The Acquisition of Second Language Speech: Studies in Honor of Professor Barbara O. Baptista*, 243–66. Santa Catarina: Universidade Federal de Santa Catarina.

Carlisle, R. and Cutillas Espinosa, J.A. (2015). The production of /.sC/ onsets in a markedness relationship: Investigating the ontogeny phylogeny model with longitudinal data. In M. Yavaş (ed.), *Unusual Productions in Phonology: Universals and Language-Specific Considerations*, 183–205. New York: Psychology Press.

Clements, G. (1990). The role of the sonority cycle in core syllabification. In J. Kingston and M. Beckman (eds.), *Papers in Laboratory Phonology I: Between the Grammar and Physics of Speech*, 283–333. Cambridge: Cambridge University Press.

Clements, G. and Keyser, S. (1983). *CV Phonology: A Generative Theory of the Syllable*. Cambridge, MA: The MIT Press.

Dickerson, L. (1975). The learner's interlanguage as a system of variable rules. *TESOL Quarterly* 9: 401–7.

Dickerson, L. and Dickerson, W. (1977). Interlanguage phonology: current research and future directions. In S.P. Corder and E. Roulet (eds.), *Interlanguages and Pidgins and their Relationship to Second Language Pedagogy*, 18–29. Neuchatel: Libraire Droz.

Dickerson, W. (1976). The psycholinguistic unity of language learning and language change. *Language Learning* 26: 215–31.

Green, A.D. (2003). Extrasyllabic consonants and onset well-formedness. In C. Fery and R. van de Vijver (eds.), *The Syllable in Optimality Theory*, 238–253. Cambridge: Cambridge University Press.

Greenberg, J. (1978). Some generalizations concerning initial and final consonant clusters. In J. Greenberg, C. Ferguson and E. Moravcsik (eds.), *Universals of Human Language*, Vol. 2, 243–79. Stanford, CA: Stanford University Press.

Harris, J. (1983). *Syllable Structure and Stress in Spanish: A Non-Linear Analysis*. Cambridge, MA: The MIT Press.

Hooper, J. (1976). *An Introduction to Natural Generative Phonology*. New York: Academic Press.

Labov, W. (1966). *The Social Stratification of English in New York City*. Washington, DC: Center for Applied Linguistics.

Labov, W. (1969). Contraction, deletion, and inherent variability of the English copula. *Language*, 45: 715–62.

Major, R. (1996). Markedness in second language acquisition of consonant clusters. In Dennis R. Preston and Robert Bayley (eds.), *Variation and Second Language Acquisition*, 75–96. Amsterdam: John Benjamins.

Major, R. (2001). *Foreign Accent: The Ontogeny and Phylogeny of Second Language Phonology*. Mahwah, NJ: Lawrence Erlbaum Associates.

Morelli, F. (2003). The relative harmony of /s+stop/ onsets: Obstruent clusters and the sonority sequencing principle. In C. Fery and R. van de Vijver (eds.), *The Syllable in Optimality Theory*, 356–71. Cambridge, Cambridge University Press.

Rauber, A. (2006). Production of English initial /s/-clusters by speakers of Brazilian Portuguese and Argentine Spanish. In B. Baptista and A. Watkins (eds.), *English with a Latin Beat: Studies in Portuguese/Spanish-English Interphonology*, 155–67. Amsterdam: John Benjamins.

Rebello, J. and Baptista, B. (2006). The influence of voicing on the production of initial /s/-clusters by Brazilian learners. In B. Baptista and A. Watkins (eds.), *English with a Latin Beat: Studies in Portuguese/Spanish-English Interphonology*, 139–54. Amsterdam: John Benjamins.

Tarone, E. (1980). Some influences on the syllable structure of interlanguage phonology. *IRAL* 18: 139–52.

Wolfram, W. (1969). *A Sociolinguistic Description of Detroit Negro Speech*. Washington, DC: Center for Applied Linguistics.

Wolfram, W. (1973). *Sociolinguistic Aspects of Assimilation: Puerto Rican English in New York City*. Arlington, VA: Center for Applied Linguistics.

Wolfram, W. (1985). Variability in tense marking: A case for the obvious. *Language Learning* 35: 229–53.

Wolfram, W. and Christian, D. (1976). *Appalachian Speech*. Arlington, VA: Center for Applied Linguistics.

Robert Carlisle is Professor in the Department of English at the California State University, Bakersfield.

10
Medial Coda and Final Stops in Brazilian Portuguese-English Contact

Paul John and Walcir Cardoso

10.1 Introduction

This study investigates the acquisition of English stops by Brazilian Portuguese (BP) speakers in the language contact situation of Montreal. The difficulties BP speakers of English have are not with the stops per se, since the same set /p t k b d g/ appears in both the BP and English phoneme inventories. The problem concerns their context of occurrence: in BP, stops occur only in onsets, whereas in English they appear additionally in *medial coda* and in *word-final* position. BP permits only a restricted set of consonants in these sites: /s l r N/. That is, in medial coda and final position, BP allows sonorants and, among obstruents, the coronal fricative /s/, to the exclusion of oral stops. When BP speakers encounter stops such as /p/ and /k/ in *cha<u>p</u>ter* or *do<u>c</u>tor* (medial coda) and *bisho<u>p</u>* or *magi<u>c</u>* (word-final), the tendency is to employ a process of i-epenthesis which permits the stops to be realized as onsets: *cha*[pi]*ter*, *do*[ki]*ter*, *bisho*[pi], *magi*[ki] (Major 1986). This epenthetic process is likewise instantiated in the L1 as a means of repairing illicit medial clusters in native words (e.g. *pacto*→*pa*[ki]*to*) and final stops in loans (e.g. *chic*→*chi*[ki]) (Cantoni and Cristófaro Silva 2008; Cristófaro Silva and Almeida 2008; Nevins 2008).[1] The occurrence

1 This is why we state that BP permits stops only in onsets. That is, the restriction is surface-true. Assuming syllable-structure to be represented underlyingly, it is always possible that stops such as the /k/ in *pacto* are at first syllabified as codas but then resyllabified as onsets via i-epenthesis. Nonetheless, it is also possible that so-called epenthetic [i] is in fact part of the UR (Cantoni and Cristófaro Silva 2008), in which case these stops never occupy a coda.

of i-epenthesis in interlanguage can thus be attributed straightforwardly to transfer.

What is not so straightforward is whether i-epenthesis in the two locations constitutes a unified process. The consensus view is to analyse medial /p/ and /k/ in *chapter* and *doctor* as codas, in which case i-epenthesis leads to resyllabification of the coda as an onset (e.g. do/k./tor→*do*[.ki.]*tor*). Regarding final /p/ and /k/ in *bishop* and *magic*, however, two opposing views have been expressed: either these are codas (the orthodox view – Blevins 1995; Selkirk 1982) or else they are onsets of empty nuclei (the view from Government Phonology – Harris and Gussmann 1998; Kaye 1990). Under the orthodox view, i-epenthesis is a unified process: in both *do*[ki]*tor* and *magi*[ki], i-epenthesis permits a coda stop to be resyllabified as an onset. Under the Government Phonology view, i-epenthesis serves two purposes: coda resyllabification in word-medial *do*[ki]*tor*, but the phonetic realization of the empty nucleus in word-final *magi*[ki].

To complicate matters, Piggott (1999) proposes a combination of the two previous views such that, depending on the language, final consonants can be syllabified either as codas or as onsets of empty nuclei. This is the position that we will be adopting in our investigation of BP-English contact.

Among the means for determining which syllabification a given language adopts, a simple measure involves the distribution of consonants in the two locations: a language that restricts final consonants to the same set as medial codas syllabifies final consonants as codas. This is the case for BP, which permits only the canonical coda consonants /s r l N/ in final position, the same set that appears in medial coda position. Conversely, a language with a mismatch between the set of final consonants and medial codas would syllabify the former as onsets of empty nuclei. English allows all consonants in its inventory except /h/ in final position, whereas medial codas are restricted to /p k f s m n ŋ l r/ (see Harris and Gussmann 1998). Consequently, English would syllabify final consonants as onsets, whereas BP would syllabify them as codas. The central purpose of the present study is to establish, via data from the developing BP ESL interlanguage system, whether this analysis is well founded.

Under our analysis, BP speakers are faced with a dual challenge when they learn English: (i) they need to expand the set of medial codas to include (among other consonants) the oral stops /p k/; and (ii) they need to acquire the novel prosodic representation of final consonants, including /p k/, as onsets of empty nuclei. Assuming that the challenge is indeed twofold, we anticipate differential acquisition of medial coda and final /p k/. To explain, under the orthodox view, BP speakers should acquire medial coda and final stops in tandem, since these have the same syllabic affiliation; under our view, we expect medial coda and final stops to be acquired separately, since different prosodic representations are involved. The central goal of our study is thus to establish whether BP speakers exhibit for the two locations simultaneous or differential acquisition of /p k/ (the only oral stops appearing in both contexts – see Harris and Gussmann 1998), with acquisition involving variable suppression of the transfer process of i-epenthesis. The findings provide invaluable evidence to determine the syllabification of final consonants.

Our study was carried out in the language contact context of BP speakers living in Montreal (Quebec), Canada, where there is access to native and L2 speakers of English in social contexts, in education (schools, universities), in the workplace, and in shops and other businesses. Such bilingual contact contexts are particularly conducive to acquisition of an L2 sound system for a number of reasons. Since the advent of the Internet, L2 learners in a non-contact context such as Brazil have considerable opportunity for exposure to spoken input, so mere degree of contact with the L2 is probably not the key point of difference. Rather, what distinguishes the contact context is the ability to interact with others in the target language. Interaction with native or native-like speakers is qualitatively different from the more passive L2 input coming from electronic media. In interactions, there is the possibility for various types of feedback on errors in the L2 speaker's output. Indirect feedback can occur when L2 speakers note that listeners have misunderstood their speech. The speakers might then realize that the breakdown in communication stems from mispronunciations that make their spoken output unintelligible (e.g. by neutralizing contrasts, thus generating homophones). Interlocutors may also provide direct feedback, for example in the form of recasts, negative reactions to mispronunciations (especially more salient and stigmatized ones) or explicit (even metalinguistic) comments on error. Motivation to progress is surely greater in a context where errors are noticed and commented on negatively. Progress is likewise enhanced through interaction since L2 speakers may request repetitions or clarifications of an interlocutor whose speech diverges in some way from their own. In brief, the potential for progress in a contact situation is inherently greater than in a foreign language context. For example, in Brazil, pronunciation errors are more likely to be tolerated (if they are noticed) or even reinforced since the majority of those around (fellow students and possibly the teacher) are generating the same inaccurate output. Given this line of thinking, we may expect BP speakers in the context of Montreal to make considerable progress in suppressing the phenomenon of i-epenthesis after medial coda and final stops.

The goal of our study, then, is to determine whether BP speakers exhibit differential acquisition of /p/ and /k/. To reiterate, the core issue is that if our participants show simultaneous acquisition of stops in the two contexts under study, our hypothesis of a distinct prosodic representation for medial coda and final stops will be falsified. In the next section, we present a review of the literature on i-epenthesis by BP speakers of English, as well as a more in-depth account of the phonological debate concerning the syllabification of final consonants. The subsequent method section presents the study we carried out to test our hypothesis of differential acquisition. This includes the profile of our Montreal BP-speaker participants, the tasks they performed and our quantitative data analysis via Goldvarb X (Sankoff, Tagliamonte and Smith 2005). The results are then presented and discussed based on our interpretations of the findings.

10.2 Background

For our purposes, the crucial observation concerning research on i-epenthesis in BP interlanguage is that most previous studies have not examined epenthesis following medial coda consonants, only following final consonants (but for certain exceptions see e.g. Baptista and Silva Filho 2007; Huf and Alves 2010; Schneider and Schwindt 2010). This limited focus is essentially due to the prevailing assumption that consonants in both contexts are codas – i.e. they bear the same prosodic status. Under this assumption, there is no reason to anticipate differential behaviour, so whatever holds for final consonants should also apply to medial codas. In due course, we will discuss arguments against this orthodox assumption, but to start with, we summarize the key findings of research carried out to date.

First, previous research has found that final voiceless stops are acquired before their voiced counterparts: ptk>bdg (Baptista and Silva Filho 1997), indicating that BP speakers are less likely to epenthesize after voiceless stops. This finding accords well with the observation that many unrelated languages instantiate a process of final obstruent devoicing (see Brockhaus 1995, on German; Gussmann 1992, on Polish; Mascaró 1987, on Catalan; and Yavaş 1994, for an overview of devoicing in interlanguage). Voiced obstruents are thus more marked in final position, triggering higher rates of epenthetic vowel repair. Next, final coronal stops are acquired before non-coronal stops: td>pbkg (Cardoso 2007). The lower rate of epenthesis following coronal stops reflects the universal tendency for coronal place to be unmarked (Paradis and Prunet 1991). This finding is also interesting partly because /t d/ are precisely the stops that do not occur in medial codas in English (Harris 1994; Harris and Gussmann 1998). In addition, stops at the end of bi-/polysyllabic words such as *attack* are acquired before those in monosyllabic words such as *pack: attack>pack* (Cardoso 2007). The higher rates of epenthesis in monosyllabic words indicates the presence of a Word Minimality Constraint (McCarthy and Prince 1993) requiring forms to be minimally disyllabic (or, from the perspective that *pack* ends in an empty nucleus, to have two phonetically realized syllables). Since the effects of this constraint are not observable in the L1 nor in the target language, the phenomenon constitutes an example of the Emergence of the Unmarked in interlanguage (Broselow, Chen and Wang 1998; McCarthy and Prince 1994).

Finally, in one of the few studies to venture beyond absolute final consonants, Huf and Alves (2010) found penultimate stops in final clusters to be acquired before strictly final stops: *tact>tack* (i.e. the /k/ in *tact* triggers lower rates of epenthesis than the /k/ in *tack*). The authors consider final consonants and final clusters as singleton and complex codas respectively. Hence, in their view, initial stops in final coda clusters are acquired before truly final codas. Under the Government Phonology view, however, final consonant clusters in English monomorphemes like *tact* are all coda-onset sequences. From this perspective, the study thus gives an indication that we may be on the right track in anticipating in our own study that medial codas are acquired before final consonants.

As suggested earlier, the primary reason previous researchers have neglected to compare epenthesis rates for medial coda and final consonants appears to be that medial stops such as /p k/ in *chapter* or *doctor* and final /p k/ in *bishop* or *magic* are thought to share the same prosodic representation: in both contexts, the stops are conventionally syllabified as codas. While a coda analysis is relatively uncontroversial for /p k/ in *chapter* and *doctor* (though see Lowenstamm 1996 and Scheer 2004), the syllabification of final consonants such as /p k/ in *bishop* and *magic*, as we indicated earlier, is open to debate. Two opposing views on final consonants can be encountered in the literature: either these are codas, which is the orthodox view (e.g. Blevins 1995; Selkirk 1982); or else they are onsets of empty nuclei, which is the view from Government Phonology (e.g. Harris and Gussmann 1998; Kaye 1990). The opposing analyses are illustrated below for the final /k/ in *magi*[k]: (1a) shows /k/ as a coda (Co), whereas (1b) shows /k/ syllabified as an onset (O) of an empty nucleus (N) (i.e. a nucleus devoid of segmental content, as shown).

Under the analysis in (1a), we expect medial coda and final /p k/ to be acquired together, since expansion of the set of coda consonants to include /p k/ should make them simultaneously available in words such as *do*[k]*tor* and *magi*[k] (that is, assuming the /k/ in *magi*[k] to be a coda). Under the analysis in (1b), which we hypothesize to be the correct one, it is anticipated that medial coda and final /p k/ are acquired at different rates, since separate syllabic affiliations are involved. Indeed, we may even predict that final /p k/ are acquired after medial coda /p k/, since only the former requires acquisition of a novel prosodic representation, namely empty nuclei (1b). Hence, the following order of acquisition is predicted: *cha*[p]*ter, do*[k]*tor*>*bisho*[p], *magi*[k].

The reasons for analysing final consonants as onsets of empty nuclei have been amply illustrated in the Government Phonology literature (Charette 1991; Harris 1994; Harris and Gussmann 1998; Kaye 1990), so we will not review them here. Nonetheless, it is worthwhile to consider three measures that point to final consonants having a distinct syllabic affiliation from medial codas in English. These measures are revealing since they do not apply to final consonants in BP. The conclusion we draw from this observation is that while final consonants are onsets of empty nuclei in English, they are codas in native BP (as in Piggott 1999).

First, there is a mismatch in English between the sets of consonants that appear in final and in medial coda position. In final position, English allows /p b t d k g f v θ ð s z ʃ ʒ tʃ dʒ m n ŋ l r/, that is, any consonant in the inventory except /h/. In medial coda position, the set is more restricted: /p k f s m n ŋ l r/, that is, only voiceless obstruents and, among the stops specifically, only non-coronals.[2] Interestingly, the set of final consonants is identical

2 Some may dispute the accuracy of this set, pointing to heterosyllabic medial clusters with initial voiced stops such as /b/ in *ob.solete* and /g/ in *ig.nite*, in addition to the coronal stops /t/ in *at.las* and /d/ in *kid.ney*. Nonetheless, such exceptions often contain a morpheme boundary (in which case they are morpheme-final) or else they fail to exhibit the level or falling sonority cline displayed by bona fide coda-onset sequences such as /k.t/ in *actor* and /n.d/

to the set of consonants appearing in word-internal onsets of unstressed syllables, an observation entirely consistent with an onset parse for final consonants. The same cannot be said of BP. In this language, an identical set of consonants is found in final and medial coda position, namely /s l r/ and the placeless nasal /N/. This distribution points to a coda parse for final consonants in BP.

Second, leaving aside clusters that arise due to suffixation, word-final consonant sequences in English are essentially limited to pairs of consonants that are also found word-internally in coda-onset sequences: hence, rt#, mp# or kt#, for example, are instantiated, but the reverse sequences *tr#, *pm# or *tk# are not. One explanation for this phonotactic restriction is, of course, that final clusters *are* coda-onset sequences in English. BP, on the other hand, does not generally allow final clusters. Only singleton consonants occur word-finally, a pattern which is again consistent with a coda parse for final consonants in this language.[3]

The third measure that leads to an onset analysis for final consonants in English concerns vowel length. Before final singleton consonants, any vowel in the inventory may occur, including long vowels and diphthongs. Before medial codas, however, usually only the set of short vowels is permitted (exceptions are limited to the coronal codas /s l n/, which do permit preceding long vowels or diphthongs, as in *pas̲.try, shoul̲.der* and *coun̲.sel*). The reason for this restriction on vowel length is that rhymes under most circumstances contain maximally two positions: either a long vowel or a short vowel plus singleton coda. If final consonants are onsets of empty nuclei, this would explain the ability of the preceding nucleus to freely harbour both short and long vowels. In BP, the same set of short vowels /i e ɛ a u o ɔ/ appears before final and medial coda consonants, although exceptionally diphthongs may also appear before /s/ or /N/ in both contexts. The inability for diphthongs to appear before final /l r/ is illustrated by disyllabic [xa.uw] *Raul* (compare with [paw.lu] *Paulo*) and trisyllabic [awda.ix] *Aldair* (compare with [kaj.ɾu] *Cairo*). For examples of diphthongs that are permitted exceptionally before /s/ or /N/, however, see [majs] *mais* 'more' and [pãw] *pão* 'bread'.

---

in *tinder*. As a consequence, Government Phonology analyses these as word-internal onsets of empty nuclei. The only consonants that unequivocally occupy a medial coda in English are thus those in the set proposed: /p k f s m n ŋ l r/.

3 Exceptionally, final clusters involving /s/ as in *biceps* and *thorax* are nonetheless permitted in BP, a fact which is consistent with the special status of /s/ in clusters in general.

In sum, according to these three measures, final consonants have an onset profile in English, but a coda profile in BP.[4] If this analysis is accurate, we can well imagine the learning challenge that acquisition of English final consonants such as /p k/ represents for BP speakers. In order to acquire English medial coda /p k/, BP speakers need only to expand the set of segments permitted in coda position to include these stops. However, to acquire final /p k/, they need to develop the novel syllabification of final consonants as onsets of empty nuclei. Since the consonant clusters that occur in BP can all be analysed as either branching onsets or as coda-onset sequences, there is no reason to posit empty nuclei anywhere in phonological representations. The challenge of acquiring final consonants in English, assuming these are indeed onsets of empty nuclei, is thus particularly elevated.

Based on this analysis, we thus hypothesize that BP speakers should exhibit differential acquisition of medial coda and final stops. The next section outlines the methodology for testing this hypothesis.

10.3 Method

The study adopts a variationist approach for data collection and analysis (e.g. Labov 2001; see Cardoso 2011 and John and Cardoso 2008 for the adoption of this approach in L2 acquisition data). To test whether medial coda and final /p k/ are acquired at different rates or simultaneously, data were collected from 18 BP adults living in Montreal, a bilingual French/English-speaking city. Among the participants, 8 speakers showed no instances of i-epenthesis, so they had apparently already acquired medial coda and final /p k/, possibly due to extended contact with English in Montreal. Consequently, we will be reporting only on the remaining 10 participants who did show i-epenthesis. These participants ranged in age from 23 to 31 years, with one 64-year-old participant. Eight of the participants had benefited from contact with English in Montreal from 1 to 4 years, while the remaining participants, with 10 and (for the 64-year-old) 18 years in Montreal, had benefited even more extensively from English contact.

4 Nonetheless, see Segundo (1993) for arguments (based on stress assignment) that final consonants in BP may in fact also be onsets of empty nuclei rather than codas.

Participants self-reported their proficiency level as beginner (3 participants), intermediate (6) or advanced (1).[5] They also self-reported 20–90% daily use of English. Even at the 20% level, such daily use is quite substantial, so they were clearly taking advantage of the language contact situation in Montreal.

Three tasks were employed to elicit spoken data: (i) real-word elicitation, (ii) non-word repetition and (iii) non-word reading aloud. For the real-word elicitation task, participants saw an image on a computer screen (e.g. a picture of a doctor) and, based on this image, verbally completed the blank in a carrier sentence (e.g. *This man is a* ___). All of the words were fairly high frequency and thus expected to be familiar to participants. Nonetheless, as preparation, the task was preceded by a training session during which the same images were shown on successive PowerPoint slides, accompanied by a recorded identification by a native speaker of English (e.g. *Doctor. This man is a doctor*). The purpose of the training session was both to remind participants of the lexical items in question and to set up an association between the word and image, thus facilitating their performance in the elicitation task. For the non-word repetition task, participants heard a recorded non-word twice (e.g. *gazoop, gazoop*). They then orally inserted the heard word at the end of a carrier phrase displayed on the computer screen (e.g. *I'd like to buy a* ___). The final task involved reading aloud the same set of non-words, which were presented in orthographic form, with stressed syllables indicated via larger lettering (e.g. *gaZOOP*).

All of the real or non-words used in the experiment were polysyllabic. The majority (e.g. *magic* and *captain, gazoop* and *toctel*) contained at most two filled nuclei.[6] Necessarily, any instances of medial coda /p k/ (e.g. *captain* and *doctor*) occur in polysyllabic forms. Our decision to eschew monosyllabic words (or, more precisely, forms with a single filled nucleus) was based on the research cited earlier showing that monosyllables such as *lip* or *book* favour i-epenthesis. That is, epenthesis is more likely in *lip* than in *bishop*. Consequently, if we included monosyllabic forms, any mismatch in i-epenthesis rates between words with medial versus final /p k/ might be due to this tendency, rather than to any distinction in the syllabic affiliation

5 The decision to simplify the methodology by employing self-reported proficiency levels rather than using a proficiency test was made principally because proficiency is not a key factor in the study – the position of /p k/ in the word is the key factor.

6 None of the words used involved medial coda or final clusters. We thus avoided examples such as *dumpster* or *forceps,* involving stops and /s/, which have been shown to be somewhat special (for more, see Cantoni 2009; Cantoni and Cristófaro Silva 2008).

of the stops. By ruling out monosyllabic forms, however, we are faced with the dilemma that there are relatively few high-frequency polysyllabic words ending in /p/ or /k/. To circumvent this problem, we incorporated tasks employing non-words (e.g. *gazoop* and *zudock*). Among the non-words, the vowels preceding /p k/ were stressed or unstressed (e.g. *ga'zoop* and *'zudock*) in equal numbers. Balancing the real words for stress placement proved more challenging: most instances of medial coda /p k/ were preceded by stressed vowels; most final /p k/ were preceded by unstressed vowels.

The participants were recorded in a quiet lab at an Anglophone university in Montreal, using an Audio-Technica AT831b lavaliere microphone attached to a Zoom H4 Digital Recorder. For the tasks involving oral stimuli (tasks 1 and 2), participants listened to the recordings over a Microsoft LX-400 headset connected to a computer.

The data were coded for various factors, including crucially *presence vs absence of i-epenthesis* (the dependent variable) and whether /p k/ was in *medial or final position* (the key independent variable). Other independent variables included in the analysis were: *word status* (real vs non-word), *task* (picture elicitation, repetition, reading aloud), *stress status* of the preceding vowel (stressed, unstressed), *proficiency level* (beginner, intermediate, advanced), and *participant.* Coding for i-epenthesis was based on an auditory analysis carried out by the first author, with borderline or otherwise uncertain tokens being verified in conjunction with the second author until an agreement could be reached. The decision to eschew an acoustic analysis (e.g. via Praat) was based on the assumption that i-epenthesis is a categorical phonological phenomenon rather than a gradient phonetic phenomenon (contra Bybee 2001).

10.4 Results

The data were analysed via Goldvarb X (Sankoff, Tagliamonte and Smith 2005), standard statistical software used in variationist/sociolinguistic studies. Goldvarb X performs a regression analysis that identifies the relative contribution of different factors to the application of a variable process (e.g. i-epenthesis). Factor weights ranging from 0 to 1 are generated, with a weight in excess of 0.5 indicating that a variable is associated with higher rates of application. In order to refine the analysis and to better identify the contributing variables, three runs of Goldvarb X were carried out, with the independent variables of proficiency level and word status progressively eliminated from the analysis. This elimination process happened either because these factors had no role in the process (for instance, whether a real or non-word was spoken had no effect on the production of epenthesis), or because they directly interfered with another relevant factor (for instance, every individual participant also belonged to a proficiency group and vice versa). The remaining factor groups were selected by Goldvarb X in both step-up and step-down regression analyses, thus indicating that the selected groups in the third run are statistically significant for the phenomenon under investigation ($p<0.05$). Consequently, we will present the results from the third run, as this provided the most insightful analysis of the data under investigation. For a discussion of Goldvarb X in the analysis of L2 data, see Cardoso (2007).

As shown in Table 10.1, the results of the final Goldvarb X analysis (664 tokens) revealed that rates of i-epenthesis were significantly higher following /p k/ in final (0.899) rather than medial coda (0.103) position. That is, the production of the target /p k/ was significantly more problematic in word-final than in medial coda position. Unexpectedly, the rates of i-epenthesis in the repetition task (0.074) were significantly lower than in the elicitation (0.803) and reading-aloud tasks (0.807). Instances of i-epenthesis in the repetition task were in fact vanishingly rare (incidentally underlining the importance of triangulating data collection). Interestingly, i-epenthesis rates were also higher when the preceding nucleus was unstressed (0.684) (*'magic*) rather than stressed (0.364) (*at'tack*). Four of the participants also showed significantly greater i-epenthesis than the others. Varying degrees of proficiency in /p k/ production are thus found; apparently, the effects of contact on the developing L2 sound system are not uniform across the participants. As indicated

Table 10.1. Factor weights and % assigned by Goldvarb X (Sankoff et al. 2005).

Factors	Factor Weights/%			
Position	final:	medial:		
	0.899/12.4	0.103/0.3		
Task	elicitation:	repetition:	reading:	
	0.803/9.6	0.074/0.4	0.807/9.7	
Stress Status	stressed:	unstressed:		
	0.364/4.1	0.684/9.2		
Participants	1: 0.213/1.5	2: 0.213/1.5	3: 0.232/1.5	4: 0.363/3.0
	5: 0.370/3.0	6: 0.485/4.4	7: 0.562/5.9	8: 0.686/8.8
	9: 0.804/11.9	10: 0.942/23.1		

earlier, the other (eliminated) variables (i.e. word status and proficiency level) did not contribute significantly to the process of i-epenthesis.

Overall, it should be pointed out that the rates of epenthesis were quite low (input probability: 0.004). All of the participants were more likely to produce medial coda and final /p k/ without [i] rather than with this epenthetic vowel, so all of our participants in the language contact context of Montreal were fairly advanced in their acquisition of this component of the English sound system. A discussion of these findings is undertaken in the following section.

10.5 Discussion

We hypothesized that final consonants such as /p/ and /k/ in *bishop* and *magic* are onsets of empty nuclei in English. They thus contrast with medial /p/ and /k/ in *captain* and *doctor*, which are syllabified as codas. BP does not permit /p k/ in either location, restricting the set of consonants in these positions to /s l r N/. This distribution suggests that, unlike English, BP syllabifies its final consonants as codas. By extension, medial coda and final stops pose a problem for BP speakers for different reasons: (i) because /p/ and /k/ are not permissible codas in BP; and (ii) because BP does not employ onsets of empty nuclei. To test the hypothesis, we collected spoken data from BP speakers living in Montreal, a language contact situation that should provide optimal conditions for acquiring the English sound system.

Our hypothesis would be falsified if the participants acquire medial coda and final /p k/ simultaneously. Such a finding would be consistent with their sharing a prosodic representation and hence with /p k/ being syllabified as a coda in both locations. This is not what we found. Significantly higher rates of i-epenthesis occurred following final /p k/ as opposed to medial-coda /p k/, a pattern consistent with our hypothesis that these consonants employ distinct prosodic representations.[7]

The results are in fact consistent with an analysis of final consonants in BP as either codas (our view, following Piggott 1999) or as onsets of empty nuclei (the Government Phonology view). Under our view, BP speakers learn a novel syllabic configuration; under the latter view, they expand the

7 It has been pointed out to us that all of the instances of final consonants were also utterance-final (e.g. always at the end of the carrier phrase). Consequently, it would be worthwhile to verify whether the same mismatch between medial coda and final consonants holds when the final consonant is utterance-medial.

set of consonants permitted as onsets of empty nuclei. Arguably, however, the greater difficulty BP speakers have in acquiring final stops is indicative of the learning challenge that acquisition of a novel prosodic representation constitutes.

Two other elements of the results were unexpected. These involve variables for which we did not formulate any hypotheses due to the scope of our study: (i) unstressed syllables favour i-epenthesis; and (ii) i-epenthesis is highly disfavoured in the non-word repetition task. The effect of stress is hard to comprehend. On the one hand, the majority of final /p k/ in the real words (*bishop, magic*) are preceded by an unstressed vowel, and the majority of medial /p k/ (*captain, doctor*) by a stressed vowel. Since stops in final position favour i-epenthesis, this might account for the observed effect of stress. On the other hand, the non-words are balanced for stress placement, so the multivariate analysis (Goldvarb X) should be able to separate out the influence of final position from the influence of stress placement. In brief, the contribution of stress to i-epenthesis is hard to explain.

A first step towards understanding why the repetition task triggers much lower rates of epenthesis involves considering the notion of i-epenthesis itself, since the term is really a misnomer. The term i-epenthesis, ubiquitous in the literature on BP, implies a process of synchronic insertion of a vowel such that, while the vowel is present in the surface form, it is missing from the lexical entry. This scenario, however, is inaccurate, since so-called epenthetic [i] is in fact part of lexical entries in BP (see arguments in Cantoni and Cristófaro Silva 2008; Cristófaro Silva and Almeida 2008). Hence, surface forms such as [kapi̲tu] *capto* '(I) capture, attract' and [varigi̲] *Varig* (Brazilian airline) are underlying /kapitu/ and /varigi/, not /kaptu/ and /varig/. The adaptation of illicit codas and final consonants in BP occurs in the lexicon itself, not in the generation of surface forms. By extension, the same surely holds for epenthetic [i] in BP English: underlyingly, *magic* and *doctor* are /madʒiki/ and /dɔkitɔr/. Put differently, there is no synchronic process of i-epenthesis that BP speakers need to suppress in order to generate accurate output in English. Instead, what is required is revision of underlying forms such that *magic* and *doctor* are /madʒik/ and /dɔktɔr/, not /madʒiki/ and /dɔkitɔr/.

We assume that syllable structure is recorded in the lexicon (Kaye and Lowenstamm 1984), so as BP speakers progress in English, becoming capable of parsing medial /p k/ in coda position and final /p k/ in onset of an empty nucleus, they rewrite underlying forms such as *magic* and *doctor* as illustrated in (2a) and (2b). The initial forms in (2a) and (2b) generate inaccurate output, with so-called i-epenthesis, whereas the revised forms generate target-like output.

2. a) /madʒiki/ → /madʒik/

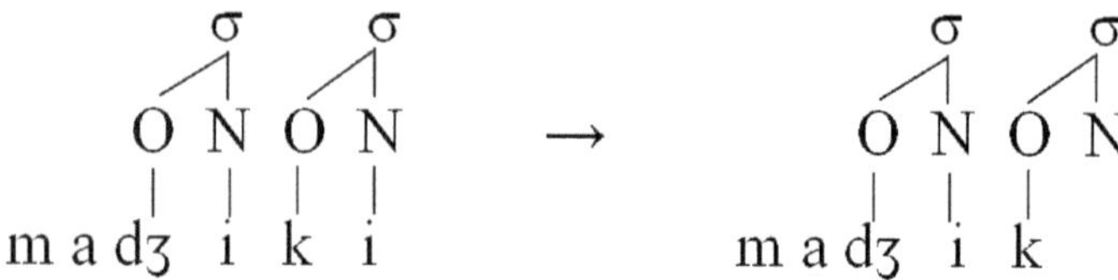

b) /dɔkitɔr/ → /dɔktɔr/

σ σ
O N O N
d ɔ k i t ɔ r
→
σ
O N Co
d ɔ k t ɔ r

One challenge for this and any other account of i-epenthesis is to explain why the presence of the epenthetic vowel is variable. Most approaches situate variation in the computational/derivational realm (i.e. in the grammar). For example, variation can be generated via optional or variable rules (Labov 1969; Cedergren and Sankoff 1974) or via multiple grammars (Kroch 1989). Variation can also be captured in Optimality Theory (OT – Prince and Smolensky 1993) via partially ordered constraints (Anttila 1997; Kiparsky 1993; Reynolds 1994), via stochastic OT (Boersma 1997; Boersma and Hayes 2001) or via lexically indexed constraints (Coetzee 2009). With respect to i-epenthesis in BP interlanguage, however, a grammatical approach to variation may not be appropriate.

We suggest that variation in BP i-epenthesis is better characterized as involving *competing underlying representations*, an approach to which Anttila (2002) refers as 'pseudo-optionality'. The idea is that, when speakers rewrite lexical entries as shown in (2a, b), they do not actually eradicate the original underlying representation; the replaced underlying representations continue to be present alongside the novel forms. Hence, at the moment of selection, the speaker can potentially access either form as a base for surface output. Initially, the ingrained habit is to access the form with an added vowel, but gradually, as speakers improve, they get more proficient at accessing the accurate form. At first, selection of the new underlying representation will be quite arduous, hence relatively infrequent and associated more with formal speech, which favours attending to desired output.

Once speakers develop the ability to represent /p k/ in a medial coda and final onset of an empty nucleus, newly acquired lexical items will presumably be recorded accurately, without an epenthetic vowel. More recent lexical entries will thus have single representations, cueing near-flawless performance. This is what we believe is happening in the non-word repetition task. By definition, non-words (e.g. *toctel, gazoop*) are items for which the participants have yet to develop a lexical representation. By having the participants insert the heard word at the end of a carrier sentence (e.g. *I can't find my* ____), we hoped to ensure that the participants processed the forms phonologically (including performing a syllabic parse), thus avoiding the possibility that they might engage in purely phonetic imitation. Indeed, there is no reason to believe that the task did not require phonological parsing. Consequently, in most cases, the participants were able to construct an accurate mental representation that could form the basis of a lexical entry (e.g. /taktəl/–/gəzup/ rather than /taki̲təl/–/gəzupi̲/). These accurate representations allow the participants to almost entirely circumvent the phenomenon of i-epenthesis that they exhibit in the real-word elicitation task.

On the other hand, in the non-word reading-aloud task, it seems that exposure to the written and not the spoken form does not necessarily enable the participants to develop an accurate mental representation. i-epenthesis thus occurs in this task at a rate similar to the elicitation task. Apparently, there is a certain tendency to revert to the L1 reflex of representing illicit medial codas and final consonants as onsets of a filled nucleus containing /i/. The absence of a vowel in the orthography (e.g. *toctel* or *gazoop*) is insufficient to trigger development of an accurate form, probably because BP speakers are used to the orthography not always reflecting the phonological form (e.g. *capto* /kapitu/ or *Varig* /varigi/).

To recap, our proposal is that competition between underlying representations is what is behind the variability of i-epenthesis in BP English. The notion of competing underlying representations is virtually absent from the variationist literature, but we anticipate that it could prove useful in accounting for variable phenomena beyond just i-epenthesis.

10.6 Conclusion

Our findings provide robust support for the view that final consonants in English are onsets of empty nuclei rather than codas. The results indicate that BP speakers in the language contact context of Montreal acquire the stops /p k/ in medial coda position before final position. If speakers exhibited simultaneous acquisition of medial coda and final stops, this would constitute convincing evidence that the stops are syllabified as codas in the two locations. More tentatively, our results are consistent with a coda parse for final consonants in BP. Our findings thus have important implications for phonological theory.

In our discussion, we also address the issue of variation. We suggest that variation ensues from the presence in the interlanguage lexicon of competing underlying representations, such that *magic* and *doctor*, for example, are represented both as /madʒiki/–/dɔkitɔr/ (the initial entry) and as /madʒik/–/dɔktɔr/ (the revised entry). Selection of the former representations results in so-called i-epenthesis, but selection of the latter leads to accurate production. Hence, acquisition really involves two steps. First comes representational acquisition: upon developing the ability to represent /p k/ in coda position and in an onset of an empty nucleus, speakers develop accurate lexical entries which compete with initial inaccurate ones. Next comes selectional acquisition: speakers gradually get better at the moment of speaking at accessing the accurate form and suppressing the inaccurate one.

The data we collected came from BP speakers living in Montreal, a language contact situation. Progress in the contact context in acquisition of the target sound system is likely spurred on by a number of factors. First, i-epenthesis is a particularly salient and stigmatized feature of the BP accent. Consequently, BP speakers in Montreal who epenthesize doubtless encounter negative reactions from native or native-like speakers. Such reactions motivate speakers to modify their lexical representations and to get better at accessing the revised forms. During interactions, BP speakers may also note misunderstandings that derive from mispronunciations, or else they receive various forms of feedback, including explicit correction from an interlocutor. In addition, BP speakers may request repetitions or clarifications when they notice a discrepancy between their own and other speakers' output. To conclude, progress in a contact situation proceeds not quite like magic ([madʒiki]~[madʒik]?), since it is gradual and variable, but a number of contextual factors nonetheless favour this progress.

References

Anttila, A. (1997). Deriving variation from grammar: A study of Finnish genitives. In F. Hinskens, R. Van Hout and L. Wetzels (eds.), *Variation, Change and Phonological Theory*, 35–68. Amsterdam: John Benjamins.

Anttila, A. (2002). Variation and phonological theory. In J. Chambers, P. Trudgill and N. Schilling-Estes (eds.), *Handbook of Language Variation and Change*, 206–43. Oxford: Blackwell.

Baptista, B. and Silva Filho, J. (1997). The influence of markedness and syllable contact on the production of English consonants by EFL learners. In J. Leather and A. James (eds.), *New Sounds 1997: Proceedings of the Third International Symposium on the Acquisition of Second Language Speech*, 26–34. Klagenfurt: University of Klagenfurt.

Baptista, B. and Silva Filho, J. (2007). The influence of voicing and sonority relationships on the production of English final consonants. In B. Baptista and M. Watkins (eds.), *English with a Latin Beat: Studies in Portuguese/Spanish-English Interphonology*, 73–89. Amsterdam: John Benjamins.

Blevins, J. (1995). The syllable in phonological theory. In J.A. Goldsmith (ed.), *The Handbook of Phonological Theory*, 206–44. Oxford: Blackwell.

Boersma, P. (1997). How we learn variation, optionality, and probability. In *Proceedings of the Institute of Phonetic Sciences 21*, 43–58. Amsterdam: University of Amsterdam.

Boersma, P. and Hayes, B. (2001). Empirical tests of the gradual learning algorithm. *Linguistic Inquiry* 32(1): 45–86.

Brockhaus, W. (1995). *Final Devoicing in the Phonology of German*. Tübingen: Niemeyer.

Broselow, E., Chen, S.-I. and Wang, C. (1998). The emergence of the unmarked in second language phonology. *Studies in Second Language Acquisition* 20: 261–80.

Bybee, J. (2001). *Phonology and Language Use*. Cambridge: Cambridge University Press.

Cantoni, M. (2009). *Categorização fonológica e representação mental: uma análise da alternância entre* [ks] *e* [s] *à luz de modelos de uso*. Master's Thesis, Universidade Federal de Mina Gerais, Belo Horizonte, Brazil.

Cantoni, M. and Cristófaro Silva, T. (2008). Verbal stress assignment in Brazilian Portuguese and the prosodic interpretation of segmental sequences. In *Proceedings of the Speech Prosody Conference, Campinas 2008*, 587–90.

Cardoso, W. (2007). The variable development of English word-final stops by Brazilian Portuguese speakers: A stochastic optimality theoretic account. *Language Variation and Change* 19: 219–48.

Cardoso, W. (2011). The development of coda perception in second language phonology: A variationist perspective. *Second Language Research* 27(4): 433–65.

Cedergren, H.J. and Sankoff, D. (1974). Variable rules: Performance as a statistical reflection of competence. *Language* 50(2): 333–55.

Charette, M. (1991). *Conditions on Phonological Government.* Cambridge: Cambridge University Press.

Cristófaro Silva, T. and Almeida, L. (2008). On the nature of epenthetic vowels. In L. Bisol and C. R. Brescancini (eds.), *Contemporary Phonology in Brazil*, 193–212. Cambridge: Cambridge Scholars Publishing.

Coetzee, A. (2009). Phonological variation and lexical frequency. In A. Schardl, M. Walkow and M. Abdurrahman (eds.), *NELS 38: Proceedings of the North East Linguistic Society, Volume 1*, 189–202. Amherst: GLSA.

Gussmann, E. (1992). Resyllabification and delinking: The case of Polish voicing. *Linguistic Inquiry* 23: 29–56.

Harris, J. (1994). *English Sound Structure.* Oxford: Blackwell.

Harris, J. and Gussmann, E. (1998). Final codas: Why the west was wrong. In E. Cyran (ed.), *Structure and Interpretation in Phonology: Studies in Phonology*, 139–62. Lublin: Folia.

Huf, J.C.C. and Alves, U.K. (2010). A produção de /p/ et /k/ em codas simples e complexas do inglês (L2) por aprendizes gaúchos. *Verba Volant* 1(1): 1–27.

John, P. and Cardoso, W. (2008). Francophone ESL learners and h-epenthesis. *Concordia Papers in Applied Linguistics (COPAL)* 1: 76–97.

Kaye, J. (1990). 'Coda' licensing. *Phonology* 7: 301–30.

Kaye, J. and Lowenstamm, J. (1984). De la syllabicité. In F. Dell, D. Hirst and J.-R. Vergnaud (eds.), *Forme sonore du langage*, 123–59. Paris: Hermann.

Kiparsky, P. (1993). Variable rules. Paper presented at the Rutgers Optimality Workshop. New Brunswick, NJ.

Kroch, A. (1989). Reflexes of grammar in patterns of language change. *Language Variation and Change* 1: 199–244.

Labov, W. (1969). The logic of nonstandard English. *Georgetown Monographs on Language and Linguistics* 22: 1–31.

Labov, W. (2001). *Principles of Linguistic Change: Social Factors.* Malden, MA: Blackwell.

Lowenstamm, J. (1996). CV as the only syllable type. In J. Durand and B. Laks (eds.), *Current Trends in Phonology: Models and Methods* 419–41. Salford, Manchester: ESRI.

Major, R. (1986). Paragoge and degree of foreign accent in Brazilian English. *Second Language Research* 2: 53–71.

Mascaró, J. (1987). Underlying voicing recoverability of final devoiced obstruents in Catalan. *Journal of Phonetics* 15: 183–6.

McCarthy, J. and Prince, A. (1993). *Prosodic Morphology I: Constraint Interaction and Satisfaction.* Unpublished manuscript, University of Massachusetts, Amherst, MA and Rutgers University, New Brunswick NJ.

McCarthy, J.J. and Prince, A. (1994). The emergence of the unmarked: Optimality in prosodic morphology. In *Papers from the Annual Meeting of the North East Linguistic Society 24*, 333–79.

Nevins, A. (2008). Review of *A Lateral Theory of Phonology: What is CVCV and Why Should it be?* by Tobias Scheer. *Lingua* 118(3): 425–34.

Paradis, C. and Prunet, J.-F. (eds.) (1991). *Phonetics and Phonology: The Special Status of Coronals*. San Diego: Academic Press.

Prince, A. and Smolensky, P. (1993). *Optimality Theory: Constraint Interaction in Generative Grammar*. Manuscript, Rutgers University, New Brunswick, NJ, and University of Colorado, Boulder, CO.

Piggott, G. (1999). At the right edge of words. *The Linguistic Review* 16(2): 143–85.

Reynolds, W. (1994). *Variation and Phonological Theory*. PhD Dissertation, University of Pennsylvania, Philadelphia, PA.

Sankoff, D., Tagliamonte, S. and Smith, E. (2005). GoldVarb X: A variable rule application for Macintosh and Windows. URL: http://individual.utoronto.ca/tagliamonte/Goldvarb/GV_index.htm

Scheer, T. (2004). *A Lateral Theory of Phonology. What Is CVCV and Why Should It Be?* Berlin: Mouton de Gruyter.

Schneider, A. and Schwindt, L. (2010). A epêntese vocálica medial em PB e na aquisição de inglês como LE: uma análise morfofonológica. *Letras de Hoje* 45: 16–26.

Segundo, S.O. (1993). *Stress and Related Phenomena in BP*. Doctoral Dissertation, SOAS, University of London.

Selkirk, E. (1982). The syllable. In H. van der Hulst and N. Smith (eds.), *The Structure of Phonological Representations*, Part 2, 337–83. Dordrecht: Foris.

Yavaş, M. (1994). Final stop devoicing in interlanguage. In M. Yavaş (ed.), *First and Second Language Phonology*, 267–82. San Diego: Singular.

Paul John is a professor of linguistics and ESL teacher trainer in the Department of Modern Languages at the University of Quebec in Trois-Rivières.

Walcir Cardoso is a professor of Applied Linguistics/Teaching English as a Second Language in the Department of Education at Concordia University, Montreal.

11 The Acquisition of English Stress by Québec Francophones

Guilherme Duarte Garcia and Natália Brambatti Guzzo

11.1 Introduction

English and French have very distinct prominence systems: while in English stress is assigned at the word level, in French prominence seems to be a property of the (phonological) phrase (PPh). Additionally, word-level stress is contrastive in English (e.g. *PREsent* vs *preSENT*). Therefore, stress is a feature that French learners of English as a second language (L2) must acquire.

The objective of this chapter is to investigate the acquisition of English stress by speakers of Canadian French (CF). CF, unlike European French (EF), is argued to exhibit word-level prominence (Walker 1984; Paradis and Deshaies 1990). In this case, producing stress per se should not be a difficulty for CF learners of English (L2ers). However, CF stress is fixed word-finally. Considering that (a) stress in English can emerge in several positions within the word, and (b) factors such as syllable weight and extrametricality play a role in stress assignment, L2ers also need to acquire a novel rhythmic pattern. Another characteristic of the L2 rhythmic pattern is the iterative building of feet, which in English are quantity-sensitive (or weight-sensitive) trochees (e.g. [æ̀kə][dɛ́mɪk] 'academic'; [pæ̀sə][dí:nə] 'Pasadena'). Although some authors argue that (Canadian) French also has foot structure (e.g. Goad and Buckley 2006), CF would still be considerably different from English, as feet would be iambic (i.e. right-headed) and non-iterative.

In this chapter, we report the results of two production experiments (one in CF and one in English) aimed at examining how advanced CF L2ers produce English stress. In other words, our focus is not on language development (i.e. whether learners actually acquire stress in English), but rather on ultimate attainment in L2 acquisition (i.e. how native speakers and advanced learners compare vis-à-vis stress production). In order to evaluate whether L2ers' rhythmic patterns mirror native English patterns, we compare L2ers' production with control data, focusing on three possible acoustic correlates of prominence: duration, pitch (F0) and intensity. To verify whether L2ers transfer acoustic cues or rhythmic patterns from their first language (L1) into the L2, we also analyse how prominence is produced by L2ers in their L1.

We found that duration is the main phonetic dimension employed by L2ers to produce target-like word-level prominence in English. Duration is also the main correlate of the alternating rhythmic patterns in L2ers' production. With regard to CF, we found no phonetic evidence for word-level prominence nor word-internal constituency, which indicates that stress and foot structure are properties that L2ers must acquire. Overall, L2ers do show target-like patterns vis-à-vis prominence and rhythm, and their use of duration is strikingly similar to the trends observed in the target language.

This chapter is organized as follows: In Section 11.2, we discuss prominence/stress in French and English, and report the results of some studies which have examined the acquisition of English stress by native French speakers. In Section 11.3, we present the methodology of our experiment. In Section 11.4, we discuss our data and present our statistical analyses. In Section 11.5, we briefly discuss the phonological implications of our results.

11.2 Stress in French and English

11.2.1 French Stress

Cross-linguistically, it is assumed that the phonological word (PWd) is the prosodic domain in which primary stress is assigned (Nespor and Vogel 1986; Selkirk 1986). In European French (EF), however, the domain of prominence is traditionally considered to be the phonological phrase (PPh), the constituent that immediately dominates the PWd (Jun and Fougeron 2000; Gussenhoven 2004). Within the French PPh, the rightmost syllable of the rightmost PWd exhibits prominence (1a). If the rightmost syllable has a schwa, prominence is placed on the preceding syllable (1b). The examples in (1) are taken from Tremblay (2007: 28).

(1) a. [ləboʃa'po]$_{PPh}$ *le beau chapeau* 'the beautiful hat'
b. [ləjɔli'mɔ̃d(ə)]$_{PPh}$ *le joli monde* 'the beautiful world'

On the other hand, some authors have argued that in Canadian French (CF) prominence is assigned in the PWd domain (Walker 1984; Paradis and Deshaies 1990). In other words, each PWd in a PPh in CF should have a primary stress (2). The examples in (2) are in Paradis and Deshaies (1990: 148).

(2) [ɛle'tɛply'gʀos]$_{PPh}$ [kʏnpɛʀ'sɔn]$_{PPh}$ [œ̃nã'fãnɔʀ'mal]$_{PPh}$
Elle était plus grosse qu'une personne…un enfant normal.
'She was bigger than a person…a normal child.'

In both EF and CF, prominence is related to greater duration (e.g. Garde 1968; Walker 1984). In EF, prominent syllables also have higher pitch (e.g. Garde 1968). In CF, however, some vowels are considered inherently long (3) and seem to exhibit a certain degree of prominence, regardless of their position in the PWd or the PPh (Walker 1984; Armstrong 1999; Tremblay 2007).

(3) Long vowels in CF:
a. all nasal vowels: /ã, ẽ, ɔ̃, œ̃/
b. some oral vowels: /ɑ, o, ɛ, ø/
c. vowels followed by /ʒ, ʀ, v, z/ in coda position

Inherently long vowels in CF are often associated with a phenomenon known as pretonic lengthening (or penultimate stress) (4). When a long vowel is in penultimate position in CF, it can arguably bear either a secondary stress (if the final vowel is long) or even the main stress in the word (if the final vowel is not inherently long). In other positions in the word, inherently long vowels are also perceived as stressed. In the examples in (4), the vowels [œ̃, ø] can be perceived as stressed [as per (3) above], even though they are in penultimate position (examples from Paradis and Deshaies 1990: 151).

(4) [lœ̃dzi] *lundi* 'Monday'
[døzjɛm] *deuxième* 'second'

Another characteristic of CF is *l'accent d'insistance*, or emphatic stress (5). Emphatic stress dislocates prominence onto a non-final syllable of the PPh, and is often associated with emotional or passionate speech. The examples in (5) are from Walker (1984: 32).

(5) [sɛˌtɛʀiblə]$_{PPh}$ *c'est terrible* 'it's terrible'
[ˌɛ̃pɔsiblə]$_{PPh}$ *impossible* 'impossible'

According to Thibault and Ouellet (1996), both emphatic stress and pretonic lengthening emerge from pitch movements in the phrasal or word domain. However, whereas emphatic stress involves a L+H* (low-high) tone combination on the emphasized syllable, pretonic lengthening results from the assignment of a H+L* tone to the target syllable.

Another characteristic of French prominence (both in EF and in CF) is phrase-initial prominence (e.g. Gussenhoven 2004; Goad and Buckley 2006; Goad and Prévost 2011). Although some instances of phrase-initial prominence in CF derive from emphatic stress, this form of prominence seems to be the result of a boundary effect (Gussenhoven 2004) (6).

(6) [ləˌmɔvɛgaʀˈsɔ̃]$_{PPh}$ *le mauvais garçon* 'the bad boy'

Phrase-initial prominence is also associated with pitch (Jun and Fougeron 2000): a high tone is assigned to a syllable of the leftmost PWd in the PPh. The syllable with phrase-initial prominence is usually the first syllable of the first PWd in the PPh (7a), but other syllables of such PWd may also bear prominence (7b). The examples in (7) are in Gussenhoven (2004: 253).

(7) a. ENfant adoptif 'adoptive child'
b. enFANT adoptif

Phrase-initial prominence, as well as emphatic stress, is arguably optional in CF. Pretonic lengthening, on the other hand, is an effect of vowel quality and is therefore not optional. However, it is not clear in the literature whether the application of pretonic lengthening overrides phrase-final (or word-final) prominence.

Stress in both EF and CF is not iterative, which has led some researchers to argue that the language has no foot structure (e.g. Jun and Fougeron 2000; Özçelik 2011). A theoretical consequence of such an assertion is that the foot (F) is not a universal domain (contra, for example, Nespor and Vogel 1986), and that PWds in certain languages may be formed directly from the combination of syllables. Nevertheless, some other scholars consider that prominent syllables correspond to foot heads in French. As a result, in phrases with initial prominence, two binary feet are constituted: the leftmost foot is trochaic, i.e. with prominence on the initial syllable, while the rightmost foot is iambic, i.e. with prominence on the final syllable (Goad and Buckley 2006) (8).

(8) [lə [[ˌmɔvɛ]$_{\text{F}}$]$_{\text{PWd}}$ [[gaʀˈsɔ̃]$_{\text{F}}$]$_{\text{PWd}}$]$_{\text{PPh}}$

Although researchers seem to agree on the fact that (Canadian) French exhibits prominence on the right edge of the PPh, two facts compromise the classification of such prominence as stress: (a) the fact that prominence can apparently shift to previous syllables, and (b) the fact that prominence does not follow any specific rhythmic pattern, but is assigned to phrasal edges (both left and right). These observations have contributed to categorizing French as an *intonation-only* language (Gussenhoven 2004). If Canadian French is an intonation-only language (as opposed to a *stress* language), then stress is a feature that English L2ers must acquire. In the next section, we present the main characteristics of English stress and briefly report the results of some experimental studies that have focused on the production or perception of English stress by native French speakers.

11.2.2 Acquisition of English Stress

Several seminal studies in the past decades have investigated English stress (Chomsky and Halle 1968; Liberman and Prince 1977; Hayes 1982; Halle and Vergnaud 1987 and many others since then). As a whole, we observe several robust tendencies in English vis-à-vis its stress patterns. In other words, stress is relatively predictable in the language. On the other hand, we should note that there is evidence that words in the lexicon already have metrical information (Selkirk 1980), which could indicate that stress in English may be less predictable than what is often assumed.

When we compare English and French, we might say that stress is one of the most explicit phonological differences between these two languages. For example, unlike French, where prominence is assigned to either the PPh or the PWd (Section 11.2.1), English licenses (primary and secondary) stress on multiple positions in a word. Another important difference between the languages is that stress in English is influenced by syllable weight, that is, heavier syllables [see (9)] are more likely to attract stress than light syllables. In verbs and adjectives, stress falls on the final syllable if it is heavy (9a) – heavy syllables may contain a long vowel or a complex coda. If this syllabic condition is not met, stress falls on the penultimate syllable (9b). Nouns, on the other hand, have penultimate stress if the penultimate syllable is heavy (9c), and antepenultimate stress otherwise (9d). Final stress is generally avoided, but may emerge if the word-final coda is complex, for example (9e).

(9) a. verbs and adjectives with heavy final syllables: *direct, supreme*
b. verbs and adjectives with no heavy final syllable: *accomplish, tired*
c. nouns with heavy penult syllable: *agenda, Arizona*
d. default antepenult stress in nouns: *Canada, quality*
e. nouns with a complex final coda and a light penult syllable: *request*

Even though stress in (i) verbs and adjectives and (ii) nouns is influenced by syllable weight, these two classes of words follow slightly different stress patterns. The differences are mostly concentrated on the word-final syllable, which requires a specific syllabic shape to be stressed. Hayes (1982) proposes a unified analysis based on extrametricality that accounts for both classes: whereas in nouns a light final syllable is extrametrical, in verbs and adjectives it is the final *consonant* that is extrametrical.

Naturally, the behaviour of word-final syllables in English makes the acquisition of its stress system more challenging to French speakers. Learners need to assign stress to different positions in a word, and which syllable bears stress depends not only on weight but also on word class and other (less predictable) factors.

Overall, one would think that final stress in English would be easier for French speakers, given their L1 system. However, in a comprehensive perception study, Altmann (2006) shows that advanced learners of English (L1 French) performed less well in words with final stress in the target language.

In a study about the processing of word stress by CF learners of English, Tremblay (2008) found that the L2ers who were able to discriminate between English words based on stress contrast were especially the ones with target-like knowledge of stress placement. On the other hand, in a study on the production of English word stress by CF learners of various proficiency levels, Tremblay and Owens (2010) found a preference for stress on the first syllable for both disyllabic and trisyllabic words. However, most of the learners did not assign stress correctly in trisyllabic words with a stressed heavy syllable. L2ers who showed a preference for stress at the left edge of the word used pitch as the main correlate, while L2ers who stressed the penultimate syllable used duration.

A crucial consequence of the differences between French and English stress is the existence of word-level constituents (i.e. feet): whereas English clearly has a rhythmic pattern, French does not. For example, the word *academic* has penultimate *primary* stress and initial *secondary* stress: (àca)(démic). Since stress is the prominence of a unit (e.g. syllable) *relative* to its neighbouring units, it is essential that learners also perceive and produce non-primary prominences in their L2.

The phonetic realization of stress in English is, as expected, very different from French (Section 11.2.1). Traditionally, stress in English is correlated with pitch (Fry 1955, 1958; Grimson 1980; Lehiste 1976). However, studies have shown that duration and intensity also play an important role in distinguishing stressed and unstressed syllables in the language (Lieberman 1960; Beckman 1986; Laver 1994; Harrington, Beckman, Fletcher and Palethorpe 1998). In other words, multiple phonetic cues signal word-level prominence in English, which likely makes stress perception and production in English even more challenging to French speakers.

Learners also need to deal with non-primary prominences, which are responsible for the rhythmic pattern in English stress mentioned above (i.e. word-level constituency). Gussenhoven (2004) shows some evidence that duration also plays an important role in distinguishing these secondary prominences from primary stress. Plag, Kunter and Schramm (2011), however, show that the evidence is not strong in North American English: if duration is in fact a cue for distinguishing primary and secondary stresses, it is certainly very subtle.

In sum, for French-speaking learners of English to be target-like, they have to first learn that word-level prominence is crucial in the language. Second, they have to be able to shift prominence within each word, since most English words will have penultimate or antepenultimate stress. Third, they need to acquire word-level constituency (weight-sensitive trochaic feet in this case), which will allow them to produce target-like rhythmic patterns. In the present study, we investigate (i) whether these three aspects are indeed acquired by advanced L2ers and, if so, (ii) how these aspects are phonetically realized in the vowels of PWds.

11.3 Methodology

If we assume that CF, as EF, has no word-level prominence, then English L2ers must acquire stress. In this case, two hypotheses can be formulated:

(i) English L2ers do not acquire word-level stress in English, therefore, what is perceived as stress in L2ers' production is perhaps the result of boundary effects transferred from their L1 into the L2 (i.e. no acoustic correlate is significant for prominence at the word level, and both L1 and L2 have similar rhythmic patterns); or

(ii) English L2ers can acquire stress in English (i.e. some syllables in the word domain are reinforced, and some rhythmic patterns can be identified), even though stress may not be produced in a target-like manner.

On the other hand, if we assume that CF does have word-level prominence and that prominence is fixed word-finally in the language, then English L2ers must acquire a different rhythmic pattern, but not stress per se. In that case, two other hypotheses can be formulated:

(i) English L2ers produce English stress using the same acoustic correlates and/or following the same rhythmic pattern (word-final stress) as in their L1; or
(ii) English L2ers produce English stress in a target-like manner (i.e. using the target-like rhythmic pattern and acoustic correlates that are potentially different from those they use in their L1).

Another hypothesis for this scenario is that CF speakers acquire stress in a semi-target-like manner, with elements from both their L1 and the L2 in their interlanguage grammar. Additionally, like some participants in Tremblay and Owens' (2010) experiment on nonce word production, they may use different acoustic correlates in order to signal stress in different positions within the PWd.

In order to test these hypotheses, two production experiments were conducted: one in CF (participants' L1) and the other in English (participants' L2). In the CF version of the experiment, the target-phrases (n=24) were formed by combinations of adjective+noun (e.g. *mauvais garçon* 'bad boy'), noun+preposition+noun (e.g. *maison du chocolat* 'house of chocolate'), and adjective+noun-adjective (e.g. *dernier candidat japonais* 'last Japanese candidate'). The carrier sentence was *Elle a vu le/la/un/une [target phrase]* ('She saw the/a/an [target phrase]'). Two words in each phrase were analysed (n=48).

In the English version of the experiment, the target phrases (n=200) were formed by combinations of adjective+noun (e.g. *adorable musician*), noun+preposition+noun (e.g. *minister of economy*), and adverb+adjective+noun (e.g. *completely frequent request*). Two carrier sentences were used: *She saw the/a/an [target phrase]* and *She saw the/a/an [target phrase] before class*. Because the number of words analysed in each phrase varied (1 or 2), the total number of words examined was 374 (final stress=98; penult stress=106; antepenult stress=136; pre-antepenult stress=34).

In both versions of the test, all vowels in the words on both left and right edges of the target phrases were considered, in order to test whether L1 boundary effects were also found in speakers' L2. Target words in both CF and English had a minimum of two syllables (e.g. *maison* 'house', *request*).

In the CF experiment, target words had a maximum of three syllables (e.g. *historique* 'historical'), while in the English experiment target words had a maximum of five syllables (*comparatively*). In target English words, stress could be final (e.g. *request, complete*), penultimate (e.g. *damage, dramatic*), antepenultimate (e.g. *senator, chemical*) and pre-antepenultimate (e.g. *secretary, comparatively*). Position of stress was not controlled in CF, as it was assumed that, if stress is present at the PWd domain in the language, it should be final for all target words in the experiment. All vowels in both English and French target words were measured for duration, pitch (F0) and intensity. The Appendix lists the words analysed in the experiments.

Participants (6 L2ers, 2 of them female; 2 English controls, 1 of them female) were recorded in a soundproof booth. All L2ers had an advanced level of proficiency in English, as they used the language on a regular basis for study or work purposes. They were all born in Quebec and lived in Montreal at the time of the experiment. Their ages ranged from 20 to 36 years, and all participants were prepubescent learners. Considering that our participants are advanced in the target language, we expect one of the hypotheses labelled as (ii) above (that L2ers can produce word-level stress in English following target-like patterns) to be confirmed.

Our French data was forced-aligned using Milne's (2012) SPLaligner. Later, a random sample of aligned sentences was manually checked. The English data was manually aligned and transcribed.

11.4 Results

Because the present study investigates the manifestation of duration, pitch and intensity in vowels in PWds, this section is divided into three parts, each of which will describe and explore the data in terms of a specific phonetic correlate. Results from each correlate will be described across all three groups of participants, namely, L1 English (n=2), L1 French (n=6) and L2 English (n=6) – the data from L1 French and L2 English were produced by the same participants. The plots used in this section include means and error bars. If two error bars do not overlap (or overlap slightly), then the values they represent are likely significantly different (overall).

The data were modelled using mixed-effects linear regressions (lmer() in R), all of which predicted the value(s) of a given phonetic correlate based on the different vowels examined. All models reported below include by-speaker random effects (which mirror the interactions or main effects included in each model) as well as a by-item random intercept. Upon inspection, all models have an unbiased residual distribution. We excluded English words with pre-antepenultimate stress from our data, to keep the analysis focused on the three stress positions found in monomorphemic words.

Recall that all participants in this study are advanced in their L2. As a result, it is expected that these L2ers will be target-like regarding the most prominent syllable in the word: in fact, L2ers (n=6) were on average 92.6% accurate in producing the correct stressed word (SD=3.8%). Only words that were accurately produced by all L2ers are considered in the analyses presented below.

11.4.1 Duration

As discussed in Section 11.2.2, duration is often considered a robust correlate of English stress in the literature (e.g. Beckman 1986; Gussenhoven 2004). This is also confirmed in our results. In Figure 11.1, target vowels are on the x-axis (V1=word-final vowel; V2–V4=word-internal vowels), and the normalized duration of each vowel is on the y-axis (duration, pitch and intensity were normalized by speaker; the values used throughout this chapter are therefore scaled and centred around mean zero, z-scores). In addition, the plots are faceted by stress position: antepenultimate, penultimate and final. In native English, duration clearly correlates with stress across all stress positions. The rhythmic pattern in words such as *academic* [(àca)(démic)] is also mirrored in the duration of each vowel in the word (e.g. plot 2 in Figure 11.1).

As suggested by the error bars in Figure 11.1, the differences in duration across vowels are significant. For example, if we examine words with *final*

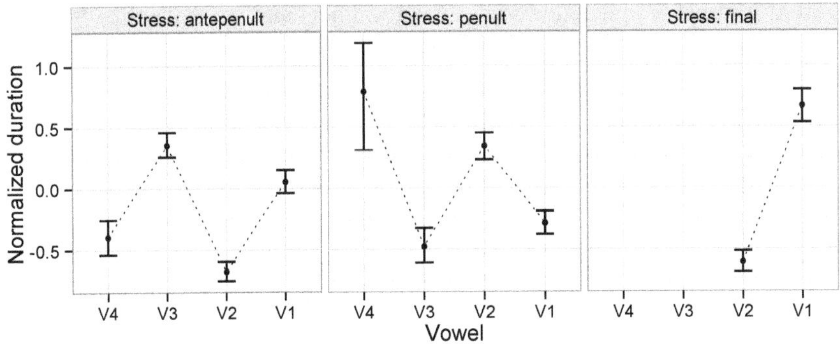

Figure 11.1. Normalized duration of different vowels in target words by stress position: English controls. V1=right edge of the word.

stress and model the standardized duration based on vowel position (V1 and V2), we find that V1 has a significant effect on duration. In other words, V2 and V1 are significantly different even when we account for by-item and by-speaker variation (V2: $\hat{\beta}=-1.78$, $t=-15.46$, $p<0.0001$), i.e., V2 is shorter than V1 by 1.78 standard deviations. Likewise, in words with *penult* stress, V1 and V2 are significantly different ($\hat{\beta}=-0.90$, $t=-12.16$, $p<0.0001$), as well as V3 and V2 ($\hat{\beta}=-0.91$, $t=-9.13$, $p<0.0001$). Given Figure 11.1, it is unsurprising that the difference between V2 and V4 is smaller for words with penult stress (V4: $\hat{\beta}=0.85$, $t=2.49$, $p=0.0133$). For words with *antepenult* stress, V1, V2 and V4 are all significantly different from V3, as suggested by the error bars in Figure 11.1.

The duration patterns in our Canadian French data, as expected, look very different. Even though we do see some gradual trend in Figure 11.2, it is no longer clear that duration is invariably different in word-final vowels. We see, however, a clear effect of penult vowel length: in a word such as *bâtiment* ('building'), for example, the penult vowel is short, whereas in *maison* ('house') the penult vowel is inherently long. As a result, whether the *final* vowel is phonetically longer relative to previous vowels depends on whether an inherently long vowel immediately precedes it. Note, too, that unlike the English data in Figure 11.1, these data do not suggest any alternating rhythmic pattern within the word – which is consistent with the analyses reported in Section 11.2.1. Therefore, we can see that the differences discussed in Section 11.2 are mirrored in the empirical data thus far.

A statistical model confirms the interaction we see in Figure 11.2, namely, that the differences in duration between V1 and V2–V3 are only significant if V2 is short ($\hat{\beta}=0.82$, $t=2.2$, $p=0.04$). No main effects are significant, which confirms that duration in itself is not a robust correlate in these data. Finally, phrase edge had no effect on duration.

Let us now examine the patterns produced by L2ers in English. The question of interest is *how* L2ers assign prominence, and whether they present target-like rhythmic patterns. The first thing we note in Figure 11.3 is its resemblance to Fig 11.1: not only are L2ers' vowels longer when stressed, but the alternating rhythmic pattern is clearly seen across syllables V1–V4 in words with antepenult or penult stress.

One interesting fact about the data presented above is that the trends observed are very similar regardless of which PPh edge we examine. For example, in a phrase such as *minister of economy*, both PWds exhibit the duration patterns illustrated above. This is particularly relevant under the assumption that French only has phrase-final prominence (Jun and Fougeron 2000; Gussenhoven 2004), since L2ers would then have to learn to assign prominence to phrase-*initial* words in the L2.

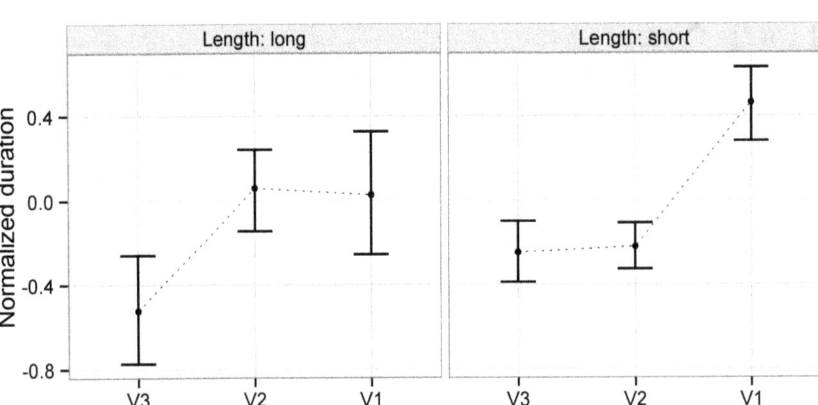

Figure 11.2. Normalized duration of different vowels in target words: French controls. V1=right edge of the word. 'Long' and 'short' refer to V2.

As suggested by Figure 11.3, V2 and V1 are significantly different even when we account for by-item and by-speaker variation (V2: $\hat{\beta}$=−1.53, t=−8.10, p<0.0001). In other words, V2 is shorter than V1 by 1.53 standard deviations. Likewise, in words with *penult* stress, V1 and V2 are significantly different ($\hat{\beta}$=−0.72, t=−11.95, p<0.0001), and so are V3 and V2 ($\hat{\beta}$= −0.43, t=−4.09, p<0.01). Given Figure 11.1, it is unsurprising that V2 and V4 are not significantly different for words with penult stress (V4: $\hat{\beta}$=0.04, t=0.13, p=0.90). For words with antepenult stress, V1, V2 and V4 are all significantly different from V3, as suggested by the error bars in Figure 11.1. Neither position in the sentence (final vs non-final) nor phrase edge (left vs right) had a significant effect on duration.

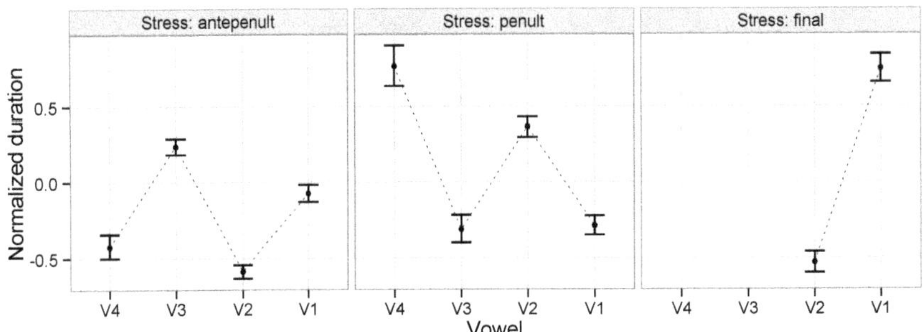

Figure 11.3. Normalized duration of different vowels in target words: L2ers. V1=right edge of the word.

11.4.2 Pitch

In Figure 11.4, we can see the normalized pitch of our English controls. Unlike Figure 11.1, we observe a trend that is less clear, in that no explicit correlation between pitch and stress is observed for all positions. In this particular case, our data could only partly capture the correlation between pitch and stress which is found in the literature (e.g. Lehiste 1976). For penult and final stress, we can see that pitch rises towards the more prominent vowel. The distribution of the data is considerably sparse (bimodal in some cases), which is likely due to our control sample size. Importantly, these results are not inconsistent with what is known about stress in English.

For words with final stress in Figure 11.4, no significant difference was found between V2 and V1 (V2: $\hat{\beta}$=−0.17, t=−1.07, p=0.28). For words with penult stress, the pitch of V3 was significantly different from V2 at α=0.05 ($\hat{\beta}$=−0.38, t=−2.04, p=0.04).

As expected, phrase position seems to have an effect on the different pitch patterns: while phrase-final words with penult stress had a descending pitch, words in non-final positions had an *ascending* (or neutral) pitch pattern overall. This difference, however, was not significant in a model that included an interaction between vowel and position (final vs non-final). Finally, for words with antepenult stress, no significant difference in pitch was found among English-speaking controls, which is not surprising given the trends observed in Figure 11.4.

In French, we can see some correlation between pitch and prominence. In Figure 11.5, the pitch of the word-final vowel (V1) is higher relative to vowels V2 and V3. The amount of variation is similar across all three

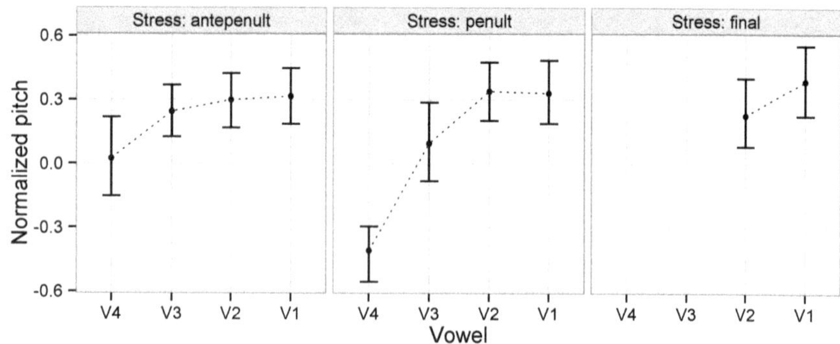

Figure 11.4. Normalized pitch of different vowels in target words: English controls. V1 = right edge of the word.

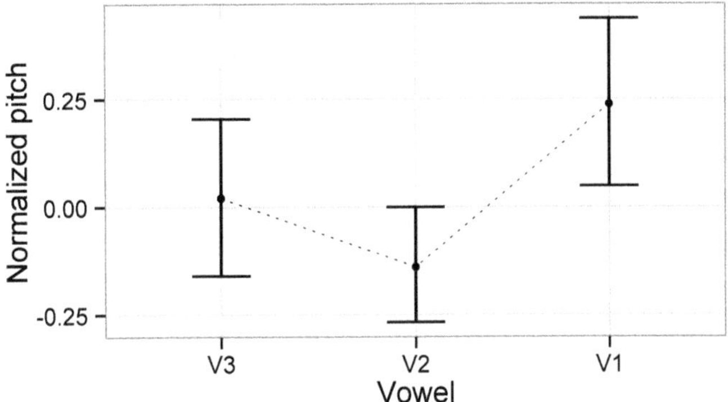

Figure 11.5. Normalized pitch of different vowels in target words: French controls. V1 = right edge of the word.

syllables (regardless of phrase edge). Therefore, our data suggest that pitch seems to play a role vis-à-vis word-level prominence in CF. However, once we take into account by-speaker (and by-item) variation, no significant pitch difference is found between V1 and V2 ($\hat{\beta}$=–0.35, t=–1.47, p=0.20) and V1 and V3 ($\hat{\beta}$=–0.10, t=–0.43, p=0.68). Unlike with duration, there is no significant interaction between pitch and the length of the penult vowel in the word.

Let us now turn to L2ers' production, shown in Figure 11.6. As with duration, we can see that L2ers' pitch patterns seem to be overall correlated with stress: higher pitch values are found in more prominent syllables (note, for example, the differences between stressed syllables and preceding syllables).

In words with final stress, V1 and V2 in Figure 11.6 suggest a significant difference. However, once we take into account by-speaker variation,

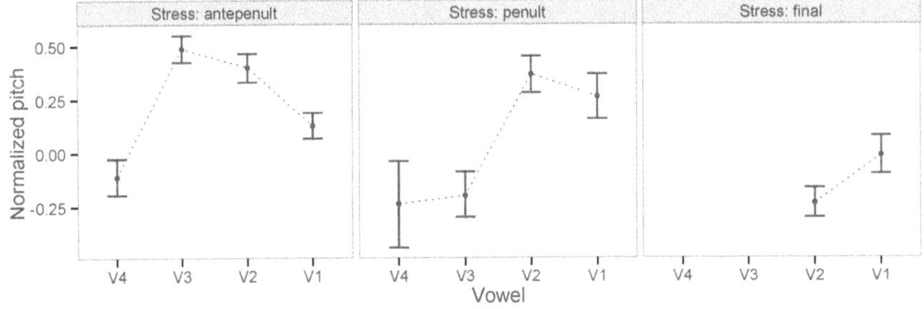

Figure 11.6. Normalized pitch of different vowels in target words: L2ers. V1 = right edge of the word.

that difference is not significant ($\hat{\beta}$=−0.09, t=−1.77, p=0.07). In words with penult stress, V2 is significantly different from V3 (V3: $\hat{\beta}$=−0.4, t=−3.03, p=0.02). V1 and V4 are not significantly different from V2. Finally, in words with antepenult stress, V1 and V4 are both significantly different from V3 vis-à-vis pitch (V1: $\hat{\beta}$=−0.52, t=−2.88, p=0.03; V4: $\hat{\beta}$=−0.53, t=−2.85, p=0.03). No interaction between vowels and position in the phrase was observed in the data.

11.4.3 Intensity

In the previous sections, we saw that L2ers' production showed a clear correlation between stress, duration and pitch. In this section, we will see that intensity, like duration, also plays a role. In Figure 11.7, for example, we see our control data, which suggest a clear correlation between intensity and stress. This correlation, however, is not as robust as expected once by-speaker variation is taken into account.

In words with final stress, for example, no significant difference is found between the intensity of V2 and V1 (V2: $\hat{\beta}$=0.10, t=0.92, p=0.47). Likewise, in words with penult stress, V4, V3 and V1 are not significantly different from V2 in our data – note, however, that the trend observed is exactly what one would expect given what is known about stress in English, i.e. a positive correlation between word-level prominence and intensity. Finally, in words with antepenult stress, V1, V2 and V4 all have significantly lower intensity than V3 (V1: $\hat{\beta}$=−1.01, t=−14.26, p<0.0001; V2: $\hat{\beta}$=−0.79, t=−11.20, p<0.0001; V4: $\hat{\beta}$=−0.37, t=−3.46, p<0.001).

In French, intensity does not seem to correlate with word/phrase-final prominence (Figure 11.8). Instead, what we see is a flat pattern for words at the left edge of the phrase, and a descending pattern for words at the right

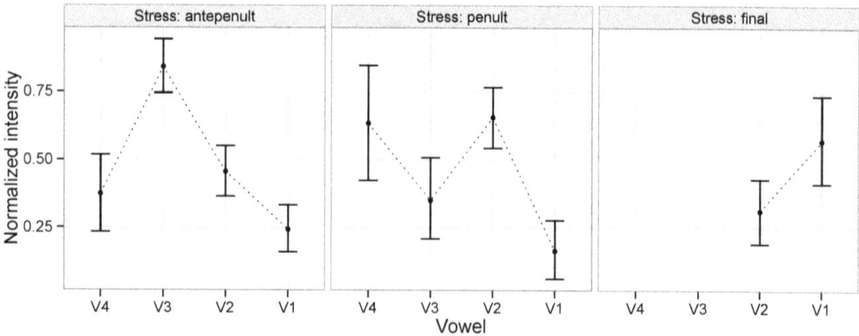

Figure 11.7. Normalized intensity of different vowels in target words: English control. V1 = right edge of the word.

edge (as expected, given this is the final word in the phrase). This result is consistent with the literature, as prominence in French is not associated with loudness. In fact, a regression model that includes an interaction between vowel and edge confirms that V3 has overall significantly higher intensity than V1 ($\hat{\beta}$=0.46, t=3.37, p<0.001), and that both V2 and V3 have significantly higher intensity than V1 at the right edge (V2: $\hat{\beta}$=0.34, t=2.42, p=0.016; V3: $\hat{\beta}$=0.48, t=2.61, p=0.009). In other words, there is no clear positive correlation between intensity and word-level prominence in our CF data (if we assume that CF PWds exhibit final prominence).

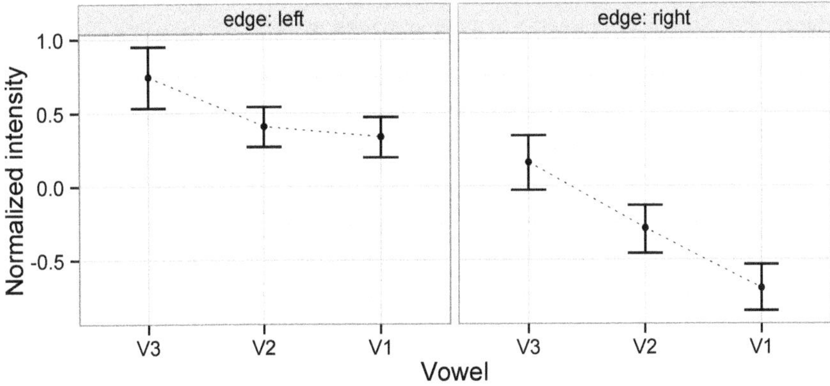

Figure 11.8. Normalized intensity of different vowels in target words by PPh edge: French controls. V1 = word-final vowel.

Looking at L2ers' production data, we see a pattern that resembles that of Figure 11.7. Stress and intensity seem to be correlated (note that very few data points with penultimate stress contain more than three vowels in Figure 11.9).

In words with final stress, penult vowels (V2) have significantly lower intensity than final vowels (V1): $\hat{\beta}$=−0.25, t=−4.35, p<0.0001. In words with penult stress, both V3 and V1 have significantly lower intensity than V2 (V3: $\hat{\beta}$=−0.36, t=−5.30, p<0.0001; V1: $\hat{\beta}$=−0.93, t=−18.77, p<0.00001). Finally, in words with antepenult stress, V1, V2 and V4 all have significantly lower intensity than V3, the most prominent vowel in the word (V1: $\hat{\beta}$=−0.99, t=−23.97, p<0.00001; V2: $\hat{\beta}$=−0.77, t=−18.63, p<0.00001; V4: $\hat{\beta}$= −0.55, t=−9.47, p<0.00001).

Importantly, the intensity of V2 and V3 in Figure 11.9 rises in relation to its surrounding vowels in words with penultimate and antepenultimate stress, respectively. This mirrors what we see in our control data (Figure 11.7).

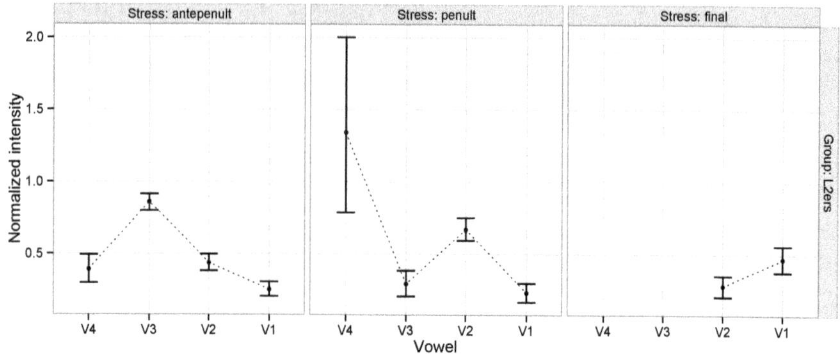

Figure 11.9. Normalized intensity of different vowels in target words: L2ers. V1 = right edge of the word.

In sum, the data show robust (and target-like) correlations between stress, duration, pitch and intensity in L2ers' production. Crucially, these patterns are clearly different from what we see in our CF data. It is important to note, however, that duration, pitch and intensity are naturally not completely orthogonal. Indeed, among L2ers' data, duration is significantly correlated with intensity (r=0.16, p<0.0001) and pitch (r=−12, p<0.0001); and intensity is significantly correlated with pitch (r=0.31, p<0.0001). Such collinearity indicates that we cannot be completely certain about the role of each of these acoustic correlates taken independently given the data.

Note, however, that all three cues examined above showed no clear correlation with L1 prominence. Even though duration is often said to be the most robust correlate of prominence in French, L2ers are not merely transferring the duration patterns present in their L1. Rather, they accurately produced the rhythmic patterns observed in our control data – indeed, rhythmic patterns are observed through duration and intensity. In other words, regardless of the orthogonality of the phonetic correlates measured, it is clear that L2ers are not merely applying their L1 patterns to the L2.

11.5 Implications and Final Remarks

Our results for duration, pitch and intensity in CF provide no evidence to support the suggestion that this language has word-level stress or word-internal constituency. Thus, what is perceived as prominence in CF may in fact be the result of phrasal boundary effects. This is in line with what some researchers have proposed for EF prominence (e.g. Jun and Fougeron 2000; Gussenhoven 2004) and for internal constituency in both EF and CF (Jun and Fougeron 2000; Özçelik 2011).

The results from our CF data have two main implications: (a) prominence may not be a property of the phonological word (PWd), and (b) word-internal constituency (i.e. foot structure) is not universal. Implication (a) contradicts the traditional notion of PWd (e.g. Nespor and Vogel 1986), according to which such constituent corresponds to a lexical stem (plus incorporated elements, such as prefixes and suffixes), and is the domain where primary stress is assigned. However, recent analyses (e.g. Vogel 2009) exclude primary stress assignment as one of the exclusive properties of the PWd.

Implication (b), on the other hand, alters the notion of the prosodic hierarchy (Selkirk 1984; Nespor and Vogel 1986) as the universal scale of suprasegmental domains in which specific phonological processes apply. In the partial representation of the universal prosodic hierarchy presented in (10), we notice that the constituent that immediately dominates the syllable (σ) is the Foot, which in turn is dominated by the PWd. If we assume that certain languages have no foot structure, then the Foot is not a universal prosodic domain, but a parametric domain (Özçelik 2011). This means that, while feet may be activated in the grammar of some languages, it may be absent in other languages. The representation in (11) illustrates the partial prosodic structure of CF. Note that the constituent that immediately dominates the syllable in (11) is the PWd.

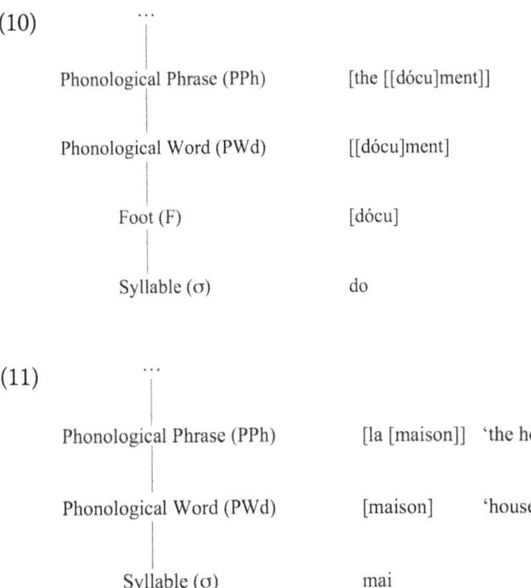

Despite the fact that CF seems to have no word-internal constituency, CF learners of English are able to acquire feet: in our results, L2ers exhibit target-like rhythmic patterns and stress, and use duration and intensity to signal both primary and secondary stresses in a way that mirrors what is observed in our English control data. This indicates that, even though foot structure seems to be absent in the speakers' L1 (see Özçelik 2011), they are able to acquire it in an L2. Pitch also seems to be used to signal primary stress, which is consistent with previous studies on English stress.

To conclude, the results indicate that, while word-level prominence and word-internal constituency seem absent in our CF data, CF speakers are able to acquire word stress and foot structure in English. Furthermore, the L2ers produce English stress with target-like rhythmic patterns and, as observed in our English control data, use both duration and intensity to signal word-internal prominence.

Acknowledgements

We would like to thank Heather Goad, Annie Tremblay, Peter Milne and Jeffrey Lamontagne for their feedback.

Appendix: Unique Items Analysed in Each Task

Note: Repeated and inflected (pluralized) words are not shown.

French Words

maison	dernière	bâtiment	moderne	élégant
président	dernier	période	heureuse	maladie
nouvelle	mauvaise	touriste	portugaise	historique
première	premier	donneur	garçon	vanille
fabrique	gâteau	cuisine	fromage	central
jolie	nouveau	fondateur	chanson	fâché
mauvais	étrange	famille	japonais	comptable
morceau	bureau	province	dessin	repoussant
chocolat	plateau	prospère	tropicale	colorée

English Words

damage	reasonable	general	fully	hospital
hurricane	hypothesis	ridiculous	request	presumably
completely	president	assaults	academic	comment
senator	quality	garage	minister	family
reasonably	possibly	probably	economy	attack
positive	analysis	event	director	soldiers
support	salute	different	negative	recruit
pyramids	complete	substance	decent	antique
chemical	adorable	impressive	orchestra	musician
pollution	review	division	frequent	cousins
inferior	eclipse	defeat	promise	miserable
physicians	impressively	dramatic	intelligent	garages

References

Altmann, H. (2006). *The Perception and Production of Second Language Stress: A Crosslinguistic Experimental Study*. PhD Dissertation, University of Delaware.

Armstrong, S.D. (1999). *Stress and Weight in Québec French*. MA Thesis, University of Calgary.

Beckman, M.E. (1986). *Stress and Non-Stress Accent*. Dordrecht: Foris Publications.

Chomsky, N. and Halle, M. (1968). *The Sound Pattern of English*. New York: Harper and Row.

Fry, D.B. (1955). Duration intensity as physical correlates of linguistic stress. *Journal of the Acoustical Society of America*, 32: 765–9.

Fry, D.B. (1958). Experiments in the perception of stress. *Language and Speech* 1: 126–52.

Garde, P. (1968). *L'Accent*. Paris: Presses Universitaires de France.

Goad, H. and Buckley, M. (2006). Prosodic structure in child French: Evidence for the foot. *Catalan Journal of Linguistics* 5: 109–42.

Goad, H. and Prévost, A.-E. (2011). *A Test Case for Markedness: The Acquisition of Québec French Stress*. Unpublished Manuscript.

Grimson, A. (1980). *An Introduction to the Pronunciation of English* (3rd edition). London: Edward Arnold.

Gussenhoven, C. (2004). *The Phonology of Tone and Intonation*. Cambridge: Cambridge University Press.

Halle, M. and Vergnaud, J. R. (1987). *An Essay on Stress*. Cambridge, MA: MIT Press.

Harrington, J., Beckman, M.E., Fletcher, J. and Palethorpe, S. (1998). An electropalatography, kinematic, and acoustic analysis of supralaryngeal correlates of word and utterance-level prominence contrasts in English. In *Proceedings of the 1998 International Conference on Spoken Language Processing*, Vol. 5, 1851–1854. Sydney, Australia.

Hayes, B. (1982). Extrametricality and English stress. *Linguistic Inquiry* 13: 227–76.

Jun, S.-A. and Fougeron, C. (2000). A phonological model of French intonation. In Botinis, A. (ed.), *Intonation: Analysis, Modelling and Technology*, 209–42. Dordrecht: Kluwer.

Laver, J. (1994). *Principles of Phonetics*. Cambridge: Cambridge University Press.

Lehiste, I. (1976). Influence of fundamental frequency pattern on the perception of duration. *Journal of Phonetics* 4: 113–17.

Liberman, M. and Prince, A. (1977). On stress and linguistic rhythm. *Linguistic Inquiry* 8: 249–336.

Lieberman, P. (1960). Some acoustic correlates of word stress in American English. *Journal of the Acoustical Society of America* 32: 451–4.

Milne, P. (2012). *SPLaligner, an Automatic Forced Alignment System for French.*

Nespor, M. and Vogel, I. (1986) *Prosodic Phonology*. Dordrecht: Foris.

Özçelik, Ö. (2011). *Representation and Acquisition of Stress: The Case of Turkish.* PhD Dissertation, McGill University, Montreal.

Paradis, C. and Deshaies, D. (1990). Rules of stress assignment in Québec French: evidence from perceptual data. *Language Variation and Change* 2: 135–54.

Plag, I., Kunter, G., and Schramm, M. (2011). Acoustic correlates of primary and secondary stress in North American English. *Journal of Phonetics* 39(3): 362–74.

Selkirk, E. O. (1980). On prosodic structure and its relation to syntactic structure. Indiana University Linguistics Club.

Selkirk, E. O. (1984). *Phonology and Syntax: the Relation Between Sound and Structure.* Cambridge, MA: MIT Press.

Selkirk, E. O. (1986). On derived domains in sentence phonology. *Phonology* 3: 371–405.

Thibault. L. and Ouellet, M. (1996). Tonal distinctions between emphatic stress and pretonic lengthening in Quebec French. *Proceedings of the International Conference on Spoken Language 96, Philadelphia*, 2: 638–41.

Tremblay, A. (2007). *Bridging the Gap between Theoretical Linguistics and Psycho-Linguistics in L2 Phonology: Acquisition and Processing of Word Stress by French Canadian L2 Learners of English.* PhD Dissertation, University of Hawaii at Manoa.

Tremblay, A. (2008). Is second language lexical access prosodically constrained? Processing of word stress by French Canadian second language learners of English. *Applied Psycholinguistics* 29: 553–84.

Tremblay, A. and Owens, N. (2010). The role of acoustic cues in the development of (non-)target-like second-language prosodic representations. *The Canadian Journal of Linguistics* 55(1): 85–114.

Vogel, I. (2009) The status of the Clitic Group. In Grijzenhout, J. and Kabak, B. (eds.), *Phonological Domains: Universals and Deviations.* Berlin: Mouton de Gruyter.

Walker, D.C. (1984). *The Pronunciation of Canadian French.* Ottawa: University of Ottawa Press.

Guilherme Duarte Garcia is a fourth-year PhD student at McGill University, Montreal.

Natália Brambatti Guzzo has a PhD in Linguistics from Universidade Federal do Rio Grande do Sul, in Porto Alegre, Brazil.

12
Factors Affecting L2 Learning across the Lifespan: Spanish Learners of English

Wendy Baker-Smemoe

12.1 Introduction

The goal of the Speech Learning Model (SLM) (Flege 1995, 2003) is to explain second language (L2) speech acquisition. As such, it postulates that as L2 learners distinguish native language (L1) sounds from L2 sounds, they are able to create new L2 sound categories. Doing so leads to accurate L2 speech perception and production. The SLM also predicts that the ability to create new L2 sound categories depends on the similarity between L1 and L2 sounds. 'Similar' L2 sounds are perceptually close to L1 sound categories (such as Spanish /i/ and English /i/ for Spanish learners of English), whereas 'new' L2 sounds (such as English /ɪ/ for these same learners) are more distant perceptually and acoustically. New L2 sounds require acquisition of a completely new sound category, and this may be easier than creating a sound category for similar L2 sounds (Flege, Bohn and Jang 1997). Other speech acquisition theories, such as the Perceptual Assimilation Model for L2 (PAM-L2), make similar predictions about new and similar sounds, although PAM-L2 focuses on L2 sound contrasts instead of individual sounds (Best and Tyler 2007).

Although the SLM has many other tenets (see Flege 1995 for a list), one of its most examined is that the learning of L2 sounds doesn't diminish in later life (Flege 1995, 2003). That is, the SLM posits that there is no 'critical period' after which it is impossible or difficult to acquire an L2, or as Flege (2003: 8) states, 'the capacities underlying successful L1 speech acquisition remain intact across the lifespan.' On the other hand, a critical period posits that maturational constraints occur that cause language acquisition to be more difficult, whether this is a diminished ability to 'induce abstract patterns implicitly' (DeKeyser 2000: 519) or a loss of neural plasticity that causes any learning to be difficult after a certain age. While the SLM acknowledges that 'age effects' occur for L2 speech acquisition, the cause of these effects, it posits, is not a critical period.

12.1.1 Studies for and against a Critical Period

Much of the recent research examining age effects and the SLM focuses on two aspects (e.g. Flege, Yeni-Komshian and Liu 1999; Flege and MacKay 2010; Flege 2003). First, this research proposes that, if there is a critical period, we should see a sharp cut-off in accuracy at some age – so that those who acquired the L2 before this period would be indistinguishable from native speakers, and those acquiring the L2 after would have very poor accuracy. One of the earliest of these studies, Johnson and Newport (1989), demonstrated a gradual decline as a function of age of acquisition (AOA) in grammaticality judgements by Korean and Chinese learners of English until about the age of 17. After 17, the learners' results more closely resembled a flat slope, and did not vary as a function of AOA. A more recent study by DeKeyser, Alfi-Shabtay and Ravid (2010) also demonstrated that a gradual decline in L2 grammatical judgement scores occurred for learners who acquired their L2 before age 18, but that such a decline did not occur for those who acquired the L2 after 18. Instead there was a flat slope suggesting that after age 18, there was a change in how the L2 was acquired. Several other studies have demonstrated similar results with varying ages for the cut-off (e.g. Abrahamsson and Hyltenstam 2008; Abrahamsson 2012).

By contrast, Flege and his colleagues have demonstrated no sharp cut off or change in L2 accuracy as a function of age. For example, Flege et al. (1999) tested this aspect of the critical period by examining 240 Korean-English bilinguals' production of English sentences and their ratings for global foreign accent (GFA) by native English-speaking judges. These bilinguals differed from each other in their AOA, from 1 to 23 years. The results of correlating these GFA scores with AOA demonstrated a gradual decline of abilities from 1 to 23 years, without any evidence of a cut-off that would be supported by a critical period. Similar results were found by Flege, Munro and MacKay (1995). Moreover, when Flege et al. (1999) ran correlations separately on early (AOA before age 12) and late (AOA after age 12) learners' GFA scores, both groups' scores correlated strongly with AOA, suggesting that there was no discernible cut-off after which AOA no longer affected GFA. Since this study by Flege et al. (1999), several studies have demonstrated differences between early learners and native speakers, and have also suggested a gradual decline in L2 speech acquisition abilities as a function of AOA (Darcy and Kruger 2012; Oh, Guion-Anderson, Aoyama, Flege, Akahane-Yamada and Yamada, 2011).

How can we reconcile the differences in the findings by Flege and colleagues with the results obtained by those advocating a critical period? One may argue that grammatical acquisition is different from phonological acquisition. As support for this explanation, in Flege et al. (1999) both grammaticality judgements and GFA were examined, and GFA was found to have a much steeper decline with increasing AOA than the grammaticality judgements had. One problem with this explanation, though, is that Abrahamsson (2012) compared age effects on both grammatical judgement tests and a test of voice onset time (VOT) by L2 learners of Swedish. He found the the results for both grammaticality judgement tests and VOT scores were similar – with AOA correlating more strongly with younger learners for both tasks.

Another possibility proposed by Flege and MacKay (2010) is that other variables are confounded with AOA – such as amount of L2 use, current age and length of residence (LOR), among other variables. These variables need to be partialed out when running correlations between AOA and any feature of L2 acquisition. Such factors have been demonstrated in several studies to affect L2 speech acquisition (see Piske, MacKay and Flege 2001).

It is also possible that the differences between Abrahamsson (2012) and Flege et al. (1999) were the result of what was tested in phonological learning. Flege et al. (1999) tested GFA, a production task that tested all aspects of L2 speech acquisition, while Abrahamsson (2012) tested a specific feature, VOT. Therefore, to adequately compare the research of these two camps, it would be necessary to carry out an analysis of both GFA and specific features of the L2 sound system in the same learners, with any confounding variables such as current age, LOR and L2 use partialed out. Because the focus of the SLM is often on the difference in acquisition of new and similar sounds, the current study will compare the perception of new and similar vowels by native Spanish learners of English.

12.1.2 Factors That May Explain Differences between Early and Late L2 Learners

The second feature of age effects that will be examined is what may cause age effects in L2 speech acquisition. Three possible factors – experiential, cognitive and social factors – are discussed below.

Experiential Factors

According to the SLM, experiential factors such as amount of L2 language use are the cause of age effects in L2 speech learning. In particular, the SLM posits that bilinguals cannot completely separate their two phonetic systems, and that the interaction between these two systems develops throughout childhood and early adolescence. Thus, the ability to separate these two systems becomes more difficult, not because of any maturational constraints, but because, as L1 categories develop throughout childhood and early adolescence, the interference from the L1 system on the L2 system becomes greater. As support for this, Baker, Trofimovich, Mack and Flege (2002) demonstrated that as L1 sound categories developed, L2 vowels were more likely to be identified by learners as instances of L1 categories. In addition, Flege and MacKay (2004) demonstrated that early and late Italian learners of English who used the L1 (Italian) more often were less accurate in perceiving English vowels. They suggested that this is because there was a greater interference from the L1 sound system for these learners, and that later learners tended to have used the L1 more often than younger learners.

This interference may be especially true for similar vowels versus new vowels, since early learners seem to improve on their perception and production of new vowels, but may not for similar vowels (Oh et al. 2011). In addition, others argue that LOR may also play a role since this indicates for how long a learner has been using the language, at least if they use the L2 often and on a daily basis (Flege and Liu 2001).

Cognitive Factors

By contrast, proponents of the critical period argue that the differences between early and late learners occur because of changes in cognitive abilities as learners age. They argue that individual differences in factors such as LOR, L2 use or cognitive abilities play little role in early learners' acquisition, whereas older learners who achieve high L2 accuracy scores usually differ from other late learners by their high language aptitude or cognitive abilities (Abrahamsson and Hyltenstam 2008). For example, DeKeyser et al. (2010) demonstrated that verbal aptitude correlated with grammaticality judgement scores for those learners who acquired their L2 after age 18, but not for those who acquired it before this time. Moreover, both DeKeyser et al. (2010) and Abrahamsson and Hyltenstam (2008) demonstrated that neither LOR nor L2 use explained differences in learners' scores – just AOA for early learners and verbal aptitude for late learners. Some cognitive abilities on these aptitude tests measure such things as analytical skills, phonetic memory, inferencing, memory for unfamiliar sound sequences, etc. (see Abrahamsson and Hyltenstam 2008: 493).

Unfortunately, it is still unclear whether cognitive factors (aptitude) differ for early versus late learners when examining L2 speech learning. In fact, it is unclear what 'aptitude' for L2 phonological learning may be. There are, however, studies that have suggested that working memory and phonological memory (i.e. the ability to recall nonsense syllables) affect whether late learners are successful in L2 acquisition (Hummel 2009; O'Brien, Segalowitz, Collentine and Freed 2007). In fact, MacKay, Meador and Flege (2001) demonstrated that phonological working memory does predict to some degree the accuracy with which L2 learners perceive L2 sounds. These two abilities therefore may be some cognitive factors that decline over the lifespan and may cause declining L2 acquisition abilities in late learners. Another possible cognitive factor is the ability to imitate previously unheard L2 sounds (Hummel 2009). However, few researchers have examined these aptitude factors to explain age effects in L2 *speech* acquisition.

Social Factors

One limitation of both Flege's research and DeKeyser's work is that neither has examined the role that specific social factors may play in explaining age effects. Some studies suggest that motivation to learn the L2, or identifying more with the L2 culture, may affect L2 learning for both early (Toohey 2001) and later (Palfreyman 2006) learners. Social factors may also include the learners' attitudes towards the L1 culture (Gatbonton, Trofimovich and Magid 2005) or their social networks (who they interact with) (Dewey, Bown and Eggett 2012). Of the three types of explanations described here (experiential, cognitive and social), social factors have been used the least to explain age effects, although they have been used to explain why some late learners perform more accurately than others (Moyer 1999).

While past research has demonstrated that age effects may be related to experiential, cognitive and social factors (see Moyer 2004), the relative importance of these three factors is still debated, especially as they relate to age effects. Indeed, it often appears that researchers fall into one of these three camps, supporting either experiential, cognitive or social explanations for why age effects occur, with little research examining all three factors in one study (but see Baker-Smemoe 2015 for a preliminary report on L2 perception).

12.1.3 Spanish Learners of English

Spanish learners of English in the United States provide an excellent group for testing age effects and whether experiential, social or cognitive factors best explain why age effects occur. Because there are so many native Spanish speakers living in the Western United States, there are many speakers who differ in their AOA, the types of speakers in their social networks, and their daily L2 use. In addition, the English and Spanish vowel systems are ideally suited for examining the difference between new and similar vowels. In previous research, it has been determined that Spanish vowels /i/, /u/ and /a/ are identified often with English tense vowels /i/, /u/ and /ɑ/ respectively, suggesting that they may be considered 'similar' across the two languages (Imai, Flege and Wayland 2002), but that the English lax vowels (/ɪ/, /ʊ/, /ʌ/) may be 'new' vowels (Flege et al. 1997).

12.1.4 Research Questions

The two goals of this study are (1) to examine age effects on both overall production accuracy and the perception acquisition of specific L2 sound features; and (2) to examine whether social, cognitive or experiential factors best explain age effects in L2 speech acquisition. In order to fulfil the two goals of this study, the following research questions are addressed:

1. Is there a difference in correlations of AOA of L2 speech abilities with GFA (a measure of overall L2 production ability) and with the perception of both new and similar sounds (a measure of one perceptual L2 feature)?
2. If so, do these differences occur for both early and late learners?
3. Is there a difference between what types of factors affect learners' L2 speech acquisition (social, cognitive and experiential) of GFA and for the perception of both new and similar sounds?
4. If so, do these differences occur for both early and late learners?

12.2 Participants

Seventy-six native Spanish speakers participated in the study. Based on their answers to a language background questionnaire, which asked their age of English acquisition (AOA), length of residence (LOR) in the United States and estimated amount of L2 use, half of the participants (38) were considered 'early learners', having learned English before the age of 14, and half (38) were considered 'late learners', having learned English after this age. An AOA of 14 was used as a cut-off for convenience, but also because a similar age (between 12 and 15) is often used in the literature (Flege et al. 1999; Abrahamsson 2012). In the case of our participants, this age

Table 12.1. Average scores of participants' experiential demographics (standard deviations in parentheses).

Group	Number	AOA	LOR	Current Age	Self-Reported English Rating	L2 Use
Early (>14)	38	6.2 (4.16) Range: 0–14	11.36 (4.68)	21 (9.86) Range: 12–53	8.6 (1.05)	56% (22%)
Late (<14)	38	28.2 (10.25) Range: 17–69	11.19 (8.82)	40 (10.80) Range: 18–72	6.7 (2.11)	60% (23%)

AOA = Age of Acquisition; LOR = Length of Residence; Self-Reported English Ratings were from 1 (I don't speak English at all) to 10 (I am a native English speaker).

provided a good cut-off since the next youngest AOA was 17. It should be emphasized that the average current ages of the two participant groups differed greatly from each other (21 for the early learners and 40 for the older learners). In addition, one of the participants' AOA was 69 years, which was considerably greater than the next oldest participant's AOA (48). See Table 12.1 for the pertinent demographics of each group.

12.3 Experiment 1: Correlations of Perception and Production and Age

The purpose of experiment 1 was to answer the first two research questions: (1) is there a difference in correlations between AOA of L2 speech abilities for GFA and for the perception of new and similar sounds, and (2) if so, do these differences occur for both early and late learners? In order to accomplish this purpose, native English speakers rated sentences produced by the native Spanish participants and the participants performed perception tasks of similar and new vowels (explained below). These scores were then correlated with AOA separately for early and late learners.

12.3.1 Global Foreign Accent

Participants were asked to read English sentences that were semantically appropriate. A total of 14 sentences were read (see Appendix for the full list of sentences). All participants reported being able to read in English before participating and all were able to read the sentences with little difficulty. They were given time to read over the sentences so that they could familiarize themselves with them before recording. Five college-aged native English speakers were also asked to read the sentences as control subjects to ensure that the listeners were rating the sentences as intended.

Ten native English speakers enrolled in a beginning Linguistics course were later recruited to listen to the sentences and rate them on a scale from 1, 'this person has a heavy non-native English accent', to 9, 'this person sounds like a native English speaker'. Each participant's scores were averaged across the sentences they produced and the scores of each of the ten raters. The late group had an average score of 4.09 (SD: 1.78), the early group had an average of 7.87 (SD: 0.84), and the native English speakers had an average rating of 8.91 (SD: 0.10).

12.3.2 Perception of New and Similar Vowels

Three native English male speakers were asked to produce words containing the vowels used in this study, *bead* (/i/), *bid* (/ɪ/), *booed* (/u/), *book* (/ʊ/), *bought* (/ɑ/) and *but* (/ʌ/), plus two other vowels not examined in this study, *bad* (/æ/) and *bed* (/ɛ/). Listeners heard three tokens of each of the three speakers for a total of 72 tokens altogether. On the computer screen were buttons, which contained words with each of these vowels. Participants were asked to click on the word that corresponded with the word they had just heard. Participants could listen to the words as many times as they wanted before making their selection, but could not change their selection once it was made. Before testing, participants verified that they knew each of the words.

The percentages of correct responses for the similar (/i/, /u/, /ɑ/) and new (/ɪ/, /ʌ/, /ʊ/) vowels were calculated. The native English speaker controls also participated in this task to ensure that the tokens were appropriate. Average percentages of accuracy for the early and late learners and the native English controls for each group of vowels are given in Table 12.2.

Table 12.2. Average percentage of accuracy in perception of new and similar vowels (standard deviations in parentheses).

	New	Similar
Early Learners (AOA range: 0–14)	0.708 (0.247)	0.822 (0.228)
Late Learners (AOA range: 17–69)	0.359 (0.192)	0.57 (0.215)
Native English Controls	0.941 (0.034)	0.970 (0.033)

12.3.3 Results

In order to determine whether both early and late learners' scores (GFA, perception of similar vowels, and perception of new vowels) were correlated with age, Pearson correlations were run (see Figures 12.1–12.3) for all participants combined and then for early and late learners individually. In addition, partial correlations were run with LOR, L2 use and current age partialed out since these three factors often confound with AOA (DeKeyser et al. 2010; Flege et al. 1999). Figures show correlations before the three factors were partialed out.

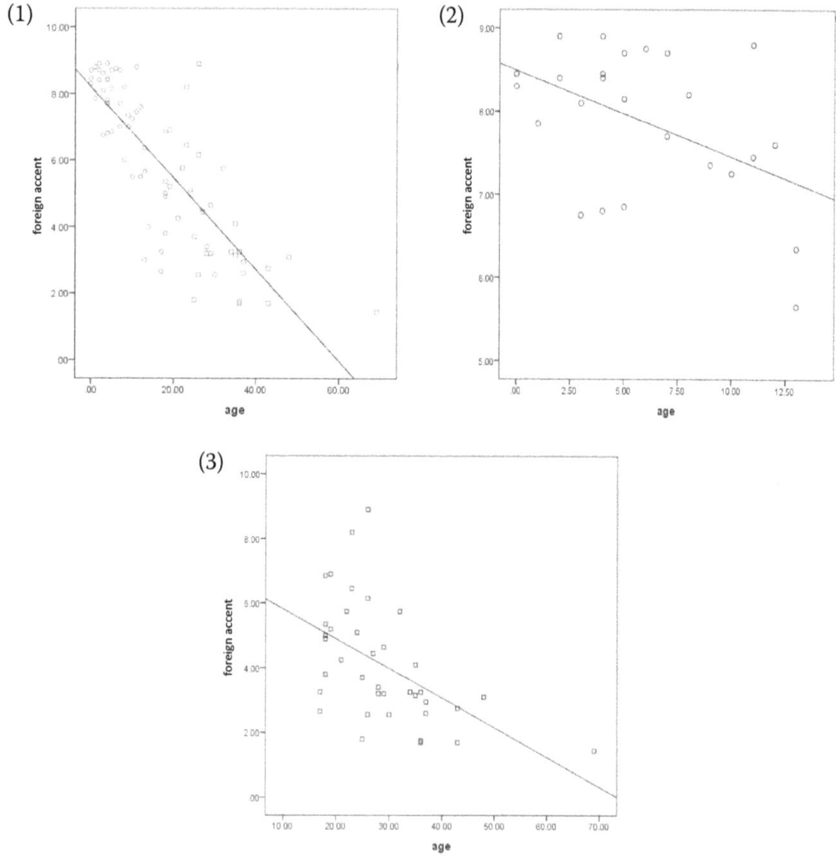

Figure 12.1. Age and GFA correlations for (1) all participants (–8.17**; –0.601**), (2) early learners (–0.685**; –0.553**) and (3) late learners (–0.568**; –0.318).
Correlations are in parentheses, with the second number in each case indicating correlations when current age, LOR and L2 use are partialed out. Shown are correlations before being partialed out.
** p<0.01.

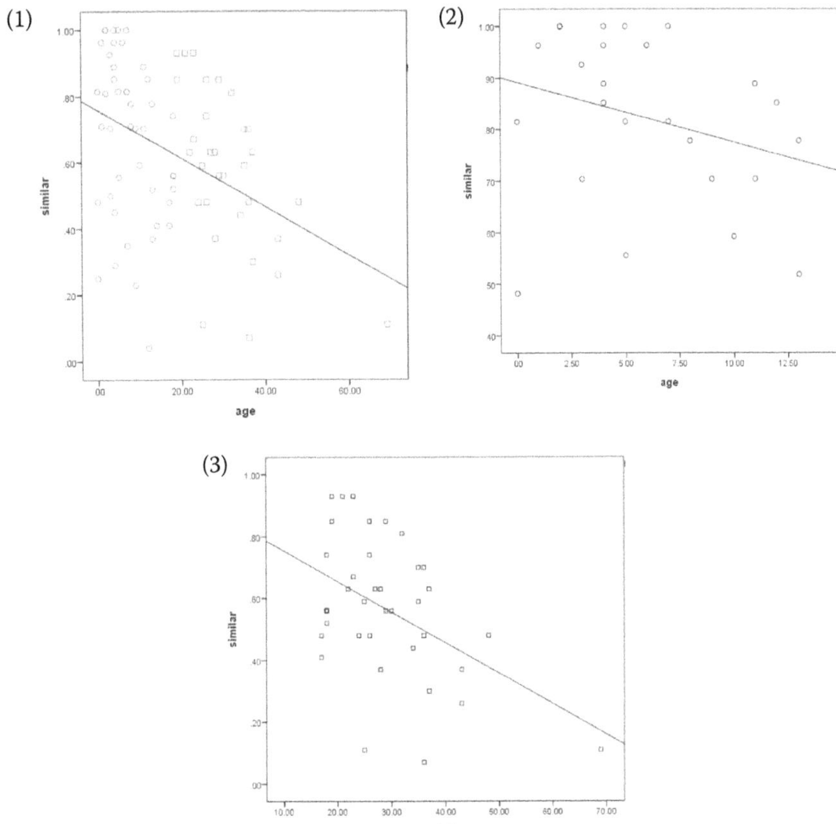

Figure 12.2. Age and perception of similar vowel correlations for (1) all participants (–0.642**, –0.405**), (2) early learners (–0.289; –0.345) and (3) late learners (–0.459**; –0.271).

Correlations are in parentheses, with the second number in each case indicating correlations when current age, LOR and L2 use are partialed out. Shown are correlations before current age, L2 use and LOR were partialed out.

** p<0.01.

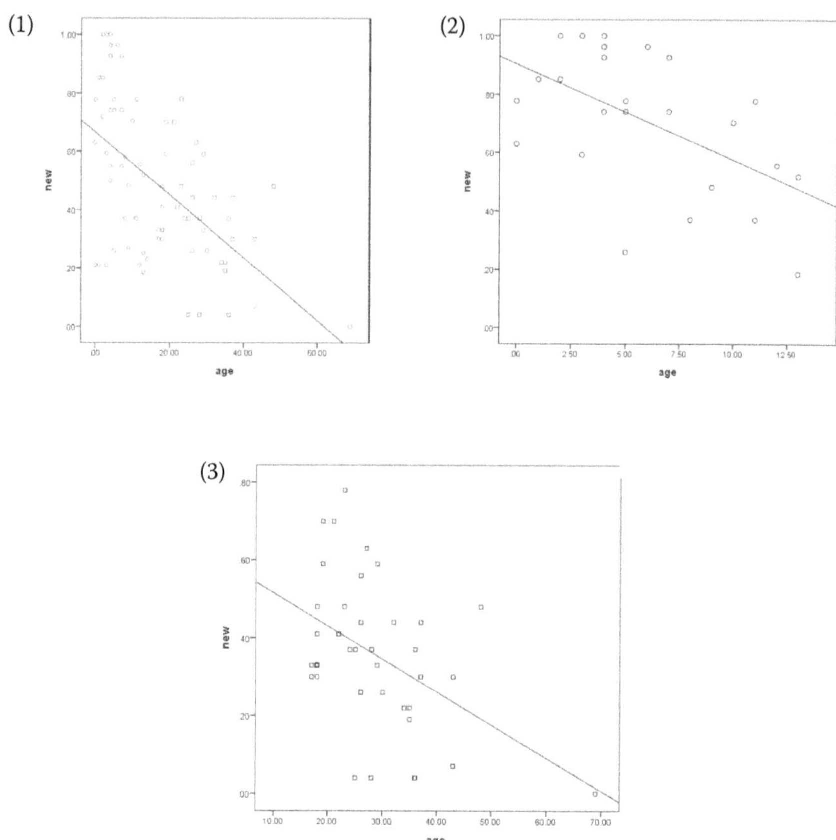

Figure 12.3. Age and perception of new vowel correlations for (1) all participants (–0.697**, –0.558**), (2) early learners (–0.549*; –0.621**) and (3) late learners (–0.442**; –0.402**).
Correlations are in parentheses, with the second number in each case indicating correlations when current age, LOR and L2 use are partialed out. Shown are correlations before being partialed out.
* $p<0.05$; ** $p<0.01$.

As these results indicate, all three measures of L2 speech acquisition strongly correlated with AOA when all participants were examined together (GFA, –0.817; similar vowels –0.642; new vowels, –0.697), and even when current age, L2 use and LOR were partialed out (GFA, –0.601; similar vowels –0.405; new vowels, –0.558), all significant at $p<0.01$. Thus, to answer question 1 of this study, we found that there was a strong correlation of AOA with all three measures of L2 speech acquisition.

To answer question 2, we found that AOA was strongly correlated with both early and late learners for new vowels (early, –0.549; late, –0.442), even when current age, L2 use and LOR were partialed out (early, –0.621; late, –0.402). Similarly, we found that AOA correlated with both early and late learners' GFA scores (early, –0.685; late, –0.568) when simple correlations were run. However, when LOR, L2 use, and current age were partialed out, the correlations were significant for the early learners' scores, but not for the late learners' (early, –0.553; late, –0.318). Surprisingly, unlike any previous studies, AOA effects were not found for similar vowels for early learners; neither when current age, LOR and L2 use were (–0.345) nor when they were not (–0.289) partialed out. In addition, there was a correlation between AOA and perception of similar vowels for the late learners (–0.459), but there was no correlation for the late learners when current age, L2 use and LOR were partialed out (–0.271).

12.4 Experiment 2: Cognitive, Social and Experiential Factors

The purpose of experiment 2 was to examine questions 3 and 4 of this study: (3) is there a difference between what types of factors affect learners' L2 speech acquisition (social, cognitive and experiential) for both GFA and for the perception of new and similar vowels, and (4) if so, do these differences occur for both early and late learners? To answer these questions, participants' production and perception scores were examined using experiential, cognitive and social factors as predictor variables.

12.4.1 Experiential Factors

As explained in Section 12.2 on the participants, experiential factors included AOA, LOR and daily English use (L2 use). How these were calculated is also explained in that section.

12.4.2 Cognitive Factors

Participants completed three cognitive tasks. Average scores for the early and late groups on these tasks are given in Table 12.3.

The first task that participants completed was a backwards digit span test used to determine general working memory capacity. In this task, participants heard a list of numbers (e.g. 1, 7, 3) and were asked to repeat them in the opposite order (e.g. 3, 7, 1). The first trial had three digits and one digit was added to each trial until the participants were no longer able to complete the task. Participants were given a score of 1 for each correct repetition and 0 if there were any mistakes. A maximum score of 20 was possible on this task.

The second task was a phonological memory task where participants heard two lists of 7 monosyllabic nonsense words and were asked to determine whether they were given in the same or a different order. These syllables followed both Spanish and English phonotactics. As with the working memory task, participants were given a score of 1 for each correct response and 0 for an incorrect one.

The final cognitive task used the Arabic phrases found in in Hummel (2009: Appendix B). These words and sentences were spoken by a native Arabic female speaker and were used in an imitation task. Participants heard these short Arabic phrases and were asked to repeat them exactly as they heard them. The phrases differed in the number of syllables from 3 to 9. None of the participants reported having learned or studied Arabic before completing this task. A trained phonetician determined the phonetic accuracy of their renditions and they were given 1 point for each syllable they were able to imitate, with a maximum score of 68 possible.

Table 12.3. Average scores on three cognitive tasks and surveys of three social factors.

	Early Learners	Late Learners
Cognitive Tasks:		
Working memory capacity	5.12 (1.84)	5.44 (1.72)
Phonological memory capacity	16.44 (3.58)	15.12 (2.88)
Ability to imitate	49.48 (5.71)	50.08 (9.71)
Social Factors:		
Number of native Spanish speakers in social network	2.08 (0.89)	2.22 (0.88)
L1 identity	6.42 (1.76)	6.76 (1.51)
L2 identity	5.32 (1.41)	6.17 (1.63)

12.4.3 Social Factors

To determine the extent that social factors affect second language phonological learning, participants were asked to fill out a survey regarding their social networks, and how much they identified with their L1 and L2 cultures. Average scores for the two learner groups are given in Table 12.3.

Social networks were identified by asking the participants to determine how many of the top three people they interacted with most were native English or native Spanish speakers, how many they were related to, and what languages they spoke with each of them. The number of Spanish speakers among these top three interactants was the score used in this analysis.

In addition, participants read 22 statements on a 9-point scale based on the Ethnic Group Affiliation (EGA) proposed in Gatbonton and Trofimovich (2008) and adapted to an American audience. Some of the statements (e.g. 'I am Latino' and 'People who don't speak Spanish do not deserve to call themselves Latino') were related to their identification with the L1 culture, while others (e.g. 'I am American' and 'I feel like I belong in America') were related to their identification with the L2 culture. The 11 statements on L1 identity were averaged for a score of L1 identity and the 11 statements on L2 culture were averaged for the L2 identity score.

12.4.4 Results

The first purpose of this experiment was to determine the relative importance of experiential, social and cognitive factors on GFA scores and the perception of new and similar sounds for both early and late learners on three measures. This was done by running three multiple regression analyses (MRA) with the following three scores as separate dependent variables: GFA, perception scores of new vowels and perception scores of similar vowels. The nine factors described above (3 experiential, 3 social and 3 cognitive factors) served as predictor variables. The results of these analyses are given in Table 12.4.

These results suggest, as previous research also does, that AOA is a major factor contributing to acquiring all aspects of L2 speech acquisition, both GFA and the perception of new and similar vowels. In addition, these results suggest that social (how strongly a learner identifies with the L2 culture) and experiential factors (L2 use) affect GFA scores. By contrast, it appears that mainly cognitive factors (ability to imitate) affect perception scores.

Table 12.4. Results of a series of MRAs for all participants, and early and late learners separately.

	GFA (adjusted R^2 scores)	New vowels (adjusted R^2 scores)	Similar vowels (adjusted R^2 scores)
All Participants	AOA 0.65	AOA 0.29	Ability to imitate 0.21
	L2 identity (–)0.05	Ability to imitate 0.11	AOA 0.14
	LOR 0.03		L2 use 0.02
	Total 0.73	Total 0.40	Total 0.37
Early Learners	AOA 0.49	Ability to imitate 0.22	Ability to imitate 0.27
	LOR 0.06	AOA 0.13	Phonological memory 0.07
		Working memory 0.09	
	Total 0.55	Total 0.44	Total 0.34
Late Learners	L2 identity (–)0.32	Ability to imitate 0.31	Ability to imitate 0.30
	Working memory 0.13	Native Spanish friends 0.08	L2 use 0.10
	Total 0.45	Total 0.39	Total 0.40

The second purpose of this experiment was to examine whether these factors play a different role in late and early L2 learners' acquisition of L2 speech perception for each of the three L2 speech acquisition tasks. To answer this research question, six similar multiple regression analyses were run: three on the early learners' scores and three on the late learners' scores for each speech perception/production task. These results are also given in Table 12.4.

The results suggest that, although AOA is a strong predictor of L2 production and perception abilities in early learners, this is not the case for late learners. Moreover, the results also indicate that social factors – identification with the L2 culture and number of native Spanish speakers in a learner's social network – play a stronger role in late learners' acquisition, and play little to no role in early learners' acquisition. Instead, cognitive factors – ability to imitate, working memory and phonological memory capacity – are greater predictors of early learners' scores on all three tasks.

This can also be demonstrated when correlations between AOA and all the other factors examined in this study were run. The results of this analysis are given in Table 12.5. As is demonstrated by the data, AOA correlates only with late learners' scores on the cognitive and social tasks. There are no significant correlations between any factor and early learners' AOA.

Table 12.5. Correlations of factors with AOA. * p<0.05; ** p<0.01.

Factor	All Participants Combined	Early Learners	Late Learners
Experiential			
Amount of L2 use	0.116	0.089	0.103
Length of residence	0.004	0.323	0.080
Cognitive			
Ability to imitate	0.283*	0.181	0.571**
Working memory capacity	0.287*	−0.168	0.317
Phonological memory capacity	0.317*	0.010	0.327*
Social			
Native Spanish in SN	0.106	0.298	0.367*
L2 identity	0.224	−0.062	0.339*
L1 identity	0.128	0.237	0.215

12.5 Discussion and Conclusion

The main purpose of this study was to identify whether L2 speech accuracy was related to AOA and whether this relationship differed for early versus late L2 learners. In addition, a second goal was to determine whether the relative importance of cognitive, social and experiential factors in the acquisition of L2 speech accuracy also differed across these two groups. The implications of the findings of this study are discussed below.

12.5.1 Critical Period and L2 Speech Learning

The results of this study verified that AOA strongly correlated with L2 accuracy scores. This was true for both overall production accuracy, as measured by GFA ratings, and for the perception of two specific phonetic features, similar and new vowels, as defined by the SLM. Such findings are similar to and verify past research on age effects (Flege et al. 1999; DeKeyser et al. 2010; Abrahamsson 2012).

However, when correlations were re-run, dividing the participants into early (AOA before 14) and late (AOA after 14), and partialing out confounding variables, three different pictures emerged. First of all, as in Flege et al. (1999), but unlike Abrahamsson (2012), a strong correlation of AOA and L2 abilities was found for late learners on their perception of new vowels. These results suggest that there is no demonstrable cut-off point that would suggest there is a critical period for L2 speech acquisition. Instead, it appears that L2 speech abilities gradually decline across the lifespan at least when testing a single feature like new vowels, as is predicted by the SLM. Secondly, for GFA, early learners' scores did correlate with AOA, but AOA did not correlate with the late learners' scores. In other words, this was typical of the pattern found in research supporting a critical period (e.g. DeKeyser et al. 2010). Some caution in interpreting this finding is needed, since support for this only occurred when current age, LOR and L2 use were partialed out. Finally, the perception of similar vowels followed a third pattern – neither early nor late learners' scores were correlated with AOA.

How can we reconcile the differences found for each of the three measurements of L2 speech acquisition? There may be many explanations, including a need for more subjects to ensure a better distribution curve. One possible explanation for the difference between GFA and new vowels is that GFA is a measurement of overall production abilities, something that may be more closely related to overall L2 proficiency (Baker-Smemoe, Dewey, Bown and Martinsen 2014). Although the raters were instructed to listen to the overall foreign accent, they most likely were influenced by fluency, speech rate and pauses, which are often associated with overall proficiency abilities (Baker-Smemoe et al. 2014). Thus, it is possible that this task more closely relates to the tasks measuring morphosyntactic abilities described by DeKeyser and others. By contrast, the new vowel perception task measures only the acquisition of specific sounds – a measurement that is more related to the interaction of the L1 and L2 and more closely fits the tenets of the SLM. This may be why this measurement followed what is predicted by the SLM.

To explain the results for the perception of similar vowels, one possibility may be that all the early and late learners were able to perceive these similar vowels with such high accuracy that there were some ceiling effects (see Figure 12.2). Indeed, the average accuracy score on similar vowels for the early learners was 82%. Similarly, Oh et al. (2011) demonstrated that early Japanese learners of English were able to produce English vowels that were similar to Japanese vowels (English /i/, /u/ and /e/) similarly to native English children after only 5 months in the United States, and late Japanese learners were able to do so after 1.6 years. In any case, what these findings also suggest is that new and similar vowels indeed are learned differently and may be affected by AOA in different ways.

The results of this first analysis, therefore, suggest that at least some of the tenets of the SLM may in fact accurately predict the effect of AOA on

L2 speech acquisition. However, they also suggest that only some aspects of the phonetic system may be learned throughout the lifespan (perception of specific L2 sounds), but others may have a critical period (GFA). The SLM, as well as any theory on age effects on L2 acquisition, would benefit from examining many aspects of L2 learning in the same study – with the goal of determining why some features may have critical periods and some may not.

12.5.2 Experiential, Cognitive and Social Factors and AOA

The second goal of this study was to examine whether social, cognitive or experiential factors best predict the individual variability found in the scores on the three L2 speech acquisition measures examined in this study, and whether their relative importance changes when examining early versus late learners' scores. When examining all the participants' scores together, it was apparent that AOA was the greatest predictor of variance in the scores of the participants.

Of the other predictor variables found to predict variability in the scores, the cognitive factor, ability to imitate, bears mentioning. Little is known about whether and what cognitive factors may be involved in L2 speech acquisition. The ability to imitate sounds has been examined in L1 acquisition research (Meltzoff 2002) and the results of this study seem to suggest it should be pursued in L2 speech acquisition research as well. This finding also seems to fit nicely with the tenets of the SLM. The ability to imitate may reflect a learner's ability to detect differences in the way that sounds are produced in the L1 versus the L2. If this is the case, then it may be that this ability may diminish as L1 categories develop; and this may be related to the SLM's explanations of why age effects occur.

When early and late learners' scores are examined separately, a better understanding of how AOA relates to the three speech measures examined in this study is possible. In these results, at least two different patterns emerge. First, for GFA and new vowels, the early learners' scores are predicted most strongly by AOA, whereas late learners' scores are not predicted by AOA at all – instead they are predicted by L2 identity scores and the number of native Spanish speakers in one's closest social network. Surprisingly, the less the learners identify with the L2, the more likely they are to score higher on the GFA. It may be that those with greater experience with the L2 have more negative feelings towards the language (but are also better at pronunciation because of their exposure). Negative attitudes towards the L2 may also be a greater motivator for them to improve their pronunciation. Along with determining the number of native Spanish speakers in their closest social network circles, these two measurements may actually be measuring L2 use – and may be a better indicator since they measure not only how often the L2 is used, but perhaps in what ways and what attitudes are felt towards it. This finding would also strengthen the SLM prediction that L2 use is one of the best predictors of L2 speech acquisition accuracy. Some caution must be given to the findings about L2 identity, however, since average scores for both early and late learners were so similar.

A second pattern developed for similar vowels – for both early and late learners, AOA was not a significant predictor. Instead, cognitive factors, especially the ability to imitate, were the greatest predictors of accuracy. Again this may be related to the ability to perceive differences in the L1 and L2 – an ability to imitate accurately L2 sounds, especially those that are very similar to L1 sounds, may aid in acquiring these sounds more quickly and more accurately.

The finding that aptitude (defined in part as some of the cognitive factors examined in this study) often plays a very different role for early versus late learners is similar to what was found in both DeKeyser et al. (2010) and Abrahamsson and Hyltenstam (2008). The current study, however, is the first to demonstrate these findings for L2 perception learning, instead of for grammatical learning. Moreover, this study may also be the first to include in the same study both cognitive and social factors and how they relate to L2 phonological learning and age effects.

Why would different factors affect early and late learners differently? One possibility is that cognitive factors decline across the lifespan – so that younger learners benefit from these abilities to a greater extent than do older learners. By contrast, for older learners, both their desire to integrate into L2 society and these cognitive factors provide the motivation and aptitude needed to more accurately use and acquire the L2. Indeed, when AOA is correlated with the factors examined in the second part of the study, it is clear that social factors only correlate with AOA for late learners (see Table 12.5). Interestingly, however, cognitive factors, especially the ability to imitate, correlate when both early and late learners' scores are combined. Again, these results need to be verified by future research, especially since the early and late learners' average scores on the cognitive and social factors were so similar.

The results of this study are merely a preliminary attempt to address many types of factors that contribute to the complicated nature of L2 phonological acquisition, especially as it relates to age effects. However, the hope is that they also demonstrate the need for examining several types of factors when attempting to predict and explain why some learners are more accurate at L2 speech acquisition than are others.

Appendix: Sentences Used in Global Foreign Accent Task

When I was nine, my favorite book was 'Miss Nelson is Missing.'
What else has Emma Thompson been in?
Do you prefer multiple choice or true and false?
After a few false starts, my uncle's business took off.
I have to pick up some hair gel at Albertson's.
Sir Thomas More's house next to the Thames was called *Chelsea.*
My *Olsen* grandma is coming for Christmas.
My sister's name is Melinda, but she goes by Mel.
Our snowman has coal eyes and a carrot mouth.
She looked cool as a cucumber, even though it was 100 degrees outside.
With every lie he told, he dug himself a deeper hole.
Who'll know if you miss class?
Do you know of anyone who'll lend me their car?
Ferdinand was that famous bull who preferred sniffing flowers to fighting.

References

Abrahamsson, N. (2012). Age of onset and nativelike L2 ultimate attainment of morphosyntactic and phonetic intuition. *Studies in Second Language Acquisition* 34: 187–214.

Abrahamsson, N. and Hyltenstam, K. (2008). The robustness of aptitude effects in near-native second language acquisition. *Studies in Second Language Acquisition* 30: 481–509.

Baker, W., Trofimovich, P., Mack, M. and Flege, J. (2002). The effect of perceived phonetic similarity on non-native sound learning by children and adults. In B. Skarabela, S. Fish and A. Do (eds.), *Proceedings of the 26th Annual Boston University Conference on Language Development.* Somerville, MA: Cascadilla Press.

Baker-Smemoe, W. (2015). What factors predict age effects in L2 perception: A comparison of social, cognitive and experiential factors. *Proceedings of the 18th International Congress of Phonetic Sciences*. The University of Glasgow, UK.

Baker-Smemoe, W., Dewey, D.P., Bown, J. and Martinsen, R.A. (2014). Does measuring L2 utterance fluency equal measuring overall L2 proficiency? Evidence from five languages. *Foreign Language Annals* 47: 707–28.

Best, C.T. and Tyler, M.D. (2007). Nonnative and second-language speech perception: Commonalities and complementarities. In O. Bohn and M.J. Munro (eds.), *Language Experience in Second Language Speech Learning: In honor of James Emil Flege*, 13–34. Amsterdam: John Benjamins.

Darcy, I. and Kruger, F. (2012). Vowel perception and production in Turkish children acquiring L2 German. *Journal of Phonetics* 40: 568–81.

DeKeyser, R.M. (2000). The robustness of critical period effects in second language acquisition. *Studies in Second Language Acquisition* 22: 499–533.

DeKeyser, R., Alfi-Shabtay, I. and Ravid, D. (2010). Cross-linguistic evidence for the nature of age effects in second language acquisition. *Applied Psycholinguistics* 31: 413–38.

Dewey, D. P., Bown, J. and Eggett, D. (2012). Japanese language proficiency, social networking, and language use during study abroad: Learners' perspectives. *The Canadian Modern Language Review* 68: 111–37.

Flege, J.E. (1995). Second language speech learning: Theory, findings, and problems. In W. Strange (ed.), *Speech Perception and Linguistic Experience: Issues in Cross Language Research*, 233–77. Timonium, MD: York Press.

Flege, J.E. (2003) Assessing constraints on second-language segmental production and perception. In A. Meyer and N. Schiller (eds.), *Phonetic and Phonology in Language Comprehension and Production, Differences and Similarities*, 319–55. Berlin: Mouton de Gruyter.

Flege, J.E., Bohn, O.-S. and Jang, S. (1997). The effect of experience on nonnative subjects; production and perception of English vowels. *Journal of Phonetics* 25: 437–70.

Flege, J.E. and Liu, S. (2001). The effect of experience on adults' acquisition of a second language. *Studies in Second Language Acquisition* 23: 527–52.

Flege, J.E. and MacKay, I.R.A. (2004). Perceiving vowels in a second language. *Studies in Second Language Acquisition* 26: 1–34.

Flege, J.E. and MacKay, I.R.A. (2010). 'Age' effects on second language acquisition. In *Proceedings of the Sixth International Symposia on the Acquisition of Second Language Speech, May 1–3, 2010, Poznan, Poland*. Retrieved from http://jimflege.com/files/Flege_MacKay_2010.pdf April 2015.

Flege, J.E., Munro, M.J. and MacKay, I.R.A. (1995). Factors affecting strength of perceived foreign accent in a second language. *The Journal of the Acoustical Society of America* 97(3): 3125–34.

Flege, J.E., Yeni-Komshian, G.H. and Liu, S. (1999). Age constraints on second language acquisition. *Journal of Memory and Language* 41: 78–104.

Gatbonton, E. and Trofimovich, P. (2008). The ethnic group affiliation and L2 proficiency link: Empirical evidence. *Language Awareness*, 17: 229–48.

Gatbonton, E., Trofimovich, P. and Magid, M. (2005). Learners' ethnic group affiliation and L2 pronunciation accuracy: A sociolinguistic investigation. *TESOL Quarterly* 39: 489–511.

Hummel, K. (2009). Aptitude, phonological memory, and second language proficiency in nonnovice adult learners. *Applied Psycholinguistics* 30: 225–49.

Imai, S., Flege, J. and Wayland, R. (2002). Perception of cross-language vowel differences: A longitudinal study of native Spanish learners of English. *Journal of the Acoustical Society of America* 111: 2364.

Johnson, J.S. and Newport, E.L. (1989). Critical period effects in second language learning: The influence of maturational state on the acquisition of English as a second language. *Cognitive Psychology* 21: 60–99.

MacKay, I.R.A, Meador, D. and Flege, J.E. (2001). The identification of English consonants by native speakers of Italian. *Phonetica* 58: 103–25.

Meltzoff, A. (2002). Elements of a developmental theory of imitation. In Andrew Meltzoff and W. Prinz (eds.), *The Imitative Mind: Development, Evolution, and Brain Bases*, 19–41. New York: Cambridge University Press.

Moyer, A. (1999). Ultimate attainment in L2 phonology: The critical factors of age, motivation instruction. *Studies in Second Language Acquisition* 21: 81–108.

Moyer, A. (2004). *Age, Accent, and Experience in Second Language Acquisition: An Integrated Approach to Critical Period Inquiry.* Clevedon, England: Multilingual Matters.

O'Brien, I., Segalowitz, N., Collentine, J. and Freed, B. (2007). Phonological memory and lexical, narrative, and grammatical skills in second language oral production by adult learners. *Studies in Second Language Acquisition* 29: 557–81.

Oh, G.E., Guion-Anderson, S., Aoyama, K., Flege, J.E., Akahane-Yamada, R. and Yamada, T. (2011). A one-year longituidinal study of English and Japanese vowel production by Japanese adults and children in an English-speaking setting. *Journal of Phonetics* 39: 156–67.

Palfreyman, D. (2006). Social context and resources for language learning. *System* 34: 352–70.

Piske, T., MacKay, I.R.A. and Flege, J.E. (2001). Factors affecting degree of foreign accent in an L2: A review. *Journal of Phonetics* 29: 191–215.

Toohey, K. (2001). Disputes in child L2 learning. *TESOL Quarterly* 35: 257–78.

Wendy Baker-Smemoe is an associate professor in the Department of Linguistics and English Language at Brigham Young University, Provo, UT.

13
English Sonorant Codas in a Brazilian Portuguese-English Bilingual Context

Rosane Silveira and Alison Roberto Gonçalves

13.1 Introduction

When we compare the syllabic inventory of English and Brazilian Portuguese (BP), the differences are striking and it is easy to predict that Brazilian learners of English are likely to face difficulties in learning the English inventory. BP favours open two-member CV syllables (e.g. *bolo*, 'cake'; *faca*, 'knife'), but clusters involving stops plus liquids are also common, resulting in CCV syllables (e.g. *troca*, 'change'; *claro*, 'clear'). As for codas, BP also allows a few consonants in this syllable position at the phonetic level when we consider word-final consonants (*mês*, 'month' [mes]; *mar*, 'sea' [mah]).[1] Although BP has words ending with the <m> and, more rarely, the <n> grapheme, these codas are produced with a nasal vowel and with no consonant gesture (*som*, 'sound' [sõ]; *pólen*, 'pollen' [ˈpɔlẽ]). BP syllabic patterns at the phonological level are (C)(C)V(C) (e.g. *três*, 'three'; *cor*, 'colour'; *ar*, 'air'; *e*, 'and').[2] English favours the CVC pattern and allows a range of syllabic patterns, which include different types of cluster in syllable onsets and codas, as well as in word-final position. Yavaş (2011) summarizes this range of possibilities as follows (C)(C)(C)V(C)(C)(C)(C) (e.g. 'texts' [tɛksts]; 'springs' [spɹɪŋz]).

1 Cristófaro-Silva and Faria (2014) explain that for the BP variety spoken in Belo Horizonte, the capital city of the state of Minas Gerais, new syllabic patterns have emerged due to the elision of word-final vowels and diphthongs. Thus, in this and possibly other BP varieties, other consonants are emerging in word-final position (e.g. *árduo*, 'arduous' [ahd]).

2 According to Cristófaro-Silva (2002), in mid-word position, BP also allows (C)V(C)(C): *perspirar*, 'perspirate' [pehspiˈɾah].

In the present study, we investigate the production of English bilabial and alveolar nasals in word-final position by Brazilians. Given that in BP these consonants have undergone vocalization in word-final position, we expect that they may lead to acquisition difficulties due to the transfer of L1 processes into the L2. The notion of transfer adopted in this paper is based on Koda (2007: 17), who defines it as the 'automatic activation of well-established L1 competencies (mapping patterns) triggered by L2 input'. Koda's definition of transfer implies that it cannot be easily controlled: both L1 and L2 are activated automatically, so that L1 information cannot be 'suppressed by learners when processing L2 lexical information' (2007: 18).

We refer to the participants of this study as bilinguals because, by the time of data collection, they had been living in an English-speaking country for a minimum of five years. We side with Grosjean (2006) who defines a bilingual individual as someone who uses two or more languages on a daily basis for social interaction. The author adds that bilinguals use the two languages for different purposes, with different people, and rarely possess the same level of fluency in all language skills. The participants are late bilinguals, given that their L1 acquisition process was stable when the L2 learning started (Butler and Hakuta 2006).

In the next section, we describe the target nasal consonants in word-final position for both English and BP, review studies on the production of English codas by Brazilians, and briefly discuss the roles played by phonological context, orthography and proficiency in L2 acquisition.

13.2 Background

13.2.1 Word-Final Nasals in English and BP

As briefly stated in the introduction, word-final nasals have different realizations in English and BP. In English, the nasal consonants are produced 'by blocking the sound from coming out of the mouth, while allowing it to come out through the nose' (Ladefoged 2001: 53). The English nasals are characterized by having a very low F1 (about 200 Hz), very low energy in the region of F2, and a third formant located around 2500 Hz (Ladefoged 2001: 34). The three English nasals, /m/, /n/ and /ŋ/, are phonetically and phonologically distinct in word-final position, as demonstrated by the examples 'clam' [klæm], 'clan' [klæn], and 'clang' [klæŋ].

BP has two nasal consonants that at the phonological level can appear in onset and word-final position: /m/ and /n/,[3] both realized with the consonant gesture in onset position only (Cristófaro-Silva 2002; Seara, Nunes and Lazzarotto-Volcão 2015). Seara (2000) conducted a thorough study to identify the acoustic characteristics of nasal vowels in Brazilian Portuguese, and she also reports acoustic characteristics for the nasal consonants in onset position. The author reports values for the three nasal formants for both the bilabial and alveolar nasals when followed by [a]. Both nasals present low FN1 (around 260 Hz), with the FN2 (/m/=840 Hz, /n/=1265 Hz) and FN3 (/m/=1789 Hz, /n/=2226 Hz) being higher for the alveolar nasal.

It is important to emphasize, however, that word-final nasal consonants are not produced with blockage of the air in BP. Instead, the preceding vowel assimilates the nasal quality and the consonant loses its consonantal gesture (Monahan 2001; Kluge 2009),[4] as demonstrated by the examples *som* 'sound' [sõ] and *pólen* 'pollen' [ˈpɔlẽ]. Consequently, in BP, different from English, there is no contrast between nasal consonants in word-final position.

13.2.2 Production of English Codas by BP Speakers

A few studies have investigated how Brazilians pronounce the English nasals in word-final position. We shall begin this review by summarizing the main findings of the studies whose focus was the production of these consonants, sometimes investigated along with other types of coda. Next, we discuss the role of phonological context, orthography and L2 proficiency in the production of English codas, as these variables are examined in the present study.

3 BP also has another consonant nasal /ɲ/, which is restricted to onset and appears in mid-word position only (e.g. *unha* [ˈũɲɐ], 'nail'), but this consonant will not be discussed here given that our focus in on nasals in coda position.

4 There is still an ongoing debate among researchers about the status of the nasal coda in Brazilian Portuguese. Some researchers follow Câmara's (1977) proposal of using the archiphoneme /N/ to transcribe these codas, based on the assumption that BP has 7 oral vowels, and that nasal vowels are actually biphonemic and should be represented by the nasal vowel followed by /N/ (e.g. Bisol 2002; Cristófaro-Silva 2002; Medeiros 2011). We side with the second position (Pontes 1972), which defends the claim that BP has 12 vowels, 7 oral vowels and 5 nasal vowels, as demonstrated by minimal pairs such as *lã* 'wool' [lɐ̃] and *lá* 'there' [la]. In this view, we dispense with the use of the nasal archiphoneme.

Aiming at identifying the rank of constraints of BP syllable structure, and the extent to which Brazilians transfer these constraints to English, Monahan (2001) examined the production of English codas, among which are nasals, by five Brazilians who were living in the United States (range: four months to three years). The author examined words containing the bilabial nasals in clusters (e.g. 'plant') and word-final position (e.g. 'clan'). The participants recorded a sentence reading test and a paragraph reading test. The results show that Brazilians tended to produce the vowel preceding the nasal consonant with heavy nasal quality, while the nasal consonant was more often produced as a nasal vowel than as a consonant. Monahan does not report the results quantitatively and it is not possible to provide more details about his findings.

Baptista and Silva Filho (2006) recorded six students from different proficiency levels reading a set of sentences containing CVC monosyllabic words ending in different types of codas, including three nasal consonants. The authors found that nasal consonants were vocalized 7.6% of the time, while 4.3% of the time the nasal consonants were fully produced, but followed by a paragogic vowel (i.e. an epenthetic vowel inserted at the end of a word; e.g. *name* [ˈneɪmi]). When the paragogic vowel was added, the nasal consonants became part of the onset of an extra syllable that was created. Although the authors do not report examples of the words included in their sentence reading test, one can infer that the cases of vowel insertion were more likely to have happened when the nasal consonant was followed by an <e> grapheme, as in 'name', as suggested by other studies of English codas (e.g. Koerich 2006; Silveira 2007). Baptista and Silva Filho (2006) aimed at investigating the role played by markedness and syllable sonority,[5] and they did not examine the data according to proficiency levels. The role of phonological context was addressed and there was a tendency for the following consonant to trigger more vowel paragoge, so the results are grouped according to place of articulation and it is not possible to visualize the results for the nasals as a group.

Kluge (2004) also investigated the production of English word-final /m/ and /n/ by 20 Brazilians, who were pre-intermediate learners of English residing in Brazil. The results of her sentence reading test also confirmed the strong tendency of learners to nasalize the preceding vowel and delete the final nasal. The author points out that the alveolar nasal was more often produced in a target-like fashion than the bilabial nasal, possibly because

5 Markedness stands for 'the relative frequency or generality of a given structure across the world's languages' (Eckman 1977: 198). Thus, a structure that is more frequently used in the world's languages is considered less marked.

the participants are more likely to transfer the L1 process to words ending in the most common spelling pattern for the coda nasal in BP, which is the <m> grapheme. The author also examined the role played by the preceding vowel and she reports that among the four vowels she investigated, [ɪ, ʌ] led to more vocalization than [i, æ] with the monosyllabic words. Furthermore, disyllabic words yielded higher percentages of target-like production of the coda nasals than monosyllabic words, and target words followed by a pause triggered higher percentages of vocalization than words followed by a vowel or a consonant. Kluge (2007) partially replicated the 2004 study by collecting data from 10 Brazilians, all intermediate learners of English. The reported findings were very similar, although the role played by the preceding vowel was not confirmed.

When assessing the effects of pronunciation instruction, Silveira (2004) collected perception and production data from two groups of Brazilians, all beginning the study of English in Brazil. Here we will focus on the production results. The researcher tested a number of word-final consonants, including the three English nasal consonants, and her goal was to assess the frequency of vowel paragoge in Brazilians' production of English singleton codas. Note, however, that the participants received no explicit instruction on the production of word-final nasals, which is our focus here.

Silveira (2004) reports results for the bilabial and the alveolar nasals, explaining that the control group (which received no pronunciation instruction) produced fewer cases of paragogic vowel after the two nasals in the pre-test (23% for [m] and 33% for [n]) than the experimental group who received four hours of pronunciation instruction (69% for [m] and 50% for [n]). In the post-test, the control group increased the percentage of tokens produced with the paragogic vowel (47% for [m] and 37% for [n]), while the experimental group reduced the percentages (53% for [m] and 38% for [n]), but continued to produce more tokens with the paragogic vowel overall. The fact that the experimental group managed to improve performance in the post-test suggests positive effects for pronunciation instruction, which seems to have been generalized to the nasals (the codas that were not the focus of instruction). It is important to highlight that all the words that were produced with the paragogic vowels were spelled with a silent <e> (e.g. 'name' and 'fine').

Zimmer (2004) investigated the production of a number of word-final consonants by 156 Brazilian learners of English from four different proficiency levels, all residing in Brazil. The researcher employed a sentence reading test containing words with different levels of frequency and non-words. Her focus was on the occurrence of a number of phonological processes transferred from the participants' L1 into the L2. For the present study, we will focus on the results regarding how often the participants produced the English nasal codas as a nasal vowel. As reported by Zimmer (2004), nasal vocalization was among the least frequent processes (12%), and clearly more recurrent in the data of the less proficient informants (levels 1 and 2).

The studies reported in the previous paragraphs relied on reading tests to gather data. Inherent in these tests is the availability of orthographic information. When considering the role of orthography in L2 pronunciation, it is important to keep in mind that most L2 learners are literate adults whose contact with the L2 relies greatly on written material (Young-Scholten and Archibald 2000; Bassetti, Escudero and Hayes-Harb 2015), especially for those who are not in a country where the target language is widely spoken. For these learners, the first contact with L2 words generally involves written input, and the availability of both acoustic and written input can affect phonological development and word learning (Bassetti, Escudero and Hayes-Harb 2015; Cutler 2015; Veivo and Järvikivi 2013). This constant access to the orthographic representations of words may lead learners to rely heavily on L1 spelling and sound correspondences when pronouncing L2 words, especially when the leaners' L1 has a more transparent sound-spelling relation (Erdner and Burnham 2005). Tasks that provide adult learners with written input, such as word-list reading or sentence reading, are expected to favour the transfer of L1 sound-spelling rules into L2 pronunciation.

Cutler (2015: 126) warns about the disadvantages of relying on orthographic information or other types of metalinguistic knowledge to create distinct lexical representations (and consequently distinct productions) as this 'other abstract speech-external information' is likely to hinder phonological representation, given that it does not help in the development of phonological categories. However, when we consider adult L2 learners, the reliance on orthographic information is inevitable. As Bybee (2001: 58) explains, 'phonetic shape is not just determined by memory representation and experience – it is also determined by the neural and motor patterns that have been laid down in childhood and reinforced by constant repetition'. For adult L2 learners, changing these patterns, which have been shaped by the L1, may require explicit instruction about how the L1 and the L2 systems differ, and about the particular characteristics of the L2 sound system and how its sound-spelling relations differ from the L1.

In this chapter, although we do not compare production generated from tests with and without orthographic input, nonetheless we expect orthography to influence the production of the target sounds in word-final position, leading the BP speakers to vocalize the target sounds frequently when these sounds are spelled with the consonantal grapheme only (e.g. 'mom', 'sun'), but not when they are spelled with the consonant grapheme followed by a silent -e (e.g. 'home', 'fine'). In the case of BP, the <me> and <ne> spellings are produced as CV syllables, as demonstrated by the words *fome*, 'hunger' [ˈfomi] and *fone*, 'phone' [ˈfoni]. Thus, to investigate further the role of orthography, we included, in the sentence reading test, words containing a silent -e grapheme, as previous studies (Koerich 2002; Silveira 2004, 2007) have shown that the presence of this grapheme leads to different types of production for obstruents.

In addition to orthography, we expect other variables to play a role in the production of the target consonants, mainly L2 proficiency. Major (2001) advocates that as L2 proficiency advances, non-target pronunciations stemming from L1 transfer diminish. This might be because with the increase of L2 proficiency, the L2 sounds are less frequently filtered through the L1 network (Kuhl 2000). Most studies reviewed in this section have controlled for the proficiency variable, except for Zimmer (2004), which investigates learners from different proficiency levels and corroborates Majors' (2001) claim. Likewise, in this study we intend to examine the extent to which L2 proficiency is related to the different productions of the target sounds. Similar to Kluge (2004), the present study investigates the role played by the following phonological context in the production of the target codas. Some of the studies reviewed in this section indicate that the phonological context could influence the production of the target codas. However, no clear tendencies were identified.

The results reported in this section confirm that both English nasals in word-final position pose difficulties to Brazilians at the production level, especially in early stages of L2 learning. The present study sets out to investigate the role played by phonological context, orthography and proficiency in the production of two English nasal consonants. Our analysis is guided by the following research questions and hypotheses (indicated by H):

1. How is the production of the target codas affected by the following phonological context?
   H1: Word-final nasals will be equally vocalized across different phonological contexts.
2. How is the production of the target codas affected by orthography?
   H2: Target words spelled with the silent -e grapheme will be vocalized less often than target words that end with the consonant grapheme.

3. How is the production of the target codas related to L2 proficiency? H3: As proficiency advances, the English nasal codas are more frequently produced with the consonant gesture.

In the following section, we describe the participants, the research instruments and the procedures for data collection and analysis.

13.3 Method

Data for this study were drawn from Silveira (2012), who recorded 62 Brazilians, 31 residing in Brazil and 31 residing in the United States at the time of data collection. For the present study, we were interested in learners with at least five years of residence in an English-speaking country, so we selected data from 24 Brazilians from the group residing in the United States (mean time of residence: 9.19 years, range: 5 to 22), 19 female and 5 male. Their ages varied from 26 to 52 (mean: 38.1) and they reported having 8 to 16 years of formal education (mean: 12.9). All the participants signed a consent form and completed a questionnaire used to gather biographical information and inquire about their language learning and use experiences. The participants' proficiency was measured by asking four English teachers to rate short speech samples in which the participants were describing images (see Silveira 2011). Based on a 12-point scale, the raters classified the group as having a mean proficiency level of 6.9 (range: 3.3 to 9.8).

Two American speakers with some knowledge of BP also recorded the test sentences and we used their data as controls to help us analyse the BP tokens acoustically and to check for rater reliability. Both native speakers were American, were residing in the United States and had a BA in the area of Humanities. One of the participants was a 23-year-old female, while the other was a 26-year-old male.

Information about how often the BP participants used English was collected with a five-point scale, which revealed that they spent from one to five hours (or more) a day using English (mean: 3.1). We also asked about their attendance of English courses in Brazil and in the United States, reported in months. Most participants had taken English courses in Brazil (70.8%, range: 0 to 124 months, mean: 32), and in the U.S. (75%, range: 0 to 40 months, mean: 11.2) The participants came from regions in southeast and south Brazil, mostly from São Paulo (8), Minas Gerais (4) and Rio de Janeiro (4), with a few from Goiás (2), Paraná (2), Brasília (1), Rio Grande do Sul (1), Espírito Santo (1) and Santa Catarina (1) states. In all the BP varieties spoken by the participants, the vocalization of nasals in word-final codas is consolidated.

The speaking data were collected by asking the participants to record a reading test containing 75 meaningful sentences (e.g. 'There is no room here.' / 'Let's play a game.'). For this study, only the 20 sentences containing the target codas were analysed. The 20 target words were all monosyllabic and were of the C(C)VC type, but only onset clusters present in BP were used (e.g. 'green', 'flame'). Each of the two target consonants was tested five times with words ending with the consonant grapheme (e.g. 'sun', 'room'), and five times ending with the consonant followed by a silent -e grapheme (e.g. 'pine', 'time'). The words were presented in three phonological contexts: followed by a pause (two tokens for each consonant), by a consonant (four tokens) and by a vowel (four tokens). The total tokens analysed were 480 (20 target words times 24 participants). No attempt was made to control for the vowels of the target words or the vowels and consonants following the target words.

The frequency of the tested words was assessed by checking their ranks in COCA (Corpus of Contemporary American English), which is a balanced corpus encompassing over 450 million words of texts of varied spoken and written genres (Davies 2015). In COCA, the frequency of the tested words ranged from 3694 for the least frequent word ('coin') to 732984 for the most frequent word ('time'), which shows a good frequency range for the tested words.

The participants were recorded during individualized meetings according to their availability, in a quiet room. Their speech was recorded using an HP notebook computer equipped with a headset and the GoldWave audio editor and recorder, and a back-up copy of the recordings was made with a portable digital recorder (Sony ICD PX312) without an additional microphone. The speech files were treated to reduce noise and increase audio volume and saved as .wav files.

Only the target words and their following context produced by each speaker underwent auditory analysis by the two researchers. First, the two researchers transcribed the tokens separately and then these transcriptions were compared. The initial agreement rate for the transcriptions was 79%. The tokens for which there was disagreement underwent a second round of auditory analysis performed by the two researchers. Cases that still led to disagreement underwent acoustic analysis performed by the same researchers and they inspected spectrograms generated in Praat and listened to the tokens as many times as necessary to reach a decision about the most adequate transcription. It is important to stress that, due to the quality of the recordings, acoustic analysis was a difficult endeavour and was used only as an additional means to help us decide on the best transcriptions. Given this limitation, we did not attempt to provide detailed classifications for the types of productions found in the data set. In the present study, the auditory analysis was deemed more feasible.

As for the procedures for acoustic analysis, in order to decide whether nasals were vocalized or not, we followed Pruthi and Espy-Wilson's (2004) and Machač and Skarnitzl's (2009) recommendations. We inspected the vowel preceding the target consonant and its surroundings in the spectrogram to locate an abrupt spectral change (indication of nasal murmur) and a region with energy concentrated in the lower frequencies. We also looked for low F1 (about 300 Hz) in the area where the nasal consonant should be displayed and for zeros in the spectrum, especially above 1000 Hz. Furthermore, we inspected the waveforms and compared them to the surrounding vowel areas to check for absence of higher-frequency components for the nasal consonants.

In order to decide on the best procedures for statistical analysis, the data set was inspected for normal distribution. The results of descriptive statistics and normality tests (Shapiro-Wilk) showed that the dependent variables frequency of vocalization and frequency of paragoge were not normally distributed; thus, in order to answer the research questions, non-parametric tests were used for within- and between-group comparisons (Wilcoxon, Kruskal-Wallis and Mann-Whitney) and correlation analysis (Spearman). For all the analyses, alpha was set at 0.05, but Bonferroni correction (i.e. dividing 0.05 by the number of comparisons) was used to adjust the probability level when multiple comparisons were run. In the following section, we report the results for the present study.

13.4 Results and Discussion

The first research question examines the production of the target consonants by Brazilian learners and how this production is affected the following phonological context. Note that, initially, the analysis focuses on the results using the target words as cases. Later in the analysis, we shall discuss the results having the participants as cases, as observation of individual variation is crucial for the understanding of second language development (De Bot, Lowie and Verspoor 2007).

Table 13.1 summarizes the results for the two types of codas, showing the two types of non-target production found in the data set: vocalization

Table 13.1. Vocalization and paragoge for the two target codas.

	/n/ Vocaliz.	/n/ Parag.	/m/ Vocaliz.	/ m/ Parag.	Total Vocaliz.	Total Parag.
Count	58	13	19	14	77	27
(percentages)	(24.1%)	(5.4%)	(7.9%)	(5.8%)	(16%)	(5.6%)
Mean	5.8	1.3	1.9	1.3	3.8	1.3
SD	6.3	1.7	3.2	1.5	5.3	1.6

N for each type of consonant: 240; Total N: 480.

of the final consonant and insertion of a paragogic vowel (consonant substitution occurred twice due to misreading by one participant and will not be discussed). Vocalization was the most frequent syllable simplification process (16%), and it was mainly present in the production of /n/ (24.1%). Paragoge (5.6%) occurred nearly equally with the two nasals, but the percentages were lower than 6% in both cases.

The overall results for vocalization and paragoge were compared running a Wilcoxon test, which revealed no significant difference (p=0.144). Mann-Whitney tests were run to compare the rates of vocalization and paragoge for each type of consonant coda and the results showed that neither vocalization rates (p=0.07) nor the paragoge rates (p=0.71) were significantly different across the two types of coda. Note, however, that vocalization rate results approached significance and this process was clearly more frequent with the alveolar nasal than with the bilabial nasal.

From these results, we can conclude that the consonant that led to higher percentages of target-like production was /m/, which is not in agreement with the results reported by Kluge (2004), who examined data from pre-intermediate learners and found that vocalization was more frequent with /n/ than with /m/. Regarding paragoge, Silveira (2004) reports that this process yielded higher rates for /m/ (59%; 53%) than for /n/ (50%; 38%) for the experimental group in both the pre- and post-tests, but not for the control group in the pretest. Silveira (2004) reports data from beginners, and we can see that the study found higher rates of paragoge for the two nasals than the ones reported in the present study, which examined data from participants of varied proficiency levels and with considerable time of exposure to English in an L2 context. Overall, these results seem to indicate that as proficiency advances, both L1 processes, but especially paragoge, become less frequent in the production of Brazilian learners of English.

Table 13.2. Vocalization and paragoge according to the following phonological context.

	/n/		/m/	
	Voc.	Parag.	Voc.	Parag.
Vowel (n=288)	16 (5.5%)	4 (1.4%)	2 (0.6%)	5 (1.7%)
Mean (SD) for Vowel	2.2 (3.7)	1.7 (1.9)		
Consonant (n=288)	33 (11.4%)	5 (1,7%)	9 (3.1%)	3 (1%)
Mean (SD) for Consonant	5.2 (7.2)	1 (1.1)		
Pause (n=144)	9 (6.2%)	0 (0%)	8 (5.5%)	4 (1.4%)
Mean (SD) for Pause	4.2 (3.3)	1 (2)		

Now we shall turn to the role played by the phonological context following the target codas and comment on the words that triggered higher percentages of L1-based phonological processes. Table 13.2 shows that the highest percentages of vocalization for the nasals occurred with the /n/ when it was followed by a consonant (11.4%). Overall, we see a tendency for the consonant context to lead to higher percentages of vocalization, which differs from Kluge (2004), who found that pause triggered more vocalization among the nasals. As for paragoge, we see no clear influence of the phonological context and our results fail to corroborate the findings of Baptista and Silva Filho (2006), who report a tendency for the target codas followed by a consonant to yield higher rates of paragoge.

Kruskal-Wallis tests were run to compare the vocalization and paragoge results across the three types of phonological context. The results corroborate hypothesis 1, as they revealed no significant differences in the rates of vocalization or paragoge due to the phonological context following the target codas.

As explained in Section 13.3, the words included in the production test were highly frequent in the COCA. Figure 13.1 displays the results per word, and a horizontal line was imposed to the bars in this graph to show the frequency of each word in COCA. The graph shows no clear pattern for frequency, and this was confirmed by running Spearman correlations that came out weak and non-significant. Figure 13.1 shows that vocalization was especially frequent with the words 'green' and 'coin', which were always followed by /k/. Possibly the presence of a velar consonant triggered more vocalization, but further studies could investigate this supposition. Conversely, the highest rates of paragoge were obtained by the silent -e words 'wine', 'line', 'game', and 'flame' (four occurrences for each), and three of them were followed by a vowel.

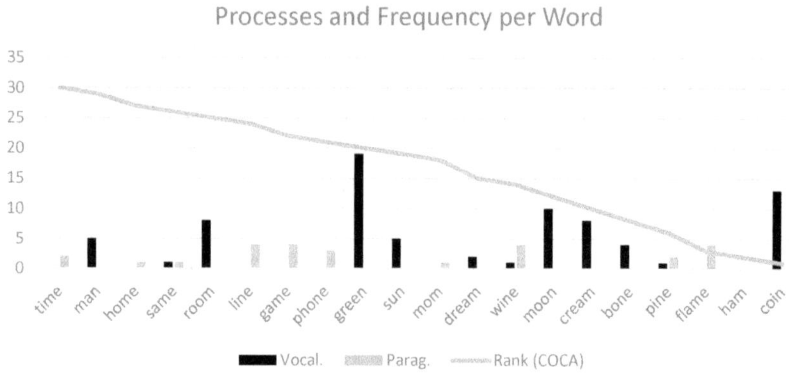

Figure 13.1. Vocalization, paragoge and word frequency.

Research question 2 investigated the role of orthography in the production of the English nasal codas, and Table 13.3 displays the results relevant for us to discuss this variable. Vocalization was more frequent when the words ended with the consonant grapheme (total=29.9%); and paragoge, as shown in previous studies (e,g. Koerich 2002; Silveira 2004), occurred more often when words were spelled with the silent -e grapheme (total=12.5%). As observed by other researchers (Erdner and Burnham 2005), orthography can be seen as playing both a positive and a negative role in production. It plays a negative role in the sense that the presence of the silent -e triggers the insertion of the paragogic vowel, which adds another syllable to the word. A positive effect of orthography may be attributed to the fact that the words ending with the silent -e also yielded lower rates of vocalization and, overall, most of them were produced in a target-like fashion (about 88% of target-like productions for silent -e words, versus about 70% for the words ending in a consonant grapheme).

Table 13.3. Vocalization and paragoge according to orthography.

	Consonant Grapheme Words (n=240)		Silent -e Words (n=240)	
	Vocalization	Paragoge	Vocalization	Paragoge
Count (%)	70 (29.1%)	2 (0.8%)	5 (2.1%)	25 (10.4%)
Mean (SD)	7 (5.9)	0.10 (0.3)	0.70 (1.2)	2.5 (1.5)

Mann-Whitney tests were run to compare the results across types of orthography. The results for both vocalization (p=0.007) and paragoge (p<0.001) came out significant, showing that vocalization was significantly more frequent for words ending in consonant graphemes than in the silent -e condition; conversely, paragoge was significantly more frequent for words ending in the silent -e condition. Comparisons were also made across type of phonological process within each type of orthography by running Wilcoxon tests. The results show that within the group of words ending in a consonant grapheme, the occurrence of vocalization was significantly higher than paragoge (p=0.01), as it is clear when we observe the results in Table 13.3. On the other hand, although the percentage of paragoge is higher than vocalization for the group of words ending in a silent -e, the statistical test only approached significance. (p=0.07). Overall, hypothesis 2 is corroborated, as the results show that orthography plays a role in the production of the nasal codas.

Finally, research question 3 examined the relationship between L2 proficiency and production of the target codas. As explained in the method section, the proficiency measure used in this study consisted of subjective rates provided by experienced English teachers, who listened to short samples of the participants' describing images. For this analysis, we looked at the results with the data set showing the performance of each of the 24 individuals, rather than tokens. Table 13.4 shows that the minimum and maximum values for vocalization are 0 and 7 (m=2.7), and for paragoge are 0 and 6 (m=1.1). As illustrated in Figure 13.2, this means that there are two participants with no occurrence of vocalization (P17 and P18) and that many participants did not insert a vowel after the codas (18 participants). Participants 3, 8, 7 and 16 produced the highest rates of vocalization, and participants 13, 12 and 1 produced the highest rates of paragoge. Note that participants 18 and 17, the most proficient ones, produced all codas in a target-like fashion, and that participants 15, 2, 19, 11 and 21 displayed high levels of target-like performance, with one case of vocalization each.

Table 13.4. Frequency of processes per participant (n=24)

	Vocalization	Paragoge
Min.–Max.	0–7	0–6
Mean	2.7	1.1
SD	2.1	2.2
Wilcoxon Test	–2.5 (p=0.01)	

Figure 13.2 shows the participants' proficiency rates (grey line), and the frequency of vocalization (black bars) and paragoge (grey bars). Clearly, paragoge is a process frequently found among the least proficient participants, though participant 10 is an exception. Furthermore, there is an overall tendency for the least proficient participants to have higher frequencies of vocalization. Spearman correlations were run and the results show a negative, strong and significant correlation between proficiency and vocalization ($\rho=-0.789$, $p<0.001$), confirming that as proficiency advances, the vocalization rates decrease. A similar tendency was found for paragoge, but the correlation was weak ($\rho=-0.375$, $p>0.05$) and not significant, maybe due to the fact that only six participants produced the target codas with a paragogic vowel, and one of them was not among the least proficient ones (P10). Thus, hypothesis 3 is partially corroborated.

Additional Spearman correlations were run to examine the relationship between proficiency, vocalization and paragoge for each type of coda. The results are summarized in Table 13.5, which shows negative, moderate and significant correlations between frequency of vocalization and proficiency for the two codas. Thus, these results indicate that as proficiency advances, the rates of vocalization diminish for the two types of coda, corroborating hypothesis 3. The relationship between proficiency and paragoge is moderate and negative for /n/ and weak and negative for /m/. Moreover, the rates of paragoge for /n/ diminish considerably as proficiency advances, as this correlation reached statistical significance, while for /m/, the correlation only approached significance. The results for the relationship between proficiency and rates of L1-based phonological processes partially corroborate hypothesis 3.

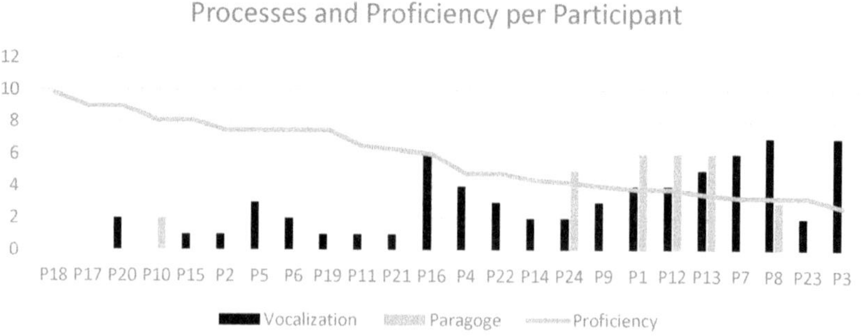

Figure 13.2. Percentage of vocalization and paragoge for each coda and participants' proficiency.

Table 13.5. Correlations for each type of consonant.

	/n/	/m/
Vocalization-Proficiency	−0.436 (p=0.03)	−0.659 (p<0.001)
Paragoge-Proficiency	−0.485 (p=0.01)	−0.370 (p=0.07)

After analysing the data set, we can conclude that vocalization is a phonological process that remains frequent in the production of the two English codas across proficiency levels, though proficiency contributes significantly to lowering the rates of vocalization. Among the nasals, vocalization tends to diminish as proficiency advances, despite the fact that /n/, the consonant that has low type frequency and productivity in BP, triggers higher rates of vocalization than /m/.

Conversely, paragoge, as demonstrated in previous studies (Zimmer 2004) tends to decrease as learners from an instructional setting become more proficient. Similarly, in the data set of the present study, which encompassed learners ranging from pre-intermediate to advanced levels, the rates of paragoge were extremely low. The role of the phonological context following the target codas was broadly examined here, and no conclusive answer can be offered. It is important to remember, however, that in BP, the occurrence of the nasal vowel in words spelled with word-final <m> and <n> is not dependent on the phonological context.

On one hand, orthography plays an important role in the production of the target codas, with the silent -e condition yielding lower rates of vocalization and, consequently, higher rates of target-like production. On the other hand, a negative effect of orthography was found, in the sense that it triggered higher rates of paragoge, thus corroborating Koerich's (2002) and Silveira's (2004) results.

13.5 Concluding Remarks

The results reported here confirm that the differences in the production of English and BP word-final nasals present a challenge to Brazilians with different levels of L2 proficiency. The phonological context following the codas seems to have little influence on the way these codas are produced, contrary to orthography, which led to different productions. The present study has shown that Brazilians, especially the less proficient ones, draw on their knowledge of L1 spelling-sound correspondence when pronouncing English words.

The results reported in the present study highlight the importance of addressing the role of orthography in L2 classrooms, pointing out the differences in spelling-sound mappings between the L1 and the L2 as a means to raise awareness about the different sound and syllable inventories of the two languages. As we can see, transfer of L1-based phonological processes diminish but do not necessarily cease as proficiency advances, not even when L2 users have been immersed in an L2 context for five years or more. It seems that, for L2 adult learners, explicit pronunciation instruction could be beneficial, as this could help them to understand more efficiently how the L2 phonetic-phonological system is organized, and how the L2 maps spelling-sound relations. This type of awareness could help to reduce transfer of L1-based phonetic-phonological processes into the L2 and to improve pronunciation, possibly in earlier stages of L2 proficiency.

References

Baptista, B.O. and Silva Filho, J.L.A. (2006). The influence of voicing and sonority relationships on the production of English final consonants. In B.O. Baptista and M.A. Watkins (eds.), *English with a Latin Beat: Studies in Portuguese/Spanish–English Interphonology*, 73–89. Amsterdam: John Benjamins.

Bassetti, B., Escudero, P. and Hayes-Harb, R. (2015). Second language phonology at the interface between acoustic and orthographic input. Introduction to special issue of *Applied Psycholinguistics* 36: 1–6.

Bisol, L. (2002). Estudo sobre a nasalidade. In M.B. Abaurre. (eds.), *Gramática do Português Falado: Novos Estudos Descritivos*, Vol. VIII, 501–31. Campinas: Editora da Unicamp.

Butler, Y. and Hakuta, K. (2006). Bilingualism and second language acquisition. In T.K. Bhatia and W.C. Ritchie (eds.), *The Handbook of Bilingualism*, 114–44. Malden: Blackwell.

Bybee, J. (2001). *Phonology and Language Use*. Cambridge: Cambridge University Press.

Câmara, J.M. (1977). *Para o Estudo da Fonêmica Portuguesa*. 2nd edition. Rio de Janeiro: Organizações Simões.

Cristófaro-Silva, T. (2002). *Fonética e Fonologia do Português: Roteiro de Estudos e Guia de Exercícios*. São Paulo: Contexto.

Cristófaro-Silva, T. and Faria, I. (2014). Percursos de ditongos crescentes no Português Brasileiro. *Letras de Hoje* 49: 19–27.

Cutler, A. (2015). Representation of second language phonology. *Applied Psycholinguistics* 36: 115–28.

Davies, M. (2015). *The Corpus of Contemporary American English*. Retrieved from http://corpus.byu.edu/coca/

De Bot, K., Lowie, W. and Verspoor, M. (2007) A dynamic systems theory approach to second language acquisition. *Bilingualism: Language and Cognition* 10: 7–21.

Eckman, F.R. (1977) Markedness and the Contrastive Analysis Hypothesis. *Language Learning* 27, 315–30.

Erdener, V.D. and Burnham, D.K. (2005). The role of audiovisual speech and orthographic information in nonnative speech production. *Language Learning* 55: 191–228.

Grosjean, F. (2006). Studying bilinguals: methodological and conceptual issues. In T.K. Bhatia and W.C. Ritchie (eds.), *The Handbook of Bilingualism*, 32–63. Massachusetts: Blackwell.

Kluge, D.C. (2004) *Perception and Production of English Syllable-final Nasals by Brazilian Learners.* Master's Thesis, Universidade Federal de Santa Catarina, Florianópolis.

Kluge, D.C. (2007). Brazilians' perception and production of English word-final nasals. Unpublished paper, Florianópolis: Universidade Federal de Santa Catarina.

Kluge, D.C. (2009). *Brazilian EFL Learners' Identification of Word-Final /m-n/: Native/Nonnative Realizations and Effect of Visual Cues.* Doctoral Dissertation, Universidade Federal de Santa Catarina: Florianópolis.

Koda, K. (2007). Reading and language learning: Cross-linguistic constraints on second-language reading development. *Language Learning* 57: 1–44.

Koerich, R.D. (2002). *Perception and Production of Vowel Epenthesis in Word Final Single Consonant Codas.* Doctoral Dissertation, Universidade Federal de Santa Catarina, Florianópolis.

Koerich, R.D. (2006). Perception and production of vowel paragoge by Brazilian EFL students. In B.O. Baptista and M.A. Watkins (eds.), *English with a Latin Beat: Studies in Portuguese/Spanish–English Interphonology*, 91–104. Amsterdam: John Benjamins.

Kuhl, P.K. (2000). A new view of language acquisition. *Proceedings of the National Academy of Science* 97: 11850–7.

Ladefoged, P. (2001). *Vowels and Consonants: An Introduction to the Sounds of Languages.* Oxford: Blackwell Publishers.

Machač, P. and Skarnitzl, R. (2009). *Principles of Phonetic Segmentation.* Prague: Epocha Publishing House.

Major, R.C. (2001). *Foreign Accent: The Ontogeny and Phylogeny of Second Language Phonology.* Mahwah, NJ: Laurence Erlbaum Associates.

Medeiros, B.R. de (2011). Nasal coda and vowel nasality in Brazilian Portuguese. *Selected Proceedings of the 5th Conference on Laboratory Approaches to Romance Phonology*, 33–45. Retrieved on 10 May 2015 from http://www.lingref.com/cpp/larp/5/paper2633.pdf

Monahan, P.J. (2001). *Evidence of Transference and Emergence in the Interlanguage.* Rutgers Center of Cognitive Science. Retrieved on 25 May 2015 from http://roa.rutgers.edu/files/444-0701/444-0701-MONAHAN-0-0.PDF

Pontes, E. (1972). *Estrutura do Verbo no Português Coloquial.* Petrópolis (RJ): Vozes.

Pruthi, T. and Espy-Wilson, C.Y. (2004). Acoustic parameters for automatic detection of nasal manner. *Speech Communication* 43: 225–39.

Seara, I.C. (2000). *Estudo Acústico–Perceptual da Nasalidade das Vogais do Português Brasileiro*. Doctoral Dissertation, Universidade Federal de Santa Catarina, Florianópolis.

Seara, I.C., Nunes, V.G. and Lazzarotto-Volcão, C. (2015). *Para Conhecer: Fonética e Fonologia do Português Brasileiro*. São Paulo: Contexto.

Silveira, R. (2004). *The Influence of Pronunciation Instruction on the Perception and Production of English Word-final Consonants*. Doctoral Dissertation, Universidade Federal de Santa Catarina, Florianópolis.

Silveira, R. (2007). The role of task-type and orthography in the production of word-final consonants. *Revista de Estudos da Linguagem* 15: 143–76.

Silveira, R. (2011). Pronunciation instruction and syllabic-pattern discrimination. *DELTA – Documentação de Estudos em Linguística Teórica e Aplicada* 27: 5–22.

Silveira, R. (2012). L2 production of English word-final consonants: The role of orthography and learner profile variables. *Trabalhos em Linguística Aplicada* 51: 15–28.

Veivo, O. and Järvikivi, J. (2013). Proficiency modulates early orthographic and phonological processing in L2 spoken word recognition. *Bilingualism: Language and Cognition* 16: 864–83.

Yavaş, M. (2011). *Applied English Phonology*. Oxford: Wiley-Blackwell.

Young-Scholten, M. and Archibald, J. (2000). Second language syllable structure. In J. Archibald (ed.), *Second Language Acquisition and Linguistic Theory*, 64–101. Oxford: Blackwell.

Zimmer, M.C.A. (2004). *Transferência do Conhecimento Fonético-Fonológico do Português Brasileiro (L1) para o Inglês (L2) na Recodificação Leitora: Uma Abordagem Conexionista*. Doctoral Dissertation, Pontifícia Universidade Católica do Rio Grande do Sul: Porto Alegre.

Rosane Silveira is a faculty member of the Department of Foreign Languages and Literature at the Federal University of Santa Catarina, Brazil.

Alison Roberto Gonçalves is a PhD student at the Federal University of Santa Catarina, Brazil.

14 The Sociophonetics of Spanish-English Contact in the United States

Barbara E. Bullock and Daniel J. Olson

14.1 Introduction

To date, the research devoted to studying variation in Spanish-English bilingual phonology in the U.S. context has largely examined the production and perception of second language (L2) learners, either Spanish speakers acquiring the majority language, English, or more commonly, English speakers learning Spanish (Carlisle 1986, 1988, 1991; Major 1986; Zampini 2008, among others). These studies assess the factors that contribute to the probability that an L2 speaker will or will not manifest a foreign accent or non-native perception (Best 1995; Flege, Munro and MacKay 1995; Munro and Derwing 1995, among others). Phonological or phonetic variation in most L2 speech studies is conceived of as deviation from a monolingual target, conditioned by a constellation of learner variables, including target language dominance and age of acquisition effects. In this way, the baseline for comparison of L2 speech is often the monolingual norm. Similarly, albeit outside the context of L2 speech, variability in the *English* sound system of Hispanics has been well researched, often as an ethnolect where Spanish inflected variability in English is viewed as a marker of Chicano identity (see Fought 1999; Godinez and Maddieson 1985; Mendoza-Denton 1999; Register 1977; Santa Ana 1991; Wolfram, Carter and Moriello 2004). Again, Hispanic English is levelled against monolingual English norms. Until recently, the *Spanish* pronunciation of Hispanics has been mostly neglected, even though it, too, must display differences that are as rich as those found in any other widely dispersed ethnolect (Brown 2005; Lipski 1987; Lynch 2009; Timm 1976; Torres Cacoullos and Ferreira 2000).

In short, the variation found in bilingual phonetic production, of both natural bilinguals and L2 learner populations, has routinely sought to attribute much of this variation to monolithic issues of transfer or interference from English. However, from a sociolinguistic perspective, an analysis of bilingual variation should seek to incorporate other socially conditioned sources of variation, both dynamic and static, beyond one's bilingualism. Variation at the phonetic level in bilingual speech may exceed the variation that is found within monolingual or majority varieties (Meyerhoff and Nagy 2008; Sankoff 2013) and, as in all communities, linguistic differences arise between bilingual speakers within the same community because individuals use their languages to project various aspects of their identities. So any study that delves into Spanish-English contact in the U.S. must attend to the complex interplay of individual and social factors that give rise to phonetic variation in all communities. For bilingual communities, we need to explore social factors that reach beyond the fact that the speakers are bilingual, or that they differ in language dominance. Sociophonetic methodologies invite us to probe socio-indexical variables in tandem with linguistic variation below the level of the categorical variable. They allow us to consider how degrees of phonetic variation, not just the presence or absence of a particular variable, might correlate with degrees of projected stances and social identities. Importantly, sociophonetic methods allow us to figure sociolinguistic variables along a continuum of 'more – less' rather than merely as endpoints 'either – or'.

It is the goal of this chapter to explore some of the variables that contribute to phonetic variation in Spanish-English contact in the United States. We begin by discussing the goals of sociophonetics and how it might be fruitfully applied in contexts of bilingualism and language contact. In particular, we focus on how to translate important constructs from bilingualism, like language mode (Grosjean 2001) and aspects of language dominance (Birdsong 2014), into empirical investigations of a bilingual's sound system that allow us to go beyond imputing all contact effects merely to interference from English. We focus on ways in which language mode and language experience, including education and literacy, are operationalized within our research as variables in empirical studies. Finally, we conclude with a discussion of the relevance of contact data for linguistics in general and for sociophonetics more specifically.

14.2 Why Sociophonetics?

In linguistics, certain types of variation in the speech signal are generally considered to be noise that needs to be filtered out in order for speakers to categorize what they hear. However, researchers in sociophonetics hold that much of the phonetic variation normally considered not to be linguistically meaningful carries social meanings. Gradient phonetic differences can serve to index properties of the speaker, such as sex, stance, group affiliation and other speaker-specific information (Di Paolo and Yaeger-Dror 2011; Foulkes and Docherty 2006; Hay and Drager 2007; Strand 1999; Thomas 2010). It has long been known that phonological variables are socially evaluated by speakers (Labov, Yaeger and Steiner 1972). For instance, the deletion or retention of postvocalic /s/ is not merely a variable rule of Spanish phonology. Rather, a speaker's choice to realize /s/ or not can be ascribed social meaning (Walker, García, Cortés and Campbell-Kibler 2014). Aaron and Hernández (2007), for example, account for the increased realization of postvocalic /s/ among Salvadoran speakers in Houston, Texas, as an instance of accommodation to the local Spanish norms. Mack (2011) demonstrated that listeners were sensitive to the presence of /s/ in the voices of Puerto Rican males who they perceived to be stereotypically gay. Bullock, Toribio and Amengual (2014) demonstrate that the maintenance or deletion of an etymological /s/ in Dominican Spanish is gendered, but that the insertion of postvocalic [s] as an intrusive segment is not. These studies remind us that the same linguistic variable in Spanish, in this case a categorical one ([s] vs zero), can be socially evaluated in different ways. Importantly, research in sociophonetics allows us to explore socially meaningful variation that is not categorical; instead, the acoustic properties of a signal that convey social meanings can be fine-grained and subtle.

The vast majority of sociophonetic studies published to date document variation among monolingual speakers, primarily of English. We would like to suggest that our understanding of the phonological systems of bilingual speakers would benefit from using methodologies that pair the replicable empirical techniques used by phoneticians with the manipulation of social and stylistic variables that are normally excluded when bilingual experiments are conducted in the laboratory. Rarely do L2 phonology/phonetic studies, which mostly target between-group differences of bilingual and monolingual speakers, allow for a manipulation of the factors that might condition variation between Spanish-English bilingual speakers in the U.S. Thus, we might learn that bilinguals differ at a phonetic level from monolinguals but we do not necessarily know under which circumstances they may do so, nor do we have any insight into variation within a bilingual group. In the next section, we turn to a discussion of some of the factors that might be expected to affect the phonetic productions of Spanish-English bilinguals.

14.2.1 Factors in Bilingualism

The effect of age of acquisition of Spanish prevalent in most of the literature devoted to bilingual phonology is less relevant as a between-subjects independent variable for the Spanish-speaking Latino population than it is for an L2 population. However, there are other factors that differentiate between individual speakers: country or region of birth, schooling or literacy in Spanish, balance of use of Spanish and English with different interlocutors, language ideologies that circulate in their communities or in society at large, their own attitudes toward language practices, the input variety they experience, etc. Many of these variables are subsumed in bilingual studies under the label of language dominance (see, for instance the Bilingual Language Profile: Birdsong, Gertken and Amengual 2012). Note that, unlike age of acquisition, which is fixed for an individual, many of these factors are more fluid, as language practices can change throughout the lifetime of an individual speaker and even throughout a single interaction. Thus, it is incumbent upon researchers to control for variables that might affect a participant's performance, including the identity of the researcher/field-worker, the language of instruction, and the setting of the data collection (Grosjean 1998; Hay and Drager 2010). In what follows, we discuss research programmes conducted in the lab and in the field, which were designed to probe the effect of some of these factors on phonetic performance.

14.3 Language Mode

In natural speech, bilinguals can operate either monolingually, speaking in one of their two languages, or bilingually, alternating between them. However, it is clear that these are not the only two categorical options. Rather, bilinguals have the ability to move along a continuum from monolingual interactions to bilingual ones. As one of the first to remark on this flexibility across a spectrum of monolingual and bilingual behaviour,

Hasselmo (1970) illustrated that Swedish-English bilinguals alternated between three different norms, or 'modes' of speaking: English-only, Swedish-American and American-Swedish. Importantly, Hasselmo noted that these three modes differed in the ratio of each language employed, with the largest percentage of English used in the English-only mode and the lowest percentage of English used in the American-Swedish mode. Furthermore, alluding to potential underlying factors driving mode selection, he pointed out that different modes were used with different types of interlocutors. English-dominant bilinguals were addressed in Swedish-American, whereas with more balanced bilinguals interaction was in American-Swedish mode. In short, bilinguals have the ability to operate along a linguistic continuum, from monolingual to bilingual language behaviour, in response to their audience, both real and imagined (Bell 1984).

The concept of *language mode*, or position along the continuum from monolingual to bilingual behaviour, has been further developed most notably by the work of François Grosjean (Grosjean 1997, 1998, 2001, 2008; Soares and Grosjean 1984). The position of a speaker along the continuum during a given interaction can be described via the relative activation of the two languages. Operation in monolingual mode in a given language corresponds with maximal activation in that language and with minimal activation of the competing language. In a fully bilingual mode, both of a bilingual's languages receive similar relative levels of activation. While there is clearly some debate about the neurological processes that may allow for alternative language selection, Grosjean (2008) demonstrates that language mode may correlate with a relative degree of activation of each of the two languages (for the Direct Access Hypothesis see Costa 2005; for Inhibitory Control see Green 1998).

Of clear importance in the study of bilinguals, language mode is difficult to operationalize methodologically, and a number of factors that can or may impact language mode have been proposed. As Grosjean (2001) states, at any given point in an interaction, driven by both psychological and linguistic factors, a bilingual must decide 'which language to use, and how much of the other is needed – from not at all to a lot' (Grosjean 2001: 2). While Hasselmo (1970) observed that interlocutors' language dominance profiles may play a role, other speaker-oriented factors such as language, attitudes and beliefs, language switching habits, and ideological or sociolinguistic differences may serve to adjust language mode. External to the interlocutors, language mode may be impacted by the context of the interaction (e.g. speech communities that are largely comprised of speakers of Language A vs those of Language B), the content of the message/

interaction (e.g. talking about topics that are more culturally, historically or linguistically related to Language A vs Language B), and even the function of the speech act (e.g. to create solidarity or distance, to make requests/ commands, etc.).

As an example, when a Spanish-English bilingual is discussing a given topic, language mode may be impacted by the perceived language profile of their interlocutor. Speaking with someone who is highly dominant in Spanish may trigger a Spanish bilingual mode; that is, the predominant use of Spanish with a few English insertions. However, speaking about the same topic with someone who is English-dominant may shift the speaker towards an English bilingual mode (see Treffers-Daller 1998 for evidence of such shifts among Turkish-German bilinguals). As such, language mode, even for the same speaker discussing the same topic, should be considered fluid and context-dependent, broadly defined.

14.3.1 Impact of Language Mode on Production

Given that language mode can be described in terms of relative activation of each of the two languages, it is logical to assume that a shift in language mode implies some shift in language behaviour. One of the most well studied of these impacts on language behaviour is the role that language mode plays in the type and quantity of language mixing that bilinguals produce. In an observational case study, Treffers-Daller (1998) recorded a single Turkish-German bilingual in three different contexts, with three different sets of interlocutors, thereby manipulating audience design (Bell 1984). The results demonstrated not only a difference in the number of code-switches, with the least amount of code-switching occurring during interaction with a German-dominant group and the most occurring during interaction with a close bilingual friend, but also in the types of code-switches produced. While conversation with German-dominant bilinguals evidenced either mostly borrowings or peripheral switches (e.g. tag switches), interaction with the bilingual friend produced more variable and complex inter- and intra-sentential switches. Poplack (1981) also found that the rate and type of code-switching differed for a single Spanish-English speaker, who participated in 'formal' and 'informal' types of interaction with the same interlocutor. Thus, language mode can vary as a function of style. These case-study findings have been replicated in experimental approaches, with participants adjusting the number of language switches based on perceived interlocutors for both French-English bilinguals (Grosjean 1997) and French-Swiss German bilinguals (Weil 1990, as cited in Grosjean 2008).

While it is clear that language mode impacts the quantity and types of code-switches that a bilingual may produce, language mode also seems to have a clear impact at the phonetic level. Specifically, production by a single speaker of a given token, both at the segmental and suprasegmental level, may differ depending on the language mode in which the token is produced. Code-switching is, by definition, representative of a bilingual language mode, and code-switching itself may have an impact on phonetic production (e.g. Antoniou, Best, Tyler and Kroos 2011; Balukas and Koops 2014; Bullock, Toribio, González Lopez and Dalola 2006; González López 2012). Of equal interest, though, is the effect of language mode on *non-switched* productions.

Khattab (2003) illustrates a case in which phonetic production varied depending on language mode in the production of rhotics in English-Arabic bilingual children. The children were recorded in two separate sessions, which effectively controlled for language mode. In one session, the children interacted with an English-speaking experimenter while in the other, with Arabic-speaking parents. While children produced more English with the experimenter and more Arabic with their parents, as expected, the researcher noted a difference between the rhotics produced for English tokens in the two contexts. Specifically, while the /r/s produced in English were most likely to be the expected English variant [ɹ], /r/s produced for English tokens in the Arabic context were the decidedly more Arabic-like [ɾ]. Similar results were found for /l/ production, with dark [ɫ] used in monolingual English coda position, and clear [l] used in English coda position during bilingual interaction (Khattab 2003).[1]

While Khattab's findings were drawn from a naturalistic speech context, in which language mode was effectively modulated by employing different interlocutors, parallel findings can be seen in experimentally based approaches. Simonet (2014) examined the mid-vowel productions of Spanish-Catalan bilinguals, a case of contact between two closely related Romance languages. Specifically, he asked participants to perform a read-speech task in two different sessions: Catalan and bilingual Catalan-Spanish. With the exception of the language of the stimuli (Catalan or

1 While evidence for shifts in language mode in production is seen in the amount of mixing (Treffers-Daller 1998) or in phonetic production, even of non-mixed stimuli, additional support for a differential role of language mode can be seen in perceptual tasks. For example, the degree of cross-linguistic activation of the non-target language has been shown to vary depending on language mode (for eye-tracking see Marian and Spivey 2003; for lexical decision tasks see Dijkstra 2005).

mixed Catalan-Spanish), all other aspects of the two sessions were similar, including the physical location and experimenter. His results demonstrated a significant difference between the Catalan mid-vowels produced in the Catalan-only mode and the Catalan-Spanish bilingual mode.

14.3.2 Language Mode and Spanish-English Contact: Evidence from the Laboratory

Two recent studies by Olson (2013, 2016) have looked specifically at phonetic variation in Spanish-English bilinguals in the U.S., examining both segmental (voice onset time) and suprasegmental (pitch range and duration) features. These two studies, described in further detail here, sought to show the potential relevance of the relatively understudied factor of language mode in bilingual speech variation and to assess the usefulness of laboratory approaches for such study.

Olson (2013) investigated the role of language mode on the production of voice onset time (VOT) in Spanish-English bilinguals. Using a cued picture-naming paradigm, in which participants were required to name visually presented objects in English or Spanish depending on the background colour on the screen, Olson examined contact effects outside the constraints of connected speech (for connected speech and VOT see Antoniou et. al. 2011; Balukas and Koops 2014; Bullock et al. 2006; González López 2012). While production in connected speech is subject to the modulating effects of utterance pre-planning (e.g. Griffin and Bock 2000), pragmatic intent (e.g. Gumperz 1982) and predictability and intelligibility (e.g. Bell, Brenier, Gregory, Girand and Jurafsky 2002), the cued picture-naming paradigm requires participants to produce tokens out of context, allowing a closer look at the underlying issues of dual language activation. The paradigm was conducted in three differing language modes, presented in three different sessions, which differed with respect to the number of English to Spanish tokens: English mode (95% English, 5% Spanish), Spanish mode (95% Spanish, 5% English) and bilingual mode (50% English, 50% Spanish). Furthermore, the laboratory approach allowed for control of word frequency, word length and cognate status, all factors that have been shown to impact segmental production.

Twenty English-Spanish bilinguals performed the picture-naming task across three different sessions, and the results were analysed for VOT of voiceless initial stops. Of note, English is considered a long-lag language with typical VOTs in the range of 30–120 ms, while Spanish is a short-lag language with VOTs in the 0–30 ms range (Lisker and Abramson 1964).

Relevant for the current discussion, results for non-switched tokens (i.e. tokens that are named in the same language as the previously named token) revealed that VOT production differed between words in a predominantly monolingual mode (e.g. 95% English, 5% Spanish), and a more bilingual mode (e.g. 50% English, 50% Spanish). Specifically, English tokens were produced with shorter lag times (i.e. more Spanish-like VOTs) in the bilingual mode relative to the monolingual mode. Correspondingly, Spanish tokens were produced with longer lag times (i.e. more English-like VOTs) in the bilingual mode relative to the monolingual mode. While this effect was subject to language dominance, it is key to note that shifts in language mode, achieved by shifting the ratio of Language A to Language B, were shown to impact segmental phonetic production. This implies that when bilinguals are in an environment in which they expect to switch languages, they perform differently from when they expect to produce only one.

As a final piece of evidence for the role of language mode in phonetic production, Olson (2016) examined the impact of language mode on suprasegmental production. While the discussion of the results for the above study on VOT focused solely on non-switched tokens, Olson (2016) examined the embedding of code-switched tokens in two different contexts: monolingual language mode (i.e. 95% Spanish or 95% English) and bilingual language mode (50/50 Spanish/English). In this study, Olson employed a reading paradigm in which Spanish-English bilinguals were asked to produce a series of controlled utterances with switched and non-switched target tokens. In this case, language mode was controlled via a contextualizing paragraph that preceded the target token, consisting of either all constituents from a single language or a 50/50 mix of Spanish and English. Moreover, language mode was further controlled by conducting the recordings over the course of three different sessions (Spanish mode, English mode and bilingual mode) conducted on separate days. Again, the laboratory environment allowed for the control of frequency, word length, semantic predictability, loan word status and pragmatic intent (e.g. all targets were placed in post-focal position).

Fourteen Spanish-English bilinguals participated in the study, with half self-identifying as English-dominant and half self-identifying as Spanish-dominant. Tokens were analysed with respect to pitch range, defined as the difference (Hz) between the f0 maximum associated with target token and the immediately preceding f0 minimum, and stressed vowel duration. The boundaries of the target constituent and vowel were marked by hand and f0 and duration values were extracted using an automated script (Boersma and Weenink 2014). With respect to pitch range, the results indicated a greater pitch range for the code-switched tokens in both monolingual mode and bilingual mode, relative to the monolingual mode, non-switched tokens. It is important to note that the difference between the non-switched and code-switched tokens was significant only for the code-switched tokens produced in monolingual mode (β=0.340, t=0.213). Similar results were found for stressed vowel duration, with code-switched tokens in both monolingual mode (β=0.158, t=3.95) and bilingual mode (β=0.094, t=2.15) produced with greater stressed vowel duration than their non-switched counterparts. Also, important for the current discussion, there was a significant difference found between the code-switched tokens produced in the monolingual and bilingual modes (diff.=−0.064, p=0.024, d=0.186).

Taken as a whole, these results illustrate that language mode, operationalized as the ratio of Language A to Language B, plays a clear role in the production of suprasegmental features. Specifically, code-switching in monolingual and bilingual modes differ with respect to pitch range and duration. While it is worth mentioning that the current results differ somewhat from the traditional 'transfer' that is seen in segmental features (e.g. VOT), potentially owing to the inverse relationship between prosodic prominence and predictability (e.g. Aylett and Turk 2004), the role of language mode is clear.

14.3.3 Manipulating Language Mode in an Experimental Setting

The above studies show a clear impact of language mode on phonetic production. Although empirical research on the role of language mode is still relatively novel, controlling for and manipulating language mode in an experimental setting will continue to be crucial for understanding and examining bilingual sociophonetics. While previous studies have experimentally manipulated language mode by changing interlocutors (e.g. Khattab 2003), changing perceived/imagined interlocutors (Grosjean 1997) and manipulating the ratio of each language present in experimental stimuli (Olson 2013; Simonet 2014), future work should examine other factors relevant to language mode. Olson, for example, in ongoing work, seeks to understand the role of physical location, testing the same subjects in both a familiar English-dominant and novel Spanish-dominant speech communities, since it is known that speakers vary in performance according to their expectations about the setting (Hay and Drager 2010; Niedzielski 1999).

The relevance of the concept of language mode to linguistics is that it forces us to think about how bilinguals' stylistic repertoires (assuming that language mode is a form of style or, at minimum, language mode impacts style) can lead to outcomes that mirror those normally imputed to L1 interference. The work overviewed here has demonstrated that Spanish-English bilinguals can manifest convergence between their languages that is not a necessary consequence of the impact of one language upon another. Instead, it is only under certain conditions, such as when a bilingual is performing more bilingually, that he/she may manifest overt signs of phonetic contact. In other words, contact effects may be dynamic rather than static.

14.4 Spanish-English Contact Viewed from the Field

Although it may be more time-consuming to collect bilingual data in the field than in the laboratory, naturalistic data play a crucial role in understanding sociophonetics, as they reflect speakers' behaviour in interaction. If the data collected in a naturalistic setting are of high audio quality and stored in uncompressed audio file formats, they are amenable to sociophonetic analysis. The Spanish in Texas Corpus project (Bullock and Toribio 2012) was constructed to permit across-the-board linguistic analyses of the dynamics of this contact variety. The data were gathered by Spanish-speaking college students in Texas, who were recruited and trained in two cities, Austin (the capital) and Edinburgh (which borders Reynosa, Mexico), to conduct semi-structured interviews in their home communities. The interviewers were equipped with two professional-quality condenser microphones with which they recorded their own voice and that of the interviewees on separate channels; this assured a good audio quality. The participants were generally friends and family members of the interviewers, whose social and family networks permitted them to sample the speech of Texans of many different social backgrounds. The metadata gathered from the participants via a survey administered in the field included biographical information about their own and their parents' place of birth and education. Participants were also queried regarding their language use and they self-rated their proficiency in Spanish on a 5-point Likert scale. The language of the interview was predominantly Spanish with occasional switches to English. In this section, we report on some of the phonetic findings from this project (Trovato 2015).

14.4.1 The Voiced Labiodental Fricative in Spanish in Texas

The variables of interest selected from the Spanish in Texas corpus are the labiodental [v] and the bilabial approximant [β]. While Spanish has orthographic <b> and <v> that correspond to etymological distinctions, the phonetic difference between them has been merged in modern Spanish to a single voiced labial phoneme that surfaces as a labial approximant allophone [β] or, in more restricted environments, as the stop allophone [b]. However, an additional phone [v] is attested in some varieties of Spanish and it has three possible sources: (i) archaisms, (ii) hypercorrect or emphatic speech, or (iii) contact with a language like English that contains the phonemic [v] (Lope Blanch 1988). The labiodental fricative is attested in the U.S. in New Mexico, leading Torres Cacoullos and Ferreira (2000) to conduct a word translation task to elicit high- and low-frequency words containing [v] in an attempt to clarify its origin. The researchers coded the productions auditorily and visually, while the participants talked. In a multivariate analysis, they considered the realization of [v] as a function of their participants' age and Spanish experience (education, proficiency and use). The linguistic factors they examined included whether the lexeme contained orthographic <b> or <v>, whether the lexeme had an English cognate with <b> or <v>, and whether it was in a high- or low-frequency word. Their results indicated that [v] in high-frequency words reflects an archaism rather than a contact feature, but that the [v] of low-frequency words appears to be due to contact, conditioned in part by orthography and the existence of an English cognate.

14.4.2 Language Experience and Spanish-English Contact: Evidence from the Field

The Spanish of Texas shares a similar source variety with that of its western neighbour, New Mexico, and speakers can be impressionistically observed to produce an audible [v]. Trovato (2015) tests the hypothesis that the [v] found in Texas is a contact feature. Here, we report on a subset of his findings. From the corpus, Trovato selected the 17 speakers (10 female, 7 male) from the El Paso region who had been interviewed by the same person. This is the closest sample point to New Mexico represented in the corpus. These individuals ranged from age 20 to 86 (mean 46/median 48) and all self-rated their Spanish reading proficiency as very good to excellent (all 4 or 5 on the Likert scale). The highest level of education they attained was high school; eight participants were educated primarily in Spanish, seven primarily in English, and one had no formal education.

From the recorded conversations, the first 50 consecutive tokens corresponding to orthographic, prevocalic <b, v> were extracted for each speaker after the two-minute mark of the recording for a total of 850 tokens, of which 487 corresponded to orthographic <b> and 363 to the grapheme <v>. All token words were of Spanish etymological origin. Two Spanish speakers coded the data auditorily as labiodental vs labial, checking the video data to confirm whether or not the upper teeth were visible on the bottom lip. Tokens were also coded for whether they occurred in an English cognate, whether the target phoneme was word-initial or internal, and whether or not it occurred in a stressed syllable onset. Only 16% of the tokens were coded as labiodental from the auditory perspective. The best fitting logistic regression using R (R Core Team 2013), included orthography, language of education, age and cognate status as external predictors of the perception of labiodental [v] vs labial [b, β], as the dependent variable. Orthographic <v> proved to be a highly significant predictor of the manifestation of [v], as did the participant's language of education. Those who were educated in English tended to use [v] more than those who were educated in Spanish. None of the other predictors contributed significantly to accounting for variation.

In order to confirm that the fricatives fell into different phonetic classes that correlated with their spelling, the tokens were analysed acoustically. Here, the orthography of the token was analysed rather than the annotators' coding of the token, to remove all question of perceptual bias. The beginning and endpoint of the fricative were demarcated in Praat V. 5.3.23 (Boersma and Weenink 2014) following the decline in intensity from the offset of the previous vowel and into the following vowel, respectively. The relative intensity (or intensity difference) between the target consonant and the following vowel was measured by subtracting the minimum intensity of the labial consonant from the maximum intensity of the following vowel. This measure correlates with constriction type; the more open the constriction, the smaller the difference between the fricative and the following vowel. The labiodental fricative [v], with a narrow constriction formed by the bottom lip and upper teeth manifests greater relative intensity than the more diffuse bilabial approximant [β] (Hualde, Nadeu and Simonet 2010). The tokens were categorized according to whether their graphemes contained <b> or <v>. On average, orthographic <v> segments were realized, as predicted, with greater relative intensity (6.4 dB) than <b> items (3.9 dB). An ANOVA indicated that this difference is statistically significant [$F(1,810)=32.97$; $p<0.001$].

14.4.3 Discussion of [v] in Texas

The predictors that contribute to the likelihood of [v] in the speech of Spanish speakers from El Paso are different from those that contribute to variation in New Mexico. The results of the auditory analysis demonstrate that the [v] is strongly correlated with orthographic <v> and that speakers whose education was in English tend to use it significantly more than do others. This suggests that, for these speakers, literate in Spanish and educated primarily in English, English has an effect on the pronunciation of Spanish lexemes containing <v>. This parallels the variation found for words of low frequency in New Mexico (Torres Cacoullos and Ferreira 2000). Word frequency was not entered as a variable for the Spanish in Texas data because this was naturally occurring speech and it was not possible to control for frequency across the tokens. A phonetic analysis of the actual productions of the speakers confirmed that <b> and <v> tokens are categorized into separate phonetic categories according to relative intensity. As predicted, the <v> tokens had a significantly higher relative intensity than those spelled with <b>, indicating that these phones are not phonetically merged for all speakers in Texas, at least in El Paso.

One possible implication of this study is that the language of education of a bilingual impacts his/her use of spelling pronunciations in Spanish more so than does his/her ability to read in Spanish. All the participants whose data were analysed here rated themselves as strong readers of Spanish. Nonetheless, it is primarily those with more education in English who produce [v] tokens. This suggests that [v] occurs as a contact feature in Texas, but one that is conditioned by a particular type of input, namely scholarly input in English, a language where orthographic <v> is almost invariably mapped to phonetic [v].

14.5 Conclusion: Interference versus Intention

We have demonstrated that Spanish-English bilingual speakers manifest phonetic features that illustrate a degree of convergence between the two languages. This does not necessarily mean that these effects are due to interference, nor that such convergence is static. The results of the laboratory experiments discussed in Section 14.3 indicate that speakers manifest more or less convergence toward English-like VOT values depending on their context-driven expectations of how much of each language they are likely to encounter (i.e. language mode). As predicted by Grosjean (2001), these bilinguals were seen to operate on a continuum from more monolingual to more bilingual modes in response to the relative frequency of languages they were exposed to during the experiment. By extension, we can hypothesize that bilinguals in real life also demonstrate more or less phonetic convergence with English according to their interactions with or their performances for more mono- or bilingual-like audiences. In short, while some convergence is evidenced, the degree of convergence is contextually dependent. In this respect, subtle forms of shifting along the continuum of language mode may serve as a stylistic resource for U.S. Spanish-English bilinguals who wish to affiliate with particular personae.

The data from the Spanish in Texas study appear at first blush to be a straightforward case of transfer from English. However, simply categorizing the outcome as a type of transfer or convergence seemingly ignores the underlying source and potential indexical value of this variation. This variation was conditioned by the factor of language of education; those with more English education produced more [v], yet we do not yet know how the [v] is socially evaluated in the community and whether it is perceived in any way as indexing a more 'majority language educated' identity than its bilabial counterpart. As the consultants were involved in a natural conversation with someone they knew, it might well be the case that they used more or less labiodental fricatives than they do in other contexts. Without a study of how this variable is received in the community, in which it is used, we cannot know whether it arises as an effect of transfer or if it is also used purposefully to signal an affiliation with a group or persona.

Sociophonetics provides an empirical framework that allows us to explore the complex interactions of socio-stylistic and linguistic variables in a more detailed way than we have in the past. It also allows us to breathe new vigour into the study of bilingual phonology, which Watson (1991: 25) has called 'the Cinderella of bilingual studies.' Contact data, though, challenges linguists in ways that data from majority or non-contact varieties does not. On the one hand, we need to know whether bilingual speakers demonstrate the same types and degrees of phonetic variation as majority speakers do. But, we also have to consider the fact that they may show types of variation that might be absent from monolingual communities, as the stylistic variation of bilingual speakers who operate in different language modes may well exceed that of monolingual ones. This implies that we need to attend to factors like language mode when working with bilingual populations and that there is a need to operationalize this construct both in the laboratory and in more naturalistic environments. Bilinguals use phonetic variations in ways that might be similar to monolinguals but the variables might carry different socio-indexical value when used by them. In sum, we may not be able to readily interpret variation in bilingual communities as deviation from monolingual norms when, instead, contact-like features may be used intentionally for socio-indexical work.

References

Aaron, J.E. and Hernández, J.E. (2007). Quantitative evidence for contact-induced accommodation. In K. Potowski and R. Cameron (eds.), *Spanish in Contact: Policy, Social and Linguistic Inquiries*, 329–44. Amsterdam: John Benjamins.

Antoniou, M., Best, C., Tyler, M. and Kroos, C. (2011). Inter-language interference in VOT production by L2-dominant bilinguals: Asymmetries in phonetic code switching. *Journal of Phonetics* 39(4): 558–70.

Aylett, M. and Turk, A. (2004). The smooth signal redundancy hypothesis: A functional explanation for relationships between redundancy, prosodic prominence, and duration in spontaneous speech. *Language and Speech* 47(1): 31–56.

Balukas, C. and Koops, C. (2014). Spanish-English bilingual voice onset time in spontaneous code-switching. *International Journal of Bilingualism*: 1–21. doi: 10.1177/1367006913516035

Bell, A. (1984). Language style as audience design. *Language in Society* 13(02): 145–204.

Bell, A., Brenier, J., Gregory, M., Girand, C. and Jurafsky, D. (2002). Predictability effects on durations of content and function words in conversational English. *Journal of Memory and Language* 60(1): 92–111.

Best, C. T. (1995). A direct realist view of cross-language speech perception. In W. Strange (ed.), *Speech Perception and Linguistic Experience*, 171–204. Timonium: York Press. .

Birdsong, D. (2014). Dominance and age in bilingualism. *Applied Linguistics* 35: 374–430.

Birdsong, D., Gertken, L.M. and Amengual, M. (2012). Bilingual language profile: An easy-to-use instrument to assess bilingualism. COERLL, University of Texas at Austin. Retrieved from http://www.spanishintexas.org

Boersma, P. and Weenink, D. (2014). Praat: doing phonetics by computer [Computer program]. (Version 5.3.83). Retrieved from www.praat.org

Brown, E.L. (2005). New Mexican Spanish: Insight into the variable reduction of 'la ehe inihial' (/s-/). *Hispania* 88(4): 813–24.

Bullock, B.E. and Toribio, A.J. (2012). The Spanish in Texas Corpus Project. COERLL, University of Texas at Austin. Retrieved from http://www.spanishintexas.org

Bullock, B.E., Toribio, A.J. and Amengual, M. (2014). The status of /s/ in Dominican Spanish. *Lingua* 143: 20–35.

Bullock, B.E., Toribio, A.J. González López, V. and Dalola, A. (2006). Language dominance and performance outcomes in bilingual pronunciation. In M.G. O'Brien, C. Shea and J. Archibald (eds.), *Proceedings of the 8th Generative Approaches to Second Language Acquisition Conference*, 9–16. Somerville, MA: Cascadilla Proceedings Project.

Carlisle, R.S. (1986). The influence of markedness on epenthesis in Spanish/English interlanguage phonology. *PALM* 2(1): 88–96.

Carlisle, R.S. (1988). The effect of markedness on epenthesis in Spanish/English interlanguage phonology. *Issues and Developments in English and Applied Linguistics (IDEAL)* 3: 15–23.

Carlisle, R.S. (1991). The influence of environment on vowel epenthesis in Spanish/English interphonology. *Applied Linguistics* 12(1): 76–95.

Costa, A. (2005). Lexical access in bilingual production. In J.F. Kroll and A.M.B. de Groot (eds.), *Handbook of Bilingualism: Psycholinguistic Approaches*, 308–25. Oxford and New York: Oxford University Press.

Dijkstra, T. (2005). Bilingual visual word recognition and lexical access. In J.F. Kroll and A.M.B. de Groot (eds.), *Handbook of Bilingualism: Psycholinguistic Approaches*, 179–201. Oxford and New York: Oxford University Press.

Di Paolo, M. and Yaeger-Dror, M. (2011). *Sociophonetics: A Student's Guide.* London: Routledge.

Flege, J.E., Munro, M.J. and MacKay, I.R.A. (1995). Factors affecting strength of perceived foreign accent in a second language. *The Journal of the Acoustical Society of America* 97(5): 3125–34.

Fought, C. (1999). A majority sound change in a minority community: /u/-fronting in Chicano English. *Journal of Sociolinguistics* 3(1): 5–23.

Foulkes, P. and Docherty, G. (2006). The social life of phonetics and phonology. *Journal of Phonetics* 34(4): 409–38.

Godinez, M. and Maddieson, I. (1985). Vowel differences between Chicano and general Californian English? *International Journal of the Sociology of Language* 53: 43–58.

González López, V. (2012). Spanish and English word-initial voiceless stop production in code-switched vs. monolingual structures. *Second Language Research* 28(2): 243–63.

Green, D.W. (1998). Mental control of the bilingual lexico-semantic system. *Language and Cognition* 1: 67–81.

Griffin, Z. and Bock, K. (2000). What the eyes say about speaking. *Psychological Science* 11: 274–9.

Grosjean, F. (1997). Processing mixed language: Issues, findings, and models. In A. De Groot and J. Kroll (eds.), *Tutorials in Bilingualism: Psycholinguistic Perspectives*, 225–54. Mahwah, NJ: Lawrence Erlbaum Associates.

Grosjean, F. (1998). Transfer and language mode. *Bilingualism: Language and Cognition* 1(3): 175–6.

Grosjean, F. (2001). The bilingual's language modes. In J.L. Nicol (ed.), *One Mind, Two Languages: Bilingual Language Processing*, 1–22. Oxford: Blackwell.

Grosjean, F. (2008). *Studying Bilinguals.* Oxford: Oxford University Press.

Gumperz, J. (1982). *Discourse Strategies*. Cambridge: Cambridge University Press.

Hasselmo, N. (1970). Code switching and modes of speaking. In G. Gilbert (ed.), *Texas Studies in Bilingualism: Spanish, French, German, Czech, Polish, Sorbian, and Norwegian in the Southwest*, 179–210. Berlin: de Gruyter.

Hay, J. and Drager, K. (2007). Sociophonetics. *Annual Review of Anthropology* 36: 89–103.

Hay, J. and Drager, K. (2010). Stuffed toys and speech perception. *Linguistics* 48(4): 865–92.

Hualde, J.I., Nadeu, M. and Simonet, M. (2010). Lenition and phonemic contrast in Majorcan Catalan. In S. Colina, A. Olarrea and A.M. Carvalho (eds.), *Romance Linguistics 2009*, 81–94. Amsterdam: John Benjamins.

Khattab, G. (2003). VOT in English and Arabic bilingual and monolingual children. In D. Parkinson and E. Benmamoun (eds.), *Perspectives on Arabic Linguistics XIII–XIV*, 1–38. Amsterdam: John Benjamins.

Labov, W., Yaeger, M. and Steiner, R. (1972). *A Quantitative Study of Sound Change in Progress 1*. US Regional Survey.

Lisker, L. and Abramson, A. (1964). A cross-language study of voicing in initial stops. *Word* 20: 284–422.

Lipski, J.M. (1987). The Spanish dialect of the Sabine River: Vestiges of the Mexican Spanish of Louisiana and Texas. *Nueva Revista de Filologia Hispanica* 35(1): 111–28.

Lope Blanch, J.M. (1988). The voiced labiodental in Mexican Spanish. *Nueva Revista de Filologia Hispanica* 36(1): 153–70.

Lynch, A. (2009). A sociolinguistic analysis of final /s/ in Miami Cuban Spanish. *Language Sciences* 31(6): 766–90.

Mack, S. (2011). A sociophonetic analysis of/s/variation in Puerto Rican Spanish. In L. Ortiz-López (ed.), *Selected Proceesings of the 11th Hispanic Linguistics Symposium*, 81–93. Somerville, MA: Cascadilla.

Major, R.C. (1986). The ontogeny model: Evidence from L2 acquisition of Spanish r. *Language Learning* 36(4): 453–504.

Marian, V. and Spivey, M. (2003). Competing activation in bilingual language processing: Within- and between-language competition. *Bilingualism: Language and Cognition* 6(2): 97–115.

Mendoza-Denton, N. (1999). Sociolinguistics and linguistic anthropology of US Latinos. *Annual Review of Anthropology* 28: 375–95.

Meyerhoff, M., and Nagy, N. (2008). *Social Lives in Language Sociolinguistics and Multilingual Speech Communities: Celebrating the Work of Gillian Sankoff*. Amsterdam: John Benjamins.

Munro, M.J. and Derwing, T.M. (1995). Processing time, accent, and comprehensibility in the perception of native and foreign-accented speech. *Language and Speech* 38(3): 289–306.

Niedzielski, N. (1999). The effect of social information on the perception of sociolinguistic variables. *Journal of Language and Social Psychology* 18(1): 62–85.

Olson, D.J. (2013). Bilingual language switching and selection at the phonetic level: Asymmetrical transfer in VOT production. *Journal of Phonetics* 41: 407–20.

Olson, D.J. (2016). The impact of code-switching, language context, and language dominance on suprasegmental phonetics: Evidence for the role of predictability. *International Journal of Bilingualism*: 20(4): 453–72.

Poplack, S. (1981). Syntactic structure and social function in code switching. In R.P. Durán (ed.), *Latino Language and Communicative Behavior*, 169–84. Norwood, NJ: Ablex Publishing.

R Core Team. (2013). R: A language and environment for statistical computing. R Foundation for Statistical Computing, Vienna. Retrieved from http://www.R-project.org/

Register, N.A. (1977). Some sound patterns of Chicano English. *The Journal of the Linguistic Association of the Southwest* 2(3–4): 111–22.

Sankoff, G. (2013). Linguistic outcomes of language contact. In J.K. Chambers, P. Trudgill and N. Schilling-Estes (eds.), *The Handbook of Language Variation and Change*, 638–68. Malden, MA: Blackwell.

Santa Ana, A.O. (1991). *Phonetic Simplification Processes in the English of the Barrio: A Cross-Generational Sociolinguistic Study of the Chicanos of Los Angeles.* Doctoral Dissertation, University of Pennsylvania, Philadelphia.

Simonet, M. (2014). Phonetic consequences of dynamic cross-linguistic interference in proficient bilinguals. *Journal of Phonetics* 43: 26–37.

Soares, C. and Grosjean, F. (1984) Bilinguals in a monolingual and a bilingual speech mode: The effect on lexical access. *Memory and Cognition* 12: 380–6.

Strand, E.A. (1999). Uncovering the role of gender stereotypes in speech perception. *Journal of Language and Social Psychology* 18(1): 86–100.

Thomas, E. (2010). *Sociophonetics: An Introduction.* New York: Palgrave Macmillan.

Timm, L.A. (1976). Three consonants in Chicano Spanish: /x/, /b/ and /d/. *The Bilingual Review/La Revista Bilingue* 3(2): 153–62.

Torres Cacoullos, R. and Ferreira, F. (2000). Lexical frequency and labiodental-bilabial variation in New Mexican Spanish. *Southwest Journal of Linguistics* 19(2): 1–17.

Treffers-Daller, J. (1998). Variability in code switching styles: Turkish-German code switching patterns. In R. Jacobson (ed.), *Codeswitching Worldwide*, 177–98. New York: Mouton de Gruyter.

Trovato, A. (2015). *The Acoustic and Auditory Differences between [v] and [β] among Bilinguals in El Paso.* Presented at the Linguistic Symposium on Romance Languages 45, Campinas, Brazil, May 2015.

Walker, A., García, C., Cortés, Y. and Campbell-Kibler, K. (2014). Comparing social meanings across listener and speaker groups: The indexical field of Spanish /s/. *Language Variation and Change* 26(2): 169.

Watson, I. (1991). Phonological processing in two languages. In E. Bialystock (ed.), *Language Processing in Bilingual Children*, 25–48. Cambridge: Cambridge University Press.

Wolfram, W., Carter, P.M. and Moriello, R. (2004). Emerging Hispanic English: New dialect formation in the American South. *Journal of Sociolinguistics* 8(3): 339–58.

Zampini, M. (2008). L2 speech production research: Findings, issues and research. In J.G. Hansen Edwards and M. Zampini (eds.), *Phonology and Second Language Acquisition*, 219–50. Amsterdam: John Benjamins.

Barbara E. Bullock is a Professor at the University of Texas at Austin.

Daniel J. Olson is an Assistant Professor of Spanish and Linguistics at Purdue University.

Index